Benjamin Harrison · *Hoosier Warrior*

1833–1865

BENJAMIN HARRISON

Benjamin Harrison

Hoosier Warrior

By

HARRY J. SIEVERS

Published by American Political Biography Press

Newtown, CT

Reprinted with the permission of the
Arthur Jordan Foundation

Published by
AMERICAN POLITICAL BIOGRAPHY PRESS

Library of Congress Catalog Card Number 96-78887
ISBN Number 978-0-945707-16-5

AMERICAN POLITICAL BIOGRAPHY PRESS
39 Boggs Hill
Newtown, Connecticut
06470-1971
Tel: (203) 270-9777 ✧ Fax: (203) 270-0091
E-Mail: APBPress@EarthLink.Net

WWW.APBPRESS.COM

This is the second printing of the first edition.

All publications of
AMERICAN POLITICAL BIOGRAPHY PRESS
Are dedicated to my wife
Ellen and our two children
Katherine and William II

This particular book is
Dedicated to:

Everett Alvarez, Jr. 08/05/64
Edward Anthony Davis 08/26/65
Jeremiah Andrew Denton, Jr. 07/18/65
John Sidney McCain   10/26/67

And all the others.

Preface

GENERAL BENJAMIN HARRISON's statue in University Park, Indianapolis, bears on its base the inscription—"Great Lives Do Not Go Out. They Go On."—These words, Indiana's memorial to her first citizen, were uttered by Harrison himself about a year and a half before he left the White House. On August 20, 1891, the President's fifty-eighth birthday, Harrison visited Mount McGregor, New York, the site of an historic mountainside where death had claimed General Grant in 1885. After dinner, the presidential party paid its respects to the memory of the great Union general who was twice President of the United States. Harrison, himself a general and a president, spoke briefly. "We are gathered here in a spot which is historic. This mountain has been fixed in the affectionate and reverent memory of all our people and has been glorified by death on its summit of General Ulysses S. Grant. It is fit that that great spirit that had already lifted its fame to a height unknown in American history should take its flight from this mountain top. It has been said that a great life went out here; but great lives, like that of General Grant, do not go out. They go on."

Benjamin Harrison went out half a century ago, but his life goes on. Fellow citizens from every section of the country, shortly after his death, raised a monument to this man who "represented what is best in public and private life." His life they carved in stone: Benjamin Harrison: "A Citizen Faithful To Every Obligation; A Lawyer Of Distinction; A Volunteer Soldier In The War For The Union; A Senator In Congress; Twenty-Third President Of The United States." Perhaps, as Henry Adams suggested, he "was the best President the Republicans put forth since Lincoln."

Historians and text-book writers (for, of biographers there have been none), following closely in the traditions of Harrison's political opponents, have kept alive much of the partisan criticism of his enemies and have written him down as an able but obscure, cold-blooded man with a strange gift for unpopularity. It has been this writer's intention to examine Harrison's early and adventurous career impartially and allow him to plead his own case before the bar of public opinion. This task has been rendered both difficult and easy by a previously unused abundance of Harrison manuscripts. In doing history a service by preserving an enormous mass of correspondence, Benjamin Harrison also did himself a service. He has hitherto been the most obscure of the post-Civil War presidents. The reason is that little has thus far been known of his acts, motives, and accomplishments before, during, and after a decade of public service in Washington. For reasons not here necessary to state, the preparation of a biography of this commanding figure was repeatedly delayed. Since honest folk can neither hate nor love what they do not know, Harrison has remained a shadow, while others less gifted have impressed the public imagination. If Harrison was a man of stature, the roots of greatness should be sought in his formative years. Neither distinguished ancestry nor chance begin to explain the raw material from which was fashioned this Hoosier Warrior. Ability, courage, and hard work brought Harrison from a shadow to a substance. Here, for the first time, I believe, is the chronicle of those forces and factors that carried him from the farm, over a battlefield, and through a courtroom to the White House.

Writing biography can be the greatest intellectual fun in the world. Add to it the spirit of a pioneer, intent upon blazing a new trail, and you have the attractive side of authorship. There is, however, the drudgery side. "Of making many books," observed the writer of Ecclesiastes, "there is no end." Indeed, without the helping hands of hundreds, writing and research could be a toilsome bore. With alacrity, then, I turn to the pleasant task of acknowledgments.

The traditionally efficient and courteous co-operation extended to me at the Library of Congress has been an unmixed blessing. To Dr. Luther Evans, Librarian of Congress, and to his staff I owe a debt twice as great as I can mention. Particular thanks are due to Mr. David C. Mearns, chief of the Division of Manuscripts, and to the following members of his able staff: Miss Katherine Brand, Dr. Charles C. Powell, Dr. Elizabeth McPherson, Mr. John de Porry, Mrs. Dorothy Eaton, Mr. Arthur Young, and Mrs. Elizabeth Fitzpatrick Gerrity.

In the National Archives, Mr. Wayne Grover and a whole host of courteous archival assistants rendered me invaluable service.

In the Indiana State Library, for me a research home second only to the Library of Congress, I wish to express my appreciation of the helpful courtesies shown me by Mrs. Hazel Hopper, Lila Brady, and their competent aides in the Indiana Division. Miss Caroline Dunn, director of the William Henry Smith Memorial Library, has never been too busy to lend an effective and willing hand. The same must be said of Margaret Pearson, archivist, and Harold Burton, curator of newspapers.

At Georgetown University, the head librarian, Mr. Phillips Temple, and the loan librarian, Miss Emily Weems, have made every effort to secure countless books, reports, and unpublished monographs covering the Harrison era.

Among other institutions whose kindly co-operation has speeded this volume to completion I must mention the Wisconsin State Historical Society, the Chicago Historical Society, the Lincoln National Life Foundation of Fort Wayne, Indiana, the Hayes Memorial Library of Fremont, Ohio, and the Historical, Memorial and Art Department of Iowa (Des Moines). In this latter depository, Claude R. Cook, curator, extended to me privileges that warm the heart of a research scholar. Likewise, the New York State Historical Society, as well as the public libraries in New York and Indianapolis, rendered me able assistance.

In the Miami University Library, Oxford, Ohio, I owe a debt of gratitude to E. W. King, genial and efficient librarian, for materials and illustrations without compare. Also, I wish to acknowledge the warm hospitality and scholarly help of Professor William J. McNiff, head of Miami's History Department.

As this biography evolved from the research to the writing stage I became increasingly more conscious of a rapidly growing debt to a multitude of friends and advisers. Dr. Charles Callan Tansill, distinguished author and scholar, has been mentor and friend every inch of the way. For personal help, encouragement, and an unstinting surrender of his time, I thank him most cordially. At Georgetown University also there have been innumerable Jesuit colleagues ever ready with valuable assistance. By a patient reading and criticism of my manuscript they more than once emboldened my spirit. With a deep sense of gratitude I acknowledge my indebtedness to Rev. Joseph T. Durkin, S.J., and to Rev. Edmund A. Walsh, S.J. To Rev. J. Hunter Guthrie, S.J., President of Georgetown, and to Rev. Gerard F. Yates, S.J.,

dean of the Graduate School of Georgetown, I express my thanks
for encouragement along the way.

Although Washington, D. C., was the literary birthplace of
Hoosier Warrior, many of the growing pains were experienced
on the soil of Indiana. Absolutely essential to the completion of
this volume have been the generous assistance and constant
encouragement of the Arthur Jordan Foundation of Indianapolis. From this group of public-spirited citizens came my commission to give Harrison his place under the sun. The devotion of
each member of the Jordan board to this project has been vital
to its completion and inspiring to this writer. In no way, however,
has the board restricted the author's obligation to write as he
believed the documentary evidence warranted. Imbued with a
spirit of public service, the Jordan Foundation has provided
secretarial assistance and a broad opportunity for important
archival research in places near and far. Here they stopped.
Neither salary nor censorship had a part in this biography. I feel
certain that Mr. Hilton U. Brown, chairman of the board, and
his associates, Mr. Bernard R. Batty, Mr. Thomas H. Kaylor,
Mr. H. Foster Clippinger, Mr. Fermor S. Cannon, Mr. Evan
Walker, and Mr. Emsley W. Johnson, Jr., all know how profoundly I appreciate their loyal assistance and constant backing.
There is but one regret. On April 12, 1950, death claimed Mr.
Emsley W. Johnson, Sr., who was then serving as vice-chairman
of the Jordan board. As a competent historian, a keen lawyer, and
a personal friend, he manifested an extraordinary interest in
every line of the biography then in progress. It is a distinct honor
to be able to pay my respects to his memory.

At the President Benjamin Harrison Memorial Home in
Indianapolis, I have found nothing but kindness and co-operation. Mrs. Ruth Woodworth, charming hostess, has spent many
an hour showing and telling me about the General's house. Here
I uncovered treasures in stacks of personal and family letters,
not to mention a goodly number of the photographs and paint-
ings which grace this volume. Also, to Mr. Gerald V. Carrier, of
the Jordan College of Music, the institution adjacent to the
home, I express my thanks.

Southern Indiana is the home of West Baden College. Here
many a debt of gratitude is owed to innumerable Jesuit colleagues. Rev. Charles H. Metzger, S.J., professor of history and

experienced critic, has read the entire manuscript. His encouragement during laborious days has been most welcome. Rev. Leo D. Sullivan, S.J., President of West Baden College, has consistently shown a spirit of interest, accommodation, and encouragement. Acknowledgments to other confreres of the cloth would read like items in the long Homeric catalogue of ships. *In globo,* I express deep appreciation and warm thanks for a charity that reflects that of the Master.

It is a pleasure for the author to record an enormous debt to Dr. Louis M. Sears of Purdue University, Freeman Cleaves of the *Financial World,* and Thomas R. Byrne, Jr., who have read much or all of this volume in manuscript and have given invaluable suggestions. Likewise, to Professor Howard K. Beale of the University of Wisconsin and to Professor Roy F. Nichols of the University of Pennsylvania, I express cordial appreciation for allowing galleys to pass under their eyes. The editorial suggestions of Dr. James Tobin of Queens College have served me well. With gratitude I acknowledge his assistance.

Scores of personal friends throughout the country have been at my elbow with services too numerous to mention and with encouragement unrestrained. I should like to mention at least the following: Mr. and Mrs. Bernard F. Gallagher, Mrs. Thomas A. Murphy, Dr. Leland Sage, Dr. Edward A. White, Rev. Herbert J. Clancy, S.J., Mr. and Mrs. Joseph A. McGowan, Rt. Rev. Msgr. Lester V. Lyons, Rev. Cornelius Gall, Rev. Paul F. Hans, Miss Ellen T. Becker, Rev. Bartholomew Fair, Rev. John Tracy Ellis, Mrs. Margaret Connolly, Miss Margaret Mary du Fief, Miss Roberta Burke, Mr. Joseph Simmons, Mr. Nicholas Devereaux, Mrs. Anna Marie Kane, Dr. James Masterson, Misses Margaret and Katherine Fennell, Mr. and Mrs. A. William Douglas, Mr. and Mrs. A. Donald Brice, Mr. and Mrs. Edward J. Lanagan, Mr. and and Mrs. Matthew E. McCarthy, Mr. and Mrs. William Angilly, Mother Philip Neri, B.S., and Rev. J. B. Tennelly. To countless others I can only mention, not express, my gratitude.

Finally, at the close of this litany, I wish to express my sincere appreciation to Very Rev. John J. McMahon, S.J., Provincial of the New York Province of the Society of Jesus. Without his endorsement, hearty co-operation, and consistent encouragement, I could not have completed this volume.

Only a secretary like Betty Pershing of Washington, D. C., can describe what an author owes to a good right hand. She typed the manuscript without protest at my penmanship or at the tired tones emanating from my Dictaphone-Time Master.

In acknowledgment of an eternally unpayable debt, I dedicate this volume to my mother and to the abiding memory of my father.

HARRY J. SIEVERS, S.J.

West Baden College
West Baden Springs, Indiana
May 24, 1952

Table of Contents

INTRODUCTION xix

I   IN RETROSPECT 3

Centennial President . . . A Preview (1789–1889).—The Solemn
Moment.—The Inaugural Parade.—A New Republican Lead-
er.—Roots of Character.—A Debt to the Past.—An Ancestral
Strain of Belligerency.—Benjamin Harrison, the Signer (1726–
91).—"Old Tippecanoe."—"Opening up the West."—John Scott
Harrison, Son of One President and Father of Another.—Mrs.
John Scott Harrison.—Married Life at "The Point."

II   PIONEER BOYHOOD AND COLLEGE DAYS 20

The Point Farm.—Carefree Days.—The Family Circle.—Log
Cabin Schooling.—Grandfather Harrison's Library.—A Quiet
Sabbath and the Golden Book.—At Farmers' College.—The
Spirit of Farmers' College: Dr. Robert Hamilton Bishop.—
Curriculum and Discipline.—Laying up a Wardrobe of the
Mind.—Sociological Beginnings.—Roots of Charity.—The Art
of Writing.—The Art of Reading.—Seeds of Patriotism.—On
the Home Front (1847–50).—Letters from Home.—Farewell to
Farmers' College.

III   LOVE, LEARNING, AND LAW 46

Matriculation at Miami University.—"Daughter of the Old
Northwest."—Rigorous Routine.—How to Win Friends and
Influence People.—A Widening Circle of College Friends.—
Off-Campus Activity and On-Campus Diversions.—"The Pious
Moonlight Dude."—New Frontiers of Knowledge.—Temper-
ance: No Life Spent in the Service of King Alcohol.—Ben's
First Elective Office.—Religious Conversion.—Prelude to Grad-
uation: Eight Months of Conflict.—Ministry vs. Law.—Legal
Leanings.—Commencement Day.

IV THE BAR AND THE ALTAR 66

A Prelude to the Study of Law.—Bellamy Storer and the Ohio
Bar.—Law Student in Cincinnati.—The Grind at the Office.—
The Bewitchings of Cupid.—The Valley of Indecision.—Time
for Decision.—A Temporary Road-Block.—A Lover's Brief:
Objection Overruled.—Premarital Bliss.—Preoccupations and
Distractions.—The Road Ahead.—Admission to the Bar and
Indianapolis Bound.

V INDIANAPOLIS 88

Farewell to "The Point."—Indiana and Indianapolis in the
1850's.—Hoosiers in Retrospect.—A Hoosier Welcome.—Self-
Reliance on a Maiden Voyage.—The Indiana Bar and a New
Breadwinner.—A Break at Last: Off to a Fair Start.—His First
Jury Trial.—Nothing Succeeds like Success.—The First Son Is
Born.—Taking a New Lease on Life.—Prelude to the Wallace
and Harrison Law Firm (1855–61).—Enter Wallace and Harri-
son.—Routine Business: The Ladder Up.—Opportunity for
Advancement.

VI THE POLITICAL ARENA 110

"Remember the Sabbath Day to Keep it Holy."—"Membership
in the First Presbyterian Church."—At the Edge of the Political Arena.—Seeds of Republicanism.—The Nebraska Bill of
Mr. Douglas.—A New Party: Campaigning for Fremont.—Political Fortunes Rise.—First Elective Political Office: City Attorney, 1857.—Dutiful Son and Party Worker.—Secretary to the
State Republican Central Committee.—Prelude to 1860.

VII THE CRITICAL YEARS, 1860 AND 1861 135

The Abolition Fever Strikes Indiana.—Reporter Nomination
Falls to Harrison.—The Campaign Gets under Way.—Harrison's Debut: The Speech that Almost Failed.—Harrison Held
Crowd . . . Stood with Lincoln.—The Campaign Continues . . .
Lincoln Nominated.—Democratic Dissension and the Concluding Months of the Campaign.—Harrison Oversteps Himself.—Campaign Highlights: Harrison Tussles with Hendricks.

VII   *(continued)*

The Fruits of Victory.—Indiana and the Union Look to Lincoln.—Lincoln Speaks at Indianapolis . . . "Silence Is King": A Memory for Benjamin Harrison.—Harrison Remembers.

VIII   THE CALL TO ARMS 162

The Urge to Volunteer.—Harrison Remains at Home.—Freedom for Work.—Sorrows and Joys.—Enter Harrison and Fishback.—A Good Investment.—The Varying Fortunes of War.—Lincoln's Call for 300,000 More Soldiers . . . Second Lieutenant Benjamin Harrison.—Recruiting Company A of Seventieth Indiana Volunteers.—A Month of Preparation (July 14—August 14, 1862).—Departure of the Seventieth Indiana for the Field.

IX   THE SOIL OF KENTUCKY 188

Colonel Harrison and the Seventieth Indiana Head for Kentucky.—Camp Ben Harrison, Near Bowling Green, Kentucky.—Camp Experiences.—A Prelude to Action.—"Our First Fight," Russellville, Kentucky.—Harrison Outwitted.—"The Fire in the Rear."

X   ON SECESSIONIST GROUND: THE WAR IN TENNESSEE   212

New Commanders and New Scenes.—The "Land of Dixie": An Old Role but New Players.—Tennessee Tenure.—Destined to Disappointment.—Student Instructor in the Military Art.—A Few Rungs up the Social Ladder.—Prologue to Atlanta: A New Year Brings New Hope.

XI   IN THE FACE OF THE ENEMY 234

Moving to the Georgia Front.—Wauhatchie in Lookout Valley.—Fighting Joe Hooker Assumes Command.—A Fight or a Footrace.—On the Eve of the Battle of Resaca.

XII   THE ATLANTA CAMPAIGN 247

Resaca.—The Aftermath and a Sobriquet.—In Pursuit of Elusive Joe Johnston.—An Acting Brigade under Fire.—Cold Steel at Peach Tree Creek.—Harrison Wears the "Lone Star": Atlanta Falls.

XIII TWIN TRIUMPHS: INDIANAPOLIS AND NASHVILLE . . 266

Riding the Wave of Success.—A Pleasant Interlude.—Revenge by Ballot.—Re-electing Mr. Lincoln.—The Decision to Return. —The Battle of Nashville.—Federals in Pursuit.

XIV BRIGADIER GENERAL HARRISON AND DESOLATED ROADS (JANUARY–APRIL 1865) 287

A Second Homecoming.—Hors de Combat.—Camp Sherman at Blair's Landing Near Hilton Head.—The March Through the Carolinas.

XV THE GRAND REVIEW (MAY–JUNE 1865) 300

From Raleigh, North Carolina to Washington, D. C.—The Grand Review.—Mustering Out.—Homeward Bound.

BIBLIOGRAPHY 319

INDEX 333

List of Illustrations

Benjamin Harrison . . . . *Frontispiece*

FACING
PAGE

The Inauguration of Benjamin Harrison, Centennial
President, March 4, 1889 8

The Inaugural Bible 8

Benjamin Harrison, Signer of the Declaration of
Independence 9

William Henry Harrison, Ninth President of the
United States 9

John Scott Harrison 40

Elizabeth Irwin Harrison 40

North Bend. The Residence of William Henry Harrison
and the Birthplace of Benjamin Harrison 41

Miami University Campus in the 1850's 41

Cincinnati, 1868 72

Bird's-eye View of Indianapolis, 1854 72

Pennsylvania Street, Indianapolis, 1854–1856 73

Ben Harrison's First Residence in Indianapolis 73

Ben Harrison's Second Residence in Indianapolis . . . 104

The Old Bates House 104

Indianapolis during Early Days of the Civil War . . . 105

Carrie and Colonel Ben Harrison, 1863 105

The Home Harrison Left Behind 136

FACING
PAGE

Chattanooga Valley from Lookout Mountain 137

Map of the Atlanta Campaign 168

Map of the Territory South of Resaca, Georgia 169

Battleground of Resaca, Georgia 200

Lithograph (1889) of the Battle of Resaca 201

Pass in the Raccoon Ridge, Whiteside 232

Hero-trio at Peach Tree Creek: Harrison, Ward,
    and Coburn 233

Confederate Works in Front of Atlanta 264

Ruins in Columbia, South Carolina, as Seen from
    the Capitol 264

Abraham Lincoln 265

State House, Indianapolis, 1865 265

The Grand Review Commences 296

Reviewing Stand in Front of Executive Mansion 296

The Grand Review from Fifteenth Street and
    Pennsylvania Avenue 297

Mrs. Benjamin Harrison, 1865 297

Introduction

BENJAMIN HARRISON was the twenty-third president of the United States. Although he has been Indiana's sole contribution to the presidential office, the Hoosier atmosphere goes back to his grandfather who was the first governor of Indiana Territory. "Ben" was the favored Christian name in the Harrison household, including the "Ben" who was a signer of the Declaration of Independence and other "Bens" in colonial and English history. After his military service in the Civil War, "Ben" was frequently referred to as "General" by his old comrades-in-arms, and this appellation gradually came into wide use.

Harrison's life was a record of steady advancement. As a young lawyer he became one of the leaders of the Indiana bar through untiring industry, unusual intellectual ability, and constant adherence to the best legal traditions of his state. In the Union Army, with no previous military experience, he displayed an aptitude for leadership that won for him a commission of brigadier general. It was in the army that he first showed a personal magnetism that made men follow him without question and that transformed the 70th Indiana Volunteer regiment into one of the best disciplined units in the armies of the West.

Harrison had a notable academic record. At Miami University he revealed intellectual gifts far above the average, and his assiduous study of the law while residing in Cincinnati provided him with the background for a legal career. He married early and was particularly fortunate in having a wife who fulfilled all the requirements of an ideal helpmate. With all these factors in his favor it was inevitable that he would command success when—barely twenty-one—he settled in Indianapolis, the new, raw, straggling capital of Indiana.

There is little doubt that his family background helped to mold Harrison. Descendant of an important family that had always played a significant role in the making of America, he was ever conscious of the fact that he should live up to the great traditions that had been established, but he always said that ancestry itself did not make the man and that he wanted no credit on that score. "Grandfather's hat," which the cartoonists were fond of drawing, was not too big for a head that had grown large with the knowledge of America's past and the bright promise of its future, but "Ben" had his own hatter. John Philip Sousa once shrewdly remarked: "Few intellectual giants have graced the presidency, but General Harrison was one of them. . . . The most brilliant speech I have ever heard was one he delivered at the Gridiron Club dinner."

Harrison had far more than mere intellectual brilliance—he had character. There was certain firmness in his make-up that defied political pressure even when it was applied by men of considerable importance in the Republican Party. There was also a balance that placed him above mere partisanship. When he knew he was right no one could dislodge him. When he was once convinced of the law and the facts he settled solidly into a conviction and could not be moved. In politics he was a leader, not a follower. This was clearly demonstrated with reference to the appointment of Mr. Brewer to the Supreme Court, as related by William Allen White. Harrison had already decided upon the nomination of Brewer when Senator Preston B. Plumb made a call at the White House and, without ascertaining Harrison's feelings in the matter, abruptly demanded the nomination of Brewer. He was enraged when Harrison gave him no assurances regarding the nomination, and he went away muttering imprecations against the impassive president. After Plumb left the White House, Harrison put the finishing touches upon the nomination and sent it to the Senate. He afterwards remarked: "I think one of the great moral victories of my life came when I put that commission back on my desk after Plumb left and conquered a despicable temptation to tear it up and throw it in the wastebasket."

It has long been evident that such an important personality deserved an adequate biography. Several attempts were made, but the official four-years' records of the administration had been lost, and the biographers were blocked. But at last Mr. Frank Tibbott, Harrison's private secretary, found the notes and tubes that he had made during the administration and was able to reproduce some twenty-five thousand letters and documents that had vanished. These were placed by the second Mrs. Harrison in the Library of Congress and became available. Of course, there were many incidents and records besides these that would be needed for a comprehensive biography. The situation impressed the Arthur Jordan Foundation, which had purchased the Harrison home. Some of the directors of the Foundation had known General Harrison personally, and they ardently believed that his contributions to the American theory of government should be made familiar to Americans. So they sought an historian.

After a long search, the Foundation selected Dr. Harry J. Sievers, at Georgetown University, Washington, D. C., who is a student of this period of American history, and commissioned him to write the life of Harrison. For three years he has worked untiringly in the Harrison manuscripts and in other pertinent collections. In this first volume of the biography, he recounts the story of Harrison's youth, his rise as a leader of the Indiana bar, his distinguished service in the Union Army, and his return to civil life in Indianapolis. It is a volume that lights up some of the dark years. It is also a volume that stresses a familiar theme—the rise of a young man from relative obscurity to the highest position in the nation. It is a typical American story, filled with items of human interest that make it good reading. Finally, it is a commentary on Americanism. Above all, Harrison was an intense American who never deviated from the faith of the founding fathers. His ancestors had helped to make America, and he continued its principles and traditions. None of our presidents entered the White House with a clearer vision of the great America of the future, and none strove any harder to make that vision a reality. This book puts Benjamin Harrison on his proper pedestal as Indiana's first citizen.

HILTON U. BROWN
Chairman of the Board
Arthur Jordan Foundation

Indianapolis
June 1952

Benjamin Harrison

CHAPTER I

In Retrospect

O N MARCH 4, 1889, it rained in Washington. At six o'clock in the morning it was drizzling, just as it had for the last five days. It rained in a leisurely, complacent way, as though without effort. The first act of everyone was to go to the windows and look out. It had poured so long that all took it for granted that it must be clear today, but there was no mistaking what was before the eye—a leaden sky, with heavy clouds chasing overhead.

By seven o'clock this March morning the capital of the United States was literally saturated with music as for four days it had been drenched with rain.[1] Martial strains stirred the souls of close to half a million people, and soon their hearts beat a joyous tempo in anticipation of the day's momentous event—the centennial inauguration of a President of the United States. Music ascended to the heavens from every corner of the town; it invaded the alleyways; it searched the public buildings; it permeated the hotels; it almost cleared the atmosphere.

At about seven-thirty there came a most welcome lull in the five-day stretch of bad weather. It actually stopped raining. There were thin spots in the sky through which the sun appeared to be struggling. The wind freshened from the northeast, to be sure, but with only strength enough to lift the dripping, sodden pennants and flags, so that they took on a semblance of gaiety, seemingly drying themselves. During the next two hours house-ridden people swarmed into the streets, more than half-con-

---

[1] There was excellent newspaper coverage of the inaugural ceremonies. See Volume 9, pp. 20–27, of the Benjamin Harrison Scrapbook Series (58 Vols.), entitled "February 28, 1888–September 18, 1890; Social and Personal and Political." Papers of Benjamin Harrison (Library of Congress).

vinced that the rain hoodoo was laid to rest. But it was a false hope that lured so many to the reviewing stands so early. At nine-thirty the clouds opened their floodgates. It rained spitefully. It pelted down, driven this way and that by a raw, sharp wind. It was a rain that forced its way into everything it touched —the kind that you feel in your bones.[2]

The storekeepers who had been offering seats in their windows for fifty cents and a dollar raised their prices to six dollars. Two or three of the larger stands were roofed over; these were packed. Although more than two hours passed before there was anything to be seen, sightseers were all in their places by ten o'clock. They stood three or four lines deep on either side of the Avenue, and filled the stands and temporary scaffoldings, waiting patiently in the soaking rain rather than lose a vantage place.

One century had been completed; a new dawn was breaking. On thousands of faces there was a light generated by a proud satisfaction with the past and a soaring hope for the future. This was a milestone for Americans, were they Democrats or Republicans, Northerners or Southerners. The people who lined the Avenue down to the Capitol nourished their own visions of grandeur. Born in the twenties, thirties and forties of the nineteenth century, these citizens had learned from their mothers and fathers about men named Washington, Jefferson, and Hamilton. Madison and Adams were still household words. Ten decades of constitutional government were being memorialized with the inauguration of General Benjamin Harrison as twenty-third President of the United States.

Coming to the presidency in his mid-fifties, Benjamin Harrison found the nation at peace with all the world and the treasury overflowing. Nor was the name of Harrison unknown in the annals of American history. Many oldsters who took their places in the inaugural crowd remembered vividly how General William Henry Harrison, hero of Tippecanoe, had, nearly half a century ago, marched triumphantly down this Avenue and had sworn the presidential oath. Among the crowd there was a grow-

2 Benjamin Harrison Scrapbook, Vol. 9, p. 28. Practically all the newspaper men compared this inauguration day with that of President-elect Harrison's ill-fated grandfather in 1841.

ing feeling "that the man on the quarter deck had inherited some
of the unadulterated blood that coursed in the veins of his grandfather."[3] As the noon hour approached, the interest heightened
throughout the ranks of the expectant throng.

The crowds in the street kept up a constant cheering, shouting
the name of Harrison, and re-echoing the cry "Four, four, four
years more." Finally, the procession from the Senate got under
way, with Marshal Wright of the Supreme Court in the lead.
The traditional order of procession was preserved, and directly
behind the members of the Supreme Court and the Sergeant-
at-Arms of the Senate marched Senators Hoar and Cockrell. The
retiring President, Grover Cleveland, and the full-bearded President-elect[4] walked side by side.

It was well after one o'clock when Cleveland and Harrison
took their places in a small railed enclosure erected in front of
the inaugural stand so gaily bedecked with flags, banners and
shields. Everything within eye's reach was handsome with color.
The plaza in front of the Capitol, the adjacent sidewalks, por-
ticos, every place of vantage from which even a glimpse of the
presidential party could be obtained, were black with people.
When the crowd saw Harrison, there was a tremendous uproar.
Bursts of cheering were renewed again and again, and not until
the new President had several times raised his hand for silence
did the rousing reception abate.

Chief Justice Fuller arose and, baring his white locks to the
rain, held a Bible in his right hand to administer the oath of
office. General Harrison removed his hat. The Chief Justice read
the oath of office in a low tone of voice and Benjamin Harrison,
with his right hand clasping the Bible, bowed his head in assent.[5]
When the ceremony was concluded, the silence was rent by another tremendous burst of applause. Finally, the President, in
a manner deliberate and free of self-consciousness as if he were

3 Clem Studebaker to Benjamin Harrison, March 25, 1892, Harrison MSS, Vol.
138.

4 Harrison was the fourth President with a full beard. From Washington to Lin-
coln all the Presidents but two wore smooth-shaven faces. See the *State* (Richmond,
Va.), March 14, 1889, a newspaper clipping in the Benjamin Harrison Scrapbook
No. 9, p. 67, Harrison MSS.

5 The inaugural Bible is kept in the Harrison Home in Indianapolis. In Harrison's own hand is written: "Here I placed my hand when I took the oath of office."

speaking from the floor of the Senate, addressed his countrymen in a loud clear voice.

While the crowd shouted its overwhelming approval—especially for the statement on pension policy—the President closed his remarks and turned to kiss his wife and daughter. With a wonderful patience, the eager and anxious spectators then waited for the inaugural parade. The downpour had tapered off into a fine but driving mist. Good humor prevailed. At last, the head of the great parade turned into Pennsylvania Avenue on the march to the White House. More than one spectator turned back the clock half a century. More than 40,000 could remember that "Forty-eight years ago William Henry Harrison, on his white horse, headed a procession of four thousand patriots along this same route."[6] On that day, Admiral Porter, then a mere lieutenant, claimed it was the finest pageant in the world. Today, the pageantry was more elegant, as 40,000 oldsters were in line to honor the grandson, many coming from sections of the country which in 1841 were trackless wastes of uninhabited territory.

The sight was inspiring, especially if one looked eastward from the Treasury where the Capitol formed a hazy, yet stately background. The broad expanse of the Avenue glistened beneath the dull sky. General Beaver rode in advance, and his head was uncovered in acknowledgment of the greetings of the great multitude. As the head of the procession reached the Treasury, a halt was called, and the presidential party, in its own carriages, turned off and drove rapidly to the White House. After a hasty luncheon the whole party, with the exception of Mr. Cleveland, repaired to the reviewing stand. As President Harrison and Vice-President Morton took their places, their cheering admirers were roused to new heights of enthusiasm. For the first time, Harrison was able to view and to realize the grandeur of the pageant in which he had taken so conspicuous a part.

Every branch of the regular service was in the first division of the review: infantry, a detachment of Marines, artillery, cavalry, naval apprentices, the National Guard of the District of Columbia. The President recognized the salute of each commanding officer by raising his hat, and he also uncovered his head as each flag was dipped in salute. Frequently, he chatted with Vice-Presi-

6 Benjamin Harrison Scrapbook No. 9, pp. 20–27, Harrison MSS.

dent Morton, warmly commending the marching of the different regiments. The entire National Guard of Pennsylvania was present under the command of Major General Hartranft. Close on their heels rode General Foraker with his Ohio troops, and after them, amid astounding applause, marched the famous Seventh of New York. Another division consisted entirely of G.A.R. Posts under the command of General Bill Warner. Another included Buffalo Bill, leading the Cowboy Club of Denver, Colorado. The band of the Flambeau Club of Dodge City sported two unique banners rounded by enormous horns. Red-shirted firemen swept through the streets like fires on the prairie. Legion, too, were the political clubs with red, white and blue umbrellas; others in white overcoats, tan-colored gloves and white ties. Last of all came the colored Harrison and Morton Clubs from Virginia, winding up one of the grandest civil and military pageants ever seen in Washington.

The new President, a man of five feet and some six or seven inches, was a stranger neither to Washington nor to the chieftains of the Republican Party. Capitol Hill remembered his election to the United States Senate in January 1881, when he succeeded Joseph E. McDonald as junior Senator from Indiana. Party leaders recalled his chairmanship of the Hoosier delegation to the National Convention in 1880, when he and his colleagues cast thirty-four consecutive ballots for James G. Blaine in that historic contest. Declining the cabinet posts tendered him by President Garfield, Harrison chose to serve his full term as United States Senator to March 3, 1887. In January of this same year, after a protracted and exciting contest, he was defeated for reelection on the sixteenth ballot by a two-vote deficit. Within a year of his defeat, Harrison delivered in Detroit what is considered one of his greatest political speeches.[7] The Michigan Club, the largest and perhaps most influential political organization in the state, was holding its third annual banquet on Washington's Birthday. General Harrison responded to the sentiment and toast: "Washington, the Republican." Proceeding to say that he felt at some disadvantage because he did not approach Detroit from the direction of Washington, he then struck the keynote

[7] Charles Hedges, *Speeches of Benjamin Harrison* (New York, 1892), p. 10.

of his victorious presidential campaign. "I am a dead statesman,"
he said, "but I am a living and rejuvenated Republican."[8]

This new Republican was bringing with him to the presidential chair a creditable background of experienced service in the
arena of public life. As lawyer, soldier and legislator, he brought
to his new position a wholesome balance of talents and abilities,
though there was nothing of the brilliant individualist in him.
People on Inauguration Day did not rank him with those early
wizards of finance, Hamilton and Gallatin, but they were specu-
lating whether General Harrison's name "would be remembered
as those of Washington, Jefferson, Jackson, and Lincoln, expo-
nents of the greatness of our Constitution," or would he "simply
be named as having been a President from the Fourth of March
of 1889 to the Fourth of March in 1893."[9] As the Columbia,
South Carolina, *Record* put it: "Time only can tell; but we do
not think that Benjamin will miss his chance to write *his page*
in the history of the United States."[10]

Yet, the diminutive, rotund Chief Executive was somewhat of
a mystery even to those admirers so loudly proclaiming his name.
He spoke in a soft, melodious voice, but behind the voice, as behind the face, was an element of strength which betokened his
ability to get there when the time came, an ability which had
carried him to this, the highest niche in the American temple of
fame. He had a habit of looking at you and still not looking at
you, and he impressed one as being a hard man to catch off his
guard.[11] His hair and whiskers were very light grey and this set
off quite well the dignity of his carriage. Beneath this sometimes

[8] *Ibid.*, pp. 9–10. Harrison spoke on the theme: "The guarantee of the Constitution that the States shall have a republican form of government is only executed
when the majority in the states are allowed to vote and have their ballots counted."
[9] Clipping of a feature article entitled "1789–1889," Benjamin Harrison Scrapbook, Vol. 9, p. 59, Harrison MSS.
[10] *Ibid.* The editor of the *Record* felt that Harrison would be assured an independence of action because "he will not be a candidate for re-election . . . and he
feels no doubt that he has but these four years in which to write *his page* in the
history of the United States, and we think he will not lose the opportunity, as did
Mr. Cleveland in the Lord Sackville matter. . . . Suppose Mr. Cleveland at that time,
instead of dismissing Lord Sackville like a valet, had treated his imbecility with
contempt, as it deserved, and had by proclamation closed the ports of the U. S. to
English vessels, then we do not hesitate to say that in that case Grover Cleveland
would have swept this country and would have been inaugurated today as President. He missed his chance; *instead of striking the lion, he kicked the donkey;*
America was laughed at; Cleveland was defeated. . . . We do not think that Benjamin will miss his chance."
[11] Benjamin Harrison Scrapbook, Vol. 9, p. 140, Harrison MSS.

Photograph by Charles M. Bell, 1889

Courtesy Harrison Memorial Home

The Inauguration of President Benjamin Harrison, Centennial President, March 4, 1889

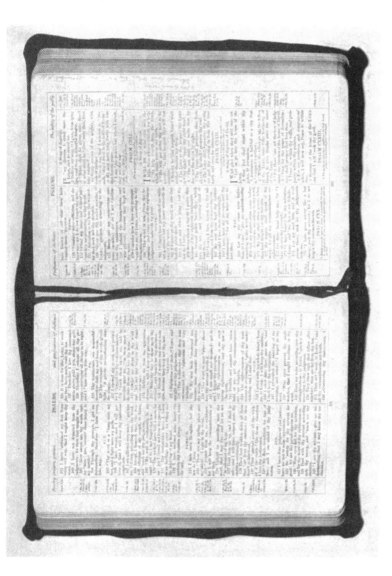

THE INAUGURAL BIBLE

Over the 121st Psalm which begins "I will lift up mine eyes unto the hills from whence cometh my help," Harrison placed his hand, while Chief Justice Melville W. Fuller administered the oath of office. Harrison's marginal notation reads: "My hand was placed here when the oath was administered. B.H."

From a Painting in the Harrison Memorial Home

BENJAMIN HARRISON
(1726–1791)
SIGNER OF THE DECLARATION OF INDEPENDENCE

WILLIAM HENRY HARRISON

NINTH PRESIDENT OF THE UNITED STATES

puzzling exterior was a dynamic and highly cultivated soul. Undoubtedly, thousands of Americans before Benjamin Harrison as well as after him have been equally honest in thought, courageous in action, firm in decision and noted for common sense. Yet, in the eyes of many of his contemporaries, Harrison so sublimated these routine traits of character that they were no longer routine.[12]

There was about the new incumbent in the White House an air of independence which was always fundamentally present in both manner and speech, even, at times, shockingly so. This spirit of independence was so startling that it mothered a profane but strikingly characteristic tale about the President while he was yet a Senator living in Washington. In the absence of his family, Senator Harrison boarded at a place called Chamberlain's in the city. Here he took his meals, and usually appropriated for his own use a rather nice table in the left hand corner of the dining room. The host of the home, in one of his reminiscent moods, recalled the fact years later and said: "You know, I like President Harrison, and I'll tell you why. At dinner frequently a group of Senators (whom I shall not name) passed Harrison by without speaking as though they didn't care a d——n for him. But what I liked about Harrison was, that he didn't seem to care a G—d d——n for them."[13]

Harrison was never in any sense a magnetic personality, though more than one friend bore witness that "his heart beat true to all the finer and nobler instincts of our nature."[14] Neither the charm of words nor the warmth of an effusive manner could he bring to the presidential office, yet by the impact of his keen intellectual ability a deep impress was to be left upon his time. In 1889, this nation, just a hundred years old, needed all the character, all the intellectual ability and acumen it could get. Then, as today, vastly complex problems demanded brains plus integrity: for-

12 John L. Griffiths, *An Address on the Occasion of the Unveiling at Indianapolis, Ind., Oct. 27, 1908, of the Statue of Benjamin Harrison* (Indianapolis, 1909), p. 21.
13 T. N. Cooper to E. W. Halford (Harrison's private secretary), May 3, 1892, Harrison MSS, Vol. 139.
14 T. R. Marshall, *Recollections of Thomas R. Marshall: A Hoosier Salad* (Indianapolis, 1925), p. 91. See also George F. Hoar, *Autobiography of Seventy Years* (New York, 1903), I, 413–21; Royal Cortissoz, *The Life of Whitelaw Reid* (New York, 1921), II, 122–23; 187–88; D. S. Alexander, *Four Famous New Yorkers* (New York, 1923), p. 183; Henry Adams, *The Education of Henry Adams* (New York, 1931), p. 320; W. H. Crook, *Memories of the White House* (Boston, 1911), Chapter 8.

eign affairs guided by a strong, yet pacific hand; a new navy to be organized; the code of international law to be given significant application; at home, a high regard for the judiciary to be engendered; our homesteads cultivated; our forests preserved; and, above all, the national peace and prosperity to be not only maintained but also enhanced. In November 1888, close to a half million American voters decreed that Harrison was the man for this task.[15]

Character is not the overnight product of high pressure and time-saving devices and mechanisms. When character and ability loom large and in some degree of eminence, they are somewhat like exquisitely carved statues. They are produced and developed by generations of disciplined ancestry and in a home environment that is vigorous and healthy. It has not been unknown that the artistic touch of genius can sometimes carve a statue in a comparatively brief span of time, but better known is the long, stern apprenticeship imperative to the exalted and respected master. So it was with Benjamin Harrison.[16] The pioneer surroundings of southwestern Ohio furnished the background of his training and apprenticeship.[17] He was fortunate in having parents who were responsive to the call of the spirit; a rural birthplace on the fringe of the unruly Ohio near Cincinnati; a practical farmer and respected statesman for a father;[18] a group of brothers and sisters, cousins and neighbors, to teach him the give-and-take code of youngsters; and at the age of 21, a newly won bride to instruct him in the stern necessity of getting out and facing the world. His home surroundings were rather ideal: tutors and the log-cabin school provided for his mental training, while the farm, the river, and the woods afforded ample opportunity for bodily development. In the midst of these natural

15 The defeated Grover Cleveland polled a popular plurality of 98,017 votes over Harrison's 478,141. The electoral vote was Harrison 233 and Cleveland 168. *The World Almanac and Encyclopaedia, 1894*, p. 376.

16 See R. B. Henry, *Genealogies of the Families of the Presidents* (Rutland, Vermont, 1935), pp. 161–88 for the ancestral beginnings of William Henry and Benjamin Harrison. See also Charles Keith, *The Ancestry of Benjamin Harrison* (Philadelphia, 1893), pp. 41–43.

17 J. Scott Harrison, *Pioneer Life at North Bend* (Cincinnati, 1867), pp. 3–15, gives the best short account. For a general and scholarly treatment see B. W. Bond, Jr., *The Foundations of Ohio* (Columbus, 1941).

18 Benjamin Harrison Scrapbook, 1853–1901, Vol. 1, Nos. 34 a and 34 b, Harrison MSS.

blessings one might be tempted to overlook an essentially important fact that Harrison was endowed with a strikingly remarkable ancestry.

Characteristically, Harrison never spoke much of his more remote ancestry, though there is ample evidence that he was in no sense indifferent,[19] once the question was raised. There was an incident in the Fremont campaign of 1856 that reveals his mind in sharply defined terms. The newly born Republicans of Indianapolis, where young Ben Harrison had his unprepossessing law office, were eager to ratify the great Pathfinder's nomination. The leaders found themselves desperately in need of speakers whose name might command respect and whose presence would serve to whip up some enthusiasm. Harrison was quietly at work in his office when a number of gentlemen came in and insisted that he make a speech to a political gathering in the street outside. Harrison protested, as he did on a number of other occasions, his lack of preparation. These men, however, were in no mood to be denied. They picked up his five-foot-seven frame and carried him downstairs, never permitting his feet to touch the ground until they had placed him on a store box that had been set up in the street. At once he was introduced as the grandson of ex-President William Henry Harrison, the man who had succeeded a Democratic President. Flustered and a bit nervous, the young speaker momentarily crossed up the political leaders by refusing to draw on the political capital of his grandfather. With an air of youthful defiance he said: "I want it understood that I am the grandson of nobody. I believe that every man should stand on his own merits."[20]

Yet, as the years passed, it became increasingly clear that he did put his Harrison heritage on a pedestal. Perhaps the most remarkable instance of this is evident when, in the spring of 1892, a perceptibly growing pressure was put on the President to stand for renomination and re-election.[21] According to Louis T. Michener, Harrison's chief political manager, it was a pres-

19 In the papers of John Scott Harrison (Library of Congress) as well as in those of his brother-in-law, John Cleves Short (Short Family Papers, Library of Congress), evidence is found that young Benjamin was not permitted to grow up in ignorance of his forebears.

20 77th Congress, 1st Session, House Document No. 154, pp. 127–28.

21 A typewritten, undated paper by L. T. Michener, entitled "Harrison Prior to the National Convention of 1892," Michener MSS, p. 1.

sure that did not respect geographical boundaries, and in some cases, even party lines. Influential men, penning letters marked "personal" and "confidential," urged him to accept a second term.[22] To all of these well-wishers and self-appointed political advisers, the President gave the same patient but firm reply, that he did not want a second term and that in good time he would decline to be a candidate. It appears that he persevered in this determination until late May, when, at last, thoroughly irked by the continual attacks, Harrison felt compelled to become a candidate. Some Democratic opponents and a number of personally hostile Republican leaders had let it be noised about that they believed Harrison's administration was marked by both personal and political failure. Harrison was particularly vexed by the statement that his difficulties in office were compounded by his administrative mistakes and by his personal inability to unbend enough.[23]

The reason behind this sudden change in plans, as alleged by the Chief Executive, left a deep impression upon Michener's memory. This political lieutenant of the '88 campaign recalled his summons to the White House where he found his chief indignant and hurt. Yet with a show of coolness and deliberate dignity that served to conceal his offended feelings, the President remarked: "No Harrison has ever retreated in the presence of a foe without giving battle, and so I have determined to stand and fight."[24]

The will to fight, it seems, had played no small part in his family history, for on his father's side he came of a long line of stern stuff.[25] The record is fairly complete. From the landing of Benjamin Harrison, the English emigrant, who came to Virginia within two and a half decades of the Jamestown settlement, down through four successive generations of Benjamin Harrisons, the ancestral line of the President manifested an average sturdiness

[22] *Ibid.*, pp. 1–2. See also Vols. 139–41, *passim*, Harrison MSS.

[23] For a summary treatment, carefully but not impartially edited, see James E. Pollard, *The Presidents and the Press* (New York, 1947), pp. 538–51.

[24] Michener MSS, p. 3.

[25] One of his direct ancestors was a member of the English House of Commons in the Long Parliament in 1649, and voted for the execution of Charles I. On his father's side, through the Willings, Benjamin was a descendant of Major General Harrison of the Parliamentary Army. See "Benjamin Harrison Scrapbooks, 1853–1901," No. 1 (1853–61), "Miscellaneous: personal and political," Harrison MSS.

of character and a more than average prosperity in the goods of this life. All five Benjamins (1632–1791)[26] were distinguished; their personal and public records are almost identical: gentlemen of education and wealth, burgesses, councilors, and militia colonels. It would be utterly false to acquiesce in the impression created by campaign biographers that President Benjamin Harrison came from "poor but pious" stock.[27]

Four Virginia generations of his name had preceded the Benjamin Harrison (1726–1791) who had signed the Declaration of Independence, but it fell to his lot to write one of the most interesting chapters in the early American history.[28] He was the first-born son of a militia colonel, county sheriff, and member of the House of Burgesses; his mother was the attractive daughter of Robert (King) Carter. It is scarcely a reflection on the early Harrison prudence to note that the Carters were one of the richest native-born American families of the day.[29] When the signer was nineteen, an undergraduate at William and Mary, lightning struck his father dead.[30] The bulk of a vast estate, with "slaves and stock thereon,"[31] fell to the young lad's possession and management. Shortly after college, having successfully supervised the administration of his father's estate, he began his public career. Entering the House of Burgesses, he gave uninterrupted service for twenty-seven years, leaving only to take his seat in the First Continental Congress. George Washington tells us that his fel-

[26] Keith, *op. cit.*, pp. 41–43, and Dorothy Burne Goebel, *William Henry Harrison* (Indianapolis, 1926), p. 2, give the arrival date of the first Benjamin as 1634. Freeman Cleaves, *Old Tippecanoe* (New York, 1939), p. 1, gives the date as 1632. The latter's explanation (p. 345) seems more accurate.

[27] One of the best epitomes of the Harrison heritage was given by the Phi Beta Kappa speaker at William and Mary College in 1855. He said: "Of all the ancient and honorable families in the colony of Virginia that of Harrison, if not the oldest, is one of the oldest . . . [and for] a period of more than two centuries, the name has been distinguished for the patriotism, the intelligence, and the moral worth of those who have borne it." James A. Green, *William Henry Harrison: His Times* (Cincinnati, 1941), pp. 4–5; also, Harrison Scrapbook No. 1.

[28] *House Document No. 154,* pp. 29–43.

[29] Cleaves, *op. cit.*, pp. 1–3. The Binghams, of Philadelphia, were perhaps a wealthier family.

[30] "News from the Maryland Gazette," *Maryland Historical Magazine*, No. 17 (1922), p. 365. The following item is listed for Friday, August 16 (1745): "Williamsburgh, July 18: Last Friday evening (July 12) a most terrible accident happened in Charles City County; when a violent thunder gust arose and lightning struck the house of Col. Benjamin Harrison of Berkeley, which killed him, and his two youngest daughters. . . ."

[31] Cleaves, *op. cit.*, p. 3.

low Virginian was summoned to this Congress in 1775 "to utter plain truths"[32] and to head the Committee of the Whole
which debated the Declaration of Independence and reported
that document as agreed to. The honor that was his in signing
the Declaration served but as a prelude to further public service
as Virginia's Governor (1781–84), and as Speaker of the House
of Burgesses (1785).[33] Nor was his domestic life less fruitful; having married Elizabeth Bassett, the charming niece of George
Washington's sister, he gave to Virginia and to America seven
hardy children, four girls and three boys.

The second youngest son was William Henry Harrison.[34] Born
February 9, 1773, it was not until his inauguration as President
in 1841 that this grandfather of Benjamin Harrison was designated "Child of the Revolution."[35] At his birthplace, on the
north bank of the James, there was more talk about the Colonial
boycott on tea and the darkening clouds of impending conflict
than there was about the new arrival.

His first eight years were quiet enough. The immense plantation, his father's shipyard and ships nearby, the mill pond and
the mill, the many slaves and the large stables combined to make
Tidewater Virginia a pleasant place in which to grow up. There
is no reason to suspect that even Benedict Arnold's invasion of
Virginia in 1781 which brought the war close to home had greatly
perturbed William Henry.[36] The day he remembered with misgivings came in April, 1791, when his father's death dashed what
hopes he had of becoming a physician.[37] The world closed in on
him. The ravages of war had left the Harrison fortunes at a low
ebb, and the subsequent depression was no respecter of persons.

The eighteen-year-old Harrison felt the pinch of an empty

32 Woodrow Wilson, *George Washington* (New York, 1896), p. 192.

33 This was his second term as Speaker, for he had defeated Thomas Jefferson for
the same office seven years previously. In the spring of 1791, on the threshold of
another term as Governor, he died.

34 Cleaves, *op. cit.*, p. 4, states that William Henry Harrison was the youngest of
seven in a family that included four daughters.

35 The phrase is attributed to the campaign orators of 1840. See Green, *op. cit.*,
p. 1.

36 The Harrison family had already been removed to a place of safety, since
Berkeley lay on the land and water routes to Richmond. The story of the plunder of
the Harrison estate by Benedict Arnold is related by Cleaves, *op. cit.*, p. 4.

37 His father had determined that he should be a physician and had pointed the
young man's education in that direction. See Green, *op. cit.*, pp. 12–14.

pocket, but by August, 1791, he succeeded in obtaining a commission in the infantry. His service with the First Regiment carried him westward to the Ohio country, where he became an aide to General "Mad" Anthony Wayne through successful campaigns against the Indians which resulted in the Treaty of Greenville in August, 1795.[38] "Opening up the West" was a fine-sounding phrase, but the bleak reality behind it signified only the perilous penetration into an Indian wilderness.

Strange as it may seem, Harrison won his greatest prize, not in successful skirmishes with the Indians, but in the comparative quiet and safety at Fort Washington, Cincinnati, where he was Commandant in 1795. There he met and married a remarkably fine young lady, Anna Symmes,[39] who not only bore him ten children, but also outlived him by almost a quarter of a century.

When he died in the White House in 1841, William Henry Harrison had enjoyed a full and important life. Biographers have done him justice so that the deeds and reputation of "Old Tippecanoe" have become a memorable part of the American tradition and heritage. There is, however, one memorial carved in stone that speaks for itself. At North Bend, Ohio, the birthplace of President Benjamin Harrison as well as the site of the ancestral home, amid century-old trees surrounding his grave, stands a majestic monument. It bears a two-fold message: a succinct biography and a well-merited tribute. On the side towards the Ohio River it reads:

"William Henry Harrison. Secretary of the Northwest Territory. Delegate of the Northwest Territory to Congress. Territorial Governor of Indiana. Member of Congress from Ohio. Ohio State Senator. United States Senator from Ohio. Minister to Colombia. Ninth President of the United States."

---

38 When William Henry was only eleven, George Washington wrote to his father, then Governor, and emphasized the great importance and necessity for Virginia to make a quick and easy road to Ohio. It was not only a question of pacifying Indians and opening up trade lanes with the West, but of tying the "back country" politically to the Atlantic states, lest it be lost to the Union. By a turn of fate, Governor Harrison's son did much to solve these problems. Green, *op. cit.*, p. 9.

39 She was the daughter of John Cleves Symmes, pioneer and Chief Justice of the Northwest Territory for a quarter of a century. Left motherless shortly after birth, she stayed in the East with her grandmother when her father made his Miami Purchase in 1788. After being educated in New York, Anna Symmes went to Ohio in 1794. Shortly thereafter she married Capt. Harrison. She died in 1864. See the long article in *The Weekly Inter-Ocean* (Chicago), October 22, 1889, in Benjamin Harrison Scrapbook No. 9, p. 19, Harrison MSS.

Facing landward and the West he served for fifty years, the inscription reads:

"Ensign of the First United States Infantry. Commandant of Fort Washington. Hero of Tippecanoe. Major General in the War of 1812. Victor of the Battle of the Thames. Avenger of the Massacre of the River Raisin."[40]

On March 4, 1889, when the last paraders had passed the reviewing stand, and twilight was thickening into night, President Harrison and his son Russell arose and walked rapidly to the White House.[41] This was his first peaceful moment all day, and it is more than likely that he spent it, as was his wont, meditatively.[42] Perhaps he mentioned to Russell how much he missed his own father, now ten years in his grave, or, perhaps, more in accord with his undemonstrative nature,[43] let his mind wander back so that forty years dropped into nothingness. He was sixteen, sitting in a dimly lighted room of a little prep school perched high on a hill just outside Cincinnati.[44] He was reading a letter from The Point, the farm he missed so much; the letter was from his father, and he smiled when he learned he had another little brother, but the rest of the letter was in a more serious vein.

. . . I can hardly express to you my satisfaction at hearing how high you stand in the estimation of your professors. I hope you will continue to be studious and attentive to your duties, and above all that you will not be unmindful to those solemn obligations you owe to God. Youth is the time to serve the Lord. Some people think to be religious you must be melancholy and morose, but it is not so. Who has so much cause to be cheerful, as he who has made his peace with God.[45]

Serious-mindedness well describes John Scott Harrison, born at Vincennes, Indiana, on October 4, 1804. His deep religious

40 For an excellent illustration of this monument see Green, *op. cit.*, between pp. 440–41.

41 Benjamin Harrison Scrapbook No. 9, pp. 20–21, Harrison MSS.

42 William Pinckney Fishback, Harrison's law partner for seven years and his acquaintance for thirty-eight years, made this observation in a long biographical account in an interview for the New York *Evening Post*, December, 1888. See Harrison Scrapbook No. 9, Harrison MSS.

43 Benjamin Harrison to his wife, Harrison MSS, Vol. 4, *passim*, 1862.

44 Farmers' College. See Ch. 2, note 50.

45 John Scott Harrison to Benjamin, October 7, 1849, Harrison MSS, Vol. 1.

convictions, which helped ease his hard and pinched career, can be more directly attributed to his mother's influence than to that of his military-minded father.[46] Scott Harrison, as he was known to his family and friends, was plainly the favorite son of both his parents. They not only confided in him, but it would almost seem that his father presumed upon this son's sense of filial duty. In the manifestation of his own magnanimity, General Harrison deprived Scott of the advantages of a West Point education, to which both had looked forward, and, while Senator in Congress, gave a commission to the Military Academy to the son of a Baptist preacher, who came to be Governor Wallace of Indiana and the father of Lew Wallace, himself distinguished by military, diplomatic and literary fame.[47] However, Scott Harrison showed himself to be no laggard or dolt, but pursued his studies and graduated at Cincinnati College under the presidency of Philander Chase, later Bishop of Ohio, and the founder of Kenyon College in Gambier. He was valedictorian of his class, and soon after began his studies for the bar. He entered the law firm of Longworth and Harrison, whose senior member was Nicholas Longworth, owner of millions in Cincinnati real estate.[48]

As his father was drawn more and more into the field of public service, eventually being appointed Minister to Colombia by President John Quincy Adams, it devolved upon the son to manage affairs at home. Forced by these circumstances to discontinue the law, Scott quietly withdrew to the North Bend farm and took charge of the family's large landed estate. As a suitable reward for this filial sacrifice and diligence, William Henry Harrison set aside for his son almost two-fifths of his 2,000-acre farm and built for him a beautiful house four miles from North Bend.[49] This new homestead and farm was familiarly known as The Point, for it lay toward the end of a long neck of land bordered on

---

46 Mrs. Harrison's Presbyterian faith is celebrated. See Green, *op. cit.*, pp. 63–64, 443–45. Even more interesting are the letters of Mrs. William Henry Harrison in the Short Family Papers, Box 56 (Library of Congress). Her husband grew interested in the things of the spirit much later in life and, while President, professed faith in the Episcopalian Church. John Scott, their son, did not join the Cleves Presbyterian Church until October 8, 1849. This may account for the fervor of the letter to his son, cited above.

47 *Weekly Inter-Ocean*, October 22, 1889, in Benjamin Harrison Scrapbook No. 9, p. 19, Harrison MSS.

48 *Ibid.*

49 Lew Wallace, *Life of Gen. Ben Harrison* (Philadelphia, 1888), pp. 48–49; also, *House Document No. 154*, p. 84.

the north side by the Big Miami and on the south by the Ohio, tapering to a point at the confluence of the two rivers.

The attractive young bride who was to become the mother of President Benjamin Harrison hailed from Mercersburg, Pennsylvania. Scott and Elizabeth Irwin, the daughter of Captain Archibald Irwin, were married at The Point on August 12, 1831.[50] Elizabeth had an equally important heritage to pass on to her children. Her grandfather, Major James Ramsey, was a Scottish gentleman who had emigrated from Glasgow to Mercersburg.[51] Near there he built a fine stone mill, established a store, and manufactured flour largely for exportation to Baltimore and Philadelphia as well as to Europe. A leaky and slow-sailing ship ruined a large quantity of flour on the way across the Atlantic, and compelled him to dispose of his business east of the mountains. Owning some large bodies of land west of the mountains, he moved to Ligonier, Westmoreland County, Pennsylvania, and there began anew, early in the 1800's. His store helped to establish his popularity in the valley, and his son, Colonel John Ramsey, laid out the town of Ligonier. It was his second daughter, Mary,[52] who married into the Irwin family back in Mercersburg, and became the mother of Elizabeth Irwin. If Elizabeth's ancestry differed markedly from Scott Harrison's, it was a difference in degree, not in kind. Along with her brothers and sisters, she was brought up to read the Scripture, memorize the catechism, and observe rigidly the Sabbath and its duties. The Irwins seemed to vie with the Ramseys in strict conformity to the Presbyterian code of living.

50 This was his second marriage. In 1824 he had married Lucretia K. Johnson, of Boone County, Kentucky, who bore him three children, Betsy Short, William Henry (who died in infancy), and Sarah Lucretia, before she herself died in 1829 (?). See Wallace, op. cit., p. 46. For the most complete account of William Henry Harrison's children and their marriages, see Green, op. cit., pp. 485–89.

51 Major Ramsey was accompanied by his sister, who later married Mr. Agnew, brother of the grandfather of the eminent surgeon, Doctor D. Hayes Agnew of Philadelphia. The Presbyterian Banner, July 27, 1889, a clipping found in Benjamin Harrison Scrapbook No. 9, p. 59, Harrison MSS.

52 The Presbyterian Banner, July 27, 1889, Harrison MSS. It is interesting to note that Mary Ramsey Irwin gave two daughters to the Harrison family in marriage. Her older daughter, Jane Findlay Irwin, married William H. Harrison, Jr., and later served President William Henry Harrison with great grace and dignity in the White House. Elizabeth, on a visit to her sister in Cincinnati, met John Scott.

It is not difficult to picture the life which Benjamin's parents lived in the two years before his birth and during the years of his infancy. It was a pinched existence. Financially, the ground all but crumbled beneath their feet, as the fortunes of farming along the Ohio were distinctly treacherous. Each major rise and fall of the river was a crisis, for, when the placid river was so low in late summer and early fall as to make navigation slow, difficult, and even impossible, that spelled hardship. Yet, come February and March, the river rolled in an "irresistible flood, furious and uncontrolled, its mighty tide covering the bottom lands for miles with its overflow, washing away its banks, and carrying off in a riot of ruin the great trees of the forest"—and this spelled disaster.[53] Yet, together, John Scott and his wife had the courage to brave these dangers of the river country and the uncertainties of pioneer life, toiling for twenty years. In that time they reared nine children. He who was destined to occupy the White House was their second-born;[54] his first wail was heard on August 20, 1833.

[53] Green, *op. cit.*, p. 409. John Scott Harrison himself delivered an address entitled "Pioneer Life at North Bend" before the Whitewater and Miami Valley Pioneer Association, at Cleves, Ohio, Sept. 8, 1866. It has been published (Cincinnati, 1867). It is excellent for the history of the settlement of North Bend and for personal anecdotes. A copy is now housed at the Indiana State Library, Indianapolis.

[54] Their first-born was named Archibald Irwin after Elizabeth's father, though the family always spoke of him as Irwin. He was Benjamin's "guardian" during prep-school and college days. Later, he rose to become a Lieutenant Colonel in the Volunteers and made a splendid record during the Civil War. He died on December 16, 1870.

CHAPTER II

Pioneer Boyhood and College Days

THE ROLLING acreage of The Point was the first home Benjamin Harrison remembered, though his grandfather's estate at North Bend, Ohio, was his birthplace and the Mecca of his boyhood pilgrimages.[1] The Point was pleasantly located at the mouth of the Big Miami, and John Scott's 600 acres ran from the river over a hill, near an old graveyard, and terminated on the bluff of a ridge. In the 1830's this little settlement tried in vain to keep pace with the rapid development of southwestern Ohio.[2] Cincinnati, the Queen City, which contained only 960 people in 1805, could boast by the 1820's of over 10,000 inhabitants. Other towns sloughed off their laggard pace, as the country of the Miami filled up with amazing rapidity.[3] No longer was there any danger from the Indians on the Ohio. Instead, the river was alive with an endless procession of flatboats, arks, and skiffs, loaded with men and women, household goods and domestic animals. From his front porch young Ben could see this pioneer parade pass before his eyes.

A great acreage yielded John Scott and his family a livelihood, rugged and pinched though it was. Corn, wheat and hay were the

[1] General William Henry Harrison's original purchase was 400 acres. This was expanded until the farm contained 2,800 acres: 2,200 in the "home farm" and a detached 600 acres to the west. This smaller piece was given to John Scott, who in 1833 was building his own homestead on it. Since the house was still under construction in August, 1833, Mrs. Harrison was made comfortable at North Bend and here Benjamin was born. See Freeman Cleaves, *Old Tippecanoe*, p. 28, and James Green, *William Henry Harrison*, pp. 415–16.

[2] See Francis P. Weisenburger, *Passing of the Frontier* (Columbus, Ohio, 1941–44), pp. 2–33.

[3] John Scott Harrison, *Pioneer Life at North Bend*, pp. 1–6.

principal crops, while the forests afforded the meat of the bear and the deer, and the streams still supplied fine fish.[4] Hogs, cattle and sheep were raised and marketed, sometimes at Cincinnati, sometimes at New Orleans.[5] Much of the family clothing was woven on the premises, though tea, coffee and sugar had to be purchased. Among delicacies there were a few chickens and turkeys for summer consumption; in the fall the fattened hog provided hams, bacon and salt pork; much of the beef was corned. The staff of life was frequently made appetizing with delicious peach and apple butter.[6]

When most of his family had grown up and he was serving in Congress, John Scott Harrison wrote to his brother-in-law, who owned a neighboring farm: "My lot in this life has been to raise hogs and hominy to feed my children and I have devoted but little time to *fancy articles*."[7] Hominy, made right on the farm, was a staple article of diet, and only when the supply of wheat and corn was low did johnny-cakes disappear from the breakfast table.

Despite his abundance of stock and produce and his willingness to find a market, Benjamin's father found himself more often than not in desperate financial straits. The periodic and protracted sickness of his large and growing family,[8] the low price of hay and the scarcity of money,[9] the severe losses caused by floods,[10] and a number of equally serious contributing factors more than once forced John Scott to the brink of losing his farm.[11] Only his mother's devotion and his brother-in-law's ready cash kept the Harrisons in possession of The Point during the

4 *Ibid.,* p. 1; also, Harrison MSS, Vol. 157.

5 John Scott Harrison to John Cleves Short, July 24, 1844, December 14, 1845, Jan. 21, 1848, Short Family Papers, Box 55.

6 Green, *op. cit.,* p. 415.

7 John Scott Harrison to John Cleves Short, January 21, 1856, Short Family Papers, Box 55. Harrison writes about the large "wheat fields" (June 29, 1842) and of sending "two fat steers to Cincinnati" (December 14, 1845).

8 John Scott Harrison to John Cleves Short, December 16, 1841, March 19, 1842, January 23, 1844, September 24, 1847 (?), and August 12, 1851, Short Family Papers, Box 55. These letters show that Scott's family was besieged constantly by illness: scarlet fever, frequent colds, pleurisy, and severe attacks of dysentery.

9 John Scott Harrison to John Cleves Short, April 17, 1843, *ibid.* See also Harrison's letter of July 24, 1844, and May 5, 1845, on the same subject.

10 John Scott Harrison to John Cleves Short, Jan. 21, 1848, Short Family Papers, Box 55: "My losses by the late flood are so heavy that I despair of recovering them without parting with a portion of my farm."

11 *Ibid.,* John Scott Harrison to Short, January 16, 1850.

entire period of Benjamin's minority.[12] Perhaps the most serious crisis occurred shortly after Mrs. Elizabeth Harrison's death in 1850, while the two older boys, Irwin and Benjamin, were away at school. On November 20, 1850, John Scott wrote in desperation to John Cleves Short, his sister's husband:

You will perhaps be surprised that one having so small a claim upon your confidence in money matters, should venture your aid again in that way. And nothing but a conviction that you will not receive my application in a spirit of unkindliness, has determined me to ask your friendly interference in extracting me again from most unpleasant embarrassments.

And here, permit me to say, that I would not make this application did I not know that I can give you such security for three or four thousand dollars as will place you beyond the possibility of loss, and at the same time offers satisfactory assurance that the interest shall be paid promptly. I propose to give as security for a loan of the above mentioned amount, a *second* lien on my property here (four hundred acres)—placing all other matters in such a way, as our friend Judge Hart will say, gives you the preference over all other liens. . . .

. . . Some months ago I mentioned my troubles to Judge Hart and he advised me to sell my farm and come to the city and live,—sell my farm, I really would, but what could I do in the city? I could not feed myself much less my children. Besides I am miserable enough here and I should be more so there. . . .[13]

The details of this relentless struggle for survival were hidden from Benjamin during his early days, and there is no question that his first decade of life at The Point was most enjoyable. He grew up, at first a slender, wiry stripling,[14] and bit by bit became a chubby, square-shouldered boy, so blond as to be almost white-

12 Mrs. Anna Harrison to John Cleves Short (her nephew), November 14, 1848, Short Family Papers, Box 56, writes that General Harrison's estate should be settled as soon as possible so "that the heirs should get the *little* that may be left for them . . . as many of them stand in need, some of them to spend in education, others to support their families. . . ."

13 John Scott Harrison to John Cleves Short, Esq., November 20, 1850, Short Family Papers, Box 55. To assure prompt payment of interest, John Scott himself proposed to make such arrangements with nearby Indiana distillers to authorize Short to draw on them every year after corn gathering, for the amount of interest due. John Scott used the river in nearby Whitewater Canal to deliver and sell corn to the distillers at Lawrenceburg, Indiana, five miles distant. See letter of John Scott Harrison to John Cleves Short, December 14, 1845, Short Family Papers, Box 55.

14 J. P. Boyd, *Life and Public Services of Benjamin Harrison* (Philadelphia, 1901), p. 26.

haired.[15] Young Ben loved to fish, hunt and swim, and it was these early predilections that forced him to solve his first problem in human relations. Before he would be allowed to set out on any of these expeditions into the woods for squirrels or out on the river for fish or ducks, his father insisted that he always have the company of an elder. Ben showed a spark of genius in complying with the paternal injunction. For "very frequently he assisted the negro who served the household in the capacity of cook; he carried wood and water for him, and helped him wash the dishes that he might better secure his company in a bout at fishing or hunting."[16] Ben liked his other schoolboy sports,[17] and used to half-walk and half-run to school in order to get there "in time to play bullpen for half an hour before books."[18]

It would be a mistake to think that Ben's days on the farm were all play. According to Congressman Butterworth, himself raised on a farm in southern Ohio,

Ben Harrison's experiences were just like ours. He was a farmer's boy, lived in a little farm house, had to hustle out of bed between 4 and 5 o'clock in the morning the year round to feed stock, get ready to drop corn or potatoes, or rake hay by the time the sun was up. He knew how to feed the pigs, how to teach a calf how to drink milk out of a bucket, could harness a horse in the dark, and do all the things we, as farmers' boys, knew how to do. He used to go to the mill on a sack of wheat or corn and balance it over the horse's back by getting on one end of it, holding on to the horse's mane while he was going up hill, and feeling anxious about the results.[19]

This farmer-legislator knowingly added that "Ben had the usual number of stone bruises and stubbed toes and the average number of nails in his foot that fell to the portion of the rest of us."

[15] *House Document No. 154*, p. 94.

[16] Lew Wallace, *Life of Gen. Ben Harrison*, p. 52.

[17] Weisenburger, *op. cit.*, p. 122: "For the young the school rivaled the home as a center of social activity. In the period before school, at recesses, and during the lunch period, games were a natural outlet for youthful energy. Pupils of various ages played scatter base, prisoner's base, stink base, poison, wood-dog and old witch. The older boys found fun in three corner cat and town ball. The latter was an early type of baseball, employing a ball made by taking a core of India rubber, wrapping it with a strong woolen yarn wound into a tight mass, and having a shoemaker cover the whole with leather. In winter of course snowballs and breast works of snow and ice permitted expression of the pugnacious spirit of growing boys."

[18] Letter from Congressman Butterworth, cited in *House Document No. 154*, p. 93.

[19] *Ibid.*

John Scott Harrison's house fronted the Ohio River; the dining room, which was the common sitting room, was large and commodious, with the usual wide open fireplace. In this room it was the custom of the family to assemble, particularly on winter evenings, around a central table. Light was obtained from the old-fashioned tallow dips, aided by flame from the fireplace, in front of which the mother would sit knitting socks for the boys and listening to the conversation, or the reading, of the younger folks.[20]

The number of socks to be darned and the number of little dresses to be made increased with amazing regularity while Ben was growing up. Besides his older brother Irwin and himself, Ben had two older sisters, Bessie and Sallie,[21] who helped feed and care for the new arrivals at The Point. Succeeding Ben in the roughly hewn cradle were Mary Jane Irwin, who soon answered to the affectionate name of Jennie, and then Anna Symmes and John Irwin—though the last two died in infancy. Before Mrs. John Scott Harrison died in 1850, five more children were born, but only Carter Bassett, Anna, and John Scott, Jr., survived and grew to maturity.[22] In addition to their own children, the John Scott Harrisons were constantly entertaining hordes of nephews and nieces,[23] and in 1848 they assumed the guardianship of two more children.[24]

20 J. E. Morison and W. B. Lane, *Life of Our President Benjamin Harrison* (Published for Lane and Morison, Cincinnati, 1889), p. 105.

21 Benjamin's two older sisters were by John Scott Harrison's first wife. Betsey Short Harrison married George S. Eaton, M.D., who had his practice in Cincinnati. "Sallie" was Sarah Lucretia Harrison, who married Thomas J. Devin of Ottumwa, Iowa. See Charles Keith, *The Ancestry of Benjamin Harrison* (Philadelphia, 1893), for genealogical chart.

22 This Anna, also called Anna Symmes, was named in honor of John Scott's mother, who was still living. The two other children who did not survive their first years were named James Findlay Harrison and James Irwin Harrison.

23 Several of John Scott's nieces and nephews lived nearby. They visited their uncle's farm frequently, and as they grew up they attended the log-cabin school. See Wallace, *op. cit.*, p. 50.

24 This guardianship is mentioned three times in the Harrison and Short Family Papers. In the John Scott Harrison Papers, Box 1, under date of November 2, 1848, is the following: "This is to certify that I, Mary R. Harrison, now residing in the parish of Point Coupee in the state of Louisiana . . . do hereby resign the guardianship as natural to my minor children, Benjamin and William Henry Harrison, and desire that Mr. John Scott Harrison of Hamilton Co., Ohio, be appointed their guardian." See also John Scott Harrison to John Cleves Short, March 20, 1862, Short Family Papers, Box 55, and E. I. Harrison to Benjamin Harrison, Feb. 9, 1848, Harrison MSS, Vol. 1.

The problem of education could have become acute, had not a small, old-fashioned log schoolhouse been erected between the Harrison homestead and the river. This cabin was of the plainest type. It had a puncheon floor and the windows were small and few; the great fireplace, filled with logs in the morning, would keep the school warm all day; for seats there were benches without backs, formed of slabs with supports of sticks fitted in augerholes. In these primitive surroundings Benjamin began his education.[25]

Though the supply of teachers was limited, the Harrison home always employed a tutor or a nurse who guaranteed that the ABC's would not be neglected. The first of these was Miss Harriet Root, the young and competent niece of a Cincinnati preacher.[26] When the children were quite small, Miss Root was their governess; she advanced with them and took her place as mentor in the log-cabin schoolhouse.[27]

Attractive Harriet Root had Irwin, John, Ben, and Jennie to teach from the beginning; later, Betsy joined her class. Her recollections of Ben are of considerable value, giving, as they do, one of the earliest pen sketches of the future Hoosier warrior:

Ben was the brightest of the family, and even when five years old was determined to go ahead in everything. He was very much ahead of his older brother, Irwin, but I held him back at the mother's request. Ben was terribly stubborn about many things. He would insist upon having his own way not only with me, but with his mother. I remember of having but one serious trouble with him, and even then I did not conquer him. I did not wish to punish him severely, but I turned him over to his mother. She corrected him and he came back quite submissive, and never gave me any more trouble.[28]

She was succeeded by Joseph Porter, a college graduate, who became a fast friend of John Scott and remained with the family a

25 Morison and Lane, *op. cit.*, pp. 105–6; also, St. Louis *Post-Dispatch,* July 1, 1888. "The old school house collapsed" in July, 1848; see Jenny Harrison to Benjamin, July 24, 1848, Harrison MSS, Vol. 1.

26 Gilbert L. Harney, *The Lives of Benjamin Harrison and Levi P. Morton* (Providence, 1888), pp. 38–39.

27 Fifty-six years later, Mrs. Harriet Root Giesy admitted that she "was dazed with the idea of going into the family as a teacher, as I was but 16 years old. As I look back upon it now I wonder that my mother consented." Unidentified press clipping, Harrison MSS.

28 This was a special dispatch to the New York *World* dated Aug. 28 (year unknown, but evidently during Harrison's presidency) from Columbus, Ohio. This newspaper clipping was found in the Harrison home, Indianapolis.

long time.[29] His classroom observations on Ben's academic progress moved him to second John Scott's intention of sending Ben to one "of the yankee colleges."[30] Familiar with the curricula of the eastern colleges, Mr. Porter told John Scott that he hoped whether Ben "graduates from Harvard or Yale, that he will take the University course at the former, for the law school at Harvard is certainly unequalled in the country."[31] After Mr. Porter came Mr. Skinner, a graduate of Marshall College, Pennsylvania.[32] Yet it was the face of Thomas Lynn that lingered longest in Ben's memory.[33]

Ben's learning was not restricted to the "wearisome and hard benches"[34] or to the assignments given by his tutors; fortunately, as a favorite of his grandparents, he could learn much at North Bend, his second home. For many The Bend was already a patriotic shrine of the Middle West where old soldiers and distinguished strangers rubbed shoulders while greeting "Old Tippecanoe."[35] As one renowned itinerant minister has recorded, in writing of William Henry Harrison and North Bend, "of his urbanity and genial hospitality and kindness, I entertain the most grateful recollections."[36] Many of the long, long line of visitors entertained by General Harrison before his death Ben was too young to remember, yet to the timeless heritage of his grandfather's extensive library he was a willing heir.

Under the keen eye of a devoted mother "who sought to provide good books, and loved to hear her children read and talk about their studies,"[37] it is not likely that Ben was long kept in ignorance of the books at North Bend. There were histories of Greece and Rome, Caesar's *Commentaries*, Plutarch's *Lives*, but

29 On one occasion John Scott Harrison had to borrow $100 to pay Mr. Porter, "my teacher." See his letter to John Cleves Short, January 23, 1844, Short Family Papers, Box 55.

30 Joseph N. Porter to John Scott Harrison, January 19, 1850, John Scott Harrison Papers, a single box in the Benjamin Harrison collection.

31 *Ibid.*

32 Harney, *op. cit.,* p. 39.

33 Indianapolis *Journal,* June 30, 1888, Scrapbook No. 6, p. 4, Harrison MSS; also, Wallace, *op. cit.,* p. 52. Wallace says his name was Flynn. The secret of Ben's fondness for Thomas Lynn has died with Lew Wallace. No written record has been discovered among the Harrison papers.

34 These were Ben's own recollections, Indianapolis *Journal,* June, 1888.

35 Green, *op. cit.,* p. 415.

36 Timothy Flint, *Recollections of the Past Ten Years* (Boston, 1826), p. 50.

37 Harney, *op. cit.,* p. 40.

the greater portion of the library was devoted to American history and biography, including the lives of Washington by Marshall and by Jared Sparks. There was no fiction. As far as the family tradition goes, General Harrison never read a novel.[38]

It is not at all likely that the General failed to share his books with young Ben, for he gave him much of his rather valuable time. There is one incident which occurred shortly after William Henry Harrison's election to the presidency that bears retelling for the light it sheds on their relationship and Ben's youth. Back on The Point farm where the orchards were prolific, the apple crop used to afford Ben great loot and much pleasure. As it was, some argued that apple-stealing back in the '40's was regarded almost a civic virtue. Apples for boys like Ben seem to have been as much of an inspiration as hard cider for the men, and the impression was popular that, no matter where they were found, they were common property and appropriate emblems of patriotic fervor. Such a delusion Ben carried with him on a trip to Cincinnati, in company with his grandfather, shortly before the latter left for the White House. The eight-year-old, early becoming tired from walking the streets and growing more than a mite hungry, could not resist the temptation presented by a stand highly piled with red-cheeked apples, and so began to fill his pockets just as he was wont to do under the favorite trees of his father's orchard (or anyone else's). Of course, there was no resistance to this till the apple-woman saw him walk innocently and unconcernedly away. Her shrieks called the attention of the grandfather to the comical situation and the account was readily adjusted. Young Ben went on munching his fruit with as much satisfaction as if its possession had not at first involved a question of law and morals.[39]

Presbyterianism flourished in southwestern Ohio during the first half of the nineteenth century,[40] although the nearest church

[38] Green, *op. cit.,* p. 429. Lew Wallace, Harrison's "official campaign biographer," says (pp. 54–55) that "at the call of the children there was notably an edition of Scott's novels." He also notes that "the son Benjamin can scarcely remember the time that he was not enthralled by Waverly, the Scottish tales, and the eastern romances. He pored over them diligently. Ivanhoe and Talisman were sources of indefinite fascination to him."

[39] James P. Boyd, *op. cit.,* p. 28.

[40] Weisenburger, *op. cit.,* pp. 175 ff.

to The Point was the edifice constructed in 1822 at Cleves, Ohio, where services were held fortnightly. Grandma Anna Harrison's $2.00 subscription and William Henry Harrison's 1,500 feet of walnut helped build the structure in which the preacher was advised to drop his Latin and Greek quotations and "to shoot low and aim straight."[41] The next nearest Presbyterian church was located at Lawrenceburg, five miles from North Bend, and it was here that Henry Ward Beecher was called to his first pastorate.[42]

Poor roads and the long distance frequently made it impossible for any of the Harrisons to attend services; yet each member of the family knew that Sundays were days apart. When Benjamin was small, the Harrison tribe, as well as their neighbors, observed the Sabbath with great scrupulousness, and "were forcibly reminded of the emptiness of all earthly pleasures and hopes."[43] The day was spent quietly, ordinary pursuits being abandoned, even letter-writing,[44] so that the call of the spirit might the better be heeded. The children's recollections of the day were far from somber or depressing. On the contrary, the young ones looked forward to Sunday afternoons, when "all assembled in the parlor and sung hymns from four o'clock until bed-time."[45]

When it was possible for any members of the family to make the trip to attend the Cleves Presbyterian church, they received an earthly reward in the form of an invitation to dinner at their grandparents' home.[46] Perhaps Young Ben and his brothers and sisters accepted the invitation with mixed emotions. They were delighted to see the table loaded with chicken and ham, and all kinds of nice pies and cakes, yet Mrs. Harrison's fixed habit

41 Green, op. cit., p. 444.

42 Ibid., p. 445. The Beechers were famous in Cincinnati. Lyman Beecher was not only President of Lane, the Presbyterian Seminary, but was also pastor of the largest Presbyterian church in the city.

43 Sallie Harrison to Benjamin Harrison, February 8, 1851, Harrison MSS, Vol. 1. It is also evident from this letter that the children desired to attend church regularly, and were awaiting the completion of a new church and the appointment of a permanent minister.

44 Jennie Harrison to Benjamin Harrison, November 26, 1849, Harrison MSS, Vol. 1: "It is Sunday and if I were not writing to my brother . . . I would not feel altogether right in doing so."

45 Sallie Harrison to Benjamin Harrison, February 8, 1851, Harrison MSS, Vol. 1.

46 Ibid., see also Green, op. cit., p. 446.

of evening Bible reading[47] was not nearly so much fun as the singing.

Ben did not need to attend church services in order to be impressed with the importance of prayer. From his earliest recollections until his devoted mother's untimely death in 1850, he heard her daily prayer: "May God bless you and keep you continually under His protecting care."[48] After fifteen years of discipline, tempered by prayers and understanding, Ben Harrison knew what was right, and it was no little consolation for him to receive, after a few weeks' absence from home, the following letter from his mother:

... you may imagine my anxiety to hear how you get along with those bad boys . . . after your Pa told me how badly they were behaving I hardly close my eyes to sleep for I felt that boys that could behave so badly, could be capable of any act. Don't fail to let us hear from you very often . . . and continue to act with that same propriety that you have heretofore . . . you don't know how thankful I feel to have such good sons and how proud I am that your teachers, and everyone, speak of your conduct in such high terms. I pray for you daily that you may be kept from sinning and straying from the paths of duty.[49]

By the fall of 1847 John Scott Harrison had determined that his two older boys, Irwin, 16, and Benjamin, 14, should have the advantages of a college education, though his first problem was securing for them an essentially sound secondary school training. He finally decided upon Farmers' College,[50] a small institution located in Walnut Hills, a suburb six miles from Cincinnati.[51] This decision taxed Scott Harrison heavily, and to his brother-in-law he confided: "Sending the boys to Cary's last week consumed all my *ready* capital. But I have corn and hay . . . both of which are cash articles in Lawrenceburg. . . ."[52] It was a sacri-

47 Cleaves, *op. cit.*, p. 332.

48 E. I. Harrison to Irwin and Benjamin, February 9, 1848, Harrison MSS.

49 E. I. Harrison to Irwin and Benjamin, July 24, 1848, Harrison MSS.

50 Farmers' College was founded upon an endowment of land and money donated by William Cary, and for a long time bore the name Cary's Academy. New York *Evening Post,* clipping marked Dec., 1888, in Benjamin Harrison Scrap Book No. 9, Harrison MSS.

51 Boyd, *op. cit.,* p. 28.

52 John Scott Harrison to John Cleves Short, November 10, 1847, Short Family Papers, Box 55. John Scott apologized for not being able to pay even the small portion of the money he owed to Short, but he promised to raise the balance of the three years' interest immediately and with great pleasure.

fice he never regretted, and one for which Ben became increasingly grateful.[53]

The President of the College, Dr. Freeman G. Cary, son of the founder, was a man of strong character. As principal of Cary's Academy, out of which Farmers' College grew, he had earned his reputation as an educator of boys.[54] His brother, Samuel Fenton Cary, was equally well known as a temperance advocate.[55] Among the young students, however, it was Dr. Freeman Cary who came in for the most discussion. To their possibly biased minds his reputation as a strict disciplinarian was certainly merited. And as might be suspected under like conditions today, the horseplay of the students kept his disciplinary talents in constant exercise. The root of the difficulty was twofold: the school buildings were located on the Cary Farm, and the president himself was a celebrated horticulturist. This situation did not make for harmony, for Mr. Cary's fine orchard of plums, cherries, apples and pears, which adjoined the college grounds, was subject to frequent raids by the boys.[56]

In this mischief, Murat Halstead, Oliver W. Nixon and Joseph G. McNutt were ringleaders—and the newly admitted freshman, Benjamin Harrison, was allowed to share in the perils and profits of these forays. As a result there was a state of belligerency existing between the president and the students, which led to frequent chapel lectures and repeated threats of expulsion. Sometimes the president would act on mere suspicion or misinformation furnished by the janitor and, when the boys would be apprehended and exonerated by a scotch verdict, there would follow profuse apologies in the chapel from the president and jubilations in the south wing, where the Halstead-Harrison crowd had their rooms.[57]

The president, being a man of hot and cold fits, was good game for the young collegians. Weekly prayer meetings were held in his room. It was not an unusual thing, when a good brother would

[53] Indianapolis *Journal*, June 29, 1888 (?), in Benjamin Harrison Scrapbook No. 6, entitled "1888: Speeches of Harrison; Biographical," p. 3.

[54] New York *Evening Post, loc. cit.*

[55] Weisenburger, *op. cit.*, p. 163. Samuel Fenton Cary was an officer of The National Division of the Sons of Temperance.

[56] This account was given by W. P. Fishback in the New York *Evening Post*, Benjamin Harrison Scrapbook No. 9, pp. 1–2, Harrison MSS.

[57] *Ibid.*; also, St. Louis *Post-Dispatch*, July 1, 1888.

be in the midst of a lengthy prayer, for somebody to start a keg filled with boulders rolling down the stairway, which was in the hall adjoining the room where the meeting was in progress. All was dark on the upper floor while this was going on, and when the soft-footed president ascended and applied his ear to the key-hole, the snoring of the occupants gave emphatic testimony to their innocence. While these incidents served as pleasant diversions in college life, young "Master"[58] Harrison was quickly introduced to the more serious side of academic life.

The really strong man on the college faculty was not President Freeman G. Cary, but the one next in seniority, a venerable and lovable old professor whom all College Hill—Carl, the faculty, and the students—regarded as "our beloved Father."[59] He was Dr. Robert Hamilton Bishop, an Edinburgh Scot, who came to America and the West when he was a young man. It was his spirit that guided the formulation of institutional policy: "The government will be mild but firm," said Dr. Bishop, "essentially parental in character . . . It will be taken for granted that every youth and young man is honest . . . that he has entered the Institution to improve, and the last thing questioned will be his integrity."[60] These were the epitome of Bishop's philosophy of education and of life.

When Ben first met him, Dr. Bishop was in the twilight of his career, having already served for twenty years as a professor at Transylvania University,[61] Lexington, Kentucky, and another twenty years as president of Miami University, Oxford, Ohio. Consequently, when he joined the faculty of Farmers' College in 1846, he brought with him a wide reputation for scholarship and for those warm qualities of sympathy and considerate attention that had won for him the respect and love of thousands of his students.[62] Within two years of his death, James Mathews,

58 Both Mrs. Harrison and Ben's sister addressed their letters to Master B. Harrison, once he left home for Pleasant Hill. See letters of 1848 and 1849, Harrison MSS, Vol. 1, *passim.*

59 James H. Rodabaugh, *Robert Hamilton Bishop* (Columbus, Ohio, 1935), p. 161.

60 A. B. Huston, *Historical Sketch of Farmers' College* (Cincinnati, 1902), p. 56; Rodabaugh, *op. cit.,* p. 166.

61 Transylvania was founded in 1780. See article in New York *Evening Post,* by Fishback, Benjamin Harrison Scrapbook No. 9, Harrison MSS.

62 Rodabaugh, *op. cit.,* pp. 76–77.

Chancellor of the University of the City of New York, felt safe in saying of Dr. Bishop that "he had a more important agency in that of directing the educational interests of the West, than any other man who lived during the same period."[63]

After three years of intimate association and diligent study under Dr. Bishop's direction, Benjamin Harrison—who was one of fifty who recited with him each day[64]—added his voice to an ever-swelling chorus of praise and gratitude. As he was leaving Farmers' College, Ben penned the following note to the Doctor:

Having for some years enjoyed the benefit of your instruction, and being now about to pass from under your care, I would be truly ungrateful were I not to return my warmest thanks for the lively interest you have ever manifested in my welfare and advancement in religious as well as scientific knowledge.[65]

At Farmers' College, Bishop continued to teach the subjects which had so attracted him while studying at Edinburgh. Occupying the chair of history and political economy,[66] he poured into the minds of the impressionable young men a philosophy pregnant with a spirit of liberalism and progressivism, and with a fervent and reasonable love of liberty, truth and virtue.[67] His broad knowledge, his youthful enthusiasm in old age, and his personal interest in each student attracted a great following.[68]

Upon Bishop's arrival at College Hill, the curriculum was liberalized to a considerable extent and students were allowed a much wider choice of subjects. Course selection was based, as the old professor used to say, on a "scale of equivalents." If a student were averse to tackling Greek or the difficult mathematics, he could avoid one of them by taking "an equivalent" in Doctor Bishop's classes. These "equivalent" classes were then unique, and very attractive to boys who thought that in this way they might work along the lines of least resistance. Bishop, however, had a way of fooling them. For example, the textbooks for the current history class were the public documents which the

63 Cited in Rodabaugh, *op. cit.*, p. 169.
64 Huston, *op. cit.*, p. 56.
65 Benjamin Harrison to Dr. R. H. Bishop, August 28, 1850, Harrison MSS, Vol. 1.
66 Huston, *op. cit.*, p. 56.
67 Weisenburger, *op. cit.*, p. 175. His sixth chapter on "Religion and Education" is well done.
68 Rodabaugh, *op. cit.*, p. 187.

old students of Transylvania and Miami Universities, who were in Congress, would dump upon the old doctor by the carload. "Here, Harrison," he would say, "take this report of the Commissioner on Indian Affairs and give us at the next recitation the leading facts as to the present condition of the Indians."[69] And so he would apportion to the boys the reports of the War Department, the Treasury, and so on, and at the next recitation short essays would be read, followed by criticism from the doctor. He was avid for facts, and frequently explained to his boys that, "Other things being equal, that man will succeed best in any given work who has the most facts."[70]

In his three years with this eminently progressive preceptor, Ben was impressed with the doctor's formula for learning. "Education," Bishop maintained, "is getting possession of your mind, so you can use facts as the good mechanic uses his tools."[71] Rules for expression, moreover, were of primary importance with this Scottish sage. He was averse to floridity of style. One of Ben's classmates, Ed Straight, had been assigned the Cuban question. For his recitation the anxious sophomore wrote a rhapsody about the "Queen of the Antilles." The old doctor's criticism was: "Not enough facts, and too much declamation."[72] It may well be that Harrison's own severe classical style, particularly during the earlier period of his public life, stems from the training he had under Bishop.

Aside from his value as a professor, Bishop's presence was a powerful stimulus to the college. Hailed by the students as the "patriot," the "sage," and the incarnation of "college spirit,"[73] he was at last asked by President Freeman Cary to formulate a new policy of discipline.[74] In response to this request the seventy-year-old educator introduced a disciplinary system that was novel in its day. The general policy in most colleges was rather harsh

69 These facts are culled from the New York *Evening Post* article by Fishback, Benjamin Harrison Scrapbook No. 9, Harrison MSS.

70 *Ibid.*

71 *Ibid.*

72 *Ibid.*

73 "Bishop became sort of a loyalty for the school; the love and admiration for him while he lived, and for his memory after his death took place of college flag and colors. In 1850 measures were begun to create in his honor the Bishop Professorship. . . . The alumni built a small cottage home for Bishop and his wife. It became a landmark in the tradition of the school after his death." Rodabaugh, *op. cit.*, p. 165.

74 *Ibid.*, p. 166.

and arbitrary. In the western schools of higher learning paddling and other forms of corporal punishment were still quite common. Bishop, however, had inherited a more democratic spirit from his associations in Scotland, and he took pains to recognize his students as men, as his political and social equals. Consequently, the policy he had declared at Miami University, and the one he now drew up for Farmers' College, read as follows: "The general principle of government of this Institution is: that every young man who wishes to be a scholar, and expects to be useful as a member of a free community, must at a very early period of life acquire the power of self-government."[75] With this attitude Bishop won Benjamin's respect and love, and consequently he had over the future president a power and influence which few professors or teachers are able to exert over those whom they teach.

In 1896, with a wisdom born of age and experience, Benjamin Harrison reflected significantly on the value of his early schooling.[76] He was thoroughly convinced that the "seeds of knowledge" ought first be planted at the tender age of eighteen months, and that the wise parent should not neglect the child until the average school-going age of six or seven years. Granted that during most of the intervening time the youngster is a scholar without opinions and without doubts, he nevertheless maintained that the early and individual attention was most desirable.[77]

Harrison's point was plain. He knew from experience that boys and girls needed at some time during their young lives the helping hand of an adult "chum," a teacher who could converse with them and bring into the open their hidden talents. Admitted, he said, that the "average youngster is lectured, teased, chaffed and petted; that he has had some moral and religious precepts imparted to him," the one important question to be asked is: "Has any man or woman had a conversation with the boy?"[78]

75 Ibid., pp. 76–77.

76 Benjamin Harrison, *Views of an Ex-President* (Indianapolis, 1901), pp. 419–25. This book, compiled by Mary Lord Harrison, his second wife, is a collection of Harrison's addresses and writings on subjects of public interest after the close of his administration.

77 Ibid.

78 Ibid.

Perhaps he was thinking of himself and his days under Doctor Bishop when he gave the following illustration:

Consider the case of a boy. He has been brought into a vast workshop, where the most subtle forces and the most intricate mechanisms are humming and whirling; into a vast picture gallery where thousands of canvases, great and small, are hung; into a great auditorium where on many stages clowns and tragedians are acting and reciting. He needs help; for a habit that will influence, yes control, his intellectual life is now being acquired. Is he to have a wandering or a fixed eye; a habit of attention or of mental dissipation?[79]

Young Ben found his help, his "fixed eye," his influential educational force at Farmers' College, and, if one may judge from his splendid collection of essays and compositions written for Dr. Bishop,[80] it is abundantly clear that he discovered in this venerable septuagenarian an adult companion with whom he was to have many a serious conversation. In later life Harrison was fond of quoting Montaigne's observation by way of contrast with his own good fortune: " 'Tis the custom of school masters to be eternally thundering in their pupils' ears, as though they were pouring into a funnel. . . . I would not have him alone to invent and speak, but that he should also hear his pupils in return."[81] Ben glibly added his own comment: "The tank may be full, but if there is no tap how shall we draw from it?"[82]

Ben Harrison's first steps along the path to higher learning were guided by the widely read and practical-minded Bishop, a man who never permitted his academic charges to forget one important principle: When you speak publicly or privately, say something people will care to remember. Harrison was one charge who made this principle his own. Not only was he successful in fashioning state papers, lectures and speeches that were distinctive for "clear, vigorous language and sound

[79] *Ibid.*, pp. 420–21.
[80] Benjamin Harrison Papers, Vol. 1, Nos. 83–143, contain over seventy pages of Harrison's essays, compositions, and sermons in their original manuscript form, all written for Dr. Bishop.
[81] Benjamin Harrison, *op. cit.*, p. 423.
[82] *Ibid.*

thinking,"[83] but even his casual conversations were remembered as remarkably worth while.[84]

While concise logic characterized his later public utterances, the young Harrison had to learn the hard way. Under Bishop's exacting eye he worked through the dry bones of Colonial and later American history. These courses, Bishop insisted, were intended to train the lawyer, the soldier and the statesman of the next generation. Consequently, the elderly professor's courses were thoroughly detailed and equally demanding. Indeed, the opening classes were more than trying, but the young Harrison was a willing subject.

Once young Ben got past his recitation on "The Character of the Men Who Made the First Discoveries in America," he found that the grind had just begun. He was required to spend long hours digging out salient facts on "The First Settlement of Maryland and Massachusetts."[85] In an era when college outlines were home-made, and short-cuts to knowledge were frowned upon, Ben spent long hours in an inadequately equipped library. He terminated his researches on the Colonies with the conclusion that: "The Puritan may be considered as the source from which all our republican principles have sprung and as such should be remembered by us with the deepest gratitude and love."[86]

Master Harrison was assigned a long period of study on the knotty problems of the American Revolution and its military and naval aftermath, the War of 1812. Minutely detailed lists of American generals, colonels and captains had to be drawn up one day; on the next, a similar list of British officers. During daily class recitation that followed, the causes of the war, battles, with exact geographical locations and results, were discussed in detail.[87] Ben was learning early the value of marshaling and interpreting facts.

---

[83] Henry L. Stoddard, *As I Knew Them: Presidents and Politics from Grant to Coolidge* (New York, 1927), p. 167: "Harrison's state papers and his subsequent lectures are an interpretation of national problems and purpose unsurpassed for sturdy patriotism. . . ."

[84] John L. Griffith's recollection of Harrison in the *Western Inter-Ocean*, March 14, 1901.

[85] Composition No. 2 for Dr. Bishop, Benjamin Harrison MSS, Vol. 1.

[86] *Ibid.*

[87] Composition Nos. 3–8 for Dr. Bishop, Benjamin Harrison MSS, Vol. 1.

Inasmuch as Bishop was one of the first in the United States to have and to teach a systematic social philosophy,[88] it is not surprising that he was no less demanding with his assignments in the field of social relations. When Ben was assigned a composition on "Some of the Leading Differences in the Modes of Living, Labor and Enjoyment of the Comforts of Life in a Savage and a Highly Advanced State of Society," he made some shrewd observations for a sixteen-year-old, the bulk of which characterized his later thinking and chivalrous conduct. Perhaps Bishop smiled when Ben reported:

The manner by which women are treated is good criterion to judge of the true state of society. If we knew but this one feature in a character of a nation, we may easily judge of the rest, for as society advances, the true character of woman is discovered . . . and appreciated. . . . Look at the position woman occupies in this country, instead of being regarded as a slave far beneath the dignity of man, she is considered a superior being, and in the eyes of many an angel, this is however, the case only when we behold them through the telescope of love, which like all other telescopes has the power of magnifying objects, and perhaps this possesses the power to a greater degree than any other, but whether we behold them through this glass or any other, she still appears worthy of the exalted position which she occupies.[89]

Shortly after his nomination as the Republican presidential candidate in June 1888, the searchlight of inquiry was turned on Harrison's private life. Was he rich? Had he accumulated great wealth in property? When the facts were made public, his good name was none the worse for the inquiry. One paragraph in the daily press summed up the findings:

General Harrison is generous to a fault. Whether public or private, a meritorious charity has rarely appealed to him in vain. He has given away money by hundreds, even thousands of dollars, year after year, and the result is that, though always having a good income from his profession, he has accumulated comparatively little property. The needs of friends, the calls for political expenses, church expenses,

[88] Rodabaugh, op. cit., p. 187. The author claims that, if anyone deserves such acclaim, Bishop might well be designated the "father of American Sociology" because he carried to America the social philosophy of Ferguson as it was interpreted and expanded according to the liberal and somewhat revolutionary principles of Stewart.

[89] Composition No. 9 for Dr. Bishop, Benjamin Harrison MSS, Vol. 1.

church charities, and the thousand and one benevolences which never fail to find a liberal man, have prevented much accumulation.[90]

This generous disposition was a growth and the seed was planted early in Harrison. Knowing his father's good nature and the ministerial background of Bishop, his preceptor, it is not surprising to read that Ben in a prep-school exercise wrote that the "Creator planted certain principles within the human heart," and that "one of the most powerful of these is that which prompts us to sympathize with suffering humanity." He added significantly that the "Creator did not design that they [the principles] should lie dormant, and if we suffer them to be hidden in our bosom, we must certainly suffer the penalty."[91]

Although Professor Bishop exercised his students in the art of biographical writing, young Ben had little talent along those lines.[92] Yet, in his third year at College Hill he came up with an interesting essay on "The Qualifications Necessary to Form a Good Historian." If a man did not have "good hard common sense," Ben claimed, it was impossible "to make a good historian out of him." To this natural qualification Harrison added sound judgment, selection of details, suitable perseverance and industry. In his conclusion he gives the key to his own later characteristic of study and research: "Before a man can do justice to any subject he must be entirely conversant with that subject, thus it is with the historian, he must study his subject until he can truly say he has mastered it."[93]

The field of politics, and particularly the presidential election of 1848, afforded Harrison ample opportunity for composition in a subject in which he was vitally interested. The three-cornered fight for the presidency in 1848 moved his pen to spell out strong sentiments against the Free Soilers, a coalition party which nominated Martin Van Buren to run on a platform of "Free Soil, free

[90] Indianapolis *Journal*, July 1, 1888.

[91] This was Composition No. 13, entitled "A Statement of the Obligation under which Every Man is to Give Assistance to the Poor and Needy According as God Has Prospered Him." In still another essay (No. 15) Harrison wrote "that only in the Noble Will of God could we have the welfare and the benefit we do." Harrison MSS, Vol. 1.

[92] The two attempted biographical sketches made by Harrison do not read smoothly. See Compositions No. 14 and 18 for Dr. Bishop, Harrison MSS, Vol. 1. In keeping with his times, Harrison wrote in full florid style.

[93] Composition No. 15 for Dr. Bishop, Harrison MSS, Vol. 1.

speech, free labor and free men."[94] "Old Van" was distinctly a used-up man in comparison with the Democratic nominee, Cass of Michigan, or the Whig candidate, old Rough and Ready Taylor, hero of Buena Vista. Ben saw Van Buren's candidacy in an unfavorable light, and wrote: "Is it not a good example of the absurdity to which party spirit leads men, for those of the free soil faction, who were, in their saner moments, true Whigs, so to be blinded by party as to see in Martin Van Buren, instead of the traitor which he is, a man fit to fill the presidential chair?"[95]

Equally important with literary composition was the companion subject, reading. In this connection Bishop taught the ineffable superiority of reading history over that of the novel.[96] When Ben was required to express his views in this field, either from expediency or conviction he followed Bishop's line of reasoning that novel reading was not only inferior but also productive of evil. At the end of a long litany of purported ills that stem directly from contact with the novel, Harrison concluded that "It unfits the mind for close application to many subjects, and I have the authority of Doctor Bishop that it weakens the mind and if carried to excess will ultimately destroy it."[97] Then, plumbing the depth of his imaginative powers, Ben told this story which affords insight into a young mind developing rapidly:

To impress more strongly upon your mind the bad effect of novel reading I will narrate an instance which came under my observation while taking a tour in the East. There was a certain young man named Brown who followed the trade of shoe-making in a certain city through which it was my luck to pass . . . he became by degrees so addicted to the damnable habit of novel reading that although he not only occupied his leisure moments in this way, but frequently en-

[94] Theodore Clark Smith has the best treatment in his *Liberty and Free Soil Parties in the Northwest* (New York, 1897). Cass of Michigan succeeded Polk as the Democratic candidate; the Whigs nominated General Taylor. The third party was formed by a coalition of three hitherto separate and hostile elements—the Abolitionist-Liberty Party, the "conscience" or antislavery Whigs of New England, and the "Barnburner" faction of the New York Democracy, which came in to be revenged on Cass for "stealing" the nomination from Van Buren. Van Buren did not carry a single state.

[95] Harrison MSS, Vol. 1.

[96] It was one of Bishop's pet pedagogical principles that "history was superior to romance" in every respect. Harrison's statement: Composition No. 2, Harrison MSS, Vol. 1.

[97] Composition for the Society, No. 2, Harrison MSS, Vol. 1.

croached on his powers of labor . . . with the result that he sought
everywhere for a Heloise . . . he became acquainted with a female
who had unfortunately been christened by that name and an intimacy
soon sprung up between them. . . .

Heloise was weak enough to consent to an interview with her ad-
mirer. They met at the appointed place of rendezvous and after walking for some time they found themselves in a retired spot . . . Brown
stopped and drawing an awl from his bosom, embraced his sweetheart
and exclaimed "Here, dear Heloise, we must die together." Saying
this he struck the awl into her bosom and it must have proved fatal
had it not stuck into the whale bone of her staves (which proves notwithstanding all that has been said to the contrary that her staves
were useful to her). He followed this with eight more blows which
inflicted as many wounds. He then attempted to kill himself and soon
fell bathed in his own blood. . . .

I will conclude by saying that the wounds were not mortal. Brown
recovered to be a wise man and Heloise to repent her interview with
the novel reader.[98]

Twelve years after he had left Farmers' College, Benjamin
Harrison, after Lincoln's call for volunteers in July 1862, began
a tour of duty as Colonel of the 70th Indiana Regiment. To his
wife he wrote: "I believe it is conceded now that our Regiment
was the first into the field under the last call. We are proud of
the position and hope to be the last to turn our backs to the enemy";[99] two days later he said: "Let the office and all its honors
and emoluments go. I would not give up the consciousness that
I am rendering humble service to my country in this hour of her
sore trial for all the honors and riches of the land";[100] and after
three months under arms: "I love to feel [I am] in some humble
way serving a country which has brought so many honors to my
kindred and such untold blessings to those I love."[101]

Those sentiments spoken on the field of battle echo strongly
the words he spoke and the spirit he imbibed at sixteen. He had
handed in an essay on patriotism, the essential theme of which
was: "True patriotism unmingled with base and selfish motives
is one of the greatest virtues a man can possess. It is one of those
few jewels which equally becomes the highest or the lowest. In

98 *Ibid.* This is in Harrison's own handwriting; the paragraph division is the
author's.

99 Benjamin Harrison to his wife, August 21, 1862, Harrison MSS, Vol. 4, 689–91.

100 Benjamin Harrison to his wife, August 23, 1862, Harrison MSS, Vol. 4,
692–93.

101 Benjamin Harrison to his wife, October 9, 1862, Harrison MSS, Vol. 4, 719–20.

JOHN SCOTT HARRISON

THE SON OF ONE PRESIDENT AND THE FATHER OF ANOTHER

From a photograph preserved in the Harrison Memorial Home

ELIZABETH IRWIN HARRISON

MOTHER OF BENJAMIN HARRISON

From a drawing preserved in Harrison Memorial Home

NORTH BEND, OHIO

The Residence of William Henry Harrison and the Birthplace of Benjamin Harrison

Miami University Campus in the 1850's, Oxford, Ohio

the King or the peasant it shines brightest of all the gems which deck the royal diadem, and yet it scorns not the brow of the humblest."[102] Yet the seed that grew into the flower of 1862 was expressed in his own boyish language:

Who would not exchange all the military glory of Napoleon or Alexander for the name of patriot? Whose ambition could ask more, whose aspirations be higher than to have his name handed down to posterity as a firm, unselfish, exampled patriot, one who holds the honor of his country above every other consideration and was ready at a moment's notice to sacrifice on his country's altar, his life, his property, his all?[103]

Before leaving the portals of Farmers' College, Ben gave evidence that Professor Bishop was not inactive in his pristine role of a Presbyterian minister. His students were required to write and preach "practice" sermons, and in many cases the young men set down what was to be the rule and measure of their lives. On one occasion Harrison set out to preach on a subject which was to be for him personally a perennial problem, declaring that "when a man suffers his business to occupy all his attention, then there is no room for religious contemplation, no time that can be devoted to the consideration of heavenly things."[104] And he might have added then, as he did a decade later, in a letter to his wife: "I feel now in the absorbing hold that my business had upon me for the last two years, I was wasting the higher part of my nature and neglecting those offices of love in my family that develop the heart and make others happy. I was too anxious to provide against bodily want, and was neglecting the cravings of the spirit."[105]

Home life at The Point had moved in its usual cycle, while Ben was away at school. Apart from vacation periods, the family did not see much of either Irwin or Ben, though they did slip

---

[102] The title was: "Of All the Generous and Ennobling Feelings which the Human Mind is Capable of Generating, Patriotism Seems to Proceed from the Holiest and Highest Source." Composition No. 6, Harrison MSS, Vol. 1.

[103] *Ibid.*

[104] Sermon No. 2 for Dr. Bishop, Harrison MSS, Vol. 1. He also asked: "What does it profit a man, if he gains the whole world, and lose his own soul?" The sermon scores the desire of earthly prosperity which diverts the mind from God.

[105] Benjamin Harrison to his wife, Dec. 4, 1862, Harrison MSS, Vol. 4, 755-58.

home to lend a hand to the plow in spring and to work with the men in the fields at harvest time.[106] Frequent letters from Sallie, Anna and Jennie indicate how much the "young men" of the family were missed, especially on those pleasanter days free from farm labor and household duties when the family plotted a fishing expedition on the Ohio,[107] or when the Miami swarmed with wild ducks and rod and reel yielded to the rifle.[108]

One of the reasons for Ben's infrequent trips home was the continued financial embarrassment experienced by John Scott Harrison.[109] In the fall of 1849 "money was so tight"[110] that John Scott seriously doubted that he could afford to keep Irwin and Ben at Farmers' College. In addition to feeling the pinch of poverty, the father of the growing household almost sickened to see his young family laid low from time to time by prevalent epidemics of cholera, smallpox, influenza, typhoid, dysentery, scarlet fever, and by the scourge of the common cold. Almost every letter Ben received brought news of illness and suffering, and in the sixth month of his departure from home he received the sad news that his baby brother, Findlay, had died.[111]

Despite the absence of money and the presence of suffering and sorrow, the family spirit was far from broken, or even low. For the family feasts at Thanksgiving and Christmas Ben always found a way to get home. The Christmas of 1849 was particularly happy and memorable, though it was the last celebration at which the children would have their mother at the other end of the long dining-room table. In late November, Ben began to anticipate some of the joy of Christmas preparations. In a letter from sister Sallie he read:

I expect you have almost despaired of hearing from me at all and indeed you have good reasons so thinking. But I have a pretty good

106 Indianapolis *Journal*, June 30, 1888.

107 Anna Harrison to Benjamin, September 14, 1849, Harrison MSS, Vol. 1.

108 Sallie Harrison to Benjamin, January 7, 1851, Harrison MSS, Vol. 1.

109 See letters of Sept. 14, 1849, October 7, 1849, and February, 1850, to Benjamin Harrison from his sisters Sallie and Jennie, Harrison MSS, Vol. 1.

110 Anna Harrison to Benjamin, December 20, 1849, Harrison MSS, Vol. 1.

111 E. I. Harrison to Irwin and Benjamin, February 9, 1848, Harrison MSS, Vol. 1. Mrs. Harrison had to tell the boys that: "There has been a sad change in our family since dear Findlay was with us, and in perfect health; he is now in the silent tomb—but his spirit is in heaven, when we think of that we can be reconciled to our loss, dear little fellow, he was a sweet child, may we all be prepared to follow him."

excuse, for we have been so busy, Jennie and I, that we have scarcely a spare moment. I have been away from home so much that my sewing has collected so much, that it keeps me very busy, and we have such a miserable girl in the kitchen that it takes part of my time to prepare our meals. Well, drawing and preparing our Christmas presents consumes time also. . . .[112]

In the messages to her boys at school Mrs. Harrison consistently exhorted them to show care in choosing companions, to avoid the evils of idleness, to use leisure time for cultural interests.[113] Nor was John Scott less vigilant, for when Ben decided that dormitory life would be more conducive to his advancement than boarding-house quarters, Ben's father wrote a letter which speaks for itself:

I sometimes feel a bit more uneasiness about you than I did when your brother Irwin was with you and you were living in a private house. I feel too you are now more exposed to many temptations incident to a college life. And yet I believe you have firmness enough to resist evil influences no matter how flattering may be the garb in which they are presented. Let your actions always be governed by the same moral influences which were experienced over you when a little boy at home, and with God's help you are safe. I hope you never lose sight of your entire confidence in your Maker both morning and evening acknowledging your manifold obligations to Him. It is said of Mr. Adams that he never went to sleep without repeating the prayer his mother taught when he was a boy. . . .[114]

From a number of "complaints" contained in letters from The Point, Benjamin had more than one account to render for his conduct. Rank negligence in correspondence, consumption of "forbidden" cucumbers, and the smoking of "long" cigars called forth epistolary anathemas from various members of the family.

[112] Sallie to Master Benjamin Harrison, November 24, 1849, Harrison MSS, Vol. 1. At Christmas time Ben was expected to play the part of Santa, and was told by John Scott that "Carter wants you to bring him some shooting crackers . . . Anna wants some candy for John Myers' children . . . Carter also wants some sky rockets . . . he sends a dollar. I think it will be poorly expended myself, but he claims it as his own property." John Scott Harrison to Benjamin, December 1850, Harrison MSS. Ben was expected to pick up these items in Cincinnati. See also letter of December 20, 1849, Anna to Benjamin. She sends him money for his trip home. Harrison MSS.
[113] E. I. Harrison to Irwin and Benjamin, February 9, May 22, and July 24, 1848, Harrison MSS, Vol. 1.
[114] John Scott Harrison to Benjamin, December 10, 1849, Harrison MSS, Vol. 1.

One day Jennie would write; the next, Sallie. Soon, a whole series of postscripts carried dire threats and warnings. On July 23, 1848, Jennie wrote to Irwin: "Tell Benja if he don't write me, we will scratch him out of our books." This letter carried an interesting series of postscripts. Sallie began:

I write these few lines by way of postscript, to give Ben a *good lecture* for not writing oftener, indeed three lines are all that have been received from him for a long, long while; it is a downright shame to neglect us all in this way, Jennie and I are always punctual about writing and of course we expect punctuality to be reciprocated . . .
P.S. . . . Please don't take offense at my lecture, you know my dear boys it was all through a spirit of kindness that I made the foregoing remarks hoping that you would profit by the scolding.
P.P.S. . . . Tell Ben Pa is quite hurt to think that he still continues to eat cucumbers notwithstanding his advice, and often said that he cannot account for his not writing, so if he wants to please his father he will change in this respect.

A third postscript to this same letter by Mrs. Harrison undoubtedly left its mark. In her maternal but insisting way she wrote:

I intended writing you last evening, but was laid up with a sick headache . . . why has not Benjamin written? Let him answer and give us frequent letters to make up for his past neglect . . . we feel constantly anxious about you. I hope you will be prudent in your diet and that Benja may abstain from cucumbers . . . If Mrs. S. family don't keep them [sic] ask him to banish them from the table so that Ben may not be tempted. . . . May God bless my sons and take them beneath his kind care.[115]

When older sister Betsey, on a visit to College Hill, found Ben and Irwin puffing away on long cigars, the remonstrance that came from home was couched in language quite restrained. Anna wrote that "Pa thinks you are very young gentlemen to be acquiring so bad a habit."[116]

Under the great strain of his mother's untimely death and the reasoned decision to complete his studies at Miami University,

[115] Jennie Harrison to Irwin and Benjamin, July 23, 1848, Harrison MSS, Vol. 1. The postscripts form part of this letter.
[116] Anna Harrison to Benjamin, June 5, 1850, Harrison MSS, Vol. 1.

Oxford, Ohio, Ben, just having turned seventeen, sat down and wrote a long letter on August 28, 1850, to Doctor Bishop:

Your kind letter expressing your sympathy with us under our multiplied afflictions was received some weeks since and I should have returned my sincere thanks for your well-wishes and good advice ere this, but that your letter came at a time when all my thoughts centered around, as most of my time was spent, around the death bed of a dear mother, and the curtain of death having at last closed the touching scene, and the first violent outbreaks of grief having subsided, a minor affliction in the shape of a poisoned right hand prevented my using my pen. . . .

Ben went on to explain that Irwin and three other members of the family had been laid low with dysentery, and "the hand of God has indeed been pressing sorely on our little household."

The triple death of mother, her baby, and a younger brother profoundly affected Ben's thinking, and in this same letter he noted that "But a short time since they were well with a hold upon life which *appeared* to be strong and now they are gone, gone to tender up their account at the bar of God." His own personal feelings he confided to the understanding doctor: "How such events should impress us with the necessity of making our peace with God! In view of these, many are the good resolves I have made for the future. How faithfully I will adhere to them only time will reveal. . . ."

The grief-stricken young man said he could not trust himself in a letter to speak of the death-bed scene, his present feelings, or future resolves. These would have to wait until "I . . . be allowed the privilege of conversing with you in person." Ben closed his letter by expressing to Bishop his warmest thanks for the love and devotion that had been showered upon him for three years, and

Though I shall no more take my seat in your classroom, I would not that this separation should destroy whatever of interest you might have felt in my welfare. But that whenever you may see anything in my course which you deem reprehensible or any advice you may suggest . . . under whatever circumstances and whatever subject, it can never meet with other than a hearty welcome. . . .[117]

[117] This is the earliest letter of Benjamin Harrison to be preserved, Harrison MSS, Vol. 1.

CHAPTER III

Love, Learning and Law

ONE MONTH and ten days after his seventeenth birthday, Benjamin Harrison set out for Miami University at Oxford, Ohio. The day before departure from The Point lingered in Ben's memory as a sad one. It was no easy task to take leave of his brothers and sisters who were now deprived of the love and care of a devoted mother. The family realized that John Scott was a wonderful father to them, yet their loss was severe. While Ben was packing his few belongings and his notes from Farmers' College, in preparation for his trip to Oxford, John Scott was in his own room writing a letter to Rev. William C. Anderson,[1] President of Miami University:

My son Benjamin, the bearer hereof, leaves home tomorrow for Oxford, with a view of attaching himself to one of the classes in your institution.

Benjamin has been for several years a student of Farmers' College in this county . . . and will hand you a statement of his standing in that school, which Doctor Bishop was so kind to give without solicitation.

It would have given me great pleasure to have accompanied Benjamin to Oxford. But my own health and that of a daughter, now in the city, will not permit my leaving home. I therefore send Benjamin alone, and commend him to your kind care and instruction.

Any aid you may be able to render Benjamin in the selection of a proper place to board will be gratefully received.[2]

Unfortunately, this letter does not reveal the conflict behind the scenes, nor does it attempt to list the reasons why Ben finally matriculated at this "Yale of the West."[3] In the fall of 1850 John Scott Harrison found himself well along the road to financial

---

[1] William C. Anderson served as President of Miami from 1849 to 1854. Though he never attended Miami as a student, he had received in 1834 an honorary M.A. degree from that institution. Anderson previously held a professorship in the Theological Seminary at New Albany, Indiana, and also taught at Hanover College in the same state. For the close relationship maintained by both these institutions with Miami University, see James H. Rodabaugh, *Robert Hamilton Bishop*, p. 161.

[2] J. S. Harrison to Rev. William C. Anderson, September 30, 1850, Harrison MSS, Vol. 1.

[3] John W. Scott, in his *A History and Biographical Cyclopedia of Butler County, Ohio* (Cincinnati, 1882), pp. 66–70, observed that "the grade of scholarship for a

ruin,[4] and was forced to abandon long-cherished hopes of sending his son to a renowned "Yankee college." This blow of apparent ill fortune was, in reality, a boon to Ben, and dovetailed nicely with a new and rapidly growing interest which first took possession of his heart back on College Hill.

Early in 1848, through the good offices of Dr. Bishop, Ben, then a freshman at Farmers' College, was introduced to Rev. Dr. John W. Scott,[5] who had come to Farmers' College in 1845, along with Bishop. The two educators had been intimate friends ever since Scott came to Miami University in 1828, a graduate of Washington College, Pennsylvania. Professor Scott, somewhat of a pioneer in the field of education for women, had succeeded in organizing a woman's college on College Hill, in the years he was teaching young Harrison and his contemporaries the rudiments of chemistry and physics.

During the closing months of his freshman year, Ben was a frequent and welcomed visitor at Dr. Scott's residence, and it was not an interest in molecules nor a yearning to master the laws of thermodynamics that attracted him. No mention is made in the Harrison Papers of Dr. Scott's pedagogical prowess. There is evidence, however, that Mr. and Mrs. Scott were blessed with two daughters and one son, Elizabeth, Caroline and John.

Carrie Scott was not so handsome as Lizzie, but she was attractive enough to win Benjamin's heart. In the eyes of this love-struck freshman Carrie was "charming and loveable, petite and a little plump, with soft brown eyes and a wealth of beautiful brown hair."[6] They grew fond of one another, and this budding romance blossomed until that frosty day in 1849 when Dr. Scott moved his school from College Hill to Oxford, Ohio, and founded a larger institution, The Oxford Female Institute. To

---

diploma was set high . . . the full curriculum was patterned very much after that of Yale; and in its palmiest days . . . when its number of students rose some years to near two hundred and fifty it obtained the soubriquet 'Yale of the West.' "

[4] This story is told in a series of letters (Jan. 12, 16, and Nov. 20, 25, 1850) from John Scott Harrison to John Cleves Short, Short Family Papers, Box 55. Immediately after having been granted a loan of $4,000 by John Cleves Short, John Scott wrote to him "your kindness relieves me for the present, at least, of parting with a home which (though sadly desolate of late) still is endeared to me by many tender and hallowed associations," November 25, 1850, Short Family Papers, Box 55.

[5] "Three of the most illustrious educators of the early West were Robert Hamilton Bishop, William Holmes McGuffey, the famed author of the Readers bearing his name, and John W. Scott." For a further estimate of their work see James H. Rodabaugh, op. cit., Chapter 4.

[6] Ophia D. Smith, Old Oxford House (Oxford, Ohio, 1941), pp. 72–73.

Ben's sorrow, he took his family and former students with him.

But Ben quickly concluded that there were striking "educational advantages" connected with matriculation at Miami University. That October day when he presented his application to President Anderson, he in no wise shared his father's regrets that he could not afford to be educated in the cultured East.

Proud of her title, "Daughter of the Old Northwest," Miami University dates her origin from a Congressional Land Grant of 1787.[7] Equally proud can she be of her location, for the village of Oxford is beautifully situated on the crown of a hill overlooking two magnificent valleys. Today's wide smooth streets and well-kept lawns give no indication of the hardships, setbacks and financial woes of the university during her pioneer days. Granted a charter on February 17, 1809,[8] it was not until the fall of 1824 that Miami's portals were opened to students, and only in the following spring was Dr. Robert Hamilton Bishop inaugurated as the first president.[9]

In the autumn of 1850, when Benjamin Harrison enrolled as a member of the junior class, he found Miami enjoying her most prosperous era under the efficient direction of President Anderson. From a nadir of 68 students the registration had risen to well over 250, while intellectual standards were maintained at a high level and hard work was the order of the day. In the catalogue he could read that the course of study "was full and thorough in all departments, and equal in these respects to that of any college in the United States."[10] Harrison was to learn first hand that this claim could be substantiated, and although Miami was the thirtieth university to be established in the United States, and the seventh state university,[11] nevertheless it compared favorably in the matter of faculty and enrollment with the more renowned institutions of the country.[12]

[7] This grant was made to John Cleves Symmes, William Henry Harrison's father-in-law. It was known as the Symmes' Purchase.

[8] James H. Rodabaugh, "Miami University, Calvinism, and the Anti-Slavery Movement," Ohio State Archaeological and Historical Quarterly, 48 (January, 1939), 66–73.

[9] A. H. Upham, "The Centennial of Miami University," Ohio State Archaeological and Historical Quarterly, 18 (1909), 322–44.

[10] Harrison MSS, Vol. 2.

[11] Donald G. Tewksbury, The Founding of American Colleges and Universities Before the Civil War (New York, 1932), pp. 70, 167.

[12] The following table, from Rodabaugh, op. cit., p. 23, illustrates Miami's position in relation to some of the other universities.

During a period of adjustment to this new university life Ben enjoyed much less freedom at Miami than he had had at Farmers' College. This was not because the laws against dueling, card-playing and dancing in any sense rested heavily on his young shoulders, nor because he felt impeded by the injunction that "no student shall wear about his person pistol, dirk, stiletto, or other dangerous weapon."[13] Rather, it was the strict daily order of study and class, varied only by class and study, which made heavy demands upon the already seriously inclined young junior.

School law said that all students must be in their rooms from 7:00 in the evening until chapel services the next morning at 7:30. After the reading of Scripture and prayers, the daily academic program got under way. Recitations and class began at 8:00 and carried through until 11:00 A.M., with the result that breakfast and last-minute "cramming" were squeezed in between a self-appointed hour of rising and chapel service.[14]

Daily recitations brought the students into direct contact with the faculty who, during Ben's stay at Miami, were "men of unusual attainments and influence."[15] At 8:00 A.M., Dr. J. C. Moffat, the soul of dignity, presided over the Latin class. He was followed at 9:00 by "Old Charley" Elliott, a scholarly and absent-minded professor who wrestled with Greek.[16] The last hour of class in the morning usually was spent in "a queer little science hall" in which Professor O. N. Stoddard endeavored to explain the mysteries of natural science.

University	Students	Volumes in Library	Instructors
Bowdoin	143	14,000	10
Dartmouth	302	14,500	12
Yale	561	25,500	31
Columbia	146	14,000	11
Princeton	237	11,000	13
Georgetown	130	12,000	17
University of Virginia	247	15,350	9
College of South Carolina	160	19,000	not given
Harvard	382	49,500	30
Miami	250	6,200	6

13 Royal Cortissoz, *The Life of Whitelaw Reid* (New York, 1921), I, 13. Reid, Harrison's vice-presidential running mate in 1892, entered Miami University the year after Ben's graduation. Reid's letters on his college life are colorful.

14 The catalogue read: "Instruction in Religion and Morality is," according to the Charter, "among the objects for which the University is established . . . ; and the students are required to be present daily at the religious worship in the chapel." Harrison MSS, Vol. 2.

15 Upham, *op. cit.*, pp. 322–44.

16 *Ibid.* See also Cortissoz, *op. cit.*, I, 15.

The boys were assigned a study period in the hour preceding and following the light meal at noon, but the time was rarely spent in the way the college authorities had prescribed. At about 11:30 A.M., the mail arrived, and this was a general signal for many to quit their books and quickly devour the news from the outside world. Immediately after lunch the rooms of the more popular men served as caucus chambers where assembled collegians swapped stories on the latest happenings at home and reviewed recently written chapters on campus love-life. Ben enjoyed similar sessions in his own room, and his roommate, John Anderson, has fortunately left us a picture:

... when we sat together in our room at Oxford ... "gowned and slippered" ... your book in hand ... picking your nose or gazing at the chance coal in the little stove ... thinking of—I won't say who— perhaps Doctor Scott ... with frowning brow descanting on Saylor's latest meanness ... or "in costume" dreading the intended bath ... [or outside] bowling on the green ... or strolling along the river bank at evening....[17]

This collegiate camaraderie did not altogether please the authorities in charge of discipline. For a period, visits of inspection were frequently made, but as discipline improved they ceased.

While Ben was acclimating himself to Oxford and a new group of friends, he was much perturbed that his family failed to write to him. Towards the end of his second week he was rewarded with a long and warm letter from his married sister, who was delighted to learn that her young student-brother "was so well pleased with the situation at Oxford" and she significantly added her sincere hope that "you will so conduct yourself that all the professors will be pleased with you." This letter was not written in a completely serious vein. Evidently Betsey suspected the worst when she asked Ben "what in the world made your lips so sore? I hope no one has been kissing you so hard they raised a blister; come confess and tell me all the particulars." Having promised to keep Ben supplied with Cincinnati papers, she concluded her letter with very pointed words of counsel, as she exhorted Ben:

Bear in mind that *now* is the time to establish your character there. And whatever reputation you *gain now*, that you will have through out your whole college life, and will have a strong bearing on your

[17] John Alexander Anderson to Benjamin Harrison, March 23, 1854, Harrison MSS, Vol. 3.

future career. I have bright hopes for you, Ben, don't, I pray you, with *your own hand* snatch from a beloved sister this fond anticipation.[18]

Ben was soon seriously distracted from his studies by the lack of news from home; even in late October only short scribbled messages gave the worried boy to understand that "a series of mishaps and mistakes too tedious to mention"[19] precluded anything like regular correspondence. They were the perennial difficulties. Jennie wrote, "Pa has not written because he wants to wait until he can send you money" (Oct. 19); "Pa was disappointed in getting his business transacted" (Oct. 26). November, however, saw a change for the better. A favorable wind chased from The Point the perennial cloud of misfortune, with the result that Ben received his first real letter from his father. John Scott Harrison expressed his satisfaction that Oxford met with his son's approval, and, like sister Bet, he urged Ben "to try hard to stand high in the estimation of both professors and fellow students."[20]

The father's enthusiastic desire to see Ben get ahead did not blind him to the ordinary obstacles which fall across the path of the young man who endeavors to stand in well with the teachers as well as with the crowd. He explained away the misconception popular in college circles that "no man can serve two masters": the faculty and the students. With Ben he insisted vigorously that one may earn "the esteem of both . . . by pursuing a straight forward, honorable course in all things . . . by showing proper respect and by giving diligent attention to all your studies." In conclusion he told him to do all this:

. . . and at the same time winning the friendship and good will of students of a kind, approvable manner, and a display of high-minded generosity and forgiveness in your intercourse with them, being always as ready to overlook an unintentional wrong as you would be to resent an intended or premeditated enmity.

It is very important in acquiring the good will of your associates, in that we should never seek to make a witty remark at the expense of the feelings of a less gifted friend or acquaintance.[21]

These words flowed from the depth of his personal experience. His own life was testimony to the value of friendship and with

18 Betsey H. Eaton to Benjamin Harrison, October 9, 1850, Harrison MSS, Vol. 1.
19 John Scott Harrison to Benjamin, October 19, 1850, Harrison MSS, Vol. 1.
20 John Scott Harrison to Benjamin, November 4, 1850, Harrison MSS, Vol. 1.
21 *Ibid.*

the air of an arm-chair philosopher he could say, "we may call forth the momentary applause of the company by flashes of our wit, but we pay too dearly for the liberty, if it is acquired by the loss of a friend, no matter how dull he may be of intellect. If he has a heart to feel, and an arm to aid, his friendship is worth preserving."[22]

John Scott Harrison's paternal but hard common sense was not wasted upon unwilling ears. Though not of the rollicking type, Ben cultivated more than a few friends. He was not selfish, "yet his love of self made him careful of his time and of his reserve powers."[23] He had his likes and his dislikes, was somewhat careless of his external appearance, and yet left the over-all impression with his fellow students as

... an unpretentious but courageous student . . . respectable in language and science . . . and excellent in political science and history . . . who talked easily and fluently and never seemed to regard life as a joke nor opportunities for advancement as subject for sport . . . [and was] impressed with the belief that he was ambitious. . . .[24]

After he had passed through the early years at Miami, Ben, in common with his classmates, found the chains of friendship forged more strongly. As a group, the junior class felt compelled to band together, to pool their intellectual efforts in an attempt to satisfy various professional demands. Here young Harrison was able to play a significant role, for, according to one of the class, "the three brightest men of the college were Benjamin Harrison, David Swing and Milton Saylor."[25] If the Greek were unusually difficult, the boys would call at Swing's room on the way to class to be coached; in return, Harrison and Saylor would help Swing over the hard places in mathematics. This group worked splendidly for themselves and for the class as a whole,

22 *Ibid.*

23 Lewis W. Ross, Ben's classmate, and later a successful lawyer in Council Bluffs, Iowa, wrote a long letter to Lew Wallace who included it as a footnote in the *Life of Gen. Ben Harrison,* pp. 60–62.

24 *Ibid.* Ross claims that Harrison's proficiency in political science and history was due "largely to the foundations laid under the instruction of Dr. Bishop at Farmers' College."

25 David Swing, of Chicago, took second honors, and Milton Saylor, later of New York City, took the first honors. Ross claimed that "Harrison in class standing and merit, ranked above the average," *loc. cit.,* p. 61. See also St. Louis *Post-Dispatch,* July 1, 1888, for a like confirmation of class standings.

and it is not difficult to see how life-friendships resulted.[26]

During these formative years Ben cultivated another very close friend. His name was John Alexander Anderson, a sophomore, and between these two seventeen-year-olds there sprang up a mutual feeling of respect and devotion that lasted for years. Shortly after the 1852 Commencement, when Ben was absent from the first alumni reunion dinner held at Oxford, Anderson wrote:

But I was very sorry indeed, then, that you did not come . . . [for] I have had so *much* real happiness with you that I think apart from your innate power of giving enjoyment, association must have something to do with it. . . . And you always bring with you a recollection of old times that no one else can produce.[27]

And after John Anderson himself had graduated and had accepted a chair of Latin, Greek and mathematics at Mount Pleasant Academy, Kingston, Ohio, Ben received another such testimonial of cordiality and devotion. Anderson wrote, "and I fear I will never be able to return to such disinterested and noble friendship . . . yet so far as I have power nothing done for you will be too great. May God bless you."[28]

Before finally deciding upon dormitory life, young Ben tried rooming at the Mansion House, a public boarding house off campus. Ben seemed to take to these new surroundings, but his father was not at all satisfied with this arrangement, "not because I was at all afraid of your contracting a habit of drinking, I have confidence in you in this regard that would not be easily shaken," but because "I was unwilling that you should necessarily have your mind so much taken from your studies, in going to and from your room for meals." John Scott was thoroughly honest in declaring that he wanted his son "to live off the fat of Oxford," and agreed that "if they feed better at the Mansion House than elsewhere, why stay there by all means, . . . but do not get in the habit of staying in the bar room."[29]

One so-called vice that Ben did not leave behind him at Farmers' College was his strong propensity for smoking long cigars, and when John Scott received repeated reports from school au-

26 *Ibid.* There is also a wealth of material in Fishback's biographical account of Harrison at Miami, Benjamin Harrison Scrapbook No. 9, Harrison MSS.

27 J. Alexander Anderson to Benjamin Harrison, December 24, 1852, Harrison MSS, Vol. 2.

28 J. Alexander Anderson to Benjamin Harrison, August 3, 1853, Harrison MSS, Vol. 2.

29 John Scott Harrison to Benjamin, November 4, 1850, Harrison MSS, Vol. 1.

thorities on the subject, he decided upon a course of vigorous action that was almost guaranteed to produce results. He sat down and penned Ben a letter in which first he expressed his own disappointment, for he had hoped smoking had been given up entirely.

> I found the other day a letter which your dear mother had written you and Irwin on that subject [cigar smoking]. I had never seen it before, and it does seem to me that you and Irwin must have forgotten the request she makes therein, or you would have never put another cigar in your mouth. Oh! how elegantly she urges you to give up the habit. She says "how *sweet* it would be to know that I had influenced you to give this habit up in the first step in a course of vice."

It was scarcely necessary for John Scott to say more; he refused to send a copy of the letter, for he knew his son well enough to say

> . . . it will be sufficient for you to remember, that a sainted mother, once made of you the request to make the sacrifice for her, to induce you at once to say, *I have smoked my last cigar,* and adhere to it with the same steadfast resolution, that you would in carrying out the wishes of your dear mother, when she was still living.[30]

Unquestionably, Ben's greatest diversion and most engaging activity centered around two buildings, the Old Temperance Tavern and the small house of Rebecca Teal. Dr. John W. Scott had bought the tavern, which was just across the street from the new college building, and established a boarding department for his newly founded Oxford Female Institute. Then Scott added several rooms in a way to connect the old tavern with the Teal house.[31] The latter was particularly important because it had a little front porch where Ben Harrison and Carrie Scott re-experienced the stirrings of love which had first sparked on College Hill. It was not long before blushing Ben was referred to by his classmates as "the pious moonlight dude."[32]

During the opening months of the school year the "men of Miami" were frustrated in their attempt to mingle with the Institute girls, and Dr. Scott locked the gates early in the evening. Only after weeks of hard pleading could Carrie persuade her father to allow the girls to receive young gentlemen at the school, and from the day that this new social policy was adopted Ben

30 *Ibid.*
31 See Smith, *op. cit.,* pp. 71–75.
32 Ophia D. Smith, *Fair Oxford* (Oxford, Ohio, 1947), p. 190.

Harrison was a frequent visitor. In summer a horse, buggy and beau gratified the village girls, who with their newly starched calico dresses and sun-bonnets found quiet contentment in an evening's drive. In winter the buggy gave way to the sleigh and impromptu races along snow-covered streets.[33]

Ben entered into this fun with high enthusiasm. He found in Carrie an irresistible charm born of bright and witty manners which overflowed with life and spirit. His own tendencies to seriousness and reserve were completely submerged in her presence. Ben was lucky in his find, for Carrie was born into a refined, cultured and religious home.[34] She was gay and fun-loving, and as a general rule in her teen-age days she disliked domestic tasks, particularly cooking and mending. An accomplished musician and painter, she was definitely artistic in taste and temperament. Her clothes, however, were not always in perfect order. "Her petticoat had a way of slipping its moorings about her slender waist and peeping from beneath her skirt." Above all, she liked to dance, and in later life when she was acknowledged as a beautiful dancer she used to say—tongue-in-cheek—"We did not dance . . . it was considered a great sin[35] at Oxford, but we managed to have just as much fun without it."

Carrie and Ben were serious young people, but they were not above a bit of mischief, especially when Carrie lured Ben from his books to some untried expedition. Once when Dr. and Mrs. Scott were away from home, the couple went buggy riding. Though it was against the rules, they slipped away to a dancing party, where Ben sat gravely apart, but Carrie danced as gaily as any girl there.[36] Carrie would change Ben within a few short years.

Although Ben was greatly interested in Carrie, he never would permit himself to forget that he came to Miami to study. His greatest opportunity for intellectual advancement came when he was invited to become a member of the Union Literary Society,

33 These details were given by Mrs. Harrison (Carrie Scott) in an interview on September 5, 1888, at Indianapolis, Indiana, Harrison Scrapbook No. 6, p. 89, Harrison MSS.

34 Scrapbook No. 9, Harrison MSS.

35 As Weisenburger observes in *Passing of the Frontier*, p. 162: in "both Presbyterian and Congregational Churches, members were arraigned for such offenses as scandal, Sunday traveling, theft, sexual immorality, profanity, card-playing, running a Sunday boat, using intoxicants, *attending cotillions* and *dancing parties,* and neglecting the means of grace, including family prayers."

36 Smith, *Old Oxford House,* pp. 73–74.

a traditional and powerful agency for good at Miami.[37] Already
fired with enthusiasm for political and literary subjects by Bishop's inspiration, Ben took advantage of this society's splendid
program of group study, public speaking and debating. Here he
found himself not only permitted to debate important religious
and political questions of the day, but also strongly encouraged
to have independent opinions and to speak them freely.

By virtue of his affiliation with the group young Harrison was
afforded excellent facilities for serious study. During the first
twenty years of its existence this association had purchased almost
2,000 books, which, in reality, formed the backbone of the university library.[38] As might be suspected, the greater part of the
university library was devoted to theology and the Greek and
Latin classics, but it was the Society library which housed a
number of important volumes in the fields of Harrison's major
interests: history, law and politics. Among the more important
acquisitions were government publications such as Senate Papers
and Documents, House Journals, Journals of Congress on domestic and foreign affairs, State Papers, and other official reports.[39]

Ben was remembered by fellow members as spending many
profitable hours in the library. When he spoke, he impressed his
fellow debaters as "level headed and thoughtful and as one who
usually made a thorough preparation." The fact that "he could
see clearly, think well on his feet, and possessed a vocabulary of
apt words constantly at his command" was not lost on them.[40]

In the 1840's and 1850's when temperance societies mush-
roomed into prominence, and the whole temperance movement
was successfully kept before the public, Miami's halls heard the

[37] Upham, *loc. cit.* These societies held charters from the state and challenged openly the right of the faculty to interfere with or control their
activities or views. By virtue of their charters they could award diplomas. Ben
received his in 1852 and it read in part ". . . Hoc diplomate notum sit BENJAMIN
HARRISON huius Societatis esse, et juvenem moribus honestis praeditum, et erudi-
tione liberali imbutum. Hisce litteris igitur cum ARTIUM OPTIMARUM CULTORIBUS
ubique gentium late commendamus. . . ." This diploma is in the possession of Mrs.
James Blaine Walker, Benjamin Harrison's daughter by his second marriage.

[38] In 1840 the 6,200 volumes in the university library were recorded as belonging to the following societies: 1,500 volumes to the Erodelphiam Society; 1,000 volumes to Miami Hall; 1,700 volumes to the Union Literary Society. See Rodabaugh,
Bishop, pp. 71–72.

[39] *Ibid.*

[40] There are several newspaper accounts wherein Ben is described by contemporaries as a member of the Union Literary Society. The best account is by Fishback
in the New York *Evening Post,* Harrison Scrapbook No. 9, Harrison MSS.

merits of the topic all too often.[41] One evening Ben was asked to debate with a veritable Demosthenes of the temperance cause. In the opening sentences of his address Ben strove valiantly to render his audience benevolent. He begged forbearance on the score that, unlike his distinguished contemporary, he could not be so entirely original as to be able to think new thoughts on the oldest subjects, yet he said he hoped that the acknowledged merits of the subject "will, . . . in some measure atone for the inexperience of the speaker, inexperience not only in making temperance speeches but in drinking whiskey." And with the wit and humor of his next remark, Ben gained a most favorable audience:

for unlike the reformed drunkard who addressed you so powerfully, I can recount no life spent in the service of King Alcohol; nor can I speak of a home made desolate by its ravages. True I have not seen his [Alcohol's] bright influence within the holy precincts of home; a father has not bowed to the tyrant, or a brother, and yet I have seen these endeared by ties of consanguinity pass from respectable positions among their fellows to a drunkard's grave, and I have seen others . . . equally respected tread the same dark road.

The keynote of his peroration was "the notorious fact that this day most of our public men drink, many to excess." Consequently, he concluded with an urgent plea for the sovereign people "to oust drunken demagogues from the legislative halls and judicial benches and fill their places with honest temperance men."[42]

As an acknowledgment of his skill in public speaking and as a personal tribute of respect from his colleagues, Ben was elected to the presidency of the Union Literary Society. In his speech of acceptance he turned a few nice phrases, as he set forth the aim of the Society by comparing its members to men engaged in military life. "For as the raw recruit," he said, "becomes familiarized with the noise and smoke of war in the sham battles of the recruiting station," so here in this hall "we accustom ourselves not only to listen without trepidation to the stern vocal dignity of an antagonist, but also to pierce through the clouds of smoke with which he seeks to enshroud his entrenchments."[43]

41 Weisenburger, op. cit., p. 163. Also see Kenneth W. Povenmire, "Temperance Movement in Ohio, 1840–1850," unpublished M.A. dissertation, Ohio State University, 1932.
42 The original manuscript is dated October 15, 1851, at Miami University. It is in the Harrison MSS, Vol. 2.
43 This oration is preserved in Harrison MSS, Vol. 2.

The main point of his presidential address was a strong encouragement to the new members that they develop and become proficient in the art of speaking on their feet. One of the greatest political assets in his public career was his own ability to make a worth-while address on almost any subject with only a moment's notice, and at the age of eighteen he was urging his contemporaries at Miami "to improve every opportunity of extemporaneous speaking." For himself and for his colleagues he set up as the model to be imitated "the beardless stripling [Patrick Henry] of the Virginia House of Burgesses" whose initial stutterings and stammerings were forgotten as his oratory won for him the title "father of his country."[44]

Harrison's crowning glory, however, was not membership in a forensic society. Far more significant was his acceptance into the Phi Delta Theta fraternity, founded at Miami University in 1848.[45] Although he was not a charter member, he was the nineteenth signer of the Greek-letter bond. After his initiation in the spring of 1851 he assumed an active role in promoting the welfare of the new-born society. Up to the time of his death Harrison enjoyed the distinction of being the only man ever elected President who had been a fraternity member during his college days.[46] During his senior year he served as secretary, and this marked the beginning of a life-long interest which was culminated when he became honored as the society's Second Founder.[47] In 1889, when Harrison entered the White House, the Ohio Alpha Chapter of Phi Delta Theta memorialized the event and predicted for the country an administration of grandeur.[48]

Although a state institution, Miami University was virtually a Presbyterian stronghold during the first fifty years of its existence.

44 *Ibid.*

45 The founder was Robert Morrison of the Class of 1849. See the *Alumni and Former Student Catalogue of Miami University, 1809–1892* (Oxford, Ohio, 1892), p. 52. Miami mothered a triad of fraternities in Harrison's day. Delta Kappa Epsilon and Sigma Chi vied with Phi Delta Theta for new candidates. See Walter B. Palmer, *The History of Phi Delta Theta* (Menasha, Wis., 1906), pp. 40–43.

46 Montgomery (Alabama) *Advertiser*, March 16, 1901. Under the same date the Indianapolis *Sentinel* carried a tribute by Hilton U. Brown and others to Harrison as one "who has been a member of this fraternity almost from its organization. Everything with which he identified himself helped the uplift of his character and loyalty. To such influences may be attributed the dignity and integrity of the organization."

47 Palmer, *op. cit.*, p. 536.

48 Morrison, some eleven years older than Harrison, became an intimate friend during their college days. Together with New Year's wishes he sent a pre-inaugural

All of its presidents up to 1873 were Presbyterian ministers, and
the trustees and professors were, in general, members of that de-
nomination.[49] In the decade between 1850 and 1860 the leading
Presbyterian divine was Rev. Dr. Joseph Claybaugh, Professor of
Hebrew Language and Oriental Literature.

Not only was Dr. Claybaugh the leading spirit in Presbyterian
ranks, but he also frequently took on the garb of an active cru-
sader on campus that students might be formally received into
the church he represented. During the twilight days of 1850, in
an attempt to "convert the sinners of Oxford,"[50] Claybaugh conducted one of his "revivals." Whether it was the eloquence of the
minister or the severe promptings of the spirit, or perhaps a fe-
licitous combination of both forces, "the young men of the University found their hearts touched, and they not only embraced
Presbyterianism, but they vowed to one another that they would
all study for the ministry."[51]

The news of Ben's formal connection with the church was received at The Point with genuine expressions of delight and
gratitude. Sister Sallie spoke for the family, when she wrote:

Pa received your letter of a few days ago, and you cannot conceive
what ineffable delight we all felt, to learn that you intended to connect your self with the church. May you never have cause to regret
this step, it is indeed, a great privilege to be members with Christ's
followers. . . . You speak of several students having given evidence of
change of heart . . . I trust that God in His mercy will smile upon
them and that they may continue steadfast to the end.[52]

---

note of interest: "Well, General Ben Harrison . . . the nineteenth signing the bond
of Phi Delta Theta, accept the congratulations of the man whose name was the first
one written to that instrument, with the hope that his administration as president
of the United States may be as successful in every way and on a much grander scale
than was his administration of the Ohio Alpha of the Phi Delta Theta Fraternity
in the crisis of 1851." Robert Morrison to Benjamin Harrison, January 7, 1889,
Harrison MSS, Vol. 56, Nos. 12608–9.

49 Rodabaugh, "Miami University, Calvinism, and the Anti-Slavery Movement,"
loc. cit., pp. 66–75. It should be noted that Presbyterian philanthropic associations
such as the Presbyterian Education Society and the Board of Education of the
General Assembly gave financial aid to Miami and to a number of its students.

50 St. Louis Post-Dispatch, July 1, 1888. Also see Fishback in New York Post, a
clipping in the Benjamin Harrison Scrapbook No. 6, p. 93, Harrison MSS.

51 Harrison's graduating class (1852) had five Presbyterian ministers, and one
Catholic priest, the Jesuit Father Harmar Denny. In the class of 1853 sixteen out of
the thirty-six graduates became Presbyterian ministers. There was also one Catholic
priest in this group. The 1854 class gave nine out of twenty-eight to the Presbyterian ministry, whereas the class of 1855 gave ten out of twenty-two. These figures
are compiled from the Alumni Catalogue, 1808–1892, pp. 54–61.

52 Sallie Harrison to Benjamin, February 8, 1851, Harrison MSS, Vol. 1.

Ben's faithful exercise of his newly won privilege to attend and participate in prayer meetings and other devotional exercises gave evidence that he was trying to serve God conscientiously. Much satisfied, John Scott penned only one admonition: "He that continues faithful, alone will obtain the victory."[53]

Before Harrison received his diploma in June 1852, he experienced quite a struggle. The elements of conflict in his soul had been slowly maturing, and the paramount problem was his lovesickness over Carrie Scott. Ben himself freely admitted to John Anderson that "my last eight months probation at college afforded me an opportunity to watch a patient through all the stages of this [love's] mysterious disease."[54] Love was only one challenge to this graduating senior now worn out by an unchecked application to hard work. He was baffled primarily by his choice of a life-time vocation. The scales seemed evenly balanced between theology and law—but there was always the question of Carrie.

Secretly they had become engaged. Though everyone on campus could see that Carrie and Ben were in love, they did not realize its seriousness. Had Ben's classmates been able to read his letters from home, much would have been revealed. Carrie's picture held a place of honor at The Point,[55] and she was assured a most cordial welcome by each of Ben's sisters.[56] Jennie wrote, "how is Carrie? I am glad I will have the pleasure of seeing her soon. I feel as if I almost knew her already . . . and I have made up my mind to love her. I feel sure it would not be a hard task to love anyone you did."[57]

Though Carrie was on his mind, so was the rapidly approaching Commencement. To obtain the college diploma both his family and his professors expected of him, Ben decided that a more serious application to study was essential. He went at the books with an intenseness that alarmed his roommate, but con-

---

[53] John Scott Harrison to Benjamin, March 13, 1851, Harrison MSS, Vol. 1.

[54] Benjamin Harrison to John Alexander Anderson, March 4, 1853, Harrison MSS, Vol. 2.

[55] "I look at my picture every day and it seems to remind me frequently of yourself and a *certain friend. Give her my love and thank her for it.*" Jennie Harrison to Benjamin, October [1851 ?], Harrison MSS, Vol. 2.

[56] "Give my love to C.S., that is if you have cultivated her agreeable acquaintance." Sallie to Benjamin, March 8, 1852, Harrison MSS, Vol. 2.

[57] Jennie Harrison to Benjamin, April 28, 1852, Harrison MSS, Vol. 2.

stant chidings for overwork did not seem to deter him.[58] Finally, a halt was called to this feverish and imprudent pace, when word came from The Point: "I hear you are not looking very well. Take care of yourself. Health ought to be the first considera- tion."[59] Under orders from home, Ben slowed down his academic pace, and, though he managed to keep the thoughts of Carrie on the periphery of consciousness, he was still confronted with choosing his state in life.

Everything pointed to his career as a gentleman of the cloth: the exceptionally deep religious character of his parents who recognized in practice the supremacy of things of the spirit; the very campus of Miami, where professors were purportedly living models of sanctity; the effect of frequent religious revivals on his thinking; and his own recent and whole-hearted acceptance of Presbyterianism and his solemn promise to enter the ministry.

Yet Ben had a mind of his own and he determined to make his own decision. If there was one thing that old Doctor Bishop had taught him, it was a healthy independence of thought. Conse- quently, this crisis saw him adopt a procedure which in later life would characterize his legislative and executive thinking. With the air of an impartial investigator, he weighed the respective merits of each career, and asked himself what course an intelli- gent "youth just emerging into manhood" should pursue.[60]

In answering this question for himself, Ben wrote: "Let it be understood I mean by profession: theology, law and physics." Then, taking for granted the long course of laborious study by which a young man prepares himself to "go forth and grapple with the stern realities of life," he considered the role of the doting parent, who, "after great expense and trouble in provid- ing a liberal education," waits impatiently to see his son "wearing a white cross," "swinging a shingle" or "dragging out a miserable existence in some obscure cellar."[61]

Harrison obviously had little taste for the pinched existence of an experimental physicist. With his choice narrowed to the altar or the bar, consideration was given to "Theology, first in

[58] J. Alexander Anderson to Benjamin Harrison, February 9, 1853, Harrison MSS, Vol. 2.
[59] Jennie Harrison to Benjamin, April 28, 1852, Harrison MSS, Vol. 2.
[60] These remarks of Harrison are taken from a manuscript in his own hand, Harrison MSS, Vol. 2.
[61] *Ibid.*

the order of importance, as it addresses itself to Christian youth with peculiar earnestness." This earnestness flowed from a realization of the "unspeakable pleasure which a faithful discharge of the duties . . . [belonging] to the ordained of God to evangelize the whole world." The minister is, in reality, God's co-worker in this glorious country of ours, for his office is "to point the inquiring soul to God, to break the bread of life, to encourage the disheartened . . . to comfort the mourner, to smooth the dying pillow, and like a guardian angel to hover around the dismal abode of poverty and wretchedness."[62]

With a warmth and vigor that possibly give a clue to his ultimate choice, Ben pondered the merits of the legal profession. In clarifying the problem in his own mind, he came to defend the profession against unjust accusers. He deemed it a strange thing, considering the connection between law and equity, that in so many communities "no invective has been thought too strong and no anathema too bitter" for lawyers as a group. He was amazed, also, that, whenever members of the legal profession had dared to join charity with their practice, they had been so often denounced as hypocrites "until it has become a generally acknowledged proposition that no honest or pious man can practice law with success."[63] By urging a reconsideration of the truth of this charge, Harrison challenged its validity and argued thus:

. . . that all rogues are lawyers may in some sense be true, but that all lawyers are rogues, no syllogistic reasoning can prove. Where is the justice in denouncing the whole profession on account of the unworthy conduct of some of its members? Shall we denounce and anathematize the practice of medicine because there are quacks (and that, too, not a few) wrapped in the dignity of an M.D.?[64]

Ben willingly admitted that "the legal profession has not yet arrived at that dignity and moral excellence to which it could be brought. . . ." Yet, in his opinion, the blame must be borne by the public whose estimate of this profession has been so low "that many who would have given a higher moral tone to it, have been prevented from entering upon it by the notion . . . that no Christian could consistently do so. . . ."[65]

62 *Ibid.*
63 Harrison MSS, Vol. 2.
64 *Ibid.*
65 *Ibid.*

Eventually, Ben made his choice and the legal profession gained another eager aspirant. Though history would confirm the choice as a happy one, his selection disappointed more than one of the Miami faculty. They had come to admire Ben and highly commended him for "the earnestness and warmth with which he entered into the duties of members of the church." He was assured that this "is the only way to enjoy religion and fulfill our communion vows," and though extremely pleased with his adherence as a communicant, one of his professors wrote:

> I had hoped besides that you would have studied Theology instead of law. I was disappointed as were others in your selection of the profession. However, a knowledge of law will be no drawback on a minister. And I hope God may yet impress you more forcibly with a desire to administer in holy things. If it is your duty to preach, you will not be happy until you do it. Some other members of your class seem to have gone the same way. I had looked for some good preachers from that class . . . but the attractions of the bar seem to have been more patent. May God give you light in every duty.[66]

On June 24, 1852, Oxford crowded to Miami's twenty-third annual Commencement exercises. Proud parents, relatives and friends of the graduates held seats of honor; only the slightly bored undergraduates felt any chagrin at the inception of the ceremonies. It must be admitted that these academic fledglings had good reason for their air of mental suffering and discomposure; even for the graduates the unusually long programme of speech-making and orchestral overtures was made tolerable only by the sobering thought that "it happens but once in a lifetime."

Ben was the third speaker of the day[67] and, although his address on "The Poor of England" was favorably received, it did not shorten the day's festivities. His family listened proudly to every word of his vigorous denunciation of nineteenth-century England, "the England of poor laws and paupers." Exploding one rhetorical question after another, he asked his sympathetic audience if they thought it were possible that Britain's "obsequious pauper and sturdy beggar" hailed from "so proud a parentage"? Or whether England's "manly race" was dying out and giving place "to Eastern slaves"? Frequently, Ben deprecated the treach-

66 J. M. Woodawl to Benjamin Harrison, December, 1852, Harrison MSS, Vol. 2. Six became lawyers.

67 Unhappily, he was listed on the printed programme as Benjamin Harris; the copy shows the last two letters of his name inked in.

MIAMI UNIVERSITY.

PROGRAMME OF THE

Exercises on Commencement Day.

JUNE 24, 1852.

MUSIC.

PRAYER.

MUSIC.

Latin Salutatory, · · · ·	David Swing, · · · · ·	*Williamsburgh.*
Poetry of Religion, · · ·	Harmer Denny, · · · ·	*Pittsburgh, Pa.*
Poor of England, · · ·	Benjamin Harrison. · ·	*North-Bend,*

MUSIC.

	James A. Hughes, · · ·	*Somerville.*
Public Opinion, · · ·	John P. Craighead, · · ·	*Dayton.*

MUSIC.

Free Thought and Free Action, }	Isaac S. Lane, · · ·	*Middletown,*
The Federal Constitution,	Lewis W. Ross, · · · ·	*Butler County.*

MUSIC.

Harmony of Contrasts, ·	Samuel Lowrie, · · · ·	*Pittsburgh, Pa.*
He is the Freeman whom the Truth makes Free, }	James H. Childs,	*Pittsburgh, Pa.*

MUSIC.

Science and Art as Aids of Christianity, }	Wm. H. Prestley,	*Pittsburgh, Pa.*
The Useful, · · · · ·	A. C. Junkin, · · · ·	*Xenia.*

MUSIC.

Mystery, · · · · · ·	David Moorow, · · · ·	*Cambridge. (Excused.)*
Oration. · · · · · ·	John Knox Boude, · · ·	*Oxford. (Excused.)*
Oration, · · · · · ·	John S. Baker, · · · ·	*Cincinnati. (Excused.)*
Death of Socrates, · · ·	Joseph Walker, · · ·	*New Concord.*

MUSIC.

Valedictory, · · · · ·	Milton Saylor, · · · ·	*Lewisburgh.*

BENEDICTION.

Intelligencer Print, Hamilton.

erous degeneration of so large a section of England's population, and finally he raised the question "how has the individual been robbed of his energy, the social circle of its virtue and purity?" Ben proclaimed that this situation was the direct result of the "Poor Laws." He labored to make clear the harm that was done "when the charitable offering is snatched from the kind hand of the benevolent giver" and substituted for it is "the compulsory provision of a legalized . . . soulless . . . benevolence."[68]

In the words of Lewis Ross, an eyewitness, Harrison's treatment of the subject showed that "he had sounded both the depths and the causes of this poverty." Writing in 1888, Ross claimed that Ben "was a protectionist at the age of 19 . . . he is a protectionist still . . . his whole career has been illustrative of his desire to save his countrymen from the poverty which oppressed the 'Poor of England.' "[69]

Finally, after the last phrases of Saylor's valedictory address, the audience freshened as the graduates prepared to receive their diplomas. For Ben the moment proved to be a fitting conclusion to his happy sojourn at Oxford. His family, his sweetheart Carrie, and several devoted friends rejoiced to handle the parchment[70] freshly wrapped in a long blue ribbon.

Ben issued from the university well equipped and uncommonly well poised. A thoughtful self-reliance and a judgment beyond his years were the elements in his character especially fostered by his life at Miami, and soon to be made manifest in the unfolding of his career. He was still very young—only nineteen—but he started home for The Point with his profession firmly fixed in mind. The only unfortunate circumstance, as he saw it, was the necessity of leaving Carrie behind to finish her final year of schooling at the Institute.

68 Harrison's address is cited in part by Wallace, *op. cit.*, pp. 63–65. The original rough draft is in the Harrison MSS (Library of Congress).

69 Cited in Wallace, *op. cit.*, pp. 60–61.

70 The diploma is in the possession of Mrs. James Blaine Walker, and the Latin reads: ". . . hoc scripto testatum volumus BENJAMIN HARRISON huius Academiae alumnum, consensu SENATUS ACADEMICI, admissum fuisse ad GRADUM PRIMUM IN ARTIBUS LIBERALIBUS. . . ." The following signatures appear on the diploma: J. C. Moffat, Charles Elliott, J. Claybaugh, W. C. Anderson, O. N. Stoddard, Thos. Matthews, R. H. Bishop, Jr., D. Lymans. Alongside of the signatures is listed the discipline which each professor taught.

CHAPTER IV

The Bar and the Altar

SHORTLY AFTER his graduation, Ben returned to The Point for a brief period of rest and relaxation. Home and family, always warmly attractive to him, were particularly inviting after his prolonged absence. Fortunately, the weather along the Ohio favored his visit at this time of the year, and the study-worn collegian described the country air as "very refreshing." To his roommate he wrote: "I hunted pretty faithfully for several days . . . the game was not abundant, . . . I found my chief reward in the exercise of the tramp."[1] He might well have added that these distractions of the rod and gun, as well as the varied chores about the farm, served the distinctly useful purpose of easing his separation from Carrie.

The evenings were pleasant. Father and son quietly talked over Ben's plans for the future. Having shared early with his father his own ambitions and deep-seated determination to make law his profession, Ben was particularly anxious for counsel as to the most acceptable city and law firm in which to take his initial steps. Indeed, he could hardly have come to a more competent counselor than his own father. For a quarter of a century John Scott Harrison was admired and respected throughout Hamilton County. As a young man he had served as Justice of the Peace of Miami Township, and during the twenty years he filled this position it was reported that he enjoyed the distinction of never having one of his decisions revoked by a higher court.[2]

1 Benjamin Harrison to J. Alexander Anderson, March 25, 1853, Harrison MSS, Vol. 2. [Throughout, the names and abbreviations found on the original documents have been preserved exactly. No attempt at uniformity has been made in this regard. Author.]

2 These biographical details are culled from an unidentified Ohio newspaper in clippings 34, 34A, 34B, in the Benjamin Harrison Scrapbook No. 1, Harrison MSS. The year was that of Scott Harrison's death in 1878.

The neighbors recalled that John Scott Harrison, in his declining years, was appointed a member of the Hamilton County Board of Control,[3] a position of importance and trust. Now, in the summer of 1852, his fellow citizens were only one year removed from sending him as their representative in Congress.[4]

Most of the legal education in Ohio was attained through study in an attorney's office, though John Scott Harrison could have enrolled his son in the law department of Cincinnati College, the only one of its kind in the state.[5] However, since the usual two years of study in a lawyer's office made a person eligible for a license to practice, and since this method had produced a singularly able body of attorneys,[6] John Scott advised Ben to go to Cincinnati and interview Bellamy Storer, a former Whig Congressman and now a prominent attorney. Bellamy was the senior member of the firm of Storer and Gwynne, and was happy to count John Scott among his personal and devoted friends.[7]

Sending Ben to Storer was a wise decision, for the latter was as distinguished for his social position as for his legal ability.[8] Hailing from New England, he was well received upon his arrival in

[3] This Board had complete supervision over the acts of the county commissioners. No money could be expended or taxes assessed without its consent. J. Scott Harrison to Benjamin Harrison, April 18, 1872, Harrison MSS, Vol. 7, Nos. 1362–63.

[4] Cf. note 2 above; Freeman Cleaves, *Old Tippecanoe*, p. 276, observes Scott Harrison's success as a "local magistrate and a justice of the peace."

[5] Francis P. Weisenburger, *Passing of the Frontier*, p. 181. This law department had only 23 students in 1850, and was in reality an outgrowth of a private law school organized in 1833.

[6] Eugene H. Roseboom, *The Civil War Era, 1850–1873* (Columbus, Ohio, 1941–44), p. 205.

[7] Carrington T. Marshall, *History of the Courts and Lawyers of Ohio* (New York, 1934), III, 892. After Storer had been Judge of the Superior Court of Cincinnati for over 16 years, John Scott wrote: "We have for several years been separated in politics, and yet I have never lost that respect and admiration for you and your private and judicial character which prompted me as 'an American' to aid with my influence your elevation to the high position you now so ably and honorably fill." John Scott Harrison to Hon. B. Storer, May 11, 1870, John Scott Harrison Papers, 1 box in the Benjamin Harrison Collection.

[8] Marshall, *loc. cit.*, contains a concise biographical account of Bellamy Storer. Born in Portland, Maine, on March 26, 1796, he was educated at Bowdoin College and graduated in 1809. Though he received his legal education in Boston, he was admitted to the bar in Maine in 1817. Later he moved to Cincinnati and, after serving in Congress for two years, was in private practice until his retirement in 1872. During this same period he also served as professor of law. He died June 1, 1875, at the age of 79. The Bellamy Storer Papers, preserved by the Historical and Philosophical Society of Ohio, yield no material after 1840. The collection is now housed at the University of Cincinnati.

the mid-West, for "to some degree a New England background served as a passport to good society and to favorable business contacts."[9]

When Ben stepped off the Ohio River steamboat at Cincinnati, he walked into a new world. As he scanned the wharves, smokestacks and church steeples, he knew for the first time what it meant to become a part of a comparatively large city population. Cincinnati was still growing, and the 1850's were transition years in Ohio's industrial progress.[10] The 1839 population figure of 40,000 had long been surpassed, as hundreds flocked westward from Pennsylvania, New York, Maryland and Virginia, as well as immigrants from Germany and Ireland.[11]

It was just past mid-century when Ben arrived, and the spirit of optimism among the people was lively and contagious. Having expanded with tremendous strides and having greatly diversified its manufacturing, the Queen City was in a splendid position to offer new citizens a sure ground for hope and material advancement.[12] Perhaps Horace Greeley's oft-quoted admonition that the young man should go west was now taking root. Surely there was good reason underlying his sage counsel for, after his visit to the city in 1850, he wrote:

. . . it requires no keenness of observation to see that Cincinnati is destined to become the focus and mart for the grandest circle of manufacturing thrift on this earth where food, fuel, cotton, timber, iron can all be concentrated so cheaply . . . that is, at so moderate a

9 Weisenburger, *op. cit.*, p. 44, and A. G. W. Carter, *The Old Court House* (Cincinnati, 1880), pp. 120–21. In Cincinnati, New Englanders were relatively few, but they were closely attached to each other. Among this New England group were such well-known figures as John C. Wright, William Green, Salmon P. Chase, and Bellamy Storer.

10 Roseboom, *op. cit.*, p. 11. ". . . despite a significant increase in manufacturing in the preceding decades, following the opening of the canal systems, the state had remained essentially agricultural with but one industrial city of metropolitan character. Even three of Cincinnati's most characteristic products, pork, whiskey and flour, were more closely related to the farm than to the factory."

11 Kentuckians originally from Virginia constituted the major portion of the early settlers in Cincinnati, and the 1839 *City Directory* listed approximately 10,000 out of a possible 40,000 names. Of these, 1,578 gave Germany as their birthplace; 1,098 gave Pennsylvania; 916, Ohio; 717, Ireland; 717, New Jersey; 673, England; 607, New York; 521, Virginia; 487, Maryland; with the rest from scattered countries and states. See Cincinnati *Gazette*, Dec. 4, 1839, cited by Weisenburger, *op. cit.*, p. 47.

12 Roseboom, *op. cit.*, pp. 11–12.

cost of human labor in producing and bringing them together . . . as here . . . such fatness of soil, such a wealth of mineral treasure . . . coal, iron, salt, and the finest clays for all purposes of use . . . and all cropping from the steep, facile banks of placid, though not sluggish, navigable rivers. How many Californias could equal, in permanent worth, this Valley of the Ohio![13]

Fortunately, Ben was not compelled to seek and select a boardinghouse from among the hundreds that offered to lodge and feed him for a minimum of five dollars a week. A room in his married sister's house awaited his coming, and both sister Bet and Doctor Eaton extended a warm welcome. This move saved the needy legal neophyte some $300 a year by his own calculation.[14]

After the usual introductions to the men in the office, and once the strangeness of the first week had passed, Ben found himself pretty much taken for granted. He had been accepted as an unpaid apprentice to make himself useful in learning the law, and now he bent all his efforts toward making his mark in the eyes of the shrewd Bellamy Storer. From the outset, while he was given an almost endless series of papers to be copied in as fair a hand as possible, neither Storer nor Gwynne neglected to assign worthwhile books for study, and frequently they coached him in those legal principles and techniques which they believed worthy of special attention.[15]

Ben's predisposition for hard work carried over from his college days, and his consistently faithful application to the prescribed readings as well as to the execution of the office tasks assigned him, greatly pleased Bellamy Storer. To his intimate college chum and former roommate, however, this almost feverish activity was a source of grave concern. After six months of silent foreboding, Anderson summoned sufficient courage to

13 Charles Cist, *Sketches and Statistics of Cincinnati in 1851* (Cincinnati, 1851), p. 257.
14 Benjamin Harrison to John Alexander Anderson, August 25, 1853, Harrison MSS, Vol. 2.
15 It worked to Ben's advantage that he could study under the direction and supervision of Bellamy Storer, for "Few lawyers have been more honored in Western legal circles . . . [and] doubtless from contact with this really noble man young Harrison absorbed, at least, strength for certain other characteristics that afterwards helped materially to constitute him the conspicuous figure he was in military and civil life." Indianapolis *Journal,* March 14, 1901.

warn Ben "you will most certainly result dangerously, if you continue your present mode of life, . . . you should have more sense than to throw yourself away by pursuing studies so closely that their attainment will be your death knell."[16]

When one considers the daily grind at the office and the long evenings at home devoted to poring over tomes of case histories, Anderson's friendly advice was evidently in good order. But neither advice nor taunts dampened Ben's quest. He refused to moderate his enthusiasm, and in reply to a query from his sister Anna as to what he did every day and how he passed his time, Ben wrote:

> I don't think it would interest you very much. I do the same things every day . . . eat three meals . . . sleep six hours and read dusty old books the rest of the time. . . . If you could see me in my office my feet cocked up and a big book with a brown paper cover on it in my lap . . . you would think me a picture of content. I suppose you have read about the Great Desert. Well, my life is as about as barren of anything funny as the Great Desert is of grass.[17]

What did succeed, however, in upsetting Ben was not the monotonous schedule of copying and studying, but the conditions under which he had to live and work. As the months passed, his hatred of city life became almost an obsession. Sometimes he managed to snatch a brief vacation at The Point, but upon his return he complained bitterly that "my experience of the country air only served to disgust me with the abominable compound of coal dust and mother earth which I am now inhaling."[18] To his family on the farm he wrote: "you think the city a very fine place but if you had to live here all the time you would soon get tired of it and long for the green grass and fresh air of Long View. It is very dusty in the streets today. It almost blinds you."[19]

Throughout the winter of 1852–53, and even in the more pleasant April days, Ben found little relief or distraction from his wearisome legal studies. At times he experienced serious mis-

16 J. Alexander Anderson to Benjamin Harrison, February 9, 1853, Harrison MSS, Vol. 2.

17 Benjamin Harrison to Anna S. Harrison, March 31, 1853, Harrison MSS, Vol. 2.

18 Benjamin Harrison to J. Alexander Anderson, March 25, 1853, Harrison MSS, Vol. 2.

19 Benjamin Harrison to Anna Harrison, March 31, 1853, Harrison MSS, Vol. 2.

givings, and on more than one occasion he confided his doubts to Anderson. Once, after he had been laid low by a hacking cough for two weeks, he wrote:

I have been reading today the most abstruse and difficult branch, that most difficult part of the law of real estate . . . remainders. I have skimmed over fifty pages and confess that I am not a whit wiser than when I commenced. Such knowledge "is not worthy of the name of wisdom."[20]

When April rolled around, with its usual thunder showers, he was delighted. "It clouded up so darkly a while ago," he wrote, "that I had to light the gas . . . and now we are having a most *drenching rain*—such showers are the temple of salvation to us poor denizens of this smoky dusty town."[21]

Despite a few lapses into homesickness and an occasional yearning for the pursuits of the farm, Ben kept his nose to the grindstone. To all outward appearances he was predominantly and enthusiastically preoccupied with his duties about the office and with his home study. Fortunately, however, he was able to avail himself of the excellent library facilities in the city, and within a few months of his arrival he was elected an honorary member of the Young Men's Mercantile Library Association.[22] By virtue of his membership he could consult the principal newspapers and periodicals of the country, and the club room often was the scene of an interesting public discussion on important political and legal questions.[23] Lest he lack balance in his social life, he tried to combine business with pleasure by sustaining his collegiate membership and interest in Phi Delta Theta activities, though a diligent regard for study prevented him from attending the annual fraternity dinner.[24]

Notwithstanding these activities, Ben still caught himself

20 B. Harrison to J. A. Anderson, April 20, 1853, Harrison MSS, Vol. 2.
21 *Ibid.*
22 The Secretary of the Association wrote to Ben on December 1, 1852, notified him of his election, and asked him to call and sign the Constitution. Ben sent the Association $4, covering one year's dues and the initiation fee. Harrison MSS, Vol. 2.
23 D. V. Martin, "History of the Library Movement in Ohio," unpublished M.A. thesis, Ohio State University, 1935, pp. 7, 26–29, 65, cited by Weisenburger, *op. cit.*, p. 182.
24 J. A. Anderson to B. Harrison, December 24, 1852, Harrison MSS, Vol. 2.

dreaming of "coy"[25] Carrie Scott. With his warm-hearted nature confined to the loneliness of a dimly gas-lighted room, he felt his separation keenly. He was not the kind to find a brother in every man, and Anderson, his college confidant, was still matriculating at Miami. Letter writing, then, was his best solace. The arrival of a letter from Carrie was a major event. At Oxford, Carrie was abnormally busy with the double burden of teaching music and sewing to younger girls as well as studying for her own graduation.

Yet he was a bit impatient[26] with what he considered infrequent letters and he complained that "she sometimes neglected *me* for a full week."[27] It became a standing joke with the post-office clerks when for days at a time they turned away empty handed the love-bewitched law student. He would return to his books but he could unearth no statute to assuage his pain at what he regarded as Carrie's cruelty. Only when he was able to set a definite date for their wedding would he enjoy saying of the jovial clerks: "I thank my stars that I shall be rid of their tantalizing shakes soon."[28]

Ben alone was unable to solve the vexing problems of an early marriage, and during the first six months of 1853 he wrestled with it day after day without coming to any definite decision. His rather full correspondence for this period reveals him frequently on the very threshold of matrimony, yet the violent conflict within prevented the final step. Failing to arrive at a decision by his own powers, he presented his problem to John Anderson, his trusted friend of college days.

Ben stated his case fairly enough. More perplexing to him than any eight hundred pages of real-estate law was the paramount concern of safeguarding Carrie's considerably weakened health. Though ostensibly finishing her own studies at her father's school, she was frequently compelled to substitute as teacher in the music classes for the ailing Miss Neal. Moreover, her free moments were spent nursing at the bedside of her sick friend.

25 *Ibid.*, December 7, 1852, Harrison MSS, Vol. 2.
26 He had been called an "impatient" suitor even at college. See Milton Saylor in Scrapbook No. 52, p. 93, Harrison MSS.
27 Benjamin Harrison to J. Anderson, September 24, 1853, Harrison MSS, Vol. 3.
28 *Ibid.*

CINCINNATI, 1868

Lithograph by Ehrgott, Forbiger and Company, 1868

BIRD'S-EYE VIEW OF INDIANAPOLIS, 1854

Courtesy W. H. Bass Photo Company

PENNSYLVANIA STREET, INDIANAPOLIS, 1854–1856

A Stone's Throw from Harrison's Office and Residence

BEN HARRISON'S FIRST RESIDENCE
IN INDIANAPOLIS ON EAST VERMONT STREET

The strain, however, was too much for her slender frame.

Anderson reported to Ben:

. . . Miss Neal's health has gradually declined until she is now not expected to live . . . poor Carrie . . . I really believe her heart will break . . . she is at the bedside continually . . . but she left once or twice today and came down and talked with me, or rather to weep. I never saw such grief. It seemed as if her frame would literally shake to pieces.[29]

This caused Ben to mull over the problem of how he could rescue Carrie, and in the meantime he prayed that "the same God who tempers the wind to the shorn lamb, will give her strength to bear up under the affliction which threatens her."[30] Finally, convinced that Carrie should get away for a rest cure, Ben made the trip to Oxford and spoke to Doctor and Mrs. Scott. They consented to allow Carrie to go East and visit her relatives[31] in Honesdale, Pennsylvania. Stimulated by Ben's visit, Carrie was able to set out alone. Evidently, the trip, the change of scenery, and the much needed rest restored her to normal health. Her subsequent letters made Ben smile again.[32]

While Carrie was away, Ben also took some time off to hunt squirrels around The Point. Here he received a letter which in all probability set the machinery of his mind in rapid motion once again. His correspondent was Bill Benton, who had been close to him at school,[33] and who was now a successful young lawyer. Under the circumstances, Benton's message must have given Ben cause for serious reflection. Here was a man his own age who had faced the same combined problem of love and law,

29 J. Alexander Anderson to Benjamin Harrison, Esq., February 2, 1853, Harrison MSS, Vol. 2.

30 Benjamin Harrison to J. Alexander Anderson, March 4, 1853, Harrison MSS, Vol. 2.

31 Dr. Scott had married Miss Mary Potts Neal, daughter of John Neal, a prominent banker and business man of Philadelphia. In addition to Carrie there was an older sister, who had married Mr. Lord and settled in Wayne County. See Scrapbook No. 9, pp. 3-4, Harrison MSS.

32 B. Harrison to J. A. Anderson, March 25, 1853, "She seems to be better than she has been since she went East," Harrison MSS, Vol. 2.

33 William T. Benton to Benjamin Harrison, March 5, 1853, "You doubtless long since have concluded that I have forgotten you and gone off to strange gods, but that is by no means the fact. Though married [on January 25], there is yet room in my heart for friends, true friends of whom I have found but few, but among whom Ben Harrison stands second to none," Harrison MSS, Vol. 2.

and had married. Now, almost three months after that step, he was well pleased with himself and all the world: "I am doing well . . . my own boss . . . making from fifty to one hundred dollars per month. Such my dear fellow is the full history of my affairs."[34]

If Benton's letter acted as a stimulant to Ben's sense of gallantry and daring, still more did a brief note from Carrie about a month later. She sent him a newspaper clipping of a duel fought in Cincinnati by a grandson of General Harrison, apparently over some slight of honor on the field of love. Ben confessed to Anderson that he felt great chagrin because Carrie added to the clipping that "she almost knew it was not me." "What amazing confidence she has," the young suitor remarked.[35]

Shortly after Carrie's little quip, if not partially because of it, Ben arrived at the momentous decision. He and Carrie must be married within the next six months. First, they proposed to visit the relatives both at Oxford and at Honesdale, and Ben gloated to Anderson: "Yes, John, we have concluded to take Niagara in on our way and tarry a day or two to view the awful sublimity of that *great* cataract . . . going . . . thence to Buffalo and New York." In outlining his itinerary Ben performed a striking act of generosity. He told John that he possibly might "not go at all. Irwin came up from home this morning; his health is very indifferent and I have offered to resign the proposed trip in his favor and take his place on the farm while he is gone. Of course it would be a great sacrifice for me to give up the only opportunity of seeing Carrie I am likely to have, but if this trip is likely to benefit his health, I would do it cheerfully."[36]

Though some of Ben's friends even yet could not believe that this was a pre-honeymoon jaunt, or that he was in earnest about his early marriage, John Scott Harrison sent them on their way with a paternal benediction and prayer that "no accident or sickness may mar your pleasure."[37] After a brief interval at Honesdale, Ben successfully passed the scrutinizing in-law test, and so

[34] W. T. Benton to Benjamin Harrison, March 5, 1853, Harrison MSS, Vol. 2.

[35] Benjamin Harrison to J. Alexander Anderson, April 20, 1853, Harrison MSS, Vol. 2.

[36] B. Harrison to J. Anderson, May 21, 1853, Harrison MSS, Vol. 2.

[37] J. Scott Harrison to Benjamin Harrison, June 1, 1853, Harrison MSS, Vol. 2.

overwhelmingly so, that a rumor sped back to Miami University to the effect that "Mr. Lord and his wife, Mr. Harrison and his sister and several friends from the city being present . . . Carrie Scott and Benjamin Harrison were this morning married." This was on July 23rd, and Anderson had all he could do to discredit the false report.[38]

Actually, the final decision to hold the nuptial ceremony in October was not made until the middle of August, at which time several factors forced Ben's determination. Carrie's health demanded that she be relieved of her duties in the Institute, and Ben felt that "this would be a good time to press for her release."[39] Moreover, Doctor and Betty Eaton's decision to sell their house in Cincinnati compelled Ben to add: "I shall be thrown out of a home in the city." Under the impact of these two emergencies, Ben went to Oxford, as he informed Anderson,

. . . for the express purpose of arranging preliminaries for my marriage!! Yes, John, it is all arranged, the consent of all the parties interested having been obtained. The time is not fixed exactly but will be sometime this fall . . . probably in October. You know my reasons for taking this step so soon and I need not dilate upon them now. Keep this a secret from *everyone*. . . . Do you consent?[40]

The hard, common-sense reply of Anderson, Ben's most trusted friend, was an adamant and unqualified refusal to give his consent. He wrote "why Ben, you are crazy . . . no, you ain't that either . . . Dr. Eaton's selling his house, and the *necessity* to keep Carrie from teaching, I predicate are the reasons. But after you are married, what then? The Point and your father at Congress. You and Irwin on the farm . . . then you are crazy." After settling down at The Point, then what? "Read law all day and talk to Carrie all night?" The rest of Anderson's letter was ribbed with

38 Anderson, who contradicted the rumor, said: "What a fool I am to lose so good an opportunity of humbugging a set of gossips that have meddled so much in our affairs in time passed. . . ." J. Alexander Anderson to Benjamin Harrison, July 23, 1853, Harrison MSS, Vol. 2.

39 Benjamin Harrison to J. Alexander Anderson, August 15, 1853, Harrison MSS, Vol. 2.

40 B. Harrison to J. A. Anderson, August 19, 1853, Harrison MSS, Vol. 2. Formal written permission was sought, however, on October 5, 1853, when Ben wrote to Doctor Scott and asked him to perform the ceremony. Benjamin Harrison to Doctor Scott, October 5, 1853, Benjamin Harrison MSS, Vol. 2.

realism; he based his opposition to the marriage on solid reasoning, not mere sentiment:

> I do not know much about your *private* financial resources, nor those of your father's *own estate,* but am under the impression that you are far from able to support Carrie as you will. You have no way to turn your mind and attainments into *cash* at present that I know of. Nor will you have for another year; then admitted like all young lawyers you must take your chances, and maybe two or three and most certainly *one* year before your profession will yield you support. . . . From Dr. Scott you can expect nothing, and your father will support you two as he has done, but will you let him? From my knowledge I should think not . . . then you need a law library which is in itself no small item, . . . Suppose that at the age 28 years, you stand free from debt, but has not your profession suffered? The axe with which you have cut your way through, is it not blunted and nicked?[41]

Of course, John left the usual loophole by admitting that "it is *you* that is to be married not *I* and every man can judge *best* for himself." He further pleaded, however:

> only Ben, remember that this world is not your *friend,* it is your enemy and . . . it requires *hard* labor to defend yourself. . . . Love is powerful as an incentive, but will it pass current for potatoes and beef? Coffee and muffins for two are not paid for by affection existing between the "two." Hard cash buys! *Where will it come from?*[42]

This bombshell shattered Ben's equilibrium. For two days he was at a loss for an adequate reply. While he protested sincerely that he took no offense at what was written, "no, not the slightest,"[43] he felt constrained to inform John that "there was but one person [his father] whom I would take any pains to satisfy beforehand." Ben frankly admitted that

> . . . many of my acquaintances, some of them good friends too, will prognosticate, as you have done, that marrying now, I "will never be

41 J. Alexander Anderson to Benjamin Harrison, August 20, 1853, Harrison MSS, Vol. 2. This extremely long and frank letter was prompted by the strongest ties of personal friendship and was written as a direct response to Ben's request for John's "consent." Even before receiving Ben's next letter, John let it be known that, even if Ben should not change his mind, he would attend the wedding. See letter of August 22, 1853, Harrison MSS, Vol. 2.

42 J. Alexander Anderson to Benjamin Harrison, August 20, 1853, Harrison MSS, Vol. 2.

43 B. Harrison to J. A. Anderson, September 7, 1853, Harrison MSS, Vol. 2.

more than half a man, if that"; and I know too how vain it would be, in general, to attempt to persuade them otherwise, . . . hence I have determined to let such people wait the issue for their consolation.[44]

Yet, Anderson was not placed in the category of a mere acquaintance. Out of fair consideration for their deep personal friendship, Ben unbent from his resolution of "watchful waiting," and attempted with boldness and eloquence to explain his motives as:

. . . first and chiefly the delicate state of Carrie's health. The anxiety of an engagement of already two years standing, and still promising a very distant confirmation have told with fearful effect upon her constitution. . . . Now, while I cannot attempt to explain the nature of the connection between the mind and the body, my observation has taught me this, that mental suspense and anxiety operate more destructively upon health than many physical causes; . . . .

You are partially informed of the delicate state of Carrie's health at present . . . sufficiently so, however, to judge, whether she is likely to survive two years more in the position she will necessarily occupy. Is she? You have already confessed to me that you did not believe she would live one. The question then, John, is narrowed down to this: Shall I marry Carrie now and thus relieve her of those harassing doubts and fears which wear away her life, or shall I agree to stand aside and let her hasten to an early grave? . . .

An aunt of mine who was married last Spring, had been engaged to the same gentleman for *five* years . . . the engagement was formed while he was in his senior year at college. He finished his college course, studied medicine three years, and practiced one before they were married. During the last two years she became melancholy and her health gradually failed, until her friends became apprehensive that she would not live to see the time fixed for her marriage. She confessed to me herself that the anxiety of mind for so long an engagement was the *sole* cause of her ill health. She is still delicate and perhaps never will regain perfect health again.[45]

The answer was evident, but Ben, now practicing before the bar of his own conscience, had only opened his case. Deciding to put all his cards on the table, he asked John if he could meet his own proposition fairly stated:

Grant your proposition that in two years I could acquire a competence, nay, if you choose, amass a fortune, secure fame world-wide. I

44 B. Harrison to J. A. Anderson, August 25, 1853, Harrison MSS, Vol. 2.
45 *Ibid.*

come laden with yellow gold and the praises of the crowd to claim
my bride . . . but she is gone, but long I seek for her in vain. I wander
to the quiet graveyard, where we have so often walked together, my
heart leads me to a humble grave over whose brown clods the turf
has already healed . . . I drop a tear, and with that first gold that
severed us for life I build a monument "sacred to her memory" . . .
and then, John, . . . what then?

On the other hand I marry Carrie now . . . the relief it would bring
to her anxious mind, and the greater care which she could give to her
bodily health, would I trust in great measure restore her health. I
should then have her long, to cheer me when worn and desponding
and watch my own health with her greater care.

Ben produced a surprise witness to testify on the advisability
of his early marriage. John's own father, Dr. Anderson, was quoted
to the effect that "if Carrie and I were not married now, this fall,
we would never be. The reason he assigned, was that I would
never live another year. In this view of the case how much better
that we should be married now?" Ben added the coy comment:
"Carrie might then watch at my bedside without impropriety. I
would die easier with her hand under my head."

Ben concluded his case "by addressing himself to the lower but
more practical view of the subject—the financial":

Now for an exposition of my pecuniary resources. Once married I
propose to take Carrie immediately to the Point and there continue
the study of my profession, still under Mr. Storer's direction. Should
I continue to study in the city after Doctor [Eaton] goes to the country, I would be obliged to go to some boarding house or hotel where
I would be a weekly expense of five dollars at least for board, washing
and so forth. My expenses then, exclusive of clothes, would be at the
smallest calculation $300 per annum. At the Point my board would
cost nothing and Carrie would probably have a good stock of clothes
to start on, this will be a small item for the first year—$300 (the
amount I would necessarily spend in the city) will *certainly* cover
every expense for the first year. I will then be in a position to convert
"my learning into cash."

The inner conflict was at an end, and but two months remained before the wedding. For Ben, the intervening days were
filled with pleasant expectation and serious preparation. Even
though September's weather was stiflingly oppressive, "he read
the law very closely," occasionally permitting himself a refreshing
dream of Carrie and the happy day ahead. "I am persuaded that

I can read as much law in four hours at The Point, where I will take proper exercise, as I now do in ten and a half. Three hours of exercise every day will change my physical appearance amazingly in the course of a year. I shall be stronger as well as wiser."[46]

Unquestionably, Ben lived those weeks on borrowed happiness. Despite the fact that the office was ever crowded with witnesses and lawyers, he felt keen satisfaction because "the story of our marriage is gradually stealing about in whispers."[47] He kept up his correspondence with Anderson, and the conclusion of one rather lengthy epistle is clearly indicative of the meditative and poetic side of a man who has erroneously been described as thoroughly cold and completely unimaginative:

> Our office is quiet now, all the tenants save myself have quit until tomorrow. Darkness is fast setting upon this page and the straggling rays of light are fleeing as if frightened to join the sun behind the western hills. A thousand sturdy muscles stretched since early dawn are now relaxed, or only exercised by the swinging of the empty bit of bucket as the honest partisan hastens with quick step and eager heart to join the loved ones at home and enjoy with them a meager meal. 'Tis night, night in a great city. Vice hidden all day long in darkened chambers now stalks boldly forth, to shock by its squalidness and misery, or tempt by its gaudy trappings in conventional respectability. But I must close.[48]

From shortly after Ben's twentieth birthday in late August until the day of their wedding, he and Carrie followed patterns of conduct wholly unpredictable but thoroughly amusing. She was intent upon keeping secret the day and the hour so as "to blind the curious."[49] When Ben visited Oxford, he found her acting and speaking in the presence of her students and friends "with as great circumspection as a nun before her abbess."[50] He added: "Her sewing she does in the privacy of her own chamber. Studiously avoiding an exposure of the suspected garments." Ben, on the other hand, steadfastly refused to be a victim of the "tyranny of a malicious and gossiping eye," for, as he put it, "con-

46 Benjamin Harrison to J. Alexander Anderson, September 7, 1853, Harrison MSS, Vol. 2.

47 Benjamin Harrison to J. Alexander Anderson, September 15, 1853, Harrison MSS, Vol. 3.

48 Ibid.

49 J. Alexander Anderson to B. Harrison, Sept. 17, 1853, Harrison MSS, Vol. 3.

50 B. Harrison to J. A. Anderson, Sept. 24, 1853, Harrison MSS, Vol. 3.

science approving, I shall act, though the whole world beside disapprove." There was a certain amount of good common sense underlying his attitude, for Ben held it as a principle that "the man who commits himself to the absurd task of pleasing everybody, is like a cork intrusted to the reversed and whirling currents of the 'Devil's Hole' [Niagara], and the one is as likely to reach the ocean as the other is to maintain a dignified individuality in society."[51]

This show of stoicism, however, was somewhat of a false front. As the days passed, Ben unbent sufficiently with Anderson to confess that "my spirits are much regulated by my moods in these times, now cheerful and talkative, and again silent, almost sad."[52] When he roused himself from these fits, he seemed to renew his confidence by his determination to succeed in spite of every obstacle, as he was quick to add:

I never lose my courage, however depressed my spirits may be. A young man with good health and a well trained mind is guilty of . . . cowardness, when he gives way to discouragement. "Faint heart" never did anything worthy of man; how then could it win "the fair lady" who prides herself upon the heroism and bravery of her lover.

By far the most trying problem for Ben was his selection of the proper wedding garments. Only the timely arrival of his brother Irwin served to tranquilize his ruffled disposition. "Together," he writes to John Anderson, "we spent almost the entire morning with tailors, boot makers, and gents furnishers." In retrospect, Ben's account of this expedition for clothing is quite significant, though at the time it was peculiarly painful:

Never did a more disagreeable, vexatious task fall to my lot: from the earliest thought of the matter to the possession of the last article, was one continued series of quandaries and perplexities, from each of

51 This statement is typical of Ben's character and thought. The idea expressed here was to grow and mature with him, and thus accompany him into the arena of public life. In this same letter he stated as a companion principle: "Neither ought a man surrender himself to any unasked advice of friends. Let him never act upon such counsels, except he can make them entirely his own. I know no greater error than to take 'advice' upon authority. Mine is the responsibility."

52 B. Harrison to J. A. Anderson, Sept. 30, 1853, Harrison MSS, Vol. 3.

which I was only released in the most desperate effort. I chose an entire suit of black, vest and all.[53]

Ben strongly suspected that his choice of a somber all-black wedding outfit would be regarded by many as an example of his lack of taste. But, like most things he did, this departure from the dictates of fashion was willful and premeditated. Not only did he select a black satin vest in place of the conventional "white vest of the drone," but he also indulged his early and growing fondness for a frock coat.[54] As he admitted:

Instead of the swallow tail and clept dress, I ordered a frock coat. I am not entirely satisfied that I was right in this latter particular, but this I know: that I will look and feel better in the old "frock"!! I am very little concerned about my appearance, however, so long as I maintain gentility and avoid poverty.[55]

Ben found it difficult to pursue his studies with requisite attention, and finally he brushed aside his legal tomes with the confession: "I am tired of the suspense and dissipation of mind incident to the anticipation of such an event. I long to have the anticipation emerge into reality."[56]

With deep respect, Ben asked Dr. Scott if he would consent to perform the ceremony. He added understandingly, however, "it will perhaps be an embarrassing part for the father to assume the marriage of his daughter, yet, if it would not be too inconsonant with your feelings, we would be glad to have it so." Ben felt it necessary to say a word also of the prospect he had of affording Dr. Scott's daughter a comfortable home and support:

For the present I shall offer a place in my father's house, where she will receive the welcome of a daughter and a sister. My present design is to "migrate" to Chicago in the Spring, when I will be able to obtain immediate admission to the Bar, and once admitted, the energetic

53 *Ibid.*

54 Scores of contemporary and later writers have mentioned Harrison and his frock coat in one and the same breath. Typical is the statement of Col. W. H. Crook, *Memories of the White House* (Boston, 1911), p. 210: "Owing to his stoutness he did not look as tall as he really was, and perhaps for this reason he wore a silk hat and a frock coat when weather conditions permitted."

55 B. Harrison to J. Anderson, Sept. 30, 1853, Harrison MSS, Vol. 3.

56 *Ibid.*

and patient pursuit of my profession will *insure* success. . . . In a word, I pledge my *best* efforts for her happiness . . . in the sincere hope that the time will meet with your approval and that you will consent to perform the ceremony.[57]

Procurement of the marriage license proved somewhat more embarrassing. Inasmuch as he had not yet attained his legal majority,[58] Ben had to be accompanied by his father when he went to Hamilton, the county seat, where they obtained the license three days before the wedding.[59]

On Wednesday evening, October 19, Ben arrived in Oxford about nine o'clock and went directly to the Mansion House, where he put up for the night.

October 20, 1853, dawned cool and brisk, and autumn wore its finest dress. Tradition has it that Dr. Scott performed the ceremony in his own home, in the first-floor front room on the west side of the house.[60] As Carrie had desired, the wedding was a simple one, with the family, a few guests[61] and no display of presents. The bride appeared in a simple gray traveling dress and Ben wore his new black suit. Immediately after the ceremony a wedding breakfast was served, and, as soon as it was polite to do so, the newly wedded couple left Oxford in a rattling old omnibus for Hamilton, thence to The Point.[62]

Uncertainty about the future lost some of its terror at least temporarily. Carrie's loving presence and encouragement replaced the anxiety of the courtship days and, thus fortified, Ben settled down to the completion of his legal studies. His application was

[57] Benjamin Harrison to Rev. Dr. Scott, October 5, 1853, Harrison MSS, Vol. 3.
[58] Ben took much good-natured jibing because of his minority status. Milton Saylor, his classmate from Miami, and later a Civil War colonel recalled at Harrison's death in 1901: "Ben married before he was 20 [sic] and had to take his father with him to get the license." Scrapbook No. 52, p. 93, Harrison MSS.
[59] B. Harrison to J. Anderson, Oct. 17, 1853, Harrison MSS, Vol. 3.
[60] Ophia Smith, *Old Oxford House*, p. 75.
[61] John Anderson had been invited, in a note dated September 24, 1853, Harrison MSS, Vol. 3: "your father told me that you are expected home the third week in October. On the 20th of that month at six o'clock in the morning (can you get off so early?) I should be very happy to see you 'at home.' You must not look for any show. It will be a plain affair with as little ceremony as possible."
[62] Smith, *op. cit.*, p. 73. The John W. Scott diary, found in the Harrison Home in Indianapolis, also records the event with stark simplicity.

vigorous, and his earlier boast that he would accomplish so much more at home now seemed to be coming true. Within a week after the wedding bells, John Anderson was apprised of the happy evening routine at The Point where Carrie "is now sitting at the fire plying her needle, while I was writing at the window. Possibly I may now and then raise my eyes from this page to watch for an instant her busy fingers. . . . Her presence and the consciousness that she is my wife . . . afford an infinitude of quiet happiness."[63]

Though Bellamy Storer's assignments for home reading and private study kept Ben well occupied with Blackstone, Coke, Littleton and statutory law during the last six months of his training, Ben went frequently to Cincinnati for consultation, attendance at court, and further personal direction. These enforced absences from home served to make Ben a daily correspondent—much to his own amazement. He narrated his dismay to Anderson:

Since I parted with you Monday afternoon, I have been doing little else than attending court and writing letters to Carrie. I have often laughed at the idea of a man writing to his wife every day. I flattered myself that I should never be guilty of a similar weakness but my manly resolve was no sooner tested than broken. And now I plead guilty to the "soft impeachment."[64]

Departures, however, meant returns to home, study, hunting and Carrie, and this latter program Ben enjoyed to the full. Whenever he was frustrated in his desire for a bit of hunting, or Carrie was too weary to sit up the night talking to him, Ben was forced to resort to the grey goose quill for his entertainment, and he aptly designated it "that mighty instrument of little men."[65] And he was soon to be afforded many opportunities to wield his pen to his own advantage.

On December 6, John Scott Harrison left for the national House of Representatives to assume his duties as the newly elected Whig from Hamilton County, Ohio. Ben spoke for the family and said: "we are all of us not a little depressed at the prospect

[63] B. Harrison to J. Anderson, October 27, 1853, Harrison MSS, Vol. 3.
[64] B. Harrison to J. Anderson, November 10, 1853, Harrison MSS, Vol. 3.
[65] B. Harrison to J. Anderson, Nov. 23, 1853, Harrison MSS, Vol. 3.

of being separated from him for so long a time."[66] John Scott himself was disturbed at the thought of "years of heartless excitement" in Washington, and in one of his first letters to his brother-in-law he complained: "I tried to make the best I can of a bad bargain, and *still my thoughts are continually wandering from the hall of legislation to my children and my home.*"[67]

Early in 1854, several months before his twenty-first birthday, Benjamin Harrison passed another important milestone in a career that was just beginning. Upon the successful completion of two years of close study, he was admitted to practice before the Ohio bar.[68] With this cherished goal happily attained, Ben and Carrie were in a position to give more careful consideration to their plans for the future. Basic to their intimate discussion of the problem was Ben's recently acquired conviction that he would under no circumstances remain in Cincinnati and attempt to build up a practice. A spirit of pride and independence nourished this view into a deep-rooted persuasion; as he confessed: "I long to cut my leading strings and acquire an identity of my own. Were I to continue on here it would be long ere that people should cease to regard me as a boy, and almost as long ere I should cease to regard myself as such."[69]

It was this reasoning that had strongly inclined Ben to settle in Chicago. Here he could be admitted to practice at any time, and, moreover, he conceived that the opportunities offered by its rapidly increasing population would be both rich and numerous.[70] Naturally, friends brought pressure to bear on him to stay

[66] B. Harrison to J. Anderson, Dec. 5, 1853, Harrison MSS, Vol. 3. John Scott dated his first letter from Washington on December 13, 1853. Anderson wrote to Ben: "your father's absence will be sorely felt by all the 'Pointers' . . . tell Sallie and Jennie that in my day *Pa* constituted all the attraction and life of the place." J. Anderson to Benjamin Harrison, December 9, 1853, Harrison MSS, Vol. 3.

[67] John Scott Harrison to John Cleves Short, February 2, 1854, Short Family Papers, Box 55.

[68] The year of Harrison's admission to the Bar in Cincinnati is variously given as 1853 and 1854. Roseboom, *op. cit.,* p. 206, places it in 1853. Marshall, *op. cit.,* III, 793, does not give any date; he only mentions his admission to the Indiana bar in 1854. The obituary account in the Indianapolis *Journal,* March 14, 1901, lists 1854 as date of admission in Cincinnati. The Indianapolis *News,* March 14, 1901, gives 1853. It is the author's opinion that 1854 is the correct date and this is based on the usual length of study required at that period.

[69] B. Harrison to J. Anderson, October 3, 1853, Harrison MSS, Vol. 3.

[70] B. Harrison to J. Anderson, September 30, 1853, Harrison MSS, Vol. 3.

in Cincinnati, "where he would have more friends and could fight his way through about as easily as in Chicago."[71] While these friendly pleadings may have caused some hesitation, it was the reception of T. B. Bryan's frank letter[72] that dissipated Ben's dream of establishing himself in Chicago, and he wrote to Anderson:

... the advantages which Chicago offers to young lawyers are not so flattering as I had anticipated but by no means discouraging. It had the effect to dissipate a very childish notion, which unbeknown to myself had (I fear) taken possession of my mind, viz: that Chicago was a place where fortunes and reputation might be acquired without the toil and crosses of a long tutelage. How noble an idea!![73]

Despite the fact that lawyers were numerous in Chicago and many new ones were coming in from the East, Ben was not completely disabused of his original plan to migrate there. He felt then, as do many legal neophytes today, that there was always room for "energetic, enterprizing young men."[74] With the suggestion, however, that he tarry in Cincinnati he did not sympathize. He refused to latch on to the hands of generous friends, and his newly found matrimonial wisdom told him that "charity given bread may nourish the body, but it does not invigorate the soul like the *hard earned* loaf." Ben resolved "to eat the hard earned loaf or starve,"[75] and he had now only to choose the site of his first endeavors.

During the early spring days of 1854 he decided on Indianapolis. It was no hasty selection. Ben and Carrie weighed the advantages and disadvantages carefully, and rumors that the Indiana capital was the city of their choice were quite current during February.[76] Finally, in March, Ben made a personal visit and inspected conditions at first hand. He met with a cordial recep-

71 J. Anderson to B. Harrison, October 6, 1853, Harrison MSS, Vol. 3.

72 Bryan described Chicago as a "young city, having the appearance of a village extended." On the other hand this same Chicago lawyer praised and preferred Cincinnati for "greater age . . . [with] far greater improvements and commercial advantages." T. B. Bryan to Harrison, October 3, 1853, Harrison MSS in Harrison Home, Indianapolis.

73 B. Harrison to J. Anderson, October 10, 1853, Harrison MSS, Vol. 3.

74 *Ibid.*

75 *Ibid.*

76 J. Anderson to B. Harrison, February 27, 1854, Harrison MSS, Vol. 3.

tion and returned to The Point favorably impressed. Letters of introduction written by his father in Washington had not arrived in time, but this mattered little, for as John Scott Harrison put it, "the fact is your *name* is introduction enough to any of the old inhabitants of Hoosierdom—the old men of Indiana who have become patriots of your grandfather and loved him as they loved no other public man."[77]

If Ben had not yet made up his mind to make the move, word from his cousin, William Sheets, must have helped. Sheets was already a successful business figure in Indianapolis.[78] At forty-nine, he enjoyed a reputation as a pioneer in the manufacture of paper, owned a paper mill, and was soon to branch out into stationery and blank books. He had been elected Secretary of State in 1832 and again in 1840, retiring from Indiana politics four years later. His social circle was also large and influential. He had married Miss Randolph, of a celebrated Virginia family and the adopted daughter of General William Henry Harrison, held a high post in the Masonic order, and was active as a temperance advocate and an early supporter of education for the deaf and dumb.[79] His letter to Ben could not have arrived at a more opportune time.

I regret that I was not home when you were in our city. I hope you met with a cordial reception, and went away favorably impressed with our Hoosier capital. We think our city promises more, in the future, than almost any other place in the West.

The young professional man who can make up his mind to make this his permanent home, and be content to grow with this place, must, in my judgment, succeed.

The mercantile part of the profession has always become in this state . . . the most lucrative. If you conclude to settle here, I advise you to make the acquaintance and secure the friendship of as many of the wholesale dealers in Cincinnati as you can, before you come. By this means you may very soon get into a good practice. Most of the members of the Bar, are moral, and some of them are pious men, but none of them very talented. I think you and your good lady would be

[77] John Scott Harrison to Benjamin Harrison, March 25, 1854, Harrison MSS, Vol. 3: "Your letter of the 22nd was received today. I had heard by Betsy's letter that you had returned from Indiana and supposed you could not have received my letters of introduction. . . ."

[78] *Indianapolis Directory, City Guide and Business Mirror; or, Indianapolis As It Is in 1855* (Indianapolis, 1855), p. 157.

[79] Indianapolis *Daily Journal*, March 5, 1872, obituary notice.

pleased with the society here. The standard of morality among the better class of society is very high. Religious privileges are very good also; in the First Presbyterian Church, old school, we have the Rev. John A. McClung, who is a rare man. Should you conclude to cast your lot among us, it will afford me great pleasure to aid in any way in my power. You must come, at once, to our house, without stopping at a hotel, and remain with us until you can find a pleasant boarding house. It will be a pleasure to introduce you to our friends. Give our kind regards to cousin Carrie.[80]

This enthusiasm matched Ben's own impressions. The die was cast. Carrie and Ben prepared to move to Indianapolis and make their own way in a new world of change and uncertainty.

[80] William Sheets to Benjamin Harrison, Esq., March 18, 1854, Harrison MSS, Vol. 3.

CHAPTER V

Indianapolis

WITH DETERMINATION in their eyes and optimism in their hearts Ben and Carrie were Indianapolis-bound. So meagre were their personal possessions that they were able to cram them into one huge box, which they shipped on ahead to the home of William Sheets.[1] Ordinarily, leave-taking would be an event filled with depression, but twin strokes of good fortune removed all shreds of regret. Ben fell heir to some property in Cincinnati on which he was able to raise $800 in cash,[2] and John Scott Harrison, who drew eight dollars a day as a member of Congress, promised a farewell present of at least $500.[3] No patrimony could have been more timely.

On the trip to Lawrenceburg, Indiana, where they were to entrain for the state capital, they both realized how much it meant to give up an old home and old friends. Nor was Ben's parting made easier when he slipped from the envelope his sister had given him a poem in her own hand: "To My Brother on His Departure from Home."[4] Once the twinges of grief had subsided, Ben and Carrie settled down to enjoy the scenery along

[1] On April 4, 1854, Benjamin Harrison paid 91¢ freight charges to the Indianapolis and Cincinnati Railroad for the transportation of one box from Lawrenceburg to Indianapolis, shipped in care of W. Sheets. See Personal Bills and Notes, 1854, 1 box, Harrison MSS.

[2] Harriet McIntire Foster, *Mrs. Benjamin Harrison* (Indianapolis, 1908), p. 9; also J. E. Morison and W. B. Lane, *Life of Our President Benjamin Harrison,* p. 107: "$800 . . . money advanced on a piece of property he had inherited from an Aunt who had married a soldier in the war of 1812." In the Indianapolis *Journal,* June 30, 1888, are the details of his desire to use this inheritance to support himself and his wife while he became established in his profession. Not being of age, however, he was unable to make a deed of sale, and a friend gave bond that the deed would be made when he attained his majority.

[3] John Scott Harrison to Benjamin, March 25, 1854, Harrison MSS, Vol. 3.

[4] Harrison MSS, Vol. 3, No. 462.

the bed of the recently completed Indianapolis and Cincinnati Road.[5] Ben remembered something of the sights he saw, and wrote home that "it was a panorama of swamps, frogless swamps and bare-legged Hoosier children."[6] Four and a half hours after leaving Lawrenceburg they arrived in their new world, Indianapolis.

In the 1850's America possessed few more interesting and more promising states than that of the Hoosiers. Its population was growing and in 1854 numbered more than 1,200,000, occupying an area of 22,000,000 acres of richly fertile soil, "nearly all of it available for agricultural purposes, and the whole capable of sustaining an immense population."[7] Coal fields, within a couple of hours ride from Indianapolis, were of fine quality; moreover, the beds lay near the surface and could be worked with great facility. These gifts alone would nourish into prominence cities like Gary, Hammond, and East Chicago, so that Indiana would emerge a leader in pig iron and steel output. Everything joined to offer natural facilities for manufacturing.[8]

Within five miles of the geographical center of the state, originally a mile-square plot of "intrenched wilderness"[9] on the west fork of the White River, was Indianapolis, the capital. Previous to 1847 it was just another American inland city whose meagre population of 4,000 knew comparatively little trade and less manufacture. By 1854, however, the inhabitants numbered[10] nearly 16,000 and the hum of machinery was heard everywhere;

5 *Indianapolis Directory, 1868* (Indianapolis, 1868), p. 53: "The Lawrenceburg and Upper Mississippi Road was originally begun in sections or several roads in 1850, a through road being bitterly and successfully opposed by the Madison Company, but was finally chartered in 1851, and finished to Lawrenceburg, 90 miles, in October 1853 under George H. Dunn, the first President. The name was changed December, 1853 to the Indianapolis and Cincinnati Road."

6 Benjamin Harrison to Anna Harrison, May 10, 1854, Harrison MSS, Vol. 3.

7 *Indianapolis Directory, 1855.*

8 "The advantages possessed by Indianapolis for profitable investment of capital and labor, in every department for industry, bear favorable comparison with those of any other city in the West. . . . A population of at least three millions, residing in Indiana and adjoining states look to us for the supply of many articles of every day use." *Indianapolis Directory, 1857*, pp. 50–53.

9 "Indianapolis was located and laid out in 1820, and on January 6, 1821 it was incorporated . . . the original town plot was one mile square." *Ibid.*, p. v.

10 To give some idea of the rapid growth of the city an examination of the population figures from 1830 to 1855 is essential: in 1830, 1,085; in 1834, 1,600; in 1840, 2,692; in 1847, 8,504; in 1855, 16,000, showing an increase in six years of almost 100 per cent. Grooms and Smith, *op. cit.*, p. vi.

eight railroads, comprising 1,500 miles of track, had been completed; seven others, totaling 900 miles, were rapidly approaching completion. Hoosiers saw that the railroads were revolutionizing their commerce, and they appreciated the fact that they themselves as well as their freight were being transported almost as cheaply by rail as they had been by water. Locomotive and car building made giant strides, and the city was rightfully heralded in her new role as one of the principal manufacturing points in the country.[11]

While public-spirited citizens and city tradesmen spoke glowingly of present and future blessings, the city was still one "of muddy boots and torn clothes," where people made "desperate attempts at finery; glass jewels and French silk dresses, which after having found no purchaser in New York, have been sent west."[12] In 1852, Madame Theresa Pulszky, visiting from Hungary in company with Kossuth's party, stopped off at Indianapolis and saw:

Some of the mothers had their babies in their arms; workmen appeared in their blouses or dusty coats, just as they came from the workshop; farmers stepped in high boots. Once more we saw that the house of the Governor is the property of the people. And yet this incongruous mass did not behave unbecomingly to a drawing-room. There was no rude elbowing, no unpleasant noises, or disturbing laughter. Had they but shaken hands less violently! I yet feel western cordiality in my stiff arm.[13]

Indianapolis occupied the middle of a shallow basin, whose surrounding area rose gradually for miles through a region "once densely covered with large hardwood trees, and in many places on the city site were extensive thickets of prickly ash and spice

---

[11] "From 1847 to 1850 several saw and grist mills, two foundries, steam engine and machine shops, a peg and last factory, a planing mill, several slaughter houses . . . were built and put into successful operation. . . . By 1857 the number of plants was greatly increased and a new variety was introduced. Two woolen factories, a large foundry and machine shop, two barrel factories, four chair and cabinet factories . . . boiler, carriage and wagon factories, etc." *Indianapolis Directory, 1857,* pp. 44–45.

[12] Jacob Piatt Dunn, *Greater Indianapolis* (Chicago, 1910), I, 188. The author quotes liberally from early diaries and writings of visitors to the city.

[13] Cited from Mme Pulszky's diary by J. P. Dunn, *loc. cit.*

wood.''[14] Hunters seldom returned unsuccessful from the chase. As late as 1842 saddles of venison sold for from twenty-five to fifty cents, turkeys ten to twelve cents, and a bushel of pigeons for twenty-five cents. The river was so full of fish that an early settler declared "a stone thrown in it anywhere, from the graveyard ford to the mouth of Fall Creek, would strike a shoal of fish."[15] Because of such abundance, the Delaware and the Miami Indians yielded the country with great reluctance. Many of them lingered in the vicinity after the treaties were signed.[16] While they had no permanent village at Indianapolis proper, their hunting and fishing camps were numerous to the north of the city site, and a traveler who passed up the river several years before the settlement related that the banks were then dotted with wigwams, and the river often dotted with canoes.

Spring was full upon Indianapolis when Ben and Carrie arrived. Their first impressions of the city and its society were in strong contradiction to the rather bizarre and false opinions formed by foreigners passing through the country. In the young couple's eyes the people seemed to be living a plain and wholesome kind of life. There was little disposition to flaunt wealth, even when it existed. Rather, the people liked to think of themselves as belonging to an older and more democratic school of thought in which wealth and ostentation did not constitute social position. The woman who "kept a girl" was socially no better than her neighbor who could not afford the luxury. Extraneous wants for the average family were few. Food and shelter, clothing and doctor's fees, along with the usual assessments for church

14 "The first history of Indianapolis was prepared by Ignatius Brown, and published as part of the City Directory of 1857. Mr. Brown was a patient delver in historical material, and in the course of the next decade . . . he revised and enlarged his work and republished it in the city directory of 1868. This second publication was more than four times as large as the first, and has been the basis of all the history that has since been published . . . errors and all." Dunn, *op. cit.*, Preface, i.

15 *Indianapolis Directory, 1868*, pp. 1–93, contains Brown's revision of the detailed history of the city from 1818 to 1868.

16 Dunn, *op. cit.*, I, 2, writes that "in October, 1818, both tribes were assembled at St. Mary's, Ohio, where Jonathan Jennings, Lewis Cass and Benjamin Parke, for the United States, made treaties with them. On October 3rd the Delawares relinquished 'all their claims to the land in the state of Indiana.' " On October 6th the Miamis also agreed to vacate Indiana.

and city, made only moderate inroads on one's financial resources.[17]

The young wedded couple was fortunate in the city of their
choice, and equally fortunate in their initial protector, William
Sheets. His home was located on the corner of Pennsylvania and
Ohio Streets, later the site of the Denison Hotel. Here, Cousin
Carrie and her lawyer husband were warmly received. They enjoyed the Sheets hospitality for a few days, while searching for
quarters where they might keep house for themselves. They
quickly found a place in a two-story frame house further up on
Pennsylvania Street. The second story was occupied by another
newly married couple, a Dr. and Mrs. John M. Kitchen.[18]

John and Mary Kitchen seemed to get along splendidly with
Ben and Carrie Harrison, and even after a half century the doc-
tor painted a pleasant word picture of his early associations with
Ben:

He was kindly, agreeable and studious, reserved even then, but at-
tracting persons to him by his intellectual qualities. He was a man of
notably clear character and made a success of everything he undertook. I do not remember that he belonged to any secret society, nor
did he, as was in that day thought necessary to every young man who
had social, business or political aspirations, join any of the volunteer
fire companies, of that period. I do not think he ever had an acquaintance with anyone that ripened into the hottest kind of friendship. I
have been hunting with him. He never pushed himself into the company of other hunters. While he was a very good shot, I do not think
he was much of a fisherman.[19]

A fire soon drove the young couple out on the streets in search
of another lodging. Perhaps this was a blessing in disguise, for
$7.00 board and rent per week[20] was certainly far beyond the

[17] For social background for the 1850–60 period see J. H. Holliday, *Indianapolis
and the Civil War* (Indianapolis, 1911), pp. 530–35.

[18] Dunn, *op. cit.*, II, 796–97. This is at variance with the account found in the
Indianapolis *Journal*, July 1, 1888, where a three-room cottage on Vermont St. is
called the first Harrison home. Evidence in other newspaper clippings, especially
in the Indianapolis *News*, March 15, 1901, seems more reliable and confirms Dr.
Kitchen's account.

[19] Indianapolis *News*, March 15, 1901.

[20] In a box marked "Bills and Notes, 1854," Harrison MSS, there is a receipted
rent and board bill to the amount of $49.00. This covered their occupancy from
April 4 to May 23. It was typical of Ben to make a pencil notation on the receipt
that a mistake of one week's board was corrected and that he was credited with
$7.00.

means of a young, unknown and clientless lawyer. Carrie, moreover, was now well advanced in her pregnancy and required
medical attention. Her physical strength was no longer equal to
household tasks, and the cost of hiring a girl, as well as mounting
doctor's fees, made Ben give pause to ways of economizing.[21] Under the press of these circumstances, he consented to Carrie's
returning to Oxford and remaining with the Scotts until their
first child should be born. He himself vowed to remain alone in
Indianapolis and to bend every effort to create and build up a
practice.

Ben's early, roseate dreams of quick success at the Indiana bar
had been rudely shattered. It was not all his fault. The nature of
law practice was peculiar at that time, and although he struggled
and searched, fees, even small ones, and clients were not easily
found. He found that he could not attach himself to any firm of
specialists, for at that time the important and lucrative fields of
corporation, patent and commercial law were not yet developed.
Actually, the leaders of the bar were—to use the phrase of the
day—"*nisi prius*" lawyers: men who were accustomed to travel
the rounds of the circuit with the presiding judge. The early Indianapolis lawyer was a professional angler; all sorts of fish came
into his net. He was compelled to pull in everything that came
along, whether it was a five-dollar case tried before a county
squire or a remunerative railroad foreclosure suit handled in
federal court. Indeed, it was not until the decades after the Civil
War that the Indiana bar assumed rank with some of the leading
legal centers of the nation. When this came to pass, some of the
older attorneys recollected that in the early 1850's it was not an
uncommon thing for the then leading legal sages to begin the
morning "with a skirmish in Squire Sullivan's court about the
ownership of a flock of vagrant geese"[22] and wind up their day's
work with a lively debate in federal court over a case involving
large interests and important principles of equity and jurispru-
dence.

21 In addition to doctor and medicine bills, Ben was obliged to foot a $51.50
bill for furniture (Tilford and Co.). He met this on April 10, 1854.

22 W. P. Fishback in New York *Evening Post*, December, 1888, Benjamin Harrison Scrapbook No. 9, Harrison MSS, which forms the substance and in some instances the verbatim account given by Charles W. Taylor, *The Bench and Bar of
Indiana* (Indianapolis, 1895), pp. 205–16.

This type of practice had its drawbacks as well as its advantages. Most fees were small, though they were fairly numerous to the lawyer whose enlarged acquaintance among his fellow citizens netted him many petty suits dealing with the collection and payment of debts, wills, mortgages, foreclosures, divorces and other routine matters. Ben's unfamiliarity with Indianapolis and its environs and his boyish appearance militated against his employment as counsel in such cases. To the new lawyer trying to break in, it was difficult to make the right acquaintances and to become known in business and social circles. Yet, as long as he was kept out by the bar of unfamiliarity, the more he was denied the opportunity of meeting many prospective clients and of studying human nature at close range. Yet, once this break-through was made, Indiana's type of professional practice gave strength, breadth and adaptability to a young lawyer's intellectual powers. It was a wonderful safeguard against merely a narrow competency in one field; more positively, it fostered intellectual activity on a front both varied and comprehensive. Of all of these possible advantages Ben was keenly aware.

He was well along the road to discouragement and financial insolvency before the tide of fortune turned. Board and food bills fell due with clocklike regularity and, with Carrie away at Oxford, loneliness engulfed him. Idleness, the ghost he feared most, stalked his path. He could not afford his own office, and clients were too few to justify borrowing any money for this purpose. Finally, his break came. Through the kindness of John H. Rea,[23] then Clerk of the United States District Court, Ben secured office space in the State Bank Building located on the triangular square opposite the Bates House. He was now in a position to meet fellow lawyers, business men and artisans. A second boon followed. By the kindness and friendship of United States Marshal John L. Robinson and his deputy, George McOuat, he was appointed court crier, at a salary of $2.50 per day.[24]

These two fortuitous events contributed immeasurably to Ben's renewed resolution to persevere. And, to help matters along, his father was never too preoccupied with the debates on

[23] Indianapolis *Journal*, March 14, 1901. *Indianapolis City Directory, 1855,* spells his name "Ray."

[24] *Ibid.* Also see Morison and Lane, *op. cit.,* p. 107.

the Nebraska Bill to forget to replenish Ben's coffers with an occasional check for $25.00 or $50.00.[25] Ben soon added to his own earnings. Tradition has it that he pocketed his first fee, a five dollar gold piece, for prosecuting and convicting a man who had obtained money under false pretenses.[26] It came the hard way. He had to hire a horse and ride a muddy road ten miles into the country to Clermont, where he tried his case before a justice of the peace whose back yard was an open-air court room.[27] A fee was a fee and no trouble was considered too great. As Ben himself remarked in later life:

They were close times, I tell you. A $5 bill was an event. There was one good friend through it all—Robert Browning, the druggist. I shall always recollect him with gratitude. He believed in me. When things were particularly tight I could go into his store and borrow $5 from the drawer. A ticket in its place was all that was required. Such friends make life worth living.[28]

Although the skies were not brightening too perceptibly, the young lawyer was able to see that at least some of the clouds were lined with silver.

Ben's diligent study of the Indiana statutes and his routine work around the court did not go unnoticed. Attracted by Harrison's show of promise, Major Jonathan W. Gordon, then prosecuting attorney for Marion County, invited Ben to assist him in the prosecution of a case known at the time as the Point Lookout burglary. Because of Gordon's reputation as one of the leading members of the bar, as well as the high calibre of the opposing counsel, Ben hastened to accept the engagement for the experience in trial work it would afford him. He felt a new pride in sit-

25 John Scott Harrison to Benjamin Harrison, May 19, 1854, Harrison MSS, Vol. 3.
26 Morison and Lane, *op. cit.*, p. 107.
27 *New York Press* (?), March 14, 1901, Benjamin Harrison Scrapbook No. 52, p. 77, Harrison MSS. The justice of the peace was John P. Martindale, uncle of the late prominent Indianapolis attorney, Emsley W. Johnson, Sr., senior member of the law firm, Johnson, Zechiel and Johnson. Mr. Johnson stated he heard his uncle tell of this Clermont case upon numerous occasions. Emsley W. Johnson, Sr., to the author, March 3, 1950.
28 *House Document No. 154*, p. 100. Also the Robert Browning of whom Ben speaks was the remaining partner of the once famous Craighead & Browning, dealers in drugs, medicines, and chemicals at No. 22 West Washington St. See *Indianapolis Directory, 1857*, p. 110.

ting with the prosecutor, and during the trial took copious notes. As a brilliant defense was made by ex-Governor David Wallace[29] and Sims Colley, two of the community's most distinguished lawyers, Ben listened intently.[30]

The trial was somewhat lengthy and, as it reached its final stages, the court determined to hold an evening session and thus allow the prosecution to close its case. This decision conflicted with Major Gordon's plans for that evening, for the chief prosecutor was most desirous of attending a lecture by Horace Mann. The physical impossibility of bilocation worked to Ben's advantage; during the supper recess Gordon told him he would have to make the concluding summary to the jury. And with that the elder man was off to the lecture.

That evening the court met by the dim light of old-fashioned tin sconces and candles. Ben was full of trepidation lest he might not acquit himself with credit, for he recognized the importance of the situation as well as the power of the men opposed to him.[31] Sitting in the dim shadow cast by the light of the one candle the sheriff had left on his desk, Ben felt somewhat fortified as he fondled the copious notes he had made during the trial. When he rose, to open the state's summation to the jury, consternation flooded his soul as he discovered that the poor lighting would not allow him to read what he had so carefully compiled. Nevertheless, he began his argument, trying again and again to make out the dim pencilings he had made. It was useless.

Straightway he abandoned all reliance on notes and proceeded to make his argument from memory. As he progressed, he discovered with growing encouragement that he remembered the evidence perfectly. Thrown upon his own resources, he made the most of his natural faculty for easy, impromptu speech. Following the judge's charge to the jury, young Harrison received con-

29 David Wallace, who succeeded as Governor in 1847, must have been known to Harrison long before his arrival in Indianapolis. While David Wallace was still a child, his father moved to Cincinnati, where he became a close friend of General William Henry Harrison. It was to his son, David, that the General gave the appointment as a cadet to West Point, passing over his own son, John Scott Harrison. Governor Wallace was well known in Indiana; he served in the Indiana Constitutional Convention of 1850 and was later elected Judge of the Common Pleas Court in 1856. He held this office until his death in 1859. J. P. Dunn, *Indiana and Indianans* (Chicago and New York, 1919), I, 420–21.

30 Indianapolis *Journal*, March 14, 1901.

31 Indianapolis *Journal*, June 30, 1888.

gratulations from every side,[32] but what pleased him most was the warm compliment of David Wallace.[33] The story had a happy ending, as the jury returned a verdict of guilty.

Shortly after this pleasant introduction to trial procedure Ben was appointed by the City Attorney to assist in the prosecution of a hotel servant charged with poisoning a guest's coffee. At the time of his assignment, Ben, like most of the citizens of Indianapolis, knew little or nothing about the nature of poison and its effects on the human body. Such knowledge came within the range of physicians and chemists, and of this latter group the city was barren.[34] As the trial was set for the next day, there was only one night in which Ben could find out all he could about poisons. He went directly to the Post Office Building to the second floor where his friend Dr. Kitchen shared an office with a Dr. Parvin. The latter was alone in the office and Ben got down to work immediately. For ten hours he studied Parvin's books and with the doctor's aid succeeded in mastering a large number of facts, medical facts, on the nature and operation of poisons in the human system. The sequel was well narrated by a local newspaper reporter:

From sun to sun the young lawyer cross examined the physician, and then he entered the court room to confound the other physicians. The long row of gray-haired and bespectacled experts were so put to it by this tow-headed boy that the sensation of the case was transferred from the crime to the prosecution.[35]

On the strength of Ben's performance the criminal was convicted, but the talk of the time was the amazing display of such knowledge on the part of a lawyer.

These moderate successes, though not highly remunerative, earned him enough prominence to induce Governor Joseph A. Wright to entrust him with the conduct of a legislative investigation.[36] His efficient execution of this task earned him further

32 *House Document No. 154*, p. 100.
33 According to the *Journal's* account, Wallace put his hand on Harrison's head and complimented him in the highest manner, predicting for him a brilliant and successful future.
34 Indianapolis *News*, March 14, 1901.
35 *Ibid.*
36 Indianapolis *Journal*, June 30, 1888.

fame, and soon clients came his way and their fees were solid food to a financially famished attorney.

Ben's happy turn in fortune came none too soon. At Oxford, Ohio, on Saturday, August 12, 1854—just eight days before Ben's twenty-first birthday—Carrie gave birth to a boy. They named him Russell.[37] Congress had recessed, and John Scott Harrison was at home resting when the news of Russell's birth came. In his own quiet way he rose to the occasion and honored the proud parents with a significantly beautiful letter. Part of his epistle was directed to Ben:

> You now stand, my dear son, in a new relation in life—a relation that will be attended with new joys and also new cares and responsibilities—that the former may outnumber the latter I hope with all my heart. And yet my experience tells me that life is very much of a mixed draught—in which the bitter and the sweet are pretty fairly —or at least equally contributed—afflictions, sometimes bring joys and again, joys afflictions, and so we are all never perfectly happy,—and never so miserable, that hope does not spread a small ray on the surrounding darkness.

And to Carrie he sent warmest congratulations and love; he asked Ben to tell her that

> I wish her all of a young mother's joy. I will not say—without a young mother's anxiety, for I believe in that very anxiety is entwined her pleasure and her joy—but I will say that I hope she may escape those many little pains and annoyances which so often afflict a young mother.[38]

As Indianapolis in late summer and early fall tended to be damp and unhealthy, Ben thought it wise that Russell should not be brought to the city until better conditions prevailed. Hence, it was decided that Carrie and the baby should stay with Dr. and Mrs. Scott until it was safe to bring Russell to live with his Harrison relatives at The Point. Ben, and Carrie too, were very anxious that the child should enjoy early in life the healthful and

---

[37] The child was named after Russell Farnum Lord who had married Carrie's older sister, Elizabeth. They were married in 1849 and made their home in Honesdale. Indianapolis *News*, Dec. 10, 1889.

[38] John Scott Harrison to Benjamin Harrison, August 19, 1854, Harrison MSS, Vol. 3.

invigorating air so traditionally characteristic of a farm. The infant grew strong and in a few weeks he found himself on display along the banks of the Ohio. This latest addition to the Harrison family, as might be expected, became quite a pet in the old house, and in the not altogether objective opinion of grandfather John Scott Harrison "he is one of the handsomest infants I ever saw."[39]

Ben cherished every piece of news he could get about his pride and joy; every tidbit kept him going in his daily efforts to build up a practice. Though he made every possible effort, his utmost endeavors netted him no great financial return. This fact, along with Carrie's protracted absence, accentuated his low spirits. Fortunately, there is preserved a letter never intended for the public eye; but it is a perfect mirroring of the future President's heart-guarded secrets. To Carrie he wrote:

My dear wife,

Tho' a letter will not go out today I cannot forbear writing you as I feel lonesome and have nothing particular to do. I met Mr. Rea at the Depot on his way to Lafayette, he expects to be gone all week, and I shall be without company both at the House and at the office.

I must bind myself more closely to my books and then I shall feel the want of company less.

. . . You do not know how disheartened I feel sometimes, at the prospect of sitting in my office, for long months, without getting anything to do. I know I should feel contented if I only had some business to occupy my attention, however trifling the profits might be. Indeed I would almost be willing to work for nothing, just for the sake of being busy. But however much I may be discouraged at the prospect, I never suffer myself to falter in my purpose—I have long since made up my mind that with God's blessing and good health *I would* succeed, and I never allow myself to doubt the result.

It is a great relief in these seasons of depression to have your society, and I long very much for it now but it seems better that you should remain where you are, for a season. I hope our place will soon become healthy; indeed, it is becoming so, at least so Mrs. Dr. N[ewcomer][40] says, the doctor himself I have not seen. I do not know whether Mr.

39 John Scott Harrison to Benjamin Harrison, September 30, 1854, Harrison MSS, Vol. 3.

40 Dr. and Mrs. Newcomer were devoted personal friends of Ben and Carrie; he was their family physician until the Civil War, and attended Mrs. Harrison at the birth of their second child.

Sheets' family have returned or not—I will leave this unfolded until tomorrow, and will add something more if I learn anything worth communicating. Much love to all the family and kisses for the Babe,

> Your affectionate husband,
> Benja Harrison.

[Wednesday morning]

I ate an oyster supper, at Dr. N's, last night, by special invitation, and after smoking a segar, went home, read awhile and retired early. This morning I feel quite brisk and much more like study. The Dr. says the sickly season is generally over by September 23rd and that the health of our place is now improving. I suppose there is no reason why you should not come out by the first of October. I will have everything ready to receive you by that time. It is quite cool this morning, and a fire in the morning and the evening will soon be necessary to comfort. I am glad cold weather is approaching; you know I always enjoy the winter season. Love to all. Write often and let me know how you and the babe get along. I had a bad dream about him last night,

> Yours,
> Ben.[41]

The first week of October had slipped by before Carrie, with Russell in her arms, finally arrived at Indianapolis.[42] They rented a more modest residence in the eastern part of the city, a one-story wooden building with three rooms, bedroom, dining room and kitchen. Outside, there was a shed where Carrie could do her cooking in summer. Since their tight budget precluded the hiring of a servant, it was Ben's good pleasure to help his wife all he could. He knuckled down to his job admirably. Before going to

[41] This letter was a personal keepsake of General Harrison and he kept it hidden away in a small drawer of the desk that adorned his office until he died. This handsome desk was removed to his home on North Delaware St. where it is preserved among other Harrison relics in the attic museum. The desk, presumably emptied out completely by the family, was discovered by Mrs. Ruth Woodworth, curator of the Harrison Home, to have concealed two intimate letters addressed to "My dear wife" and "Dear Carrie" under dates of September 19, 1854, and January 5, 1855. The Arthur Jordan Foundation of Indianapolis, restorers and present owners of the Harrison Home, gave the Library of Congress photostatic copies of these letters on July 12, 1940, now listed as A.C. 6322 among the papers of Benjamin Harrison.

[42] Among the Benjamin Harrison Collection (Library of Congress) there is one box marked "Personal Notes and Bills, 1854." The rent receipts show that Ben had paid one board bill from July 15 to August 28 for $13.00. (This was for himself at a rate of $2.00 per week.) There is another rent receipt for $32.72 covering August 29–October 9 ($5.00 per week for one person). The subsequent bills, beginning with Oct. 9, 1854, show him renting for Carrie, himself, and the baby.

his office in the morning, he sawed all the wood Carrie would need for the day. When he came home for his noon day meal, he would fill up a water bucket and attend to the other chores about the house.[43]

At the office his luck seemed to improve. During the fall months, at least, his law business was prosperous enough to allow him to have a shingle made for over his office door, and also to have printed 300 business cards bearing the inscription:[44]

B. HARRISON

ATTORNEY AT LAW

INDIANAPOLIS, INDIANA

Will give prompt attention to all
business entrusted to his care.

Special attention given to the
collection of claims.

OFFICE IN STATE BANK BUILDING

In his advertising Ben was also able to list eight references of character from reputable firms and men in New York, Chicago, Baltimore, Cincinnati and Indianapolis.[45] It was a wise investment but brought only a modicum of business. What came his way was chiefly notarial work, writing deeds, petty cases before justices of the peace, probate work and collections, together with an occasional appearance in the circuit court.[46]

Despite his most strenuous efforts, Ben simply could not seem to make ends meet. His first essay as an independent attorney was

43 New York *Mail and Express,* an undated newspaper clipping in Harrison Scrapbook No. 52, pp. 83–86, Harrison MSS.

44 In 1889 this inscription was copied from one of the original cards (then yellow with age and in the possession of William Sheets' family). Ben paid a printing bill of $2.00 for this work on Nov. 7, 1854, "Personal Bills and Notes, 1854," Harrison MSS. See also the Chicago *Weekly Inter-Ocean,* May, 1889, a clipping in the B. Harrison Scrapbook No. 9, p. 94, Harrison MSS.

45 From Cincinnati, Ben listed Hon. Bellamy Storer, Lewis Whiteman, and Samuel H. Hart & Co. The New York reference was his brother-in-law, Russell F. Lord, Superintendent of the Delaware and Hudson Canal. The others were: Joseph Reynolds, Baltimore; John B. Anderson, New Albany, Indiana; Thomas B. Bryan, Chicago; and William Sheets, Indianapolis. See B. Harrison Scrapbook No. 9, p. 94, Harrison MSS.

46 New York *Mail and Express,* an undated newspaper clipping in B. Harrison Scrapbook No. 52, pp. 83–88, Harrison MSS. Also "Personal Notes and Bills, 1854," Harrison MSS.

a distinct financial failure, so that he was forced to borrow money. Fortunately, his family[47] and friends, like Robert Browning, the druggist, stood by him in these dark hours.

And as if the financial burden were not heavy enough, Ben was saddled with concern over the failing health of his two dependents. From almost the time of her return to the city Carrie was ill, and little Russie did not develop in normal fashion. Shortly after their first Christmas together—and not a very merry one at that—Ben scraped enough money together to allow Carrie and the babe a health vacation. Their destination was twofold, the Scott home at Oxford and the Harrison farm at The Point. Not long after their departure, Ben wrote:

. . . I forgot to tell you to write often, but I suppose you will not need the caution. I know you and the babe will be cared for, both at the Point and at Oxford, but as no one loves you as I do, so no one will take as good care of you as I would. . . . I wish I were able to send you some money as you should have your teeth fixed etc., but I am now reduced to two dollars myself. I will try to send you some in a day or two, though I am sure I have no idea where it is to come from.

Sid Mear's party I am told is to come off Wednesday. Nothing of interest has transpired since you left. Take good care of our sweet boy and of yourself also. Say to Irwin that if he will bring you out I will not go down, as money is too scarce to be squandered un-necessarily. I would like very much to visit Oxford and will do so if funds are more plenty. If Irwin is coming out however it would be as well for you to come with him. Love to all.[48]

The year 1855 could not have begun less inauspiciously than it did for Benjamin Harrison. With two dollars in his pocket and the dread uncertainty as to where or when the next dollar would come, no one could blame him for feeling discouraged. He was not alone in this plight, for a large majority of his fellow citizens

[47] John Scott Harrison to Benjamin, Oct. 29, 1854, Harrison MSS, Vol. 3. The following excerpt is typical: "Irwin is hauling his wheat to Lawrenceburg and I will try to make you a small remittance. . . . Anna insists (unsolicited) that she will give you her lot—She is a noble girl and her heart is as big as her body—you might take it and give her your obligation to refund when she needs it. The amount would be worth more to you now than double that amount six years hence."

[48] The original of this letter is preserved in the Benjamin Harrison Home in Indianapolis; a photostatic copy is housed in the Library of Congress as A.C. 6322, Harrison MSS.

in Indianapolis believed themselves equally ill-starred on New Year's Day, 1855. The financial panic that had occurred in the West during the fall of 1854 dealt a heavy blow to the general business of the city.[49] The free state-stock banks had generally stopped payment, and their notes, which formed the great bulk of the circulation, were passing at a heavy discount. Railway and other enterprises were greatly embarrassed, and nearly all those in progress suspended operations. Traders and manufacturers were cramped, and general distrust prevailed among business men. Even the bankers' convention, held at the capital on January 7, failed in any way to ease the situation or alleviate the suffering of the community;[50] two weeks later the mayors of the several cities of the state met in convention at Indianapolis, "for consolation and mutual improvement, but without any visible result."[51] This condition was further aggravated by the poor physical health of the citizenry, as the month of January saw the outbreak of a smallpox epidemic. The disease spread so rapidly during February that construction of the city's first hospital was begun.

All Ben could see was black: more money borrowed from court clerk John Rea;[52] additional bills from doctors treating Carrie and Russell at Oxford;[53] and a steady decline in the number of clients who stopped at 32½ West Washington Street and walked up one flight to the desk called Harrison's Law Office.[54] To make matters worse, John Anderson, Ben's closest friend and one to whom he looked for encouragement, wrote him a letter that came close to being the proverbial straw that broke the camel's back.

[49] For the most detailed treatment of the effects of the 1854 financial panic on Indianapolis see *Indianapolis Directory, 1868*, pp. 69–72.

[50] This convention attempted to classify the notes of the suspended banks and fix discount rates according to the value of their securities. These rates were accordingly fixed, but not adhered to even by those who made them, and the discounts were raised or lowered at the caprice of the brokers, entailing great losses on the community, and making large sums for the operators in the business. Ignatius Brown, in *Indianapolis City Directory, 1868*.

[51] *Ibid.*

[52] Indianapolis, January 13, 1855, Harrison MSS, Vol. 3. Under this date was a promissory note signed by Benjamin Harrison to the effect: "due John Rea for money borrowed one hundred and six dollars to be paid in good bankable currency." Ben paid $80.00 on January 30, 1855.

[53] "Personal Notes and Bills, 1855," Harrison MSS.

[54] *Indianapolis Directory, 1855*, p. 77.

On February 2, 1855, the same man who had objected to Ben's early marriage again wrote somewhat pessimistically:

I wish you had settled in some other place. It doesn't strike me Indianapolis will ever be much of a business place—seats of government rarely are—Washington, Columbus, Lexington—however, it is polite to follow up present openings—and reputation once acquired you can move to a more suitable locality.[55]

Then, paradoxically, in the midst of misery and want, Ben met the right man. It may have been prophetic that the meeting resulted from the gentleman's ambition for political office. He was William Wallace, a successful lawyer, the son of former Governor David Wallace and the brother of Lew, who was both a military man and a romantic novelist in later life. William was not to be left far behind. Political ambition impelled him to fish in troubled waters,[56] and in March, 1855, he approached young Harrison and asked him to become his law partner, since a competent helper would leave him free to campaign.

The meeting occurred about three months before the 1855 city elections, scheduled that year for early May. The account comes down to us in Wallace's own words. After speaking of his earlier acquaintance with Harrison and his favorable impressions of him as a lawyer, he relates:

It happened in the year 1855. I had received the nomination for Clerk of Marion County on the People's Ticket. The canvass required a good deal of time, and I concluded to offer my young friend a partnership. I met him on the street one day, and told him I had some good clients and a fair practice, and that if he would go into the office and take care of them while I was canvassing for office, we

[55] John A. Anderson to Benjamin Harrison, February 2, 1855, Harrison MSS, Vol. 3. The letter was not entirely one of pessimism. John had heard reports of Ben's initial success in the Point Lookout burglary prosecution and of his merited praise at the hands of Wallace. He added "My own congratulations to those already received upon your successful debut."

[56] Financial and social conditions favored the emergence of a new political party that would promise reform and stability. The People's Party of 1854, of which Wallace was a member, made just such promises of timely aid. It was composed of Free-Soil Democrats, Anti-Slavery Whigs, Know-Nothings and Temperance men, and in the October elections it carried the state and elected a majority of both houses of the legislature. See J. P. Dunn, *Indiana and Indianans*, I, 492.

BEN HARRISON'S SECOND RESIDENCE
IN INDIANAPOLIS ON NORTH NEW JERSEY STREET

THE OLD BATES HOUSE

Abraham Lincoln spoke from first balcony, rear of car, February 11, 1861

From J. P. Dunn, *History of Greater Indianapolis*   *Courtesy W. H. Bass Photo Company*

INDIANAPOLIS DURING THE EARLY DAYS OF THE CIVIL WAR

View of Washington Street, East from Meridian, 1862

CARRIE AND COLONEL BEN HARRISON, 1863

would share the profits. I think this was the only partnership agreement we ever had. I was defeated for the office, so we continued the practice of law together.[57]

The newly constituted law firm of Wallace and Harrison prospered, and, while Will Wallace stumped Marion County, Ben Harrison succeeded not only in satisfying Wallace's former clients but actually procured many new ones.[58] One may be sure that the new junior partner never regretted his immediate acceptance of Wallace's proposition. A letter to his devoted teacher and guide, Doctor Bishop, clearly reflects his changed fortune and rejuvenated spirits:

... You will I am sure be glad to hear that I am doing *very well* in my profession. I have formed a partnership with a son of ex-governor Wallace's and our prospect of increased business is good.[59]

Prospects for increased business were good; better, perhaps, than even Ben himself imagined. From the "quiet kind of business"[60] that Wallace had built up by March, 1855, the firm rose rapidly to new heights. At the end of one year the Wallace and Harrison cash ledger listed a sum total of $1369.00 credited to incoming fees.[61] This success was due primarily to the firm's collection work undertaken for two large out of state business houses: Dibble, Work and Moore, of New York City, and

57 Indianapolis *Journal*, June 30, 1888.

58 Wallace was willing to attribute this success to Harrison whom he characterized as a young man of "superior intellectual qualities . . . and sterling worth." *Ibid.*

59 Ben still felt he owed a tremendous debt of gratitude to Doctor Bishop. He speaks of the secular knowledge gathered under Bishop as forming but a "small part of the debt of gratitude I owe you. The kind interviews which you repeatedly gave me on the subject of my soul's future interest, are gratefully remembered by me and were I trust not without influence in bringing me to Christ." Benjamin Harrison to Robert Hamilton Bishop, March 11, 1855, Harrison MSS, Vol. 3.

60 By this description Wallace meant "some collections and a good deal of probate business." Indianapolis *Journal*, June 30, 1888.

61 One book entitled "Cash Ledger: March 22, 1855–October 6, 1865" for Wallace and Harrison Law Firm, Harrison MSS. This is only one item in an abundance of material covering every aspect of the legal and financial dealing of the law firm. Incoming Correspondence (1853–61), as well as the Wallace Letter-Press Books, are available in the Harrison Collection at the Library of Congress.

Thatcher, Shaw and Co., of Boston.[62] As business increased, their reputation was enhanced and this contributed to the upward spiral. Reputable business and law firms from nearby Louisville and Cincinnati as well as from Philadelphia and Baltimore now employed Wallace and Harrison as their Indianapolis agents.[63]

On the domestic front the type of practice was more varied, and perhaps more interesting, yet it proved as profitable as the collection work done for out of town clients. Foreclosures, for example, sometimes netted a fee as high as $100.00,[64] but these were exceptions to the general rule. Five per cent of the total sum of bills collected was considered a fair commission, but lawyers could not always obtain that high a rate.[65] It was the multiplicity of the ordinary fees of anywhere from one to five dollars that was the backbone of the domestic income. The cases themselves were ordinary: sales, contracts, tax reports, minor collections, wills and general counsel.

The comparatively lax divorce laws of the state provided another lucrative source of income. The state had the unenviable reputation for affording wide facilities for loosing the conjugal bond, and it was not uncommon for lawyers in distant cities to contact Wallace and Harrison either by letter or, more directly, by sending the interested party directly to Indianapolis. Such cases as these usually brought in good fees, and not too infrequently a bit of humor also. From Milford, New Hampshire, came the following hand-delivered letter:

The bearer is a gentleman from Amherst in this county . . . [who] has a *devil* for a wife and wants to get rid of her. Your laws offer greater facilities for procuring divorce than ours. I understand there

---

[62] Wallace seems to have been responsible for adding these two houses to their lists of clients and references. Dibble, Work and Moore carried "an extensive assortment of staple goods, hosiery etc., etc.," according to their letter to Wallace and Harrison, January 1, 1858, 1 box "Legal Correspondence, 1853–1858," Harrison MSS.

[63] In Louisville, Prentice, Henderson and Osborne, as well as the John Smiat & Co., were the two most important clients. They were credited with paying fees of $150.92 and $222.52, respectively, in 1857. The Philadelphia firm of Lippincott, Coffin & Co., ranked second only to Dibble, Work and Moore in fees paid. Cash Ledger, Harrison MSS.

[64] Wallace and Harrison Cash Journal, March 22, 1855–October, 1861, lists under date of July 28, 1855: "Indianapolis Brownsburg RR. Co., fee for foreclosure of mortgage of Jones and wife $100.00." Harrison MSS.

[65] Cash Journal, Aug. 9, 1856, Harrison MSS, reveals that a fee of $20.00 was charged for the collection of $400.00 for Peterson and Quick.

has been a change in your law for divorce and that in order to avail of your old law a residence in your state must be obtained. . . .[66]

Also, according to the Indiana statute, abandonment was considered good cause for divorce within one year, or in a shorter time if the court was satisfied that there was no probability of reconciliation. This piece of legislation served to attract a number of cases from neighboring Ohio, and as one Buckeye attorney wrote to Wallace and Harrison:

> Your state has the rather unenviable reputation for its facilities for divorcing people, but in the present case, I am satisfied that it would be better in every way for both parties to be released from their conjugal obligations. . . .[67]

In 1859, however, the Hoosier divorce laws were made more stringent; consequently, cases coming to hand after that date were rather summarily dismissed so far as the law firm was concerned. Even pressure and the bait of giant fees could not make the partners accept the case of the pretty public-school principal from Brooklyn, New York. She was a reputable person and a close friend of Cyrus B. Smith, former mayor of the city. Her attorney let it be known that she "had the money to pay a lawyer" to institute divorce proceedings against her husband, who was allegedly "a loathsome sot when in liquor."[68] Wallace and Harrison refused to handle the case on the plea that the new state legislation ruled out the possibility of suit being brought in Indianapolis.[69] Neither attorney, in view of the high grade and lucrative practice of the past three years, considered divorce cases a financial imperative any longer. It should be also observed that the firm was on the point of dissolution because Wallace had gained his political office.

For Benjamin Harrison personally—apart from his successful partnership with Wallace—the years 1855-60 were a period of

66 O. W. Lull to Wallace and Harrison, May 24, 1857, "Legal Correspondence to Wallace and Harrison, 1 box 1853–1858," Harrison MSS.
67 C. M. Olds (Columbus, Ohio) to Wallace and Harrison, "Legal Correspondence," November 26, 1858, Harrison MSS.
68 W. A. Donaldson (Brooklyn, New York) to Wallace and Harrison, "Legal Correspondence," October 28, 1861, Harrison MSS.
69 Wallace and Harrison to W. A. Donaldson, Letter Book: June 2, 1860–November, 1861, 440–41, Harrison MSS.

progress. Sworn in, early in 1855, as notary public,[70] Ben continued to nourish his ambition to be appointed Commissioner for the Court of Claims. He exploited the political influence of his father in Washington,[71] at least to the extent that the proper kind of "weighty" recommendations accompanied his application. His efforts were rewarded and he received the appointment.[72] His various duties kept him fully occupied with legal work, sometimes too much so. In his quest for financial security he frequently failed to reciprocate Carrie's tender affection, but it was not long before he reproached himself for these "wounds" of neglect.

Though he himself failed frequently to cultivate those social graces which sometimes pave the road to success, his intellectual ability and his individuality as a lawyer were never lost sight of. It was to be expected that men such as Bill Benton, Ben's lawyer friend and college acquaintance, sent an occasional note of congratulations on Harrison's expert practice in the federal courts,[73] but, when strangers wrote to the firm in the same vein, the praise was even more acceptable. The letter from Crane and Mason, Greencastle, Indiana, attorneys, reflects in some degree Ben's progress and rise to legal eminence, in the eyes of neutral observers:

We have to write to you on a confidential matter and trust in any event whether you consider us right or not you will consider this letter and the subject broached in it and our connection with the case below stated as matters of professional confidence that are only to be known to you and to us. Our client had the pleasure of hearing Mr. Harrison in the case of Tom vs. Tom at our last common pleas court and had sense enough to join in the universal opinion that that was a masterly effort, and when from reasons of our own we declined prosecuting the case below stated, wishes us to receive your aid. We

[70] See "Legal Correspondence of Wallace and Harrison," September 22, 1855, Harrison MSS.

[71] John Scott Harrison to Benjamin, July 28, 1855, Harrison MSS, Vol. 3. "I enclose a letter from Hon. G. E. Pugh in regard to your application for the appointment of Commissioner. I thought my honorable friend was going to treat my request with silent contempt. But it seemed he preferred to let the 'day of grace' go by than make a show of friendship."

[72] *Indianapolis Directory, 1857*, p. 66.

[73] W. P. Benton to Benjamin Harrison, Esq., March 26, 1859, "Legal Correspondence to Wallace and Harrison, 1 box 1858–1859," Harrison MSS.

write to know . . . if you will undertake the case with us and to inquire what fee you will charge for so doing.[74]

If any proof were needed that Harrison warmly welcomed this new surge of material prosperity, or that contentment with his lot in Indianapolis was increased a hundredfold, striking evidence is afforded by the young lawyer's steadfast refusal to accept a tempting offer to leave the city of his choice and settle in the small but thriving community at Shelbyville, Indiana. C. H. Boggess, speaking for the citizens of Shelby County, made the offer in the following terms:

We as the citizens of Shelby County want to know from you immediately whether you can locate in our town for the purpose of practicing law, and until after the election, canvass the county . . . as a central committee may direct.

Provided a sufficient number of responsible citizens of our county will give you three hundred dollars, seventy-five dollars on the first of September, seventy-five dollars on the first of December, seventy-five dollars on the first of March and seventy-five dollars on the first of June, we are willing to bind ourselves so far as to make it secure. I am fully satisfied . . . you can do well here, if you will come now. We have a paper ready now to make up the amount when we hear from you. If you can, let us know by return mail.[75]

Ben chose Indianapolis, and for the next half century, except for his senatorship and presidency, he identified himself with the "Heart of Hoosierdom." His fortunes and his fame grew with the city. The bar, however, did not remain the sole campus of his activity. In the Fitful Fifties Ben Harrison surveyed the changing political patterns of his day, witnessing the growing strength of midwest political figures and the birth of a new political party with which he would choose to cast his lot.

[74] January 27, 1860, in "Wallace and Harrison Legal Correspondence, 1860–1861," Harrison MSS. The case involved sale and collection and was accompanied by a four-page detailed explanation. See also the letter of Sample to Wallace and Harrison, May 4, 1859, "Legal Correspondence, 1858–1859," Harrison MSS, for an expression of a similar opinion: "if it be possible, let Mr. Harrison come here, say tomorrow or next day. If he is only here to advise, I can do all the work. . . ."

[75] C. H. Boggess to Benjamin Harrison, August 20, 1855, Harrison MSS, Vol. 3. Even a year and a half later the invitation was still open for Ben to remove to Shelbyville and pressure was brought to bear that he might reconsider his earlier decision. See S. Alter to Benjamin Harrison, January 20, 1857, "Legal Correspondence, 1853–1857," Harrison MSS.

CHAPTER VI

The Political Arena

BEFORE the Civil War, the two most engrossing and vital interests in Indianapolis were religion and politics. It was a day of serious thinking, and, like many another American who came up from the ranks, Benjamin Harrison was characteristically a child of his own times. It was an era when simplicity keynoted both the lives and the homes of practically all the Indianapolis citizenry. Travel was rare; even the luxury of a vacation was unknown to most people. Amusements were few, and secret societies, the Masons and Odd Fellows excepted, were unpopular and regarded with suspicion. No one could deny that religion was a main factor in life at the Hoosier capital, and everyone was willing to admit that it governed not only the moral conduct of the people, but their social relations as well. Churchgoing was proper, reputable and even fashionable, whether people were formally inducted church members or not.[1]

Amid the almost universal simplicity of sparsely furnished homes one could usually find in the parlor, or sitting room, a handsome center table. On it were a lamp and the family Bible, and this was symbolic of the role that religion played in the lives of the common people, and of the central place it was accorded in the home.[2] The fact that Indianapolis was a community of workers whose labors were hard and long[3] in no sense

[1] J. H. Holliday, *Indianapolis and the Civil War* (Indianapolis, 1911), especially Chapters 1–2, "The Settlement and Its Life," and "Religion and Politics."

[2] Logan Esarey, *A History of Indiana* (Indianapolis, 1918), II, 523: "It was a great period for searching the Bible. Every preacher and thousands of laymen studied the Book with utmost attention in order to more narrowly examine the foundations of their faith and creeds."

[3] Stores were opened by six o'clock generally, and as a rule none closed before nine in the evening. Factories and mechanics began work at seven and quit at six, with an hour's intermission at noon. Doctors, lawyers and public officials were at work early, and the banks ran from eight to four. See Holliday, *op. cit.*, pp. 531–32.

served as an excuse for putting aside daily prayer or in any way abbreviating Bible reading within the family circle. To Ben and Carrie this daily ritual was something of a twice-told tale; they knew it well from their earliest days.

Under these conditions the commandment ordering a strict observance of Sunday was obeyed with unbending rigidity.[4] On this day, set aside for holiness and awe, no work was to be done save the works of mercy and necessity. The people were not to give themselves over to their own wills, not to follow after any worldly pleasures. Rather, the entire day was to be spent in religious devotion and solemn worship, in the sanctuary or in the home. Public worship occupied the greater part of the day, as morning and evening church attendance with the usual psalm singing and sermon were focal points of activity. At home came the Bible reading, or the catechism, around the fireside, or a lesson from some religious work with solemn admonitions from parents to children.[5]

It was no great sacrifice for Ben and Carrie to contribute their share to the religious life of the community. Although they hailed from a farm, they did not find it difficult to go along with the city customs. Ben saw to it that all possible work was completed by Saturday, and the routine in the Harrison household differed only slightly from that of their neighbors:

The wood and kindling were all laid up for the Sabbath fires; the shoes were blackened and the Sabbath apparel arranged, and everything was done to make it possible to keep the Sabbath as a day of complete rest from secular toil. Sabbath cooking was reduced to a minimum. Two meals on the Sabbath day was the universal custom,

4 "The Sunday is kept at Indianapolis with Presbyterian strictness. No trains start, letters do not go, nor are they received, so that a father, mother, husband or wife, may be in extremity and have no means of communicating their farewells or last wishes, if Sunday intervenes." J. P. Dunn, *Indiana and Indianans*, I, 503. This practice was somewhat relaxed by the time of Ben and Carrie in the city.

5 These details are drawn largely from "The Diary of William Owen," in *Indiana Historical Society Publications*, IV, 493–94. Violations of Sunday observance carried severe sanctions: "the psalm singing Presbyterians believed that the church was responsible for the conduct of its members, and that church discipline was the principal means by which the members were to be kept within the straight and narrow way. . . . hour upon hour was spent in church courts. . . . offenders . . . [received] public admonition and rebuke before the whole congregation. The congregation claimed the right to know how the Session dealt with the offender who violated the laws of God and the church."

and one of these was usually cold, . . . If in the evening the children
were hungry, they could be allowed to "cut a pie" or have a cold piece
of bread and brown sugar, or more likely rye bread and sorghum
molasses.[6]

The solemnity of the services and the abstinence at table were
designed to implement and secure the church tradition which
taught that God's wrath was certain to descend upon the man or
the people who forsook or desecrated His holy day.[7]

Almost the first question asked about newcomers to Indianapolis was: "What church will they go to?" Ordinary strangers
might spend some time in deciding upon a church,[8] and one's
chief friends and associates often were determining factors in
their choice. Ben and Carrie, however, were destined to membership in one of the four Presbyterian churches, for previous to
their nuptial vows they had dedicated themselves as formal com-
municants in the faith of Calvin and of Knox. No doubt, their
almost immediate association with the First Presbyterian Church,
located on the east side of Circle Street,[9] was recommended because William Sheets, their cousin and benefactor, had been
elected an elder by the Session in 1853.

Fortunately, the church records, which describe Mr. Sheets as
"one of the best known men in Indianapolis in the religious
and also in the commercial life of the middle part of the last century,"[10] are extant also for the period of Harrison's arrival in the

6 *Ibid.,* p. 494.

7 "Riding and visiting were tabooed, even walking for the walk's sake was not regarded favorably. On Sunday the business establishments were shut, except possibly
some of the saloons that kept a back door unlocked." Holliday, *op. cit.,* p. 539.

8 *Indianapolis Directory, 1855,* lists four Presbyterian, one Associate Reform
Presbyterian churches; and seven Methodist chapels. Christians, Baptists, English
and German Lutherans had two churches, while Catholics, Episcopalians, and
Evangelicals, one each.

9 Rev. Dr. John A. McClung was pastor. The hours of Sunday worship were
10:15 A.M. and 7:15 P.M., with Sabbath school at 2:00 P.M. and prayer meeting every
Thursday evening.

10 *Indianapolis, First Presbyterian Church, Centennial Memorial, 1823–1923*
(Greenfield, Ind., 1925), p. 423. This is a record of the anniversary of the founding
of the church, "together with historical material, session records, sermons, addresses
and correspondence relating to its life and work during the century."

city in 1854. They clearly indicate that the young lawyer and his wife entered into church life early and fully. Of Carrie, the record reads:

> Mrs. Benjamin Harrison belonged to a younger group; she too was a power. Her tastes were artistic, her creations in needlework lovely and her vitality charming. She laughed readily and her gaiety and intellectual gifts made her delightful to the younger women coming into the church.[11]

Ben's contribution to his church was of a much more serious nature—quite in keeping with his character; during a membership that was to extend over almost a half-century he shouldered the burdens of an elected officer. His first church trust came in 1857, when he was made a deacon; four years later, despite his still youthful age of 28, he was elected the sixteenth elder of the Session, an office he filled until his death forty years later. The appraisal of the Session bears testimony to Ben's early zeal:

> When he came to this place in 1854 at the age of twenty-one, he lost no time in uniting with this church and taking up such work as he found to do. He became a teacher in the Sabbath School,[12] he was constant in his attendance on church services; his voice was heard in prayer meetings; he labored for and with young men, especially in the Y.M.C.A.[13] And in whatever way opened, whether public or private, he gave testimony for his faith and the lordship of his Master.[14]

While attendance at the Presbyterian church was executed with clocklike regularity, still there was another, and, in the eyes of many, a more pleasant side to ecclesiastical membership. As a central institution of the community the church successfully provided its members with a pleasing social life, and under this heading the church social stood out. Held under the auspices of the

11 *Ibid.,* p. 66.

12 "Before he went to war young Harrison was Superintendent of the Sunday School and Mrs. Harrison had charge of the infants." *Indianapolis Journal,* July 1, 1888, in B. Harrison Scrapbook No. 6, p. 6, Harrison MSS.

13 "The Young Men's Christian Association was organized on the 21st of March, 1854 . . . and successfully pressed forward in a useful work . . . a library . . . a series of lectures by distinguished persons . . . a city missionary appointed, and sabbath schools organized." *Indianapolis Directory, 1868,* p. 63 of Brown's *History of Indianapolis.*

14 *Centennial Memorial,* p. 141.

ladies' sewing society these gatherings took place sometimes at the church, but more usually in the home. At these afternoon meetings they did sew for some worthy cause or other, but as one writer, manifesting a sense of humor, said: "We had no newspaper, but we had a sewing society."[15] In the evening, when the men and young people came, a substantial supper was served. These socials afforded Carrie a wide field for church work, but Ben frequently attended them as a matter of obligation. He never excelled as a raconteur, and he was shy; nevertheless, he brought himself to unbend as the occasion required. As he continued his attendance at these bi-monthly meetings, his personality slowly unfolded and one of his Bible class boys claimed he "has seen him sit for hours with a party of men who are telling good stories and laugh heartily at every one."[16]

There was also the church festival, a function more uncommon and entirely different from the mere routine entertainments. In reality, the festival was a small-scale commercial enterprise for raising funds, at which refreshments were partly contributed and partly bought. When these entertainments were advertised as Oyster Suppers—a delicacy dear to the heart of Benjamin[17]—an admission fee was charged, and as a rare dessert ice cream was offered at "ten cents a saucer." In the off-weeks "donation parties" were popular: a group of friends would swoop down upon the home of the pastor and present gifts, and eat the supper they had brought with them. These affairs usually abounded in good fellowship, and contributed largely to the enriched social life of the community.[18]

Bread-winning and church-going were matched by the enthusiasm for politics of the mid-nineteenth-century Hoosier. Each man recognized within himself a political capacity, so great that he would willingly undertake to hold any office from postmaster to congressman. This engaging confidence was inspired perhaps by the fact that it was the individual citizen and his neighbors

15 *Ibid.*, p. 65.

16 An undated clipping from the Washington *Post* [February 28, 1889 ?], B. Harrison Scrapbook No. 9, p. 7, Harrison MSS.

17 Harrison MSS, Vols. 4–6, *passim*. See especially the letter of March 4, 1865, Benjamin to Carrie: "I soon got to be expert in opening them [oysters] and took two or three dozen with *great* relish," Vol. 6, 1110–11, Harrison MSS.

18 Holliday, *op. cit.*, p. 535.

who had organized the government on state as well as local levels. All the political and social institutions around him were his own handiwork, or at least bore the imprint of his own mind and hand. At the time of Harrison's arrival in Indianapolis, the stump speaker commanded as large an audience as the wandering preacher in the field or the newspaper paragrapher in the press.[19]

The almost universal attraction to politics among members of the legal profession was widely acknowledged. Fired with local pride and sectional prejudice, the two most common incentives for political spellbinders,[20] these men prepared early to do political battle throughout the decade prior to the actual "Disruption of American Democracy."[21] Benjamin Harrison himself, though just of voting age, was contemporary with the political strife current in Indiana. He heard the heated debates over tariff, banking, slavery and immigration. He witnessed the almost complete disintegration of the old political parties, and was about to take a part in the new alignment. He would have been blind had he not sensed that the leaders of the Democratic party were apprehensive.[22] And on the other hand one might not blame him for failing to recognize "the young Republican colt, a cross with Whig, American, anti-slavery and temperance strains," now "cavorting dangerously, responsive to neither bit nor spur."[23]

Unfettered by any blind devotion to his grandfather's and even his father's name and political beliefs, he decided to back this new "political" horse, and in 1856, after two years of watchful waiting, he threw in his lot with the insurgent Republican Party and campaigned actively for the presidential nominee, John Charles Frémont.[24] It was a step that shocked the conservatism

19 Esarey, *op. cit.*, II, 600–3.

20 Charles Zimmerman, "The Origin and Rise of the Republican Party in Indiana, 1854–1860," *Indiana Magazine of History*, 13 (1917), 407–8; Kenneth M. Stampp, *Indiana Politics during the Civil War* (Indianapolis, 1949), p. 3.

21 See Roy F. Nichols, *The Disruption of American Democracy* (New York, 1948), pp. 20–40.

22 "With good reason did Democrats fret as their supremacy waned. They saw their old time majorities of 20,000 dwindle down to a mere technicality. . . . Strong political captains, harmonious and jubilant in victory were now sniped at by discordant groups of bickering, jealous, half-hearted supporters . . . the carefully and costly built political machine was going headlong into a ditch." See Esarey, *op. cit.*, II, 654–55.

23 *Ibid.*

24 Benjamin Harrison to John Anderson, November 5, 1856, Harrison MSS, Vol. 3.

of his family so much that his brother John tauntingly remarked that "Ben was the only Republican in the family and the more shame for him."[25] In leaning toward the cause of Frémont the young lawyer parted company, politically speaking, with his own father. John Scott Harrison warned his son that "he was all too strongly tinctured with Republicanism."[26]

As Harrison settled into a self-supporting legal career, one of the great crises of American history was approaching. The slavery question was setting the country ablaze. Where might an earnest, religiously inclined young man, the son of a Whig Congressman and the grandson of a Whig president, be expected to take his stand? Though most political observers in Indiana would have said that he must go with the Republicans as did most of the Whigs,[27] Ben's own father disassociated himself with the Republican party at an early date and joined the ranks of the American Party.[28] The story behind this political break between father and son is worth relating, and though their personal relations were sometimes severely strained, they were never broken.

When Benjamin arrived in Indianapolis, John Scott Harrison was just completing his first term as a Representative in Congress from the second Ohio district.[29] During his early months of struggle with the law, Ben was also undergoing a political apprenticeship, his father serving as the master-politician. In all probability, John Scott meant this as an academic study through which his son might keep himself well informed on national affairs. The fifty-five-year-old Whig certainly never intended that his prolific

[25] [Jennie Harrison Morris ?] to Benjamin Harrison, July 23, 1860, Harrison MSS, Vol. 4: "Dear Ben: I was really provoked at John Harrison this morning. Somehow the conversation turned to politics and to your different views to that of your family. John said that 'Ben was the only Republican in the family and the more shame for him.' . . ." Letter unsigned, but in the handwriting of Ben's sister, Mrs. Jennie Harrison Morris. It was written from Indianapolis.

[26] John Scott Harrison to Benjamin, March 29, 1857, Harrison MSS, Vol. 3.

[27] Stampp, op. cit., p. 22.

[28] Eugene H. Roseboom, The Civil War Era, 1850–1873, p. 320; see also George H. Porter, Ohio Politics during the Civil War (New York, 1911). For the actual founding of the party see Walter R. Sharp, "Henry S. Lane and the Foundation of the Republican Party in Indiana," Mississippi Valley Historical Review, 7 (1920–21), 93–112.

[29] Weekly Inter-Ocean, October 22, 1889, a clipping in B. Harrison Scrapbook Vol. 9 (part 2), Harrison MSS. J. S. Harrison was a candidate for Congress in the second Ohio district for two successive terms and was elected in 1852 and 1854.

correspondence should serve as a course in practical politics for young Ben. For his son he envisaged a future above politics—which he candidly characterized as a "drug, which should never be found in a gentleman's library or parlor . . . and fit only to scent the beer house."[30] Even after the Wallace and Harrison law partnership was formed, John Scott laid a strict injunction upon Ben to stick to his law practice and to avoid politics, for "none but knaves should ever enter the political arena."[31]

Moreover, he instructed his son that the public as well as the private lives of politicians were "surrounded by temptations, . . . [and] many inducements to stray from the proper path."[32] Despite these admonitions to avoid the perils and pitfalls of political life that John Scott so freely gave to his son, he himself performed faithful service in Congress. During one of the most critical periods in history he could boast: "I have not been absent from my seat for a single day for nearly five months and . . . I have never paired off with anyone . . . except for a few hours to join a continual session of thirty six hours in order to take some repose and some refreshment."[33] This meant, of course, that during his formative days Ben had a political pipe line direct from Washington. The messages which came from his father served in no small way to color his own political thinking. From the parent who warned him to stay out of politics came the first seeds of "new republicanism."

The political party to which Ben pledged his earliest allegiance was a fusion party brought into existence by the strong and heterogeneous local reactions to the Kansas-Nebraska Bill.[34] The germs of this new political alignment were spread broadcast during May and June, 1854. The distressing reports penned by Congressman Harrison in Washington to lawyer Harrison in Indianapolis on the momentous question of slavery extension

30 John Scott Harrison to John Cleves Short, February 2, 1854, Short Family Papers, Box 55.

31 John Scott Harrison to Benjamin, December 28, 1855, Harrison MSS, Vol. 3.

32 John Scott Harrison to an unnamed correspondent, July 14, 1854, 1 box of John Scott Harrison Papers in Harrison MSS. The congressman claimed he put all his faith and trust in the "night and morning prayers of a pious mother."

33 John Scott Harrison to Benjamin, May 19, 1854, Harrison MSS, Vol. 3.

34 Andrew W. Crandall, *The Early History of the Republican Party, 1854–1856* (Boston, 1930), p. 20.

were infectious with "republicanism," though the author himself would not join the embryonic party.[35]

The high drama of the Nebraska Bill as it made its way through Congress was not lost on John Scott Harrison; neither was it lost on Ben. He knew well the story of how Stephen A. Douglas introduced the Kansas-Nebraska Bill in the Senate in January, 1854, and he followed closely the struggle in the Senate. From the other side of Capitol Hill, John Scott Harrison wrote:

> The great question now before Congress and the country, as you are apprised, is the Nebraska Bill of Mr. Douglas. It proposes *virtually* to repeal the Missouri Compromise, which forbids slavery beyond the line 36 degrees 30 minutes. . . . I would be the last man in the world to interfere with any of the constitutional rights of the slave holding states. But when they ask me to aid in breaking down a *solemn compact* made when Missouri was admitted to The Union *with slavery,* they ask more than I am willing to do. The truth is, there was no necessity of forming the territory at this time, . . . and still less, to introduce the slavery clause into the bill. A bill passed [by] the House last session, sought to leave the slavery question out of the matter, but was not acted upon by the Senate and therefore failed to become a law. Mr. Douglas, and his slavery clause, is bait for southern waters, when he comes to fish for the presidency.[36]

On May 8th, the battle over the Nebraska Bill began in the House. From that day until the 22nd, the floor of the House was in a blaze of excitement as the majority leaders tried to force a vote. Everybody then knew that the Douglas forces could carry it; what is more, everybody knew that speech-making availed nothing. The minority, however, contested every inch of ground.[37] John Scott Harrison, who admitted that he never had "the gift of gab," now proudly counted himself in that die-hard group.[38] He was quick to share with Ben the intimate details of the struggle. Nor did he hedge in his sharp denunciation of the "deformed and loathsome Nebraska Bill,"[39] whose passage would not only ring down the curtain on the Whig

35 Roseboom, *op. cit.,* p. 320; Allan Nevins, *The Ordeal of the Union* (New York, 1947), II, 414–16.

36 John Scott Harrison to John Cleves Short, February 2, 1854, Short Family Papers, Box 55.

37 Nevins, *op. cit.,* II, 154–55.

38 J. S. Harrison to Benjamin, September 30, 1854, Harrison MSS, Vol. 3.

39 J. S. Harrison to Benjamin, May 19, 1854, Harrison MSS, Vol. 3.

Party in Ohio and Indiana, but would also crystallize the nation's parties into new forms. This, in the words of the angered Douglas, meant "civil war, servile war, and disunion."[40]

John Scott Harrison told Ben that the regular debates on the bill would close shortly; the fight on the amendments, however, would then begin, and

This may last for several days ... but as the Pacific Railroad bill is set for Wednesday by a special order and as it will take a two-thirds vote to set it aside, I apprehend on Tuesday night the House will feel best about the small hours.[41]

Notwithstanding his bitter animosity to the "iniquitous" Nebraska Bill, John Scott Harrison refused to do violence to his Presbyterian conscience by resorting, he added, to any "revolutionary mode of defeating it." The conservative old Whig confided to Ben that he had been approached by the Bill's desperate enemies who

... suggested that if the Bill cannot be defeated in any other way ... that some of its opponents will leave the House and thus prevent a *quorum.* I have been asked how I felt in regard to this step. I have answered that I was opposed to the passage of the Bill but would not feel justified in resorting to any such revolutionary mode of defeating it. I have spoken against it ... I shall vote against it in any and all shapes, but further than this I couldn't go. If the majority pass this bill ... upon them must rest the responsibility.[42]

The fires of personal animosity burned fiercely on the floor of the House. Sufficient heat being generated, the forging of new parties was made easy. At home at Indianapolis, young Ben was not missing a trick, though his political insight came by proxy through his father. On an eventful day in May the bitterly partisan Alexander H. Stephens of Georgia arose to speak. The shrill-voiced remarks of this parliamentary manager of the Nebraska Bill[43] precipitated John Scott Harrison and the minority group

40 Nevins, *op. cit.,* II, 316–18.

41 J. S. Harrison to Benjamin, May 19, 1854, Harrison MSS, Vol. 3.

42 *Ibid.*

43 Nevins, *op. cit.,* II, 155. The author paints a vivid picture of Stephens whose gaunt body, small, sickly-looking frame, beardless, wrinkled parchment skin, and shrill voice gave him a certain physical resemblance to John Randolph of Roanoke.

into a fit of almost uncontrollable rage. Tempers flared on both
sides. Immediately, a detailed account of the outbreak was on its
way to Indianapolis:

You will have seen by the papers how near we have come to having
a personal collision in the House. Mr. Campbell[44] was endeavoring
to reply to something that was said by Mr. Stephens of Georgia charging opponents of the bill with being factious, when he was loudly
called to order and not suffered to proceed. He persisted in denouncing the act as arbitrary . . . when a Mr. Edmunson of Virginia reached
over at him calling him very hard names and drew his fist as if to
strike him. . . . Campbell maintained his ground with great firmness
. . . members rushed to the scene of action from all quarters of the
House. I found myself rushing to Campbell's aid over the tops of the
desks. My friend Governor Aiken of South Carolina . . . who sits next
to me . . . seized Edmunson and held him. . . .[45]

The vigorous action of the Speaker saved the day. He ordered
the Sergeant-at-arms to use the mace of the House, had the irate
Virginian arrested, cut off debate, declared the sitting adjourned,
and thus prevented a general and perhaps bloody fight.[46] With
this last attempt at filibustering by Campbell, the opposition
had worn itself out. On May 22nd the Nebraska Bill became
law. Not only had the Missouri Compromise been repealed, but
also the ambiguous popular sovereignty principle was substituted. Two important results flowed from this legislation. Parts
of the Northwest were legally open to Negro slavery and a strong
sectional foundation was given to the embryonic Republican
Party.[47] The die was cast for April, 1861.

The years 1854–1856 were critical not only in national politics,
but also in the career of John Scott Harrison and his son. In the
cooling-off period immediately after the heated struggles over
the Nebraska legislation, they gave serious thought to the manifold political problems confronting the country. Up to this time
they had both shared an understandable admiration for the Whig

44 Lewis D. Campbell of Ohio headed a bitter filibustering group.

45 John Scott Harrison to Benjamin, May 19, 1854, Harrison MSS, Vol. 3.

46 Nevins, op. cit., II, 156 ff. John Scott Harrison mentioned these details at
great length in his letter of May 19th.

47 Reinhard H. Luthin, The First Lincoln Campaign (Cambridge, Mass., 1944),
p. 37.

Party of William Henry Harrison,[48] but now, with the collapse of Whiggery, they felt compelled to draw up separate political creeds.[49]

After his strenuous opposition to the Nebraska Bill, John Scott found his political reputation spread far beyond the confines of his congressional district in Cincinnati, and even beyond Ohio's borders. It was no secret that the name of Harrison was still open sesame for political advancement. To many it was still the sign and emblem of effective political revolution. Even in the Hoosier capital in 1854 several old-line Whigs, stimulated by resurrected memories of the Log Cabin and Hard Cider campaign in 1840, started to boom John Scott Harrison for the presidency in the 1856 election. These old-timers had a peculiar faith in the power of a name—so much so that in October, 1854, they created a special committee to invite the son of Old Tippecanoe to come to Indianapolis and make arrangements to lead their forces in the next presidential election. Ben got the whole story from his father in a letter that was intended to spike these booming presidential guns:

> I received two or three days ago the letter of invitation to Indianapolis and have made up my mind not to attend. I received a letter . . . saying . . . it was the intention of my friends to nominate me there and then for the presidency, or at least make arrangements for a subsequent meeting for that purpose. These intimations would keep me away if nothing else. If any such foolish movement is made I do not want to be made *particeps criminis,* as you lawyers say . . . [they have] calculated too largely on the potency of a *name.*[50]

While his father was scoffing at the idea of leading a resurgent political group in 1856, young Ben endeavored to carry out that early paternal advice which bade him hold himself aloof from all political entanglements. Besides, his efforts to build up a substantial legal practice allowed him no other course of action. Even after his successful partnership with Will Wallace in 1855, the young lawyer's chief interest was to provide a decent living for Carrie and Russell. As long as he could write: "Business engagements have crowded me pretty close,"[51] there seemed little danger

48 *House Document No. 154,* p. 125.
49 Crandall, *op. cit.,* pp. 21–22, 269–71.
50 John Scott Harrison to Benjamin, October 29, 1854, Harrison MSS, Vol. 3.
51 Benjamin Harrison to J. A. Anderson, Nov. 5, 1856, Harrison MSS, Vol. 3.

that he would jump on some political bandwagon. Actually, Ben had learned his lesson of "political non-intervention" so well that he felt bound to admonish his father against making any political mistake in Ohio by accepting a third-party candidacy for governor.[52]

This voluntary segregation from politics, however, was short-lived. A growing intimacy with Will Wallace, whom Ben described as a "devoted politician and something of a *rover* by nature,"[53] persuaded him to help Wallace and the new party in the canvass. Although their partnership agreement left Ben "with the entire responsibility and labor of the office . . . and the courts,"[54] he volunteered to help Wallace stump Marion county in his campaign for the county clerkship.

This was Harrison's first bow in the direction of the Republican Party.[55] Shortly thereafter, he made his first stump speech at a meeting at Acton, Indiana, where he stood on a railroad track and addressed all of 15 or 20 people.[56] Because of the strong Southern element in Indiana's population[57] Ben's remarks on the slavery issue were conservative, with more emphasis on the evils of sectionalism than those of slavery. Evidently, he executed his task successfully, since this maiden effort earned him the invitation to campaign in Shelby County which C. H. Boggess tendered.

Ben seemed to enjoy this first incursion into Hoosier politics. His clear presentation and easy manner of speaking made him wholly acceptable to small-town audiences. The deeper he delved into the issues, the more he felt the need of thinking things out for himself. Step by step he weighed the pros and cons of the slavery issue, that "alarm in the night," now alerting the country to a possibly unprecedented conflagration. Like his father, he

52 John Scott Harrison to Benjamin, August 2, 1855, Harrison MSS, Vol. 3. His father replied: "You need not fear of my making a mismove in regard to the candidacy for Governor of Ohio. I have never for one moment entertained the least idea of running."

53 Benjamin Harrison to J. A. Anderson, Nov. 5, 1856, Harrison MSS, Vol. 3.

54 *Ibid.*

55 In Indiana, the Republican Party did not officially adopt that name until the presidential campaign of 1856 was well under way. The fusion ticket of 1854 and 1855, however, represented the mainstream of Republican thought. See Zimmerman, *art. cit.*

56 *House Document No. 154*, p. 127.

57 Stampp, *op. cit.*, p. 22. See also George W. Julian, *Political Recollections, 1840–1872* (Chicago, 1884), pp. 136–37.

was opposed to the extension of slavery, and up to the time of his political debut, they both took the conservative position that the institution of slavery was entitled to such protection as the Constitution and laws of the country offered it.[58] On this latter point, however, Ben began to waver.

By June, 1856, he had shifted his political views on the slavery question sufficiently to give full approbation to the anti-slavery gospel enshrined in the national Republican platform drawn up at Philadelphia.[59]

The way was clear for an open break, politically speaking, between father and son. John Scott Harrison had lined up in Congress with the American Party to fight to the bitter end the successful election of Nathaniel P. Banks of Massachusetts, a recently baptized Republican, as Speaker of the House.[60] He felt so strongly on this issue that he wrote to his brother-in-law the following indictment of the "ultra" North:

> The bane of the present congress is the fanaticism of fifteen or more preachers of the gospel who have soiled their robes by entering the arena of politics and who seem to believe that the furtherance of Christ's kingdom upon the earth can only be advanced by an indiscriminate warfare upon the slave-holder. These men all vote for Banks ... and reject with haughty pride all mention of a compromise in a moderate Anti-Nebraska man. *"Banks* or *nothing"* is their war cry. We resist them. These false prophets carry with them all the ultramen of the North and unfortunately for the country they have a plurality in the house.[61]

This furious anti-abolitionist blast was only intensified a month later by the premeditated neglect with which Speaker Banks treated Congressman Harrison. The latter wrote to Ben: "I am not on an important committee ... Banks gave me a low seat on account of my opposition to him."[62]

During the summer of 1856 the political gap between the two men widened perceptibly. It was a period of increasing sectional fanaticism and party sensitivity. The controversy which followed

58 *House Document No. 154,* p. 127.

59 Crandall, *op. cit.,* pp. 179–85; 195–98; Stampp, *op. cit.,* p. 23.

60 Nevins, *op. cit.,* II, 415.

61 John Scott Harrison to John Cleves Short, January 21, 1856, Short Family Papers, Box 55.

62 John Scott Harrison to Benjamin, February 25, 1856, Harrison MSS, Vol. 3.

Preston Brooks' caning of Senator Sumner served only to fire tempers to white heat.[63] Scott Harrison, about to retire from the House, wrote with a great sadness: "We have fallen upon evil times . . . I regard the course of the Republicans in the House as extraordinary and almost revolutionary."[64]

As the various factions prepared for the presidential battle of 1856, John Scott Harrison drew consolation in the early May reverses that the Republicans suffered in Indiana. He chided Ben on his political waywardness: "I see by the papers that your Republican ticket was badly beaten. If you want to be successful, you must run up the *true blue* American flag."[65] John Scott himself did precisely this very thing. He not only declared openly for the election of Millard Fillmore on the American ticket, but also co-operated actively in piling up proofs of Frémont's Catholicism—a line of attack most effective in defeating the Republican candidate.[66] He campaigned in Ohio and Kentucky for the "cause of conservatism throughout the country."[67]

This active course on his father's part somewhat embarrassed Ben. People began to believe that he was tempted to toss over his newly adopted Republican principles and switch back to the position adopted by the Fillmore supporters, yet they reckoned without consulting the twenty-three-year-old Republican. Anderson, who had been privy to the rumor that his old college chum had now turned his political coat, wrote from New Albany:

Of course politics is the engrossing topic of your town and I very much fear that you individually have gone astray from the principles which I endeavored to instill in your youthful mind and will throw away your vote upon Millard Fillmore at the approaching election as your father has announced him as his preference.[68]

[63] Nevins, *op. cit.*, II, 443. For Harrison's attitude on the unfortunate affair, see Charles Anderson to Hon. John Scott Harrison, M.C., August 3, 1856, in John Scott Harrison Papers, 1 box, Harrison MSS.

[64] John Scott Harrison to John Cleves Short, August 24, 1856, Short Family Papers, Box 55.

[65] John Scott Harrison to Benjamin, May 9, 1856, Harrison MSS, Vol. 3.

[66] Vespasian Ellis (editor of the *American Auburn*) to John Scott Harrison, September 3, 1856, in John Scott Harrison Papers, 1 box, Harrison MSS. See also Nevins, *op. cit.*, II, 507–8.

[67] Committee of the American Party to John Scott Harrison, October 15, 1856 (Lexington, Ky.), in John Scott Harrison Box, Harrison MSS.

[68] J. A. Anderson to Benjamin Harrison, October 2, 1856, Harrison MSS, Vol. 3.

To a man who had dedicated himself to the new Republican Party and had addressed the people of Indianapolis more than once in support of Frémont's nomination and candidacy, this letter from Anderson called for a sharp reply. On election eve Ben penned a short, decisive note to Anderson that left no doubt for which candidate the future president would cast his first vote in the morning:

> ... You do me great injustice in your allusion to my supposed politics. I am *Frémont* all over and all the time ... have made a good many speeches for him in this and adjoining counties, and am now waiting (rather despondingly) for news of his election.[69]

Harrison's election-day forebodings for Frémont were fully realized. After the ballots in the presidential contest were counted, Democrat Buchanan enjoyed a popular plurality over the Western Pathfinder that ranged close to half a million votes,[70] though his margin of victory in the Hoosier state was only 20,000.[71] The balance of power was held most decisively by the Fillmore supporters.[72] In the family battle of politics, the first round went overwhelmingly to John Scott Harrison. Despite this Republican defeat on three fronts—city,[73] state and country, Ben's confidence was not seriously diminished nor was his political allegiance the least bit shaken.

The Republican leaders determined to fight on stubbornly, and even after the November disaster the halls of Congress resounded with protests on the treatment of Kansas. Eastern seaboard Republicans were already talking about Frémont's "victorious defeat."[74] In Indianapolis, the first ray of sunshine broke through on November 22nd and shattered thoroughly the passing gloom of two weeks before. At a special election held to fill

---

69 Benjamin Harrison to J. A. Anderson, November 5, 1856, Harrison MSS, Vol. 3.

70 Buchanan: 1,838,169; Frémont: 1,341,264; Fillmore: 874,534. The figures from the *World Almanac and Encyclopedia, 1894* (New York, 1894), p. 117.

71 W. D. Foulke, *Life of Oliver P. Morton* (Indianapolis, 1899), I, 58.

72 Nevins, *op. cit.*, II, 511, for the national scene. In Indiana the Fillmorites held the political balance of power; see Stampp, *op. cit.*, p. 24.

73 The city election in Indianapolis took place on May 6, 1856. 2,776 votes were cast and the Democrats elected the whole ticket, with 10 out of the 14 councilmen. W. R. Holloway, *Indianapolis* (Indianapolis, 1870), pp. 106–7.

74 Nevins, *op. cit.*, II, 514.

vacancies in the office of Mayor and City Clerk, more than 3,000 crowded to the polls. For the first time in several years the Democrats found themselves defeated, and the Republicans indulged in wild demonstrations of delight.[75]

On January 7, 1857, when Oliver Perry Morton, recently defeated Republican gubernatorial nominee, began to address a meeting of Republicans in the capital, he realized that he was facing an enthusiastic and rejuvenated group. He coined for them a new battle cry and pledged a vigorous political leadership. Taking his keynote from the bloody fields of Kansas, Indiana's next governor thundered: "Our creed is plain. We do not assail slavery where it exists entrenched behind legal enactments, but wherever it sallies forth, we are pledged to meet it as an enemy of mankind."[76]

The political atmosphere in Indianapolis was charged with expectant Republicanism, and the party willingly accepted Morton's leadership. Under these circumstances it was not hard for Ben to realize the full import of the ominous news that his father continued to send from Washington. The retiring American Congressman wrote:

. . . the Republicans of the House seem never to tire shrieking for Kansas. . . . The theme is so delightful to their ears that they have forgotten the election is over. . . . The shrieks can no longer make votes for John C. Frémont. Why will they not let the country rest?[77]

Ben's reply to his father's political query has not been preserved, but it is evident that inactivity was no part of his plans. With a law practice growing more steady and lucrative, he felt safe in making for himself an important decision. Shortly after the incorporation of the new city charter was accepted by the Councilmen,[78] Harrison let it be known that he accepted the call of the Republican Party to stand for the office of City Attorney at the coming May elections. This unmistakably public profession of faith in the principles of the Republican Party came

[75] *Indianapolis Directory, 1868*, pp. 70–71.

[76] Foulke, *op. cit.*, I, 59.

[77] John Scott Harrison to Benjamin, December 2, 1856, Harrison MSS, Vol. 3.

[78] The general charter law, adopted in 1853, was amended by the Legislature in 1857, and accepted by the City Council on March 16, 1857. See Holloway, *op. cit.*, p. 108.

as a distinct shock to John Scott Harrison, whose reaction was one of bitter protest. He actually refused to come to Indianapolis and stay with Ben.

Without paternal encouragement, and despite family coolness, Ben entered into the political fray with warm enthusiasm. Both parties were putting forth all their strength in order to gain control of the newly organized city government, with the result that the canvass was animated and bitter. Colorful demonstrations by day were surpassed in brilliance only by the great torchlight processions at night. Fireworks and balloon ascensions were common to both parties, but the Republicans stole a march on the Democrats in their theatrical demonstrations of slavery as a moral, social and economic evil.[79]

Though feeling ran high during the campaign, the election held on May 5th came off without incident. Harrison was victorious[80] in a contest that saw a new high of 3,300 votes cast. Each party elected a portion of its ticket, so that neither could claim a clean-cut triumph, a fact which rendered Ben's personal victory more satisfying. Almost immediately he entered upon the duties of his new office, duties not unfamiliar from his occasional role as assistant prosecuting attorney in Marion County.

Political ambition accounts in large part for Ben's acceptance in 1857 of an election as City Attorney of Indianapolis, a position paying only $400 a year. By doing so he cut himself off for a full year from practice and took a place that most men well launched in the legal profession, with a growing clientele, would have eyed disdainfully. As a state Senator or as Congressman he would have held a position of dignity, but the City Attorney was usually a political hack. It was his familiarity with the work that made him willing to consider such an office. He did not plead financial necessity as the compelling motive. Actually, his principal reason for seeking the berth seems precisely that which, a year later, would force him to choose between a candidacy for the legislature and the secretaryship of the State Republican Central Committee. There is no question that at this period of his life he aspired

79 Zimmerman, op. cit., pp. 360–61, 366.
80 Official notification came from the City Clerk's Office on May 7, 1857. The document read: "It has been certified by the Board of Inspectors, that Benjamin Harrison has been elected City Attorney in the city of Indianapolis for the term of one year, at an election held in said city on the fifth day of May." Harrison MSS, Vol. 3.

to political prominence—an ambition not confined to his own heart—for his father finally reversed himself and wrote: "I look forward to a period in the future when you may occupy a high position among the political men of Indiana."[81]

While he was settling down to his new office routine, Ben determined to redress the grievances felt by his family at what they regarded as political conduct unbecoming a Harrison. This was a likely time for a reconciliation, if possible, or, at least, an understanding about divergent political views. John Scott Harrison's departure from Congress in March, 1857, left the door open for a family reunion, and happily Ben took the first step. He realized that his father, now crowding sixty, was in for a lonesome time, once he returned to The Point. Carter, John and Anna were away at school, while Irwin impatiently awaited his father's return to accept an army commission procured by the retiring Congressman from President Pierce.[82] Only Sallie and Jennie, both eligible for marriage, were still at home to care for a father, whose four years in Washington had aged him considerably.

Ben's peace offering was tendered in the shape of a more faithful correspondence with his father, whose personal affection had never waned. John Scott's inevitable loneliness was forestalled by the frequency of Ben's weekend visits[83] as well as by the attentions Carrie showered on her father-in-law whenever he made the trip to Indianapolis. These mutual visits did a great deal to build up the warmth and devotion that had been somewhat strained by politics. Political questions would still crop up for discussion, but principles were now debated in a quiet, detached and dispassionate manner. Neither would change his political views, but a closer understanding was manifested by both father and son.

As a matter of fact, Ben's devotion to the Republican cause in-

81 John Scott Harrison to Benjamin, January 29, 1858, Harrison MSS, Vol. 3.
82 Irwin Harrison to Benjamin, February 21, 1857, Harrison MSS, Vol. 3: "I received a letter from Pa the other day telling me he had seen the President . . . he told him my commission . . . had been fixed . . . I hope in the cavalry." Three weeks later, John Scott wrote Ben that President Pierce had authorized a Captain's commission for Irwin at a salary between $1,200 and $1,500 a year. John Scott Harrison to Benjamin, March 14, 1857, Harrison MSS, Vol. 3.
83 This was particularly true after June, 1857, when Carrie's absence in the East left Ben free to travel. Harrison MSS, Vol. 3. John Scott could also visit his married daughter, Betty Eaton, at nearby Long View.

creased to such a degree that an attempt at proselytism within the family circle was not considered out of place—not with his father, but with elder brother, Irwin. The latter's commission had carried him to the Kansas Territory, and by lengthy correspondence Ben believed he had converted his brother and made him ready for the Republican Party. Just before Christmas, however, a letter from Irwin scathingly indicted Republicanism in action and bitingly denied even a passing flirtation with that political doctrine:

... I write you this evening to correct your very wrong impression of my turning *Republican*. I don't know but I should feel insulted—that I *an American, a Know-Nothing,* should so far forget the principles of our party, as to affiliate for a moment with a set of men so *corrupt* as the Republicans. Six months residence in Kansas has done anything but impress me with the honesty or purity of the said party. I am sorry that *you* could not have the opportunity that I have had, of having your *eyes opened,* for I am sure your political posts would have beaten time to the *True Goose now and forever.* As for Governor Walker I look upon him as one of the most corrupt, intriguing little rascals I ever had the misfortune to know. Should he appear as a candidate for the Presidency in 1860, as I think he will, I will resign, and stump the country against him, exposing his corruption while Governor of Kansas. But enough of politics....[84]

New Year's Day, 1858, fell on a Friday. Ben took a quick glimpse backwards and a long look to the future. His carelessly kept diary reveals one resolution: "January 1, 1858—Stopped use of tobacco in every form ... Wallace, Haughey, Browning and myself."[85] Three days later, in usual Sabbath form, Carrie and Ben attended services in the First Presbyterian Church. According to the second of four entries in the diary, the Rev. Mr. Cunningham delivered a sermon entitled: "The Fashion of This World Passeth Away."[86] For the young man wrestling with the serious problems of his own future, the homily afforded adequate food for reflection.

Young Harrison was truly in a reflective mood. His one-year

[84] Irwin Harrison to Benjamin, December 13, 1857, Harrison MSS, Vol. 3.
[85] The diary of Benjamin Harrison, 1858, Harrison MSS. For a man so detailed in other pursuits, one is amazed to find only four entries in this diary: January 1, 3; February 8, and April 3.
[86] Diary, January 3, 1858, Harrison MSS.

term as City Attorney was more than three-quarters completed, and he appeared uninterested in standing for re-election. Perhaps Ben was out for bigger game now that the Republican sway in city politics was complete and growing increasingly stronger.[87] Additional money and prestige can be two of nature's most compelling arguments—the kind that rarely slip from the periphery of consciousness—especially when a young man possessing a revered name has a political future that promises high. In view of the Harrison background, it is not surprising to learn that in the spring of 1858 the leaders of the new party were considering the advantages and merits of Benjamin Harrison's candidacy for the State Legislature. With Ben this was no light matter. He pondered it well. Was it a step in the right direction? Would he be charged with mere political opportunism? If he should choose to run and were successful, would his new duties preclude adequate attention to his law practice?

These and kindred problems Ben mulled over for the better part of three weeks. Finally, he decided to present the question to his father. At least he could give counsel born of both interest and experience. His letter elicited an almost immediate reply:

I received your letter of the 25th yesterday. In regard to your becoming a candidate for the legislature, I hardly know what to advise you. If you were obliged to leave home to attend to the legislature in case of your election, I would think it a bad policy. But as you would be at home, at least among your *Business,* if not attending to it, I do not believe that it would seriously affect your practice—except so far as it might create an impression abroad that *you had turned politician* and would probably neglect business entrusted to your care. I certainly would not consent to run unless I thought the prospect of being elected was pretty good.

I do not believe that there is anything in the future of the Republican Party that would justify a man in making very great sacrifices to sustain its falling fortunes.

If the "Little Giant" does not make some unforeseen blunders—he has completely *spiked* the guns of the Republicans and taken from them their only effective battle cry. If the Kansas and Nebraska imbroglio is to be kept up—which God in His mercy avert—Mr. Douglas must lead the present Republican sentiment—and consequently the party—and all that portion having democratic antecedents (and their name is legion) will *gladly* receive Mr. Douglas as their leader. A few

---

[87] In the May 1858 election in Indianapolis the Republicans elected an entire ticket and a majority of the Councilmen. *Indianapolis Directory,* pp. 74–75.

of your old Whigs may kick at this—but it will do no good—the majority of your leaders are renegade democrats and they will ship you all in....

Some of the leading Republican newspapers have pretty strongly hinted at a willingness to take Mr. Douglas for their candidate in 1860. ... You have noticed that the Commercial—that sore through which the Republican party of the country ejected their venom and filth—has already pretty clearly indicated its willingness to fight with the Douglas banner.

I look forward to a period in the future when you may occupy a high position among the political men of Indiana. But a false step now might spoil all. If I were in your place, I would content myself with a general endorsement of the doctrines of the Republican Party. And would not be *too ardent* in my support of all these (so called *Republican principles*) or you may find some of them are fallacious and will not stand the test of true patriotism . . . and therefore you will not long be popular with the American people. . . .[88]

Days of speculation followed. Ben's indecision and hesitancy caused wonderment throughout the circles of his friends, and finally all talk of his candidacy for the State Legislature ceased. A few more intimate friends knew the story from the inside. The young City Attorney was offered the important political post of Secretary to the State Republican Central Committee. When he heeded this call of his party by a ready acceptance of the position, more than one of his contemporaries regarded this move with suspicion and regret. Was this not accepting another "political hack"? Ben thought otherwise; history, it seems, would be willing to confirm his good judgment. When one considers his mature years as public servant and a leader of Indiana Republicanism, this early decision to become Secretary of the State Central Committee seems prudent. First of all, it was a guarantee for state-wide introduction and familiarity with the leading figures in the new party. Secondly, in the effective execution of his office he would have no choice but to learn—from the bottom up—the essential details of organizational procedure. The collection of campaign funds, and their expenditure in an age of increasingly costly canvasses would also be an experience of no little value.

At the Bates House, Indianapolis, on July 10, 1858, an important meeting of the State Republican Central Committee was

[88] John Scott Harrison to Benjamin, January 29, 1858, Harrison MSS, Vol. 3.

convened.[89] In an effort to build up and put into smooth working order an efficient state machine the Committee passed several resolutions. One was an assessment of $25.00 on each thousand Republican votes in every county, taking as a basis the vote cast for Oliver Perry Morton, the gubernatorial candidate in 1856. As a start in his office, Harrison found himself responsible for the collection and distribution of these funds.[90] Two other resolutions passed at that meeting, however, were more significant, both to the party in general and to Benjamin in particular:

> Resolved: that this committee deem it of vital importance to the success of the Republican Party in Indiana in the coming contest that there should be a thorough organization of the party throughout the state, extending into the counties, townships and road or school districts: and that the Republican committees for the several counties be requested to have complete lists of all the voters in their counties made, designating them as *Republican, American, Buchanan, Douglas,* and *doubtful;* that they be requested to send copies of such list to the secretary of this committee at as early a day as possible, or at least the aggregate of each class of voters.
>
> Resolved: that the members of this committee be requested to write the chairman at least once a month giving him information of the prospects of the political conditions of their localities: and that the members also be recommended to keep up correspondence with each other during the canvass.[91]

These instructions, of course, put Ben in contact with political chieftains ranging from Congressmen to County Chairmen. He usually closed his letters by saying: "I am directed by the Committee to call your attention particularly to the resolution in reference to the raising the necessary funds and to request your *prompt* and *energetic* action in this matter."[92]

The opportunities for political advancement and political *savoir faire* that the faithful exercise of this office could bring

[89] Benjamin Harrison to the Hon. D. D. Pratt, July 27, 1858, Harrison MSS, Vol. 3.

[90] This power was in virtue of a resolution offered by Mr. Brown, of Randolph: "Resolved: that the Secretary of this committee be constituted its treasurer and that the funds contemplated . . . be placed in his hands as much as practicable and be held subject to the order of the chairman." See Benjamin Harrison to Hon. Will Cumback, July 27, 1858, Harrison MSS, Vol. 3.

[91] *Ibid.*

[92] Several such letters were sent out under date of July 27, 1858. See Benjamin Harrison to Hon. D. D. Pratt, to Hon. Will Cumback, etc., Harrison MSS, Vol. 3.

were not neglected by the twenty-five-year-old secretary. Moreover, so strong was the imprint of this experience that almost twenty-five years later, while serving in the United States Senate, he remembered the importance of this early political post. To his Indiana political confidant, Louis T. Michener, he expressed the hope that "our folks will make an effort to get some good secretary on our State Committee and keep the rooms open and the work going on."[93]

Despite the prominence of political affairs during 1858 and 1859, these were by no means the all-absorbing interest. The neighbors of Ben and Carrie may have expressed wonderment at the arrival of an old crib crated and shipped from The Point. Was it for three-and-a-half-year old Russell, who now objected to being called "baby"?[94] Members of the family were charmingly delicate in their inquiries. From Kansas, brother Irwin wrote: "If modesty would not prevent, I should like to inquire after another nephew or niece that I have dreamed of as being at your house. I should like to know *his* or *her* name ... if a boy, and you give it my name, I will make my will in his favor, *provided* that I never marry."[95]

Irwin's letter arrived two weeks late. On Saturday, April 3, 1858, Ben wrote in his diary for the fourth and last time that year: "Our Little Girl Born About Noon ... after Carrie had gone through severe labor for about twelve hours ... doctor had to use forceps...."[96] Thus it was with the arrival of Mary—forever to be called Mamey—that Russell was superseded as the baby of the family. The newcomer, according to sister Jennie, was "a perfect little beauty ... prettier than Russell." Poor Carrie came

93 Benjamin Harrison to Louis T. Michener, December 8, 1882, Harrison MSS, Vol. 12, No. 2574 (a Tibbott transcript). This letter was written in Washington and directed to Michener in Shelbyville, Indiana.

94 John Scott wrote: "Your grandma who thinks of everything and everybody, insists that I shall send the old crib to Lawrenceburg tomorrow to be put enroute for Indianapolis. It is so richetty [*sic*] ... I am afraid it won't stand the journey." J. S. Harrison to Benjamin, February 8, 1858, Harrison MSS, Vol. 3. Ben heeded his father's warning on the dilapidated condition of the crib. See "1858 Personal Bills, Checks, Notes, etc.," Harrison MSS. Under date of June 5, 1858, "paid $2.50 (bill of March 17th) to Tilford Furniture Co. for one crib mattress and repairing crib."

95 Written from Camp Bateman, Kansas Territory, to Benjamin, April 17, 1858, Harrison MSS, Vol. 3. About to marry, Irwin confessed: "I suppose you think his chances are poor, yes, very poor, to make anything with the above proviso."

96 Diary, April 3, 1858, Harrison MSS.

in for little or no credit for this bundle of natural pulchritude,
for Jennie added: "I think she must be pretty ... sure enough ...
I suppose like her father ... of course."[97]

If we can believe the Indianapolis City historian, "the year
1859 was another year of unbroken progress, but of meager interest. All that can be told of it can be condensed into a dozen
words. Buildings going up, the city spreading in every direction,
business increasing."[98] The same short formula may be properly
applied to Benjamin Harrison. His law practice was blossoming;
his commission as Notary Public was renewed for four years,
signed by Governor Asbel P. Willard;[99] above all, the horizon of
his political future was promisingly bright.

[97] Jennie Harrison to Benjamin, June 22, 1858, Harrison MSS, Vol. 3.
[98] Holloway, *op. cit.*, p. 110.
[99] August 5, 1858, Harrison MSS, Vol. 3. The commission has been preserved.

CHAPTER VII

The Critical Years, 1860 and 1861

THE YEAR before young Harrison came to Indiana, *Uncle Tom's Cabin* was playing nightly to a full house in the state capital.[1] Thousands in the city were reading the book. People remembered Edward May saying that "the negro was either a man or brute."[2] South of the Ohio, during those days, he was a chattel, a part of the stock, like a horse. North of the Ohio he was not a social or political entity, but he was a human being. Then came *Uncle Tom's Cabin* to impress upon its readers that the Negro was a man of feeling, who could suffer as deeply as other men. Few believed that the novel recorded events that ordinarily happened to slaves, but everybody knew that it described things that might happen to any slave, and which had occasionally happened to some of them. The book was widely read in Indiana, not only for its story, but also because the Beechers were prominent in the state and because the composite character of Uncle Tom was believed to have been drawn, in part at least, from an old Indianapolis Negro, formerly a slave, who was known as "Uncle Tom" and whose humble home was always called "Uncle Tom's Cabin."[3]

Soon, Helper's *Impending Crisis* was widely circulated and avidly read. Harrison himself had a hand in arranging a lecture program in 1856 that cheered Charles Sumner's presentation of an abolitionist creed. On the same lecture platform one

1 Ignatius Brown, *History of Indianapolis from 1818 to the Present*, in *Indianapolis Directory, 1868*, pp. 66–67.

2 Jacob Piatt Dunn, *Indiana and Indianans*, I, 504 ff.

3 Dunn, upon whom I have drawn heavily for these facts, goes on to say (pp. 504–6) that Uncle Tom "was very religious, was a favorite of Henry Ward Beecher, and his family coincided with that in the book. It was said that Mrs. Stowe visited his home, while at her brother's in Indianapolis."

year later, Horace Greeley, editor of the New York *Tribune*, the most widely circulated Republican journal, was afforded an equally warm welcome by the city.[4] For a brief span the citizens supported a new Republican newspaper, the Indianapolis *Daily Citizen*.

Events such as these served to divide the community in which Harrison lived into sharply opposed political camps. Men of the Republican, Democratic and American parties engaged in contests marked by intense partisan feeling and much bitterness. Men of one stripe would believe anything of their opponents. The Democrats opposed prohibition; therefore, their adversaries denounced them as a party of whisky-drinkers. As the slavery question became prominent in Indianapolis,[5] the Democrats denounced the opposition as "nigger lovers" and "Black Republicans,"[6] and tempers flared. Devotion to party became almost a religion; party discipline, an eleventh commandment. Little wonder that men's eyes were frequently blinded to the truth.[7] As Secretary to the Republican State Central Committee, Harrison became experienced in political methodology and began to regard party declarations as almost infallible.

As the dawn of 1860 broke, political fires burned brightly. A wild conflagration was certainly possible, and perhaps only the November presidential election would indicate whether a conflict was "repressible" or "irrepressible."[8] Nothing daunted, by the middle of January, Harrison had reached his decision to stand for nomination on the Republican ticket for the office of Supreme Court Reporter of Indiana.[9] His aim was high. The

[4] Brown, *op. cit.*, pp. 71–73. These lectures were under the auspices of the Young Men's Christian Association in whose activities Benjamin Harrison played a prominent part.

[5] *The American Eagle* (Paoli, Indiana), February 2, 1859; March 15, 1860.

[6] *Old Line Guard* (Indianapolis, Indiana), January 7–November 3, 1860, *passim*.

[7] J. H. Holliday, *Indianapolis and the Civil War*, pp. 542–43.

[8] For the most up-to-date and usable bibliography and treatment of this subject see Howard K. Beale's chapter, "What Historians Have Said About The Causes of the Civil War," in Bulletin 54, *Theory and Practice in Historical Study: A Report of the Committee on Historiography* (New York, 1946), pp. 53–102.

[9] The first Reporter of the Supreme Court of note was A. G. Porter, later Governor of the state. Under the old Constitution the cases had been reported by Judge Blackford, who used to hang the proofs in the Law Library so that attorneys might point out any errors. Porter's brilliance resulted in recommendation by the Supreme Court Judges and to election by a large majority in 1854. He and Harrison were always friendly and in 1888, Ben appointed him Minister to Italy. See Dunn, *op. cit.*, II, 716–18.

CHATTANOOGA VALLEY FROM LOOKOUT MOUNTAIN

Harrison wrote of the "carnival of death" behind this leafy curtain.

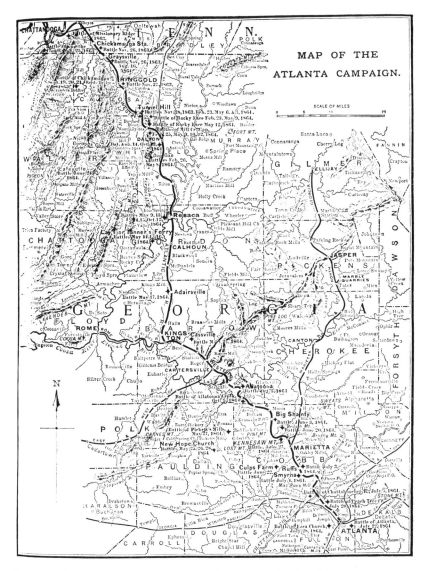

From *The Mountain Campaigns in Georgia; or, War Scenes on the W. and A.*
Published by the Western and Atlantic R.R. Company

MAP OF THE ATLANTA CAMPAIGN

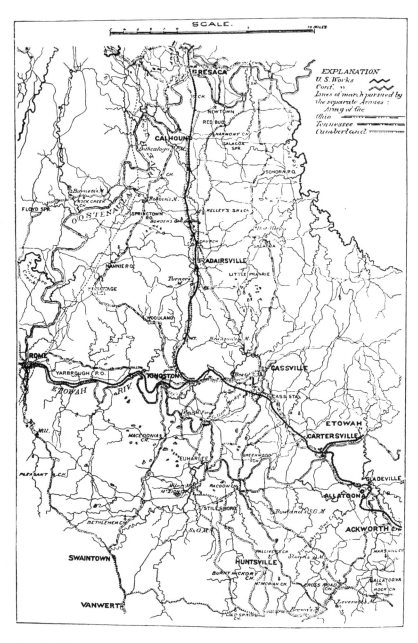

Reproduced from the *Memoirs of General William T. Sherman*
(New York, D. Appleton and Company) by permission of author and publishers.

MAP OF THE TERRITORY SOUTH OF RESACA, GEORGIA

post was not only a dignified one, but most lucrative. Immediately, he found himself confronted with a hard fight from two quarters. He faced formidable opposition in his own party; and he also realized that, even if he should be successful on the convention floor, he was in for a "dog-fight" type of campaign against the Democratic nominee, Michael C. Kerr. The latter also was destined for Washington, a man whose talents and popularity would win for him the Speakership of the House of Representatives.[10]

Indianapolis played host to both state conventions in 1860. Early in January the Democrats assembled and fired the first shot in what proved to be one of the most decisive political campaigns in history.[11] Viewed from Washington, the Indiana stakes were high. The state was a "political prize, ranking third in northwestern states in convention and electoral votes."[12] Democrats and Republicans alike considered the Hoosier vote indispensable to national success, and state party leaders determined to carve out strong tickets from the best possible political timber. The contest promised to be "unprecedented in interest and bitterness,"[13] and the political strategists believed that "victories in pivotal Pennsylvania and indispensable Indiana in October . . . all but marked the inevitability of Lincoln's victory."[14]

On January 11th the Douglas Democrats seized control of the state convention. With the zeal of insurgents they repudiated the Buchanan administration by nominating Thomas A. Hendricks for Governor. Politically, it was an excellent choice. This forty-year-old Hoosier lawyer was a most "available" candidate and had already attained a high degree of personal popularity.[15]

10 *Ibid.*, pp. 562–66. Kerr died in office. See *Biographical Directory of the American Congress, 1774–1949* (Washington, D. C., 1950), p. 1407 for details on Michael Crawford Kerr.

11 Reinhard H. Luthin, *The First Lincoln Campaign*, p. 226: "The campaign of 1860, besides being one of the most momentous in American History, was one of the most remarkable insofar as the winning candidate, Abraham Lincoln, did not represent a majority of the voters."

12 *Ibid.*, p. 4.

13 Brown, *op. cit.*, pp. 78–80.

14 Luthin, *op. cit.*, p. 226.

15 See John W. Holcombe and Hubert M. Skinner, *Life and Public Services of Thomas A. Hendricks* (Indianapolis, 1886), pp. 202–4. Hendricks had just resigned his post as Commissioner of the General Land Office. His removal from the field of active politics, while serving in this latter office, had made him the man upon whom

The remainder of the Democratic slate was filled with popular and capable men. The two candidates in whom Harrison manifested a personal interest were David Turpie, nominee for Lieutenant-Governor,[16] and Michael C. Kerr, the party's selection for the office of Reporter of the Supreme Court. The ensuing campaign was calculated to be, as Turpie himself called it, a battle of political giants.[17]

This challenge to forge an equally strong ticket was accepted by the Republicans on Washington's Birthday. Their convention nominated Henry S. Lane, "the steadfast disciple of Henry Clay,"[18] for Governor. The latter's vigorous activity in founding Hoosier Republicanism, his proficiency as a stump speaker, and his overwhelming popularity with the rank and file insured strong leadership.[19] The second place on the ticket was filled by Oliver P. Morton, whose leadership had already been demonstrated in his vigorous campaign for Governor in 1856. It was no political secret that the two top candidates on both tickets were aiming at higher political berths.[20]

Though the head of the ticket was nominated "without too much show of a struggle,"[21] the nomination for Reporter of the Supreme Court was a real battle that was carried to the floor of the convention. Finally, the contest was narrowed down to three aspirants: Mark L. De Motte, an ex-congressman from Indiana's 10th district; John F. Miller of St. Joe county, afterwards United States Senator from California; and Benjamin Harrison of Marion County. According to De Motte, the fight was "vigorously waged,"[22] but Harrison, by a rousing speech to the convention,

---

a divided party could most easily unite. Kenneth M. Stampp, *Indiana Politics during the Civil War*, pp. 17–19.

[16] An Indianapolis lawyer who was to succeed Harrison in the U. S. Senate in 1887.

[17] According to Dunn, *op. cit.*, p. 562, citing Turpie's own book, *Sketches of My Own Times* (Indianapolis, 1903).

[18] Stampp, *op. cit.*, p. 27.

[19] Walter R. Sharp, "Henry S. Lane and the Foundation of the Republican Party in Indiana," *Mississippi Valley Historical Review*, 7 (1920–21), 93–112.

[20] "If the Republicans carried the state, Mr. Lane was to be elected to the Senate, Mr. Morton succeeding to the governorship; if our party (quoting Turpie) prevailed, similar changes were to be the result. The result in October carried out in part this arrangement . . . the future in some degree carried it still further . . . all four . . . became senators." Dunn, *op. cit.*, I, 563.

[21] Fort Wayne *Sentinel*, February 25, 1860.

[22] An undated newspaper clipping in Benjamin Harrison Scrapbook No. 52, p. 91, Harrison MSS.

won the nomination. It was the young lawyer's first major political move within the party, and in later years he remembered it and talked about it frequently.[23]

John Scott Harrison wrote to his son that he was "gratified at your success in the convention . . . [I] hope that your election may be as triumphant as your nomination was flattering."[24] But the politically battle-wise father rebuked Ben for voicing "some very complimentary things of Mr. C. Clay of Kentucky." He feared that his son was damaging his political chances before he even went before the Indiana electorate.

In John Scott's eyes, as well as in the opinion of many Kentucky and Indiana citizens, Cassius Marcellus Clay was nothing less than a political apostate. Hailing from Kentucky, traditionally a citadel of Whiggery, and claiming direct descent from Henry Clay, America's renowned Compromiser, middle-aged "Cash" Clay shocked every conservative Kentuckian, when he bent every effort to organize the Republican party in the blue grass country and campaigned vigorously for the election of Frémont. He had charged to him innumerable anti-slavery speeches and was considered by conservatives to be as dangerous as Charles Sumner of Massachusetts. Clay was thinking along the same lines as Benjamin Harrison, though the Kentuckian was prudent enough to moderate his anti-slavery views while he engineered his own boom for the Republican Presidential nomination.[25]

Before the Republicans in Indiana adjourned their Indianapolis convention, they gave evidence in their platform that John Scott Harrison was entirely correct in issuing his paternal admonition: "You may rely upon it that the people of Indiana are not prepared to adopt . . . the very ultra . . . anti-slavery sentiments of Mr. 'Cash' (as he calls himself)."[26] This was no understatement. The platform retreated noticeably from the advanced position on slavery extension reached at Philadelphia four

23 De Motte recalled: "We all met in Washington. I was a member of the House of Representatives; General Harrison was a Senator from this state, and John F. Miller was Senator from California. One evening we met and whiled away the hours until almost midnight recalling the events of the contest." Benjamin Harrison Scrapbook No. 52, p. 91, Harrison MSS.

24 J. S. Harrison to Benjamin, February 24, 1860, Harrison MSS, Vol. 4.

25 Luthin, *op. cit.*, pp. 114–16.

26 J. S. Harrison to Benjamin, February 24, 1860, Harrison MSS, Vol. 4.

years earlier.[27] Without doubt, the "irrepressibles" in the party were bitterly disappointed, while the "accommodators" were well pleased with their handiwork, particularly since the Indianapolis platform was far from reaffirming the power and duty of Congress to exclude slavery from all the territories. Actually, the platform merely denounced the doctrine that the Constitution by itself carried slavery into the territories and vaguely promised to oppose slavery extension by all constitutional means.[28] So innocuous a statement of policy displeased Ben Harrison, for it did not resolve the issue of slavery extension; it only deferred it.

Benjamin had a mind of his own; what is more important, he was willing to express it. Even though he had been chided by his father for entertaining and echoing radical sentiments, the young politician must be credited for paying close attention to John Scott's further remark: "I like to see a candidate honest and outspoken."[29] In favoring the candidacy of Cassius Clay, the ardent young Republican felt that he was backing the man who would do most to check the spread of slavery. As his own campaign notes[30] demonstrate, he was certain that he was holding the same ground as Henry Clay and Daniel Webster. With telling effect he cited Henry Clay's early speeches, usually ending with the Kentuckian's famous remark made during the Compromise debates of 1850, when in his intense anxiety for peace he went as far as his conscience would permit in concession to slavery. Clay had declared again and again that he would never vote to extend it over territory then free:

As long as God allows the vital current to flow through my veins, I will never, never, by word or thought, by mind or will, aid in admitting to one rood of Free Territory the Everlasting Curse of Human Bondage.[31]

27 Stampp, *op. cit.*, p. 29.

28 "The rest of the platform aroused no opposition. It demanded the immediate admission of Kansas as a free state, a homestead law, and the construction of a transcontinental railroad. It also proclaimed Republican devotion to the Union." *Ibid.*

29 J. S. Harrison to Benjamin, February 24, 1860, Harrison MSS, Vol. 4.

30 "1860 Campaign Notes," a small notebook, six inches by three-and-a-half inches, which Ben used in the 1860 campaign. Harrison MSS.

31 *Ibid.*, p. 5.

Ben, it seems, was pretty much alone in these thoughts. Not only his father,[32] but also a majority of the Indiana delegates to the Republican National Convention,[33] favored the nomination of the conservative Mr. Bates for president. This momentous event, however, was still almost three months removed. In the meantime it was imperative that the Republican nominee for Supreme Court Reporter stump the state, meet the people, and address their political assemblies.

Traditionally, Hoosier politicians were and are an energetic breed; hence, it caused no wonderment that the nominees for state office did not wait for the national convention of 1860 to define party policy before launching their own campaigns. Perhaps few foresaw the magnitude of the impending crisis; somehow, even a smaller number possessed a clear concept of the underlying issues at stake. Even so, there was not the slightest semblance of apathy among the electorate.[34]

On March 10, Lane and Morton opened the Republican canvass at Terre Haute. The role of party keynoter fell to Oliver Perry Morton.[35] The opening shot was directed right at the heart of slavery. Here, Morton proved himself a notable exception to the rule that most of the speakers on both sides tended to ignore the real issues. Political wisdom dictated that the Republicans adopt Morton's speech as their campaign textbook. Lane, conservative by nature, was allowed to fill a position in which he could adapt his remarks to fit popular sentiment in different parts of the state.[36]

The remainder of the state ticket was not idle. Harrison made his first speech in the campaign at the thriving town of Lebanon, seat of Boone County, about twenty-five miles due north of Indianapolis. This youngest of the Republican candidates was only

---

[32] J. S. Harrison to Benjamin, February 24, 1860, Harrison MSS, Vol. 4.

[33] Howard K. Beale (ed.), *The Diary of Edward Bates 1859–1866* (Washington, D. C., 1933), p. 102.

[34] See Stampp, *op. cit.*, pp. 31–48.

[35] Indianapolis *Daily Journal*, March 13, 16, 1860; also W. D. Foulke, *O. P. Morton*, I, 67–72. For a briefer treatment, see Charles M. Walker, *Sketch of the Life, Character, and Public Service of Oliver P. Morton* (Indianapolis, 1878), pp. 31–35.

[36] James A. Woodburn, "Henry Smith Lane," *Indiana Magazine of History*, 27 (1931), 283–84. It was possible for Lane's position on slavery to shift remarkably.

twenty-seven, exceedingly boyish in appearance, short of stature and slim of figure. He did not begin to take on flesh till several years afterward.[37]

A large crowd, collected in a grove, was awaiting the appearance of Caleb Blood Smith,[38] the day's principal speaker. An accomplished orator and a one-time enthusiastic Whig of the old school, Smith was one of the mighty in the Republican Party. He was chairman of the Indiana delegation to the National Republican Convention and also filled the post of delegate-at-large. From his vivid memory he could have spun for young Harrison, or for anyone who would lend him an ear, many a colorful yarn about the enthusiastic log-cabin campaign and presidential victory of William Henry Harrison in 1840.[39] He cherished a hope that the victory fires of twenty years ago might be rekindled this year. Caleb Smith was never a profound thinker, but as a storyteller he had few equals. He was gifted with an eloquence that charmed his hearers and could always arouse his audience to a high pitch of enthusiasm.[40]

This Lebanon husting was opened by Mr. Smith, and, according to all reports,[41] he made one of his better speeches. The people alternately laughed and shouted as he poked fun at the candidates on the Democratic ticket and blistered them with his sarcasm. Nevertheless, with a wisdom characteristic of seasoned campaigners, he said little on the pertinent election issues. He had little to say about the Dred Scott decision, little about Kansas, but a good deal about the split in the Democratic Party. To the burning question of slavery there was scarcely a reference.

When Smith had accepted the thunderous applause and had bowed out, the crowd began to wander away from the speaker's

[37] This description was the eye-witness account of William Henry Smith, then connected with the *Atlas,* an Indianapolis afternoon paper published by John D. Defrees, later a warm devotee of Lincoln and a close friend of Harrison. W. H. Smith, "Personal Recollections," a newspaper clipping in Harrison Scrapbook, Vol. 52, p. 102, Harrison MSS.

[38] Louis J. Bailey, "Caleb Blood Smith," *Indiana Magazine of History,* 29 (1933), 213–39.

[39] John B. Martin, *Indiana: An Interpretation* (New York, 1947), p. 46.

[40] Harrison Scrapbook, Vol. 52, p. 102, Harrison MSS.

[41] Smith's account in the Indianapolis *Daily Atlas.* He had heard Caleb Smith many times. He also knew Harrison personally, but he had never heard him speak in public previous to this meeting.

stand. Although Benjamin Harrison was to be the second speaker, political anonymity cloaked him. Probably not more than fifty persons in the audience had ever heard of him. The chairman of the meeting undertook to introduce him and, had he continued a minute or two longer, the scheduled speaker would have found no one in front of him, so rapidly were the people departing. The embarrassing situation, however, was short-lived. The *Atlas* reporter gives the happy sequel in these words:

Mr. Harrison had the same sharp, rasping voice that became famous in after years, and with almost his first utterance he caused the crowd to pause. Some stopped a moment to look at the boyish figure as he stood on the stand, with his fingers in his trouser pockets.

Another sentence shot out, reaching to the very verge of the crowd and more of them paused to listen. They began to get back toward the stand, drop into their seats, or lean against some of the trees. Those who had got some distance away looked back and saw the deserted seats being filled up, and they, too, came back.[42]

Within ten minutes, stump-speaker Harrison had the crowd "straining to hear the terse and rugged sentences as they fell from his lips."[43] There was no attempt at star-spangled oratory, no flights of eloquence, no amusing anecdotes. Ben got down to facts immediately, warning his audience of the dangers that menaced the country. He had courage, if not wisdom, with him, for he went so far as to prophesy concerning "the insidious inroads of the slavery power . . . unless the people arose in their might and put an end to them."[44] The remainder of the speech was a clear and logical presentation of the issues, as the young candidate understood them. Harrison discussed the slavery issue in such a way that the people of Lebanon could not mistake his mind on the subject. They understood that with him the whole question revolved around the one central idea that the extension of the slave territory must stop; that to yield to the demands of the Southern leaders could end only in making all the country slave territory. First and last he stood with Abraham Lincoln in the railsplitter's

[42] W. H. Smith, "Personal Recollections," Benjamin Harrison Scrapbook, Vol. 52, p. 102, Harrison MSS.
[43] *Ibid.*
[44] *Ibid.*

declaration that a house divided against itself could not stand, and that the country must become wholly free or wholly slave.[45]

Harrison's open espousal of Republicanism—a force looming ever larger on the horizon—gave him the advantage of having the offensive in the campaign. Certainly, during the first two months of the Indiana canvass, his Democratic opponents were clearly on the defensive. Strangely enough, the historic Democracy which had the "one best hope of saving the Union was threatened with hopeless discord."[46]

Indiana Democracy, however, was not long content to leave the initiative with the Republicans.[47] By April, Hendricks, David Turpie and other party leaders inaugurated a more active program of stump-speaking.[48] Soon, practically all of the opposing candidates paired off to begin a series of joint debates. Leading the parade were the gubernatorial candidates, Lane and Hendricks, who attracted by far the larger crowds throughout the state. Frequently, the character of their respective political harangues was determined more by the geography of the state than by their own personal convictions. In the north the Republican leaders found that abolitionism was a strong and popular speaking point; in the communities of southern Indiana, however, their battle cry rang out as a plea for non-interference with slavery in the states, and for its non-extension into the territories. With so shifting and illogical a platform, Harrison could not agree. His sense of logic protested and he soon made up his own permanent set of campaign notes. It was June before he could put them to effective use, following a post-convention lull in the state campaign.

In mid-May of 1860, Chicago's wigwam welcomed the national Republican forces. Harrison was not a delegate, though a great flurry of excitement and interest swept through the family cir-

[45] This had been Lincoln's warning at the Republican state convention at Springfield, Illinois, June 16, 1858. See A. J. Beveridge, *Abraham Lincoln* (Boston and New York, 1928), II, 577.

[46] James G. Randall, *The Civil War and Reconstruction* (Boston, 1937), p. 174: "no other party (than the Democratic) had both the likelihood of success if united, and the ability to hold the country together if successful."

[47] Stampp, *op. cit.*, p. 33.

[48] Indianapolis *Daily State Sentinel*, April 30, 1860.

cle because Ben's married sister, Sallie, misread the newspapers and believed that he was going to Chicago in that capacity.[49] W. R. Harrison, of Indianapolis, not Benjamin, was the delegate chosen.[50]

Harrison scrutinized the columns of the Indianapolis *Daily Journal* for an account of the part played by the Indiana leaders assembled in the two-story wooden wigwam.[51] Inasmuch as his stump partner, Caleb B. Smith, was chairman of the Hoosier delegation, as well as one of the delegates-at-large, Harrison probably knew beforehand the plan of the Indianans. His own earlier preference for Cassius Clay faded rapidly as the choice of Hoosier Republicanism narrowed down to Bates of Missouri or Lincoln of Illinois. The final decision rested primarily with Smith,[52] a politician who was willing to be convinced one way or the other. Seemingly attracted and won over by the offer of a cabinet position, Smith threw his influence behind Lincoln, and at the Indiana caucus on May 15 he successfully stifled the pro-Bates element. Four days later, on the third ballot, Lincoln was nominated. Indiana voted solidly for her former illustrious resident.

Despite his callow political youth, no one realized more clearly than Benjamin Harrison that the party of his choice was becoming a formidable organization partly by virtue of the Democratic family troubles.[53] Both before and after Lincoln's nomination in Chicago, the bitter controversy between President Buchanan and Senator Douglas of Illinois—a feud of long standing[54]—was chiefly responsible for the hopeless split within Democracy. Ben and his

49 Sallie (Harrison) Devin to Benjamin, April 20, 1860, Harrison MSS, Vol. 4: "I see by the papers you have been appointed a delegate at the Chicago convention . . . What time shall I meet you there?"

50 Cincinnati *Enquirer*, February 24, 1860.

51 For a detailed description of the work of the Indiana delegation at Chicago, see Charles Roll, "Indiana's Part in the Nomination of Abraham Lincoln for President in 1860," *Indiana Magazine of History*, 25 (1929), 1–13.

52 Luthin, *op. cit.*, pp. 140–42; see also his "Indiana and Lincoln's Rise to the Presidency," *Indiana Magazine of History*, 38 (1942), 385–405.

53 George Fort Milton, *The Eve of Conflict* (Boston, 1934), pp. 370–480. This section recounts the dismal story of the Democratic party in its death throes.

54 See Philip G. Auchampaugh, "The Buchanan-Douglas Feud," *Journal of the Illinois State Historical Society*, 25 (1932), 5–48; Louis M. Sears, *John Slidell* (Durham, N. C., 1925), and the same author's "Slidell and Buchanan," *American Historical Review*, 27 (July, 1922), 712–24.

Republican fellows did not conceal their joy on April 30, when the cotton-state delegates stalked out of the Democratic national convention at Charleston, South Carolina. The inevitable break had occurred. Contrasted with Republican solidarity at Chicago, this bewildering disruption of the Charleston conclave was viewed by Democrats with serious regret. There was no mistaking this omen. The death knell of the Democratic Party was slowly tolling.

Down the road of disunity went the Democrats. At Baltimore in June the northern Democracy named Stephen A. Douglas for President. The Charleston "bolters" subsequently convened in Baltimore and Richmond before they could emerge with a national ticket composed of Kentucky's John Breckinridge and Oregon's Joseph Lane.[55] During the interval between the conventions at Charleston and Baltimore, as we have seen, the Republicans had gleefully nominated Lincoln and Hamlin.

As if this devasting split between the North and the South did not augur sufficient ill for Democracy, a new party, bearing the name National Constitutional Union, entered the arena of national politics. Composed of former American or Know-Nothing Party members, this party met in convention at Baltimore and put forward as candidates two conservatives: Senator John Bell of Tennessee for President and Edward Everett of Massachusetts for Vice-President.[56] Early in May, Horace Greeley tagged this Bell-Everett combine as "The Old Gentlemen's Party."[57]

Harrison's father gave his active support to the Constitutional Unionists, for he had found it impossible to cast his lot with either the Republicans or the Democrats.[58] Ben learned of his

[55] John C. Breckinridge, of Kentucky, was Vice-President under Buchanan (1857–1861) and a leader of the Southern Democrats. Joseph Lane was United States Senator from Oregon. See Emerson D. Fite, *The Presidential Campaign of 1860* (New York, 1911); and Randall, *op. cit.*, pp. 176–81.

[56] The vice-presidential nominee, Edward Everett, was a good front man. Having served as Secretary of State, Minister to Great Britain, and President of Harvard, he was sufficiently well known and did not resort to crusading. "Like Bell, he adopted a colorless and negative attitude . . . to avoid offending the South." Randall, *op. cit.*, pp. 104, 181.

[57] New York *Daily Tribune*, May 11, 1860.

[58] Actually, John Scott Harrison did not trifle with offers from the Ohio Democrats; in 1861 he refused to accept their nomination for the office of Lieutenant Governor. Scrapbook No. 52, pp. 83–86, Harrison MSS. That he was a Bell-Everett supporter is clear from his letters to Ben, June through October, 1860, Harrison MSS, Vol. 4.

father's new political allegiance quite early in the campaign, but this paternal devotion to the cause of the Constitutional Unionists in no wise served to soften the son's stump assaults on John Bell. Under the caption, "Ben Harrison vs. John Bell," the Paoli *American Eagle* wrote:

> The grandson of General Harrison, candidate for Reporter of the Supreme Court of Indiana, said in his speech in the Court House at Rockport on last Tuesday that inquiry has been made into John Bell's record, and it was ascertained to be similar to that of Breckinridge and Lane. "Freemen of Spencer County" (said the speaker) "will you vote for Bell and Everett? Better for you to place your heel, and grind them into the dust."[59]

No man is a prophet in his own country, and when Benjamin's tour of political duty brought him to Lawrenceburg, Indiana, for a speech, one so well versed in Scripture as he was ought to have given some heed to that pregnant Biblical admonition. Yet in this territory so familiar to him from his boyhood days, Harrison's Republican zeal outran his political prudence and his usually reliable sense of history. Zeal without knowledge has been called the sister of folly, and once Ben had read the stinging rebuke penned him by his own father after the Lawrenceburg address, he knew he had classed himself among the foolish.

Fortunately, in one sense at least, John Scott Harrison was "too sick to be out of the house" on that June afternoon on which his son sharply assailed the "slave oligarchy and the slave aristocracy" of the South. Even so, when the Cincinnati *Gazette* printed an extended report of Harrison's Lawrenceburg speech, this gentleman of the old school was so deeply incensed that he severely lectured his son on the necessity of observing the canons of veracity in public addresses. More especially did he berate Ben's "use of terms of reproach and scorn towards Southern gentlemen." To Scott Harrison, whose four years in Washington gave him many a friend from the South, these charges by an inexperienced, overzealous stump speaker, even if he was his flesh and blood, were sheer calumny. The young man was perhaps shocked into sober reality by his father's chiding question: "How can I trust men whom I know have been *educated* to hate any man

[59] *American Eagle*, October 4, 1860.

South of the Mason and Dixon line? As much as I hate Democracy I do believe there is more safety in that than in Republicanism as at present defined."[60]

John Scott Harrison did not content himself with a flat contradiction of Ben's attack on the Southern gentry as "all wrong . . . because it is not true." He ventured to teach his son an important lesson. "You will allow me to correct you . . . I have resided in Washington and you have not . . . and I assure [you] . . . there is not in this land a more religious, moral, upright people than those of Washington City." If this bit of reproof did not entirely deflate the young Republican warrior, whose emotions had evidently dulled his historical acumen at Lawrenceburg, Ben was thoroughly humbled by his father's timely reference to the revered memory of William Henry Harrison. It hurt Ben deeply, as he read:

Your speech going out as it does in the *Gazette* will reach the eye of many a friend of your Grandfather who will regret to see such sentiments emanating from a grandson. . . . They will regard him a little on the agrarian order. I am confident that a man loses by such sentiments. He may collect a few of the uneducated and prejudiced crowd . . . but he will soon lose with intelligent men.

I had hoped that you would never find it necessary to talk about "slave oligarchy or slave aristocracy." . . . Let me advise you not to use these terms . . . leave them to Chase and Giddings *et id omne genus.*[61]

This was a bitter potion for Ben to swallow, but he downed it manfully. He learned his lesson well. Blackguardism had no place in his oratorical attempts during the remainder of the campaign. Within a month, David Swing, the man who had wrested first academic honors from Ben at Miami in 1852, wrote him a letter of congratulation. Paradoxically, Swing, now a member of

[60] John Scott Harrison to Benjamin, June 12, 1860, Harrison MSS, Vol. 4.

[61] *Ibid.* Of all John Scott's letters to Ben of a political and personal nature, this is one of the longest and most important. This was no mere political squabble. At the outset, John Scott admitted: "I do not of course concur in all that you said on that occasion [at Lawrenceburg], and do not propose to contest with you the leading principles of the policy you advocate." His main purpose was to teach his son a lesson in character formation. Once he had thoroughly reproved him for his ill-starred section on the South and her people, he concluded his letter by saying: "The main body of your speech was good and the sentiments were such as would need little objection from any of your opposition. . . ."

the cloth, wrote from Oxford, Ohio, to compliment his former college fellow "on the high character of your political addresses." One paragraph of this letter reveals Harrison's progress:

I am glad to read many notices of the high character of your political addresses. While we were together in college my only doubts about your future were based upon your apparent want of health of body. You will not consider it flattery, if I say to you that you always had the *mens sana*. But your almost rugged appearance of the present makes me feel that there is nothing in the way of your great success in life.[62]

Perhaps even more pleasing to Ben than Swing's meed of praise was a friendly letter from his father, the first since the latter's scolding after the intemperate speech at Lawrenceburg. John Scott designed to pay high tribute to his son's intellectual honesty:

While I would have been glad on your account, as well as my own, that you could have felt it your duty to pursue a more conservative political course, I shall not doubt that in adopting a more ultra one, you are governed by the honest convictions of your judgment.[63]

May, June, and July had been highlighted by an almost endless series of national conventions. The political excitement and interest of these gatherings had somewhat detracted from the luster of the keen struggle within the states themselves. In August, however, as the Indiana campaign entered its final phase, the canvass rivaled the heat in intensity. Stump-speaking under a broiling sun was no pleasure; only the close proximity of the state elections scheduled for October 9 gave the inspiration and strength necessary for final perseverance. During these twilight days of the political battle, Harrison did most of his campaigning

[62] David Swing to Benjamin Harrison, July 10, 1860, Harrison MSS, Vol. 4. Swing concluded by saying: "My sympathies are all with you not only from our oneness in the *Church* and *State* but from the fact that we were classmates in other days . . . give my kindest regards to Carrie . . ."

[63] John Scott Harrison to Benjamin, July 23, 1860, Harrison MSS, Vol. 4. The long delay in writing was caused by John Scott's many political engagements. He claimed he felt neither irritation nor unkindness toward Ben, though he did promise: "I will not hereafter interfere with your political course."

in what is known as the "pocket district" of Indiana.[64] Quite coincidentally, it was during this part of the state canvass that some of the more interesting episodes of Ben's early career occurred.

On one occasion, Harrison was billed to speak in the town of Rockport, located at the very southern tip of Indiana. As in most of his other campaign trips, horse-and-buggy transportation was secured, but the novelty of driving over the country in a wagon had long since left Ben.[65] Actually, he was a tired, travel-worn and campaign-weary gentleman when he arrived in town to address an audience that was none too friendly. This latent hostility was nothing personal; rather, it was an attitude along the Kentucky border that was reserved for Black Republicans. On his way to Rockport, Harrison took out his diminutive book of political notes and began to prepare his speech. He planned to make his whole speech an answer, point by point, to some recent statements made by Hendricks, the Democratic candidate for Governor.

This particular political assembly was well attended, and this political novice was careful to make an exceptionally benevolent introduction. He built up Hendricks with a view to knocking him down by quoting from the latter's own statements in the press. When it came time to read the clippings, Harrison pulled out his little note book. He was momentarily startled. Feverishly he searched its pages, but in vain; the one he wanted could not be found. Only his quick wit saved him from serious embarrassment. "Gentlemen," he said finally, "I carefully pasted that extract from Mr. Hendricks' speech in my note book, and I am sure I used good mucilage, but it has disappeared. It simply goes to show that not a thing Thomas A. Hendricks says will stick."[66] This unexpected bit of merriment drew loud cheers and applause from the crowd. Indifferent, hostile glances melted into warm smiles of approval.

The real highlight of the campaign, as far as Benjamin Harri-

[64] Lew Wallace, *Life of Gen. Ben Harrison*, pp. 81–83. Ben's careful preparation of his speeches during this stretch drive brought their own reward. They were well received. The "pocket district" is the extreme southwestern sector of Indiana, centering about Evansville.

[65] Indianapolis *News*, March 14, 1901.

[66] An undated newspaper clipping in the Harrison Scrapbook, Vol. 52, p. 92, Harrison MSS.

son was concerned, came upon him most unexpectedly. In late August he arrived at the town of Rockville in Parke County, where he was scheduled to make an appearance at the courthouse. He was much alarmed when he discovered that Thomas Hendricks had a meeting for the same hour at the same place. The people were clamoring for a joint debate. Harrison hesitated a moment, while he sized up the situation. Mr. Hendricks was a formidable platform opponent, the leader of the Democratic Party in the state, a speaker and debater whose reputation was national. When pressed to debate with this man, Ben made a very apt reply: "This is, of course, a very unfair proposal. Mr. Hendricks is at the head of the Democratic ticket, while I am at the tail of the Republican ticket."[67] Finally, however, Ben agreed to a joint meeting.

The courthouse was jammed. John Davis and Daniel Voorhees, two of Indiana's leading Democrats, occupied prominent seats along with Mr. Hendricks. Benjamin Harrison was not even offered a chair. He sat on the edge of a desk, with his feet dangling not quite to the floor, and waited his turn. Hendricks rose. The two hours allotted to him turned into four. He was overwhelmed with applause. Taking his seat, he generously suggested that the spectators remain and give ear to his youthful opponent.[68]

Ben, arranging his papers, faced a profound silence. The audience stared at him blankly. One thing he knew for certain. This crowd, after four hours, was weary of speech-making. He began by complimenting Hendricks, though his words did not come from his heart.[69] Then, with workmanlike precision, he stated a proposition, and declared that earlier the Democrats had conceded its truth. This caused a stir in the crowd, a little short of sensation. Before any demonstration could be made for the point

[67] Wallace, op. cit., p. 83.

[68] There is an abundance of source material for this famous meeting between a future President and a future Vice-President. The most readable account is in House Document No. 154, pp. 129–30, written by the late Ross F. Lockridge, Jr., on whom I have drawn heavily. Wallace, op. cit., pp. 82–86, contains several colorful details omitted in Lockridge's condensed account, and there are any number of newspaper accounts readily available in the Harrison Scrapbooks, especially Vol. 52, pp. 77–92.

[69] During the Atlanta Campaign in the spring of 1864, Harrison was induced to mention Hendricks' name in a letter to his wife. Praising Gen. O. O. Howard, he wrote: "He is a good deal like Tom Hendricks in his manner and tone of voice. He has that same easy, gentle, persuasive mode of speech, but one is not led to look for deceit and cunning beneath it, as I always was in Hendricks." Benjamin Harrison to his wife, March 22, 1864, Harrison MSS, Vol. 5, pp. 963–64.

Harrison had scored, Mr. Voorhees, the "Tall Sycamore of the Wabash," stood up in a stately manner and denied the truth of Harrison's charge. Like the report of a pistol, the clear voice of the little lawyer came back at him: "Fellow Citizens, the denial to which we have listened induces me to amend my assertion. I now say that every Democrat approved the proposition, except Mr. Voorhees. He was then a Whig."[70]

With a spontaneity that distinguishes an American political audience, a tremendous yell of approval burst out. From this demonstration Harrison took it that the house was well stocked with Republicans. With new-found pleasure and charm, he took up Mr. Hendricks' points, and answered them briefly one by one, supporting each statement with facts from his note book.[71] He demolished his opponent's position with a calm confidence that would later always characterize him as a speaker. Rockville Republicans were wont afterward to remark: "Such a drubbing as the little fellow did give them. And he was so clean about it. No abuse, no blackguarding. I would walk a hundred miles to see it done over."[72] The chairman of the meeting remarked afterward: "I have heard a good many political debates in my day, but I never heard a man skin an opponent as quickly as Ben Harrison did Hendricks that day."[73] The story spread through the state, and the Republican candidate for Reporter of the Supreme Court soon enjoyed a reputation that considerably strengthened his chances for election.

As this 1860 war of words was drawing to a close, its complement was found in the spectacular political demonstrations that were conducted throughout the state. In many respects, Ben's first major Hoosier campaign was almost as colorful as the victorious fight of his grandfather in 1840, those unforgettable days of "Tippecanoe and Tyler Too." Each closing day of the state canvass in 1860 was marked by "speeches, day and night, torchlight processions, and all kinds of noise and confusion."[74] At In-

[70] Wallace, *op. cit.*, p. 85.

[71] In the Harrison MSS, Vol. 4, pp. 613–22, there is a ten-page typewritten account of the argumentation used in this joint debate. It is culled directly from the Indiana newspaper, the *Parke County Republican*, August 29, 1860.

[72] Wallace, *op. cit.*, p. 86.

[73] *House Document No. 154*, p. 130.

[74] Indianapolis *Locomotive*, September 29, 1860.

dianapolis, citizens turned out by the thousands to cheer "Abe's Boys, the Rail Maulers, and the Wide-Awakes."[75] Columns marched to the flourish of trumpets and to the beat of drums. Vibrant symbolism, perhaps; yet this display afforded a strange premonition of the approaching tragedy of war.

During the final days of the state campaign the battle was bitterly waged. The Democrats, sensing the imminence of defeat, turned frantically to alarmist tactics.[76] Their battle cry was a variation of the theme that a Republican triumph meant the certain inauguration of the "irrepressible conflict." At best, the Democrats argued, this signified a peaceful disunion; at worst, it meant a bloody civil war for mastery in the Union. Neither alternative was a happy one.

The majority of the Indiana electorate appeared unafraid. On October 9, the citizenry went to the polls and gave over their state administration to the Republicans by a substantial majority.[77] Along with his ticket, Harrison was swept into office, with a majority of 9,688. A flood of congratulatory messages came rolling in to Ben and Carrie, and no joy was more unrestrained than that of the Harrison family. At The Point, however, there were mixed emotions. John Scott Harrison certainly cherished his son's success. He even despatched sister Anna to Indianapolis with a special message of "sincere congratulations on *your* success."[78] However, his own pride and spirit of integrity compelled him to add in a letter to Ben:

Although I was opposed to the principles of your party, I mention . . . my having thus early sent forward my congratulations on the election of a more national man than Lincoln . . . I have great faith that Providence will yet find for us some way of escape . . . and save our country from the scourge of a "higher law" President.[79]

[75] Logan Esarey, *A History of Indiana*, II, 656–61.

[76] Stampp, *op. cit.*, p. 46.

[77] Lane and the Republican ticket carried the state by nearly a 10,000 majority. Of the eleven Congressmen, the Republicans elected seven. The southern part of Indiana remained true to Democracy and returned four Representatives to Washington. Indianapolis *Daily Journal,* October 12, 13, 14, 1860.

[78] John Scott Harrison to Benjamin, October 15, 1860, Harrison MSS, Vol. 4.

[79] There is some ambiguity in Scott Harrison's use of the term "higher law" here. It is quite probable, however, he is referring to Mr. Seward, whose famous statement that "there is a higher law than the Constitution which regulates our authority over the domain" branded him as a radical and unacceptable to the Chicago convention of 1860. Like many others, John Scott believed that, if Lincoln were elected, Seward and his doctrine would dominate the administration. Hence his

Although John Scott Harrison entertained the desire to visit Ben in Indianapolis during his hour of victory, his efforts to defeat Lincoln during the remaining month of the presidential campaign kept him at home.[80] A planned family reunion at Ben's modest home was not canceled, but merely postponed. John Scott was a political die-hard, yet his sense of humor did not desert him. In a letter to Ben he quipped:

> When your enthusiastic Republicans *subside* a little . . . or when we turn the tables on you and become as enthusiastic over the election of John Bell, I will come out . . . and promise to be very forbearing towards you Republican gentlemen who crowed before you were out of the woods.[81]

If Indiana had reason to boast in October, the state was not alone.[82] November brought unrestrained joy. The Hoosier majority for Lincoln surpassed by almost 15,000 votes the victory obtained by Harrison and the state ticket only a month before.[83] The sweep of Indiana Republicanism for its presidential nominee was thorough and complete. Not since 1840 had the Democrats lost the state in a national election; not until 1876 would they win it again.[84]

The state leaders of the victorious young party were soon in serious conference at Indianapolis. Victory, as they all understood, had to be used with propriety and discretion. Since a political revolution had taken place within their commonwealth, Hoosier leaders believed that every effort must be made during the months previous to Lincoln's inauguration to give the lie to

---

pious *quod Deus avertat* in writing to Ben. John Scott Harrison to Benjamin, October 15, 1860, Harrison MSS, Vol. 4.

[80] *Ibid.* John Scott Harrison faithfully stumped Ohio and Kentucky for the Constitutional Unionists, Bell and Everett. He mentioned one such meeting to Ben: "I addressed a meeting of Union men at Carrollton, Ky., on Saturday last. I think there must have been three thousand people present."

[81] *Ibid.*

[82] Important Republican victories in Pennsylvania and in Ohio presaged the election of Lincoln in November. See Stampp, *op. cit.*, p. 47; Luthin, *op. cit.*, pp. 197–201.

[83] In Indiana, the official tabulation showed the following presidential vote: Lincoln 139,033; Douglas 115,509; Breckinridge 12,294; and Bell 5,306. Indianapolis *Daily Journal*, December 4, 1860. It is interesting to note that Hendricks and Turpie ran about 10,000 votes ahead of Douglas, while Lane, Morton and Harrison ran some 3,000 behind Lincoln. Esarey, *op. cit.*, p. 661.

[84] Stampp, *op. cit.*, p. 48.

the South's warning that the latter's election would disrupt the Union.[85]

The action of the Hoosier statesmen was certainly timely and above all intimated to the defeated Democrats that they need have no fears of Republican radicalism. The situation throughout the nation, however, was otherwise. Two days after Lincoln's election, South Carolina felt herself yielding bit by bit to an ever-growing spirit of agitation and unrest. Mrs. Mary Chesnut recorded in her diary the talk she heard on the streets of Charleston. It ran like this: "Now that the black radical Republicans have the power I suppose they will Brown us all."[86] On this sentiment the southern lady wrote: "No doubt of it." Within a month South Carolina was ready to leave the Union. On December 20, 1860, the state issued an ordinance of secession. To the Gulf States this was as a sign from heaven. Almost immediately they followed South Carolina's daring lead.

Everyone knew that Abraham Lincoln had been elected on a platform that judged that all the material and spiritual welfare of the nation was directly attributable "to the union of the States." What the people did not know was the mind of Lincoln, but the South feared for the worst. They could not easily overlook the clause in the Republican platform: "We hold in abhorrence all schemes for Disunion, come from whatever source they may."[87]

December, 1860, and January, 1861, were confused and dismal days. By February 1, the South was far along the road to secession. Up North, in the meantime, there was much talk. Some Unionists cheered, others blanched at the mere mention of Seward's doctrine of an "irrepressible conflict." Men of all parties looked hopefully to their political leaders for guidance and statesmanship equal to the crisis. Too often they found neither.[88] Instead,

---

[85] Dwight L. Dumond, *The Secessionist Movement* (New York, 1931) and the same author's edited work, *Southern Editorials on Secession* (New York, 1931), give the best general treatment to this problem.

[86] *A Diary from Dixie,* pp. xxii, 1, cited by Randall, *op. cit.,* p. 184. The entry for Nov. 8, 1860, was filled with phrases such as: "Look Out:–Lincoln is elected"; "The die is cast"; "The Stake is life or death."

[87] A summary of the Republican national platform is given in Wallace, *op. cit.,* p. 252.

[88] Stampp, *op. cit.,* p. 49.

they found politicians grouped together with the ideals and the motives of ordinary business men. A supreme interest in party advantage and in personal profit during this hour of growing emergency all too frequently obscured sound thinking. Perhaps bigoted partisanship and narrow self-interest loomed too large during these critical weeks, yet there was a feeling that the man in Springfield, Illinois, could assuage the fears of the South by a forthright declaration of friendliness.[89] A strange silence prevailed.

Indiana, meanwhile, had sworn in her new state officers. On January 13, 1861, in the presence of retiring Governor Abram A. Hammond and of his own law partner, Will Wallace, Benjamin Harrison took the oath "to support the Constitution of the United States and the Constitution of the State of Indiana and faithfully discharge his duties as Reporter of the Supreme Court of the State of Indiana."[90] The next day, Henry S. Lane took office as Governor. In his address to the Legislature he did little to alleviate Democratic forebodings. Rather, he branded the South and her sympathizers by solemnly stating: "The doctrine of secession . . . is a dangerous heresy."[91] Events moved rapidly. Two days later, on January 16, according to plan, Lane was elected United States Senator, while Oliver Perry Morton became Governor. Then appeared at Indianapolis what to many seemed an ominous sign.

[89] Randall, *op. cit.*, pp. 222–23, presents a highly critical picture of the "Sphinx from Springfield" and observes that "few Presidents have launched upon their tasks with prestige as slight as that of Abraham Lincoln. . . . In the East especially he was distrusted and regarded as inadequate to the crisis which confronted him . . . there were many who snobbishly dismissed him as a 'simple susan'."

[90] The original Commission, as signed by Gov. Hammond, and attested to by Will Wallace, Notary Public, is preserved under date of January 13, Harrison MSS, Vol. 4. Harrison's commission was for a term of four years.

[91] Martin, *op. cit.*, p. 60. On this day John Scott Harrison wrote a very pessimistic letter to Ben: "papers are full of bad news. I think your Republican friends are assuming great responsibility. They talk of not treating with armed traitors . . . [but] we want to save Kentucky, Tennessee, North Carolina, Virginia, Maryland etc., etc., . . . are these states not worth an effort? If we can save them, there is hope that the horrors of Civil War may be prevented." As Randall, *op. cit.*, p. 223, observes: "Many thought Lincoln would be President only in name, and that Seward would be the directing force in the new administration." On this point Scott Harrison wrote Ben that "Seward can save us if he will—will he do it? I confess I believe not. He has until now folded his senatorial robes about him with pharisaical sanctity, as if his garments were unspotted and now that the conflagration is almost past subduing he proposes suggesting a remedy . . . away with such *patriots*." J. S. Harrison to Benjamin, January 14, 1861, Harrison MSS, Vol. 4.

In view of the threatening attitude assumed by the Southern states it was deemed proper by the newly elected Hoosier Assembly to unfurl the American flag from the State House dome, and the ceremony was fixed for January 22, 1861. After an elaborate parade the flag began to be raised. Suddenly, the staff broke and with the flag tumbled down the dome to the roof. A feeling of shock and fear shot through the great crowd. Silently they dispersed, deeming the event ominous of trouble.[92]

The ensuing month of February was one of mystery and expectation. Lincoln was slowly making his way to Washington. In Indiana, Benjamin Harrison and his Hoosier contemporaries joined the rest of the country in keeping a close watch on the actions and the statements of the President-elect. Though each succeeding day made this pre-inaugural period one of intense indecision,[93] most of the American people hoped that Lincoln would break his long silence by dropping some clue to his contemplated policy.

The grave problem of national disunity was catapulted by public discussion into the crisis stage. The people still looked to the new political incumbents for guidance. The Republicans, shortly to take over the presidency, were definitely on the spot. Either they would act, and act decisively, or else fall into disrepute. By mid-February, when Southern secession became a reality, most of recently elected Republicans began to take one of three positions. Some took the view that secession might as well be acquiesced in; others tried to find a satisfactory basis for compromise; the third and more numerous group insisted that secession was rebellion pure and simple, and as such could only be answered with military force.[94]

On this critical issue of secession and Northern reaction to it Benjamin Harrison stood with his party in Indiana, and there could be no mistaking that these men were prepared to take up arms to preserve the Union. As early as November 22, 1860, Oliver Perry Morton, party chieftain and now Governor, pointed

---

[92] *Indianapolis Directory, 1868*, pp. 78–80.

[93] For an excellent and scholarly treatment of this historical period between Lincoln's election and his inauguration see Wood Gray, *The Hidden Civil War* (New York, 1942), pp. 31–50.

[94] *Ibid.*, p. 34.

out in forceful language that compromise or acquiescence in disunion would be fatal to American nationality.[95] It was known to
every party member that compromise or acquiescence in secession
"would almost certainly lead to the disruption and overthrow of
the Republican Party."[96] Although these sentiments were entertained by local leaders like Morton and Harrison, this was not
the important question in February, 1861. The universal concern was the secret locked in Lincoln's heart. With what group
would he stand? What policy or plan was evolving within the
secret recesses of his mind? In the hope of hearing some kind of
answer from the lips of the one man who could reassure their
anxious hearts, the people of Indianapolis, on February 11, 1861,
awaited the personal appearance of the "strange man from Illinois." Even the more enthusiastic and optimistic of his followers
felt that Lincoln would not condescend to break his pre-presi-
dential silence, despite the fact that he owed so much, in a political sense, to Hoosier Republicans.

His speeches to date along the route had been all too reserved,
"colorless, if not actually trivial."[97] If Charles Francis Adams and
his contemporaries distrusted Lincoln as "an absolutely unknown
quantity . . . perambulating the country, kissing little girls and
growing whiskers,"[98] the crestfallen Democrats of Indianapolis
were no less suspicious on the afternoon of his scheduled arrival
in their city. The Democratic *Daily Sentinel* fanned the fires of
distrust when it published an editorial entitled: "Mr. Lincoln's
Visit to Indianapolis":

> Mr. Lincoln is a theorist, a dreamer, and perhaps, an enthusiast in
> his convictions. He is not a practical man, and for that reason will be
> deficient in those qualities necessary to wisely administer the govern-
> ment. He lacks will, purpose and a resolute determination to success.
> For those reasons Mr. Lincoln will be an uncertain man; and today,
> with a full knowledge of his views upon the present condition of our
> public affairs, it will be impossible to predict what his action will

[95] Foulke, *op. cit.,* I, 86–96. Morton's keynote was struck in the following words:
"We must then cling to the ideal that we are a nation, one and indivisible, and that
although subdivided by state lines . . . we are one people . . . we must therefore do
no act, we must tolerate no act, we must concede no idea or theory that looks to or
involves the dismemberment of the nation" (p. 90).

[96] Gray, *op. cit.,* p. 37.

[97] Randall, *op. cit.,* p. 222.

[98] Charles Francis Adams, *Charles Francis Adams, 1835–1915: An Autobiography*
(New York, 1916), p. 82.

be. At a time when it requires a man of nerve, will and purpose to administer the Government successfully, it is most unfortunate that the administration of our public affairs should be confided to such hands.[99]

Benjamin Harrison, however, did not share this pessimistic view of the man whom political opponents delighted in taunting as "the Sphinx from Springfield." To Indiana's new Supreme Court Reporter who had supported Lincoln's candidacy as earnestly as he had his own, the President-elect appeared as a "great simple hearted patriot."[100] He took an active part in preparing a warm welcome for the man who in little over a year would be his Commander-in-Chief in a prolonged war to preserve the Union.

The detailed arrangements for Lincoln's reception were completed, and the right and left wings of the procession knew their precise movements a long time in advance.[101] The care taken by the committee on arrangements and the efforts of the Young Republicans to provide a fitting welcome for their national leader would not go unacknowledged. As Harrison later stated of Lincoln, "he was not unappreciative of friendship, not without ambition to be esteemed . . . whose overmastering and dominant life's thought was to be useful to his country and to his countrymen."[102]

Toward evening, the Indiana capital was in readiness. Hotels and business houses spread their bunting, and the main streets were thronged. An excursion train of eight cars came in about half past four and stopped at the crossing selected for Lincoln's arrival and an old gentleman with a carpet sack in his hands got

99 Indianapolis *Daily Sentinel,* February 12, 1861. The concluding sentence read: "In his present tour, the President-Elect will come into contact mostly, if not entirely, with office seekers, and he will have little opportunity to ascertain the true sentiment of the country upon the issues that threaten the dissolution of government." Seventy-five years later, Randall, *op. cit.,* p. 223, would write: Lincoln's "preoccupation with hordes of office seekers to the neglect of weightier matters, his social awkwardness, his caution, interpreted as timidity, in approaching critical problems, his inexperience in the management of great affairs, all contributed to the unfavorable impression."

100 Benjamin Harrison, *Views of An Ex-President,* p. 473.

101 The Indianapolis *Daily Journal* for February 11, 1861, carried the full program for the reception.

102 Harrison, *op. cit.,* p. 473. Harrison spoke these words at the Lincoln Day Banquet of the Marquette Club, Chicago, February 12, 1898.

out. The cry rose that he was Mr. Lincoln, and a rush and scramble was made for him. He enjoyed the joke, seemingly, but hurried on, elbowing his way with sturdy independence, and succeeded in leading off several hundred noisy urchins as far as the Bates House.[103]

Finally, at five o'clock, the train carrying the President-elect and his suite arrived. Lincoln received the national salute of thirty-four guns, and the grand procession got under way. At Bates House, Governor Morton made a speech of welcome and introduced Lincoln to the people. The newly elected leader placed the question of preserving the Union in the hands of the people themselves:

> I appeal to you . . . to constantly bear in mind that with you, and not with politicians, not with Presidents, not with office-seekers, but with you is the question: Shall the Union and shall the Liberties of this country be preserved to the latest generations?[104]

Benjamin was in the audience, and has left his impressions of the moment: "it seemed to me hardly to be a glad crowd, and he not to be a glad man. There was no sense of culpability either in their hearts or in his; no faltering; no disposition to turn back, but the hour was shadowed with forebodings."[105]

Lincoln made a profound impression on Benjamin Harrison on that occasion. Thirty-eight years later, after Harrison himself had piloted the ship of state for four years, he could recall:

> Before us stood our chosen leader, the man who was to be our pilot through seas more stormy and through channels more perilous than ever the old ship went before. He had piloted the lumbering flat-boat on our western streams, but he was now to take the helm of the great ship. His experience in public office had been brief, and not conspicuous. He had no general acquaintance with the people of the whole country. His large angular frame and face, his broad humor, his homely illustrations and simple ways, seemed to very many of his fellow-countrymen to portray a man and a mind that, while acute and powerful, had not that nice balance and touch of statecraft that the perilous way before us demanded. No college of arts had opened

103 Indianapolis *Daily Sentinel,* February 12, 1861.
104 The Claypool Hotel now stands on the site of the old Bates House. On the Washington Street side is a bronze memorial plaque bearing these words.
105 Harrison, *op. cit.,* p. 473. For a detailed and interesting account of this episode see George S. Cottman, "Lincoln in Indianapolis," *Indiana Magazine of History,* 24 (1928), 3 ff.

to his struggling youth; he had been born in a cabin and reared among the unlettered. He was a rail-splitter, a flatboatman, a country lawyer. . . . The course before him was lighted only by the lamp of duty; outside its radiance all was dark. He seemed to me to be conscious of all this, to be weighted by it, but so strong was his sense of duty, so courageous his heart, so sure was he of his own high purposes and motives and of the favor of God for himself and his people, that he moved forward calmly to his appointed work; not with show and brag, neither with shrinking.[106]

The next day, Lincoln resumed his slow journey to Washington and Harrison continued in his duties as Reporter of the Indiana Supreme Court decisions. He tried, also, to maintain his law practice. This double burden meant long work hours during the day and, more frequently than not, hours borrowed from the night. More and more, Ben found that the law was a jealous mistress. Though he could spend but little time with Carrie and the two children, he took consolation in the knowledge that his work was for them and for the new home he hoped soon to give them. To make this possible he busied himself with texts, indices, syllabi and clients.

February and March passed without incident. Lincoln now held the reins of government. An expectant attitude on both sides had been maintained. Although conflicting declarations had been made, at least the evil day when declaration must be translated into violent action was delayed. By April 12, Harrison found that he had collected enough material to publish his volume of reports. The better to secure himself from interruption while making the index to the volume, he took refuge in a basement room of the old First Presbyterian Church on the Governor's Circle. Here he was when the news of the firing on Fort Sumter was brought to him.[107]

[106] Harrison, *op. cit.*, pp. 473–75.
[107] Wallace, *op. cit.*, pp. 86–87.

CHAPTER VIII

The Call to Arms

No ONE PRESENT in Indianapolis upon that fateful Friday evening of April 12, 1861, ever forgot the telegraphic despatch which announced that the Charleston batteries had opened fire on Fort Sumter. By morning, all the citizens had been alerted by the alarming news of what certainly meant civil war.

Through the long Saturday that followed, business was at a stand. . . . The streets were black with breathless multitudes awaiting the tidings of the seventy loyal men in an unfurnished fort, bombarded by ten thousand raging rebels. At ten o'clock a despatch was announced, "Sumter has fallen."[1]

By late evening the spirit of war pervaded the hearts of young and old alike. Excitement grew as flags waved and patriotic music sounded.[2] The young men of Harrison's age took their cue "from the wet eyes of old and venerated citizens."[3] Into their young and eager hands was falling a trust, the sacred trust of fighting to preserve the Union.

This was Harrison's difficult hour. In early manhood, still two years shy of thirty, the fighting blood of his fighting grandfather raced through his veins. The immediate urge to take up arms was

1 W. D. Foulke, O. P. Morton, I, 114.

2 J. P. Dunn, Indiana and Indianans. Chapter 21 of the first volume was contributed by John H. Holliday, a resident of Indianapolis during the Civil War. Soon after the war, Holliday founded the Indianapolis News, of which for many years he was the editor. Jacob Piatt Dunn claims that Holliday's "personal familiarity with the subject, coupled with extensive research given in preparation of this article, make it a contribution to local history especially worthy of preservation." Actually, Holliday published this work under his own name in 1911 as Vol. 4, No. 9, of the Indiana Historical Society Publications.

3 Foulke, op. cit., I, 114.

terribly pressing. Momentarily, he hesitated. Could he, in all fairness, leave Carrie and the two children? What would be the better thing? Tomorrow was Sunday, and perhaps in the peace and quiet of the sanctuary a right decision could be made. Ordinarily, this active Presbyterian elder would have found the worship hour a splendid opportunity to ponder his future in the war at hand.

It was useless, however, for the day was "as complete an obliteration of Sunday"[4] as Indianapolis had ever seen. From every pulpit the preachers rallied Christians to the support of their country's cause.[5] Following the religious services two immense mass meetings were held, and resolutions were passed, pledging to the government "the lives, the fortunes and the sacred honor of the people of Indiana, in whatever capacity and at whatever time the country might require them."[6] Under these conditions, certainly, the possibility of his making a dispassionate decision seemed all the more remote.

In the days that followed, Hoosierdom mobilized for war.[7] In response to Lincoln's call for 75,000 men for three months, Indiana volunteers soon began to pour into the capital by train, on horseback, and on foot. Practically every activity other than preparation for war was brought to a pause.

Responsibility always rested heavily upon Harrison's shoulders, and, after Sumter fell, his ultimate decision to remain at Indianapolis severely taxed his discretionary powers. Considering himself a prominent member of the political party that "talked of not treating with armed traitors,"[8] he sensed an additional obligation to exercise his patriotic virtue on the field of battle with the same vigor as he had on the political rostrum. Although he had kept his silent counsel during those torturing days of waiting, prior to the bombardment in South Carolina,

4 Indianapolis *Daily State Sentinel* and *Daily Journal*, April 15, 1861.

5 Kenneth Stampp, *Indiana Politics during the Civil War*, p. 71. Also Foulke, *op. cit.*, p. 115: "The country's cause was the theme at the churches; it was in the prayers, in the sermons and in the songs."

6 Foulke, *op. cit.*, p. 115.

7 Stampp, *op. cit.*, p. 73, notes: "for the present at least the episode at Fort Sumter had cleared the air and brought unity to Indiana and to the Republican party —indeed, unity out of disunion."

8 John Scott Harrison to Benjamin, January 14, 1861, Harrison MSS, Vol. 4.

this silence was in no way indicative of a lack of interest or of a policy of salutary neglect. Two months before Sumter's surrender, Harrison's father had remarked:

You say but little of politics, and yet I know you feel a deep interest in the result of the present crisis. Bearing as you do the name of one of the founders of the Republic, you must hope and pray for its perpetuity.... I confess to you I can scarcely see a single star in this night of gloom.[9]

Frequent parades, the roar of cannon and the bluster of martial music[10] did not render his decision to remain at home any more easy. Only the two-pronged consideration of his material welfare and of his manifold domestic obligations snapped his dream of military glory. The sober reality Harrison faced in mid-April, 1861, deterred him from offering to Governor Morton his services as a volunteer. His responsibility was by no means confined to the support of Carrie and the two children—Russell nearly seven and Mamey just turned three. A third child was expected; when Lincoln issued his first call for volunteers, Carrie was in the seventh month of her pregnancy. Harrison also had to reckon with two more dependents in his growing household. His younger brother, John, lived with the family while attending an Indianapolis school,[11] and Harry Eaton, a nephew from Cincinnati, increased the family circle to six.[12] Had charity and kindnesses to his family ceased here, perhaps no serious inroads would have been made upon Benjamin's financial resources. This was not the case, however, for his meticulously kept expense account reveals cash loans and outright gifts to his brother Carter and to his sister Jenny.[13]

Under these circumstances Harrison chose the more practical course. He returned to his law office and resumed his duties as

[9] John Scott Harrison to Benjamin, February 7, 1861, Harrison MSS, Vol. 4.

[10] Indianapolis *Daily State Sentinel*, April 17, 23, 27, 1861.

[11] John Scott Harrison to Benjamin, January 14, 1861, Harrison MSS, Vol. 4.

[12] Harry Eaton was sister Betty's boy. Perhaps Ben was repaying his own debt of gratitude for lodging and keep with the Eatons during his days of legal study in the Queen City. See Betty Eaton to Benjamin Harrison, February 6, 1861: "Thanks for asking Harry to come and live with you. I take great pleasure in knowing he will share with your own little ones your kindness." Harrison MSS, Vol. 4.

[13] Almost excessive charity within the family circle was one of Ben's strong points all his life. Often, it was practiced at a great sacrifice to himself and his own family. "Personal Notes and Bills for 1860–1862," Harrison MSS.

Supreme Court Reporter. Despite a consistently good income from his partnership in the Wallace and Harrison law firm, and the prospect of increased revenues from his lucrative post as Reporter,[14] he still found it difficult to make ends meet. Consequently, he continued to borrow money from his life-long friend, Albert Gallatin Porter, a man destined to be Governor of Indiana from 1881 to 1885 and minister to Italy during Harrison's administration as President. At this time, the young lawyer was indebted to Porter for almost three thousand dollars and was paying a semi-annual interest on his note that fell just short of one hundred dollars.[15]

Harrison deemed that his place was in Indianapolis where he could satisfy his civil and domestic obligations. Yet, love of country engrossed him and he was hard pressed in abiding by his decision. Fortunately, however, Indiana was soon ready to place some 12,000 troops in the lines, and this number was more than double the quota assigned the state by Lincoln's directive.[16] Harrison gained no little consolation from the knowledge that Indiana was first among the states to fill the volunteer quota. Consequently, when Governor Morton offered to oversubscribe,[17] it was time to forget his initial disappointment at being left behind. It would be important for him to execute his professional and civil duties with a clear mind and an undivided heart.

Harrison gave himself to his work a bit too conscientiously. Long hours, it is true, increased the family treasury, but the physical strain soon began to tell. This oversteady application to work, a habit formed in college and developed in Storer's law office, effected a perceptible change in Benjamin's manner. He had little time to devote to his wife and children. Though Carrie maintained an understanding silence, one wonders if she did

14 Benjamin Harrison's Ledger for 1854 to 1867 (Ac. 1698 Add. 8) Harrison MSS, indicates that he had many suits in the Marion County Common Pleas Court during 1861.

15 Among Harrison's "Notes and Bills" for 1859 is the following item: "Indianapolis, Indiana, August 30, 1859 . . . Received of Benjamin Harrison, Esq., $88.50 in full for the first half year's interest on his notes for $2,950 to me. A. G. Porter." Harrison MSS.

16 David Stevenson and Theodore Scribner, *Indiana's Roll of Honor* (Indianapolis, 1864, 1866), I, 20. For a more colorful account see Irving McKee, *"Ben-Hur" Wallace* (Berkeley and Los Angeles, 1947), pp. 31–46.

17 Kenneth P. Williams, *Lincoln Finds a General* (New York, 1949), I, 60–62.

not share the sadness of Mary Owens, who said of Lincoln that "he was deficient in those little links which make up the great chain of woman's happiness."[18] It was not long, however, before John Scott Harrison was apprised of his son's overindulgence in work. Almost immediately a letter issued from The Point: "You must take care that you do not overtax yourself . . . for what is wealth and honor without *health?*" Had John Scott concluded his paternal exhortation there, it would have been nothing more than a routine admonition. In his shrewdness, however, and from the intimate knowledge he possessed of his son, he added a paragraph, the wisdom of which the younger and immature man learned to appreciate only after three years' absence in the army:

I have thought that a professional man when he leaves his office in the evening should leave the study and care behind him and direct his energies to the enjoyment of his family and innocent social pleasure. I do not know, however, that this is always practicable, and yet as far as possible I think it ought to be observed . . . too much care and study is apt to make a man unsocial and morose . . . and professional men should remember that their families have claims upon them as well as their clients or patients.[19]

The overworked lawyer seems to have accepted the gentle warning with a gracious determination to strike a happy balance between work and play. He attempted to make time in which to enjoy the comforts of home after working hours, yet he himself would have been the first to admit that his efforts were none too successful. The time-consuming labors of his Supreme Court task, added to the strenuous demands of his regular practice, seemed to deprive him completely of the normal hours for leisurely living. His root fault stemmed from an excess of virtue, for Benjamin Harrison in his reading and study was a very miser of time, never wasting a moment.

He had discovered that a Supreme Court Reporter was a com-

18 David Donald, *Lincoln's Herndon* (New York, 1948), p. 188.
19 John Scott Harrison was not too harsh on his son. The father added in the next sentence: "I am grateful to learn of the confidence reposed in you by the Church. He who wears worthily the honors of the Church of Christ, cannot fail to be the worthy recipient of the honors of his country . . . would to God that more of our office holders were God-fearing men." J. S. Harrison to Benjamin, February 7, 1861, Harrison MSS, Vol. 4. It is well to bear in mind that Ben's duties as a Presbyterian elder were not slight. See *Centennial Memorial of The First Presbyterian Church* (Indianapolis, 1925), p. 122.

bination of civil servant and private business man. Although keeping and editing the detailed records of court trials and judicial decisions necessarily entailed long hours of solitary work, the undertaking carried its own reward. Harrison the civil servant recorded and published the decisions, while Harrison the private business man found a ready market for the sale of his work in bound volumes. State officials, including the Governor, leading members of the Indiana bar, and various state institutions were eager and certain customers. The price averaged around $4.50 per volume, and the ultimate personal gain was no trifling sum.

He was honest enough to reveal the ambition motivating his labors. "I hope to make out of this office . . . enough to pay for my house and lot."[20] Yet the question he raised in his own mind was whether the sacrifice and effort were really worth the guaranteed income. This daily preoccupation was a grind from which both he and Carrie suffered many inconveniences, though his wife was quite willing to make the sacrifice for a home they could call their own. Regret did not take hold until Harrison had entered the army and was separated from his wife well over six months. Then he yearned for reunion with her in order to "appreciate the unselfish and confiding love you have manifested for me." He proceeded to make a conscience-cleansing confession:

I now see *so many* faults in my domestic life that I long for an opportunity to correct. I know I could make your life so much happier than ever before . . . what need we care for earthly riches, if we can only be rich in the love of God and each other.[21]

Before the Civil War was three months old, a black cloud of personal sorrow temporarily engulfed the Harrison home. Carrie lost at birth the child whom she and Ben awaited as their "third pet."[22] Their sorrow was intense and prolonged despite the many consoling messages of sympathy that poured in from relatives and friends. Yet, the rare beauty and warmth of the condolences expressed by John Scott Harrison, who knew this type of sorrow only too well and too frequently, certainly revived their spirits:

[20] Benjamin Harrison to his wife, August 23, 1862, Harrison MSS, Vol. 4, Nos. 692–93.

[21] Benjamin Harrison to his wife, November 30, 1862, Harrison MSS, Vol. 4, No. 748.

[22] On June 13, 1861, Ben noted his expense for a child's coffin and box for the grave, amounting to $10.50.

I hear with sorrow the loss and disappointment you sustained in the death of your little babe but few will doubt that your loss has been her infinite gain. She has exchanged a world of sin for one of purity and bliss. . . .

You have lost a little one, too young to know and love you . . . but God in his mercy is sparing to you two bright and intelligent children who have learned to do this . . . and you should, and do feel grateful that He has been disposed to withhold what would have been still a more bitter cup. Such afflictions fall more heavily upon the bereaved mother . . . and Carrie has our sincere sympathy. . . .[23]

Early in June, however, came the event that served, at least partially, to lift the Harrisons from the doldrums. It was the startling report that the Eleventh Indiana Volunteers,[24] under the command of Colonel Lew Wallace,[25] had made an effective raid upon Romney, Virginia, forty-six miles southwest of Cumberland, Maryland. This news of a Confederate retreat was more than timely, for, after two months of uneventful war, the Indianapolis public was starved for news of action. Up to this moment, neither citizens nor soldiers had much to cheer about. The Eleventh had merely been at Evansville, Indiana, policing the Ohio River instead of winning glory on the field of battle. Now came the report that Hoosier troops had marched over the mountains and had won no mean skirmish.[26]

While they contributed to the spontaneous applause that greeted this news of the rebel retreat, Ben and Carrie took a personal joy and delight in the Eleventh's success. Each had a brother in this regiment, Lieutenant Irwin Harrison and Private Henry Scott, each of whom had enlisted for three months. Ben

[23] John Scott Harrison to Benjamin Harrison, June 25, 1861, Harrison MSS, Vol. 4.

[24] Called the Eleventh Regiment because the units began with the Sixth, following the Mexican War's Fifth.

[25] Wallace first took over the state's Adjutant General's office and, when Indiana's quota was more than met, resigned his office to become a colonel. Lew Wallace was the brother of Harrison's law partner, Will Wallace, and the entire Wallace family had been intimate with the Harrisons since the territorial days under Governor William Henry Harrison.

[26] The military importance of this small event is vividly described by Williams, *op. cit.*, I, 70–73, as "a good example of the unexpected repercussion that a small event can have"; he remarked that "nothing Stonewall Jackson's famous 'foot-cavalry' ever did was much better than that." As Irving McKee, Lew Wallace's biographer points out, the Eleventh was credited with frightening Joe Johnston from Harper's Ferry and with the reopening of the Baltimore and Ohio to Union traffic (*op. cit.*, pp. 37–38).

yielded readily to his brother's almost immediate request for "a pair of Captain's shoulder straps."[27] Of his brother-in-law, Henry Scott, he inquired about his "chance of promotion of any kind" and suggested that Lew Wallace might have some position "in his gift."[28]

Judging from his correspondence, it is quite evident that Ben had taken a keen and fraternal interest in Henry Scott's welfare. Shortly before the outbreak of the war, Henry had come to make his home with the Harrisons, and by the head of the family he had been treated more like a brother by blood than by marriage. In short order, he had begun to read law with Wallace and Harrison, supported by the remunerative duties of a Notary Public.[29] When Will Wallace was nominated for the Clerkship of Marion County and was necessarily absent from the office a great deal, Ben Harrison relied more and more on the ability and services of Henry Scott. When he had marched away with the Eleventh Indiana in early May, he was sorely missed at the office. Toward the end of his term of enlistment, the question of signing up for three more years had been raised. His sister Carrie was definitely against it, and, although work-weary and distressed at the thought of being deprived of his valuable services for so long a period, Ben penned to Henry one of his characteristically deliberate letters:

Carrie tells me she has urged it upon you very strongly not to enter for the three years service, upon the ground that I needed you at home. I need not say that you were more useful to me than anyone I have ever had in the office and about home, but notwithstanding all this, I would not have you to do anything you might esteem a reproach on any such account.[30]

It would not have been typical of Harrison to conclude his message with so brief and simple a statement of the problem. As

27 Irwin Harrison to Benjamin Harrison, June 24, 1861, Harrison MSS, Vol. 4: "You promised me while a Lieutenant to give me a pair of shoulder straps," Irwin wrote, "I will now accept them, and you will *please* send me a pair of Captain's straps . . . direct your letter to Capt. A. I. Harrison. . . ."

28 Benjamin Harrison to Henry M. Scott, June 3, 1861, Harrison MSS (Harrison Memorial Home, Indianapolis).

29 Benjamin Harrison Scrapbook Series, Vol. 1, p. 13, Harrison MSS.

30 Benjamin Harrison to Henry M. Scott, June 3, 1861, Harrison MSS (Indianapolis). This letter was discovered hidden in Harrison's old desk.

he had felt constrained to express his views on the re-enlistment problem that faced Lincoln and the Northern soldiers, he added:

It might be that many a man entered for 3 mos. service, whose circumstances were such that he could not enter for 3 years. We are all governed a good deal by the question "What will people say or think?" I do not know what I should do under similar circumstances. It is a question for *you*, but in determining it, do not suffer any consideration for my supposed convenience to influence you one way or the other . . . I shall get along very well and should you return (which God grant you may), whether it be after three months or three years, you will find a place for you in my family and in my office.[31]

The concluding paragraphs of this long letter were charged with concern for Henry's moral welfare. The young soldier was warned to "avoid with more care the *vices* of the camp than you would the enemy's *bullets* . . . they are more deadly. . . . By your priceless and immortal soul, let not the ribaldry of companions keep you from Scripture reading and prayers."[32]

Eventually, however, neither patriotism nor human respect were determining factors in Henry Scott's decision to leave military service at the end of three months. Under constant drill and the other rigors of army life, his health broke badly. Strangely enough, just about the time John Scott Harrison was writing to Indianapolis on his fears that "this hot weather will kill more of our men in camp than the balls of the enemy in the field,"[33] young Henry Scott, a sick man, was entraining for Indianapolis. True to his promise, Ben gave young Henry a warm welcome to the family circle. Through Carrie's special care the ex-soldier was soon restored to tolerable health, and before September was far spent he was back in the office rendering able assistance to the law firm.

Henry Scott's return was a stroke of good fortune for Harrison, who was complaining that Will Wallace was unable to pull his half of the legal load. He used to refer to Wallace, the Republican candidate for Clerk of Marion County, as the man who had not

31 *Ibid.*

32 Ben's concern for Scott's spiritual welfare was deep. "I hope you have not forgotten to remember your Creator in the camp. . . . I hope to have you returned to us not only safe in body but with a soul unscarred with sin. You have our daily prayers that God would make you his own and keep your heart in innocence." *Ibid.*

33 John Scott Harrison to Benjamin, August 2, 1861, Harrison MSS, Vol. 4.

done a lick of work since his nomination, and bitingly added "nor for some months before."[34] Henry Scott's presence temporarily filled the breach, but with Wallace's success at the polls in November, the law firm of Wallace and Harrison hastened to the brink of dissolution. Finally, in December, 1861, with mutual good feeling, the six-year partnership was terminated. Both men had taken long and successful strides down the highway of law and politics.

Less than two weeks had passed before Benjamin Harrison had associated himself in his second important legal venture. William Pinkney Fishback, a rather polished speaker and quick-witted Indianapolis attorney, was glad to accept second place in the new firm.[35] On December 11, 1861, they hung out their newly painted Harrison and Fishback shingle at 62 E. Washington Street.[36] Henry Scott soon took space with them and, though not yet qualified to affiliate as a third member in the firm, performed valuable service as a Notary Public. This new combination of legal talent was extremely friendly. "Pink" Fishback, as he was known, was the scourge of everything lazy, and he fitted in perfectly with Harrison's capacity for work. He had known Ben intimately from their school days, when Harrison evidently had created a very fine first impression by his ready eloquence:

I remember his facility in extemporaneous speech amazed me . . . a faculty which he has improved wonderfully. In all my knowledge of him I never knew him to trip in a sentence. He seemed to see about two well-rounded sentences ahead of him all the time.[37]

34 Benjamin Harrison to Henry Scott, June 3, 1861, Harrison MSS (Indianapolis).

35 Fishback was late of Conner and Fishback, recognized attorneys in the city, and had seen Harrison in action on several occasions. Fishback declared that "of all the men I have known in professional life, Ben Harrison is the most diligent, painstaking and thorough." Wallace, *op. cit.*, p. 174.

36 This new office of Harrison and Fishback was located over Munson and Johnson's store. The new partnership was widely advertised. Indianapolis *Daily Journal*, January 1, 1862.

37 Lew Wallace, *Life of Gen. Ben Harrison*, p. 173, cites a letter he received from W. P. Fishback, under date of July 13, 1888, wherein Fishback places his first meeting with Harrison at Miami in 1850. A thorough search of the *Alumni and Former Student Catalogue of Miami University, 1809–1892* (Oxford, Ohio, 1892) yields no evidence of Fishback's presence at the institution. Internal evidence based on Fishback's letters and other statements in the press indicate a close association with Harrison during his days at Oxford.

Harrison had come a long way since his first law partnership in 1855. Now he was widely known in every county of the state. His apprehension was quick and sure, but his genius lay in application and a determination to master every question which came before him. Not content merely with painstaking work on briefs, he enjoyed the contests of the courtroom. Six years of practice had contributed no little to Harrison's maturity along legal lines. Just before they disbanded, Wallace was asked: "What impression did Harrison make among lawyers?" From the reply it is not difficult to understand Fishback's satisfaction in associating himself with Harrison, whom Wallace characterized as possessing:

... admirable qualities as a lawyer ... quick of apprehension, clear, methodical and logical in his analysis and statement of any case. He possessed a natural faculty of getting the exact truth of a witness either by direct or cross-examination. In this respect he has but few equals.... Always exacting from Courts and Jurys their closest attention and interest in the cause ... when ... demanded ... illustrating the rarest powers of the genius orator. He is a hard worker, giving to every case the best of his skill and labor, so that he never went unprepared, trusting to good luck, the want of skill, or the negligence of the other side.[38]

Another factor that considerably brightened the prospects was Harrison's own growing reputation within the Republican Party. He had climbed several rungs of the ladder of political popularity and influence, said reports that reached his father back on the Ohio farm. John Scott Harrison, who still occasionally scoffed at the Republican party and advised his son against too close a connection with politics and politicians, now wrote in a somewhat different strain:

... you have a more influential position in your own party than perhaps you are aware.... I heard a wealthy merchant of Lawrenceburg say not long since that he regarded you the strongest and most influential man of your age in the state ... that ... is of course known to the powers at Washington.[39]

[38] Indianapolis *Journal*, June 30, 1888.

[39] John Scott Harrison to Benjamin Harrison, July 10, 1861, Harrison MSS, Vol. 4.

By reliability rather than any striking talents or political connections, Harrison lifted his firm to the front rank among Indianapolis law offices. Business men liked him because he was instinctively conservative in his advice, and because he devoted untiring attention to their cases. An example of the confidence he enjoyed with men of business was afforded by James L. Hill & Co., insurance dealers of Springfield, Illinois. The company had a particularly obnoxious debtor, picturesquely described as a "slippery dog, wide awake and will need very close watching."[40] The actual business of collecting the company's claim was entrusted to Harrison with a show of confidence that speaks for itself: "If you see any chance, please do with the claim as if it were your own. I have entire confidence in you . . . shall rely entirely upon your sagacity."[41]

The increased volume of business that fell to the new law firm enabled Harrison to realize a greater income than he had anticipated, although he had been relying confidently on the profits from the publication of Volumes 15 and 16 of the *Indiana Reports*.[42] Consequently, he felt himself in a position to make a new investment, and the need that stood highest on the Harrison list was a new home.[43] Good fortune, in the person of Albert Gallatin Porter, gave more than a gentle knock at the door. Ben and Carrie were very alert to what they considered a grand opportunity. Porter, their friend and creditor, unexpectedly came into the possession of some property and was anxious to dispose of it. Since he was aware that the Harrisons had put up with crowded quarters for a long period, Porter proposed to sell them

40 James L. Hill & Co. to Benjamin Harrison, Esq., November 5, 1861, Harrison MSS, Vol. 4. Evidence is also given that Harrison was not slow to use his famous name as a recommendation and a guarantee of integrity.

41 *Ibid.* From Harrison's handwritten notation on this letter we know that the claim was collected and the case disposed of much to the satisfaction of the Hill Co.

42 Testimony of John Caven, the man Harrison appointed as his deputy in the Office of Supreme Court Reporter after he himself entered service. An unidentified newspaper clipping in B. Harrison Scrapbook, Vol. 52, p. 94, Harrison MSS.

43 Concern over these crowded living conditions was frequently expressed by John Scott Harrison, especially when it came to boarding young Johnny during his schooling days. John Scott Harrison to Benjamin, December 26, 1861, Harrison MSS, Vol. 4, writes: "But I am unwilling to impose too much of a burden upon you. Your family is large, perhaps too large for your comfort. . . . I have therefore to ask that if John is in any way of your family convenience and comfort—in the least degree—you will provide him some cheap but respectable boarding house."

both house and property, allowing cash payments on time. Further than this, he gave Harrison the advantage of extending his previous notes as long as he desired.[44]

The property was located on the southeast corner of Alabama and North Streets, and the house, though somewhat remodeled, was a good example of old-style architecture. It was a frame building two stories high, with small upstairs windows, common in residences at that time. An old stable, set back on the alley of the same lot, was a welcome part of the purchase that was made almost immediately. Moving-in day was a happy occasion.

As might be expected, the pleasure and enjoyment of a new home also entailed some sacrifices, mostly financial. On this account, Harrison soon made himself the scapegoat. He felt constrained to work twice as hard in order to meet his newly incurred financial obligations. Fishback noticed how heavily his partner carried his new responsibility:

> During the time I was his partner he worked like a slave. He was Reporter of the Supreme Court and prepared the "syllabuses" or "syllabi," as the case may be, at his home at night. He was working to pay for his house, and came near wrecking his health by over work.[45]

While Benjamin Harrison was wrestling more or less successfully with his many problems throughout 1861 and the early weeks of 1862, the nation was not faring so well. After absorbing the initial shocks of the civil war, the people grew more and more accustomed to marching troops and blaring bands. Actually the Northern war feeling that ran so high after Sumter's surrender and was intensified by the Union reverse at Bull Run[46] had slackened perceptibly during the waning days of 1861. Perhaps at Indianapolis, Harrison was not fully aware of the Eastern

[44] Mr. Porter came into the possession of the property through some kind of trade and was glad to sell to Harrison. "He said he would sell it on time and give him as long as he wanted to pay . . . so the property was purchased for something like one thousand dollars . . . Harrison making two payments on it before he went to war and the rest afterwards." Indianapolis *Journal*, July 1, 1888.

[45] Wallace, *op. cit.*, p. 174.

[46] Wood Gray, *The Hidden Civil War*, pp. 52–60: "The reverse at Bull Run seemed only to intensify the unity and determination of the section and led to demands for a more vigorous and ruthless prosecution of the war . . . the defeat of our army has created another Fort Sumter rising of the people in their might," reported an observer.

trend toward dissatisfaction, for on December 1, 1861, the report of the Secretary of War showed that volunteering in the Midwest had far outstripped that of the rest of the nation.[47] Indiana could hold her head high. With a population only slightly larger than that of Massachusetts, the Hoosier state had raised twice as many men for the war. As far as Harrison could see, all seemed well as long as partisanship was subordinated to the war effort.

But this era of harmony did not last, and this was painfully true in Indiana. The Democratic party was being successfully regenerated, particularly by press campaigns, and soon stood as a group of sturdy opponents to the war. Indianapolis was the scene of a bitter press duel between the Republican-sponsored *Journal* and the Democratic-edited *Sentinel*. The evils of actual violence and the threats of violence against lukewarm supporters of the war were argued editorially. The subject of personal rights, violated in the practice of arbitrary arrests, also was hotly discussed.[48] This, Harrison could see with his own eyes, but there were numerous other indications sufficient to convince even the most optimistic souls that the war temperature, by the end of 1861, had reached an astonishing low.

President Lincoln, in early 1862, was continuing his search for a general. McClellan's sustained inactivity afforded no grounds for satisfaction. Actually, it was the source of much distrust in official circles at Washington.[49] Unless decisive victories should be won, there was more than a likely chance that foreign intervention and internal lethargy would combine to make the civil war a hopeless contest for the Union.

This was the gloomy and complex picture as Benjamin Harrison saw it on New Year's Day, 1862. Three days later, his father, ever imbued with a healthy skepticism of Republicans in general and of Lincoln in particular, wrote with his usual candor:

[47] The states of this section furnished nearly three-fourths as many troops as the rest of the North combined. *War of Rebellion, Official Records of the Union and Confederate Armies,* Series 3, I, 698–708; hereinafter abbreviated as *Official Records.* Gray, *op. cit.,* p. 62, also points out: "Ohio alone, with Illinois not far behind, had provided more troops than all New England."

[48] For one of the most satisfying treatments of this constitutional phase of the civil war controversy see James G. Randall's *Constitutional Problems under Lincoln* (New York, 1926) and his later work, *The Civil War and Reconstruction,* especially pp. 382–404.

[49] Williams, *op. cit.,* I, 147–49.

Our affairs of a public nature look to me very dark. I have long since utterly despaired of the country. We have no man suited to the emergency. Greatness has departed from both the American farm and camp. One arm alone can save us. . . . I fear that arm will not be outstretched until we have emerged from such an ordeal as no nation has ever been called to pass for its purification. . . . "Good Lord, deliver us," should be the prayer of all our people.[50]

Harrison was willing to concede the seriousness of the situation, but from his vantage point in Indianapolis the clouds were not so black and threatening. As a matter of fact, several signs seemed to augur swift success for the Union armies. Widespread dejection and impatience were quickly dispelled by the forward movement in the spring of 1862. Early in February, Grant's dramatic capture of Forts Henry and Donelson served to open the Mississippi as far as Vicksburg and, followed shortly by Farragut's taking of New Orleans and success in Missouri, revived the hopes of an early Northern victory.[51] To Indianans the "bloody battle of Shiloh, and the occupation of Memphis and Corinth appeared indicative of the imminent collapse of the Confederacy."[52] Throughout the North much was expected of General McClellan, who had drilled and organized his troops until they were, according to his report, "wild with delight & egear [sic] to try their own hand in the fight."[53]

"Little Mac," the man who had written derisively about the regiment which he had found "cowering on the banks of the Potomac"[54] after the battle of Bull Run, was purportedly ready. All he needed was good weather, for he promised that "when the roads were better, this army will move on to the South and victory."[55] These were encouraging words, and Northern minds were infected with confidence. One cannot blame Harrison and his friends for brushing aside any doubt concerning the immediate success of the Northern cause, for so confident was the Washington government that it had fielded an army sufficiently large

50 John Scott Harrison to Benjamin, January 4, 1862, Harrison MSS, Vol. 4.

51 Gray, op. cit., pp. 78 ff.

52 Stampp, op. cit., p. 133. Even southern Indiana, predominantly pro-Southern in sympathy, "grew more optimistic, and business revived with the expectation that the Mississippi would soon be open again to western commerce." Indianapolis Daily Journal, February 17, 18, April 10, May 1, June 14, 1862.

53 Gray, op. cit., p. 78.

54 Williams, op. cit., I, 241.

55 Gray, op. cit., p. 78.

to crush the rebellion that in April, 1862, the War Department stopped recruiting.[56]

With the advent of summer, 1862, this bubble of early confidence burst, and a wave of disappointment and disillusionment swept the country. Want of a determined policy threatened to dash every previous hope of victory. McClellan's advance up the Yorktown Peninsula had been stopped in the Seven Days' Battle, and, after "Little Mac's" abortive campaign of three months and a week, it was a confident Lee who watched the Union forces in · their "flight across the swamps."[57] On the western front, inactivity also prevailed. Union lethargy rendered the April victory at Pittsburgh Landing almost fruitless. Now, fear crept abroad and stark disaster threatened, as General Bragg, after assembling a large Confederate force at Chattanooga, entered Kentucky and threatened Ohio and Indiana. Benjamin Harrison in later years vividly recalled these perilous days:

> Buell was returning from Tennessee, Kirby Smith coming through the Cumberland Gap, and McClellan had been defeated on the peninsula. It seemed as if the frown of God was on our cause.[58]

As Harrison added, "this was not the heyday of success." This was gross understatement, for in Indiana, as in the majority of other Union states, war enthusiasm had yielded to general apathy. Among the Hoosiers the public depression was particularly great. As an antidote, Governor Morton joined with seventeen other state executives in memorializing President Lincoln on June 28 to the effect that "the people of the United States are desirous to aid promptly in furnishing all reenforcements that you may deem needful to sustain our Government."[59] Within three days, Lincoln had placed his grateful acknowledgment in the hands of the various governors. He told them that he concurred in their views

56 Stampp, *op. cit.*, p. 133. This premature halt to recruiting was loudly protested and severely criticized. Governor Morton of Indiana led the opposition to this move. See Foulke, *op. cit.*, I, 179.

57 Williams, *op. cit.*, pp. 214–41, a severe indictment of McClellan.

58 Charles Hedges (comp.), *Speeches of Benjamin Harrison* (New York, 1892), p. 117. This was the high point of General Harrison's famous address to the 14th reunion of the Seventieth Indiana Regiment, held at Clayton Village, Hendricks County, on September 13, 1888.

59 Indianapolis *Daily Journal*, July 7, 1862. The text of this communication was republished on this day along with Lincoln's reply under date of July 1.

and suggestions. Consequently, on July 1, he decided "to call into service an additional force of 300,000," suggesting and recommending that "these troops be chiefly of Infantry."[60]

Governor Morton faced the serious problem of implementing his promise, for he discovered that the enthusiasm he voiced far outstripped that of the ordinary citizen upon whom fell the task of meeting the new state quota. To insure a generous response to the President's request for more troops, Morton resorted to a special proclamation to the people. First he appealed to their pride, telling them that "up to this hour Indiana occupies a most exalted position connected with the war . . . her troops have been in almost every battle . . . with uniform and distinguished gallantry." Then came his direct and forceful request for manpower:

I therefore call upon every man, whatever may be his rank and condition in life, to put aside his business, and come to the rescue of his country. Upon every man individually let me urge the solemn truth, that whatever may be his condition or business, he has no business or duty half so important to himself and family as the speedy and effectual suppression of the Rebellion.[61]

The response was distinctly disappointing.[62] Although for two or three days the newspapers carried reprints of the Governor's strong appeal, it went practically unheeded. Morton was thoroughly dejected, and he was not the kind of man to hide his feelings. It was in this despondent mood that Benjamin Harrison found him on the morning of July 9, 1862.

Accompanied by his former law partner, Will Wallace, Harrison arrived at the Governor's office shortly before noon to discuss a political matter. Though the Governor was by no means jovial, he received his two political lieutenants in a cordial manner. At the close of their conference, he asked them to step into his inner room on the east side of the Old State House, where he led them to the window. A bit puzzled, Harrison and Wallace stood there with Morton. In silence they watched a score of work-

60 Ibid.
61 Indianapolis Daily Journal, July 7, 1862.
62 Ibid., July 12, 1862.

men engaged in the erection of a new building. Ten minutes dragged by. Morton did not say a word.

Then the Governor shattered the strange silence. He was thoroughly appalled, he said, by the weak response of his people to the presidential call for volunteers. He was even further plagued by sights such as all three were now observing. He mumbled something about the able-bodied men laboring so unconcernedly in the pursuits of private enterprise. "See here," he exclaimed, "look at those workmen across the street, toiling to put up a new building, as if such a thing could be possible when the country itself is in danger of destruction."[63] The Governor was thoroughly alarmed.

He had thought his own presence in the field might serve as an example to the people of the state and thereby stimulate recruiting. Lincoln had not approved of the plan, and Morton's request for active service had met with a categorical refusal.[64] Now, he unburdened his troubled soul to Harrison and Wallace:

Gentlemen, there is absolutely no response to Mr. Lincoln's last call for troops. The people do not seem to realize the necessities of the situation. Something must be done to break the spirit of apathy and indifference which now prevails.[65]

Harrison felt that the Governor was appealing to him personally.[66] Hence, without hesitation, he replied: "Governor, if I can be of any service, I will go."[67]

Morton refused to make a snap decision. His reply was a few moments in coming, and when it did it was a compromise answer. "You can raise a regiment in this Congressional district right away; but it is asking too much of you to go into the field with it. You have just been elected Reporter of the Supreme Court.

---

[63] *House Document No. 154*, p. 110. Wallace, *op. cit.*, pp. 179 ff., describes Morton pointing to the men cutting stone and then saying: "These men are following their own private business, so that it has come to be a serious question what I shall do next to arouse them."

[64] Foulke, *op. cit.*, p. 181.

[65] *House Document No. 154*, p. 110.

[66] Morton's biographer alleges that "Harrison had told Morton, sometime before, that whenever it was necessary for him to go, the Governor was to inform him." Foulke, *op. cit.*, p. 184.

[67] *House Document No. 154*, p. 110.

But go to work and raise it, and we will find somebody to command it."[68]

This suggestion that he enlist others for a task that he himself would be avoiding failed to appeal. He refused emphatically to concur in Morton's compromise solution. He would not recruit others for battle and then stay at home himself. Faced with this ultimatum, the Governor not only acquiesced in Harrison's determination to go with the troops, but offered him command of the regiment. Complete ignorance of military tactics forced him to reply: "I do not know as I want to command the regiment . . . so, if you can find some suitable person of experience in such matters, I am not at all anxious to take the command."[69] Before the interview ended, Morton agreed to hold in abeyance his offer to commission Harrison colonel of the regiment about to be formed. However, he commissioned him a Second Lieutenant, "fully empowering him to enlist volunteers for said regiment and when enlisted to muster them into the United States service."[70] As they walked down the capitol steps, County Clerk William Wallace became Lieutenant Harrison's first recruit.[71]

When Harrison left Wallace at the State House steps, the freshly commissioned officer did not, as one might suspect, go directly home and break the news to an unsuspecting wife. He stopped first at a store, purchased a military cap, engaged a fife-player, and then returned to his office. After he had flung a flag out of the window, he sat back quietly and waited for Company A's second recruit. That evening he confided the news to Carrie, who made the sacrifice as bravely as he himself had done.[72] Her acceptance of the call of duty played no small part in encouraging

68 Wallace, op. cit., pp. 179–80.

69 Ibid., p. 180.

70 From the Adjutant General's Office of the Indiana Volunteer Militia, Indianapolis, Indiana, July 9, 1862, the following commission was issued: "BENJAMIN HARRISON has been appointed a Second Lieut. in the 70th Regiment Indiana Volunteers, to be organized in the sixth congressional district of the State, in pursuance of general orders no. 49 issued at this office. He is fully empowered to enlist volunteers for said regiment and when enlisted to muster them into the United States Service. By order of his Excellency, O. P. Morton, Governor. (Signed) L. A. Z. Noble, Adt. Genl. Indiana." Harrison MSS, Vol. 4.

71 Indianapolis Daily Journal, July 12, 1862, and July 16, 1862, wherein mention is made of "Our County Clerk, William Wallace, Esq., who is a high private in his [Harrison's] Company."

72 An unidentified newspaper clipping in Scrapbook Vol. 9, Harrison MSS.

her husband. She possessed a deep faith—so deep that it wrung from the pen of James Whitcomb Riley the following tribute:

> Yet with the faith she knew
>   We see her still
> Even as here she stood—
> All that was pure and good
> And sweet in womanhood—
>   God's will her will.[73]

During the next two days the recruiting was discouragingly slow. Only when the morning edition of the Indianapolis *Daily Journal* was in the streets on Saturday, July 12, did the fires of patriotism glow at all. A large advertisement notified "all friends of the Union" of a grand rally scheduled for Masonic Hall that evening at eight o'clock. Old men were invited to contribute aid by counsel and means; the young were urged "to let the spirit of '76 kindle in your breast and prove yourselves not unworthy keepers of the Ark of Liberty."[74] The principal speakers were to be General Ebenezer Dumont, Governor Morton, County Clerk William Wallace, and Supreme Court Reporter Benjamin Harrison.

It was soon evident that a second meeting place would have to be assigned to handle an overflow crowd. Long before eight o'clock, Masonic Hall was so closely packed that a man could scarcely edge his way in. Enthusiasm grew with the increasing numbers, and after the State House Grove was designated as the second meeting place, the crowd assembled there surpassed that at Masonic Hall. The speakers decided that they would address both assemblies in turn.[75]

At Masonic Hall, Governor Morton made the opening address and then presided over the meeting. He stressed repeatedly the utter necessity of sacrificing private interests for the public welfare, and then closed on a note of confidence. "He had faith that the people would come to the rescue and save the Government."[76] The Governor then introduced General Dumont, famous for his

[73] Dunn, *Indiana and Indianans*, III, 1411. Riley gave this tribute upon the occasion of Mrs. Harrison's death, October 25, 1892.

[74] Indianapolis *Daily Journal,* July 12, 1862.

[75] Indianapolis *Daily Journal,* July 14, 1862.

[76] *Ibid.*

early rout of the Confederate forces at Philippi.[77] His appearance was greeted with loud and prolonged cheering. Sensing the rising patriotic fervor of the crowd, the general keyed his remarks so as to endorse point by point Morton's appeal to furnish a goodly number of volunteers. The Governor had put the cards on the table and they were face up:

> Indiana must do her duty or our country is lost. From 5,000 to 6,000 Indianians had been lost to us defending the best government in the world, and if we now dishonor the cause in which they sacrificed their lives, we disgrace their memory.[78]

At this point, according to the newspaper reporters, William Wallace and Benjamin Harrison returned from addressing the larger meeting at the State House Grove. Both were immediately called upon to speak. Wallace rose first and captured the crowd by his sincerity. He explained how "on the day before Mr. Benjamin Harrison and [myself] had been appealed to by Governor Morton to give [our] services to the country." Hence, he said, he was convinced that "the hour had come when every man should respond to his country's call for volunteers." He concluded by disclosing the fact that he had already volunteered and was ready to go "with a knapsack on his back and a musket in hand."

Benjamin Harrison spoke with equal simplicity and sincerity. The *Journal* recorded his remarks as follows:

> Benjamin Harrison, Esq., Reporter of the Supreme Court, said that his determination to volunteer was the result of deliberate judgment. He had calculated the cost and though the sacrifices to him were great, both in a personal and a business point of view, he had determined to take the step and he would keep his word. He could not weigh the questions of profit or tender ties of home against the duty he owed his Government. And he had no more interest in the country than any of those to whom he was speaking, and it came home to all. He trusted many would give their names now, and that their example would work a good leaven in the hearts of his hearers that would make it uncomfortable for those who can go to remain at home.[79]

[77] "At Philippi the Confederates were completely surprised by Cols. Kelley and Dumont, and beat so hasty a retreat that the affair received the local name of the 'Philippi Races'." See Rossiter Johnson, *Campfire and Battlefield* (New York, 1894), p. 45.

[78] Indianapolis *Daily Journal*, July 14, 1862.

[79] *Ibid.* At the conclusion of Harrison's speech, the recruiting books were opened at both meetings. The *Journal* reported that "with energetic efforts two companies are to be raised in as many weeks in this city and county."

At the conclusion of Harrison's speech, a number signified their intention of volunteering, while still another group subscribed over $1,500 "to aid in recruiting and for support of the families of those enlisting." The impetus given to the raising of the Seventieth Regiment by this meeting was immeasurable.

On July 14, recruiting officers were appointed in all the congressional districts of the state, with power to enlist men for the term of "three years, or during the war."[80] In Indianapolis "the stars and stripes were flung to the breeze from a number of windows," and so lively was the recruiting that two days later indications were that the city and the county would furnish at least three companies.[81]

During the first week, two factors combined to keep the fires of patriotism burning brightly. First were the various bounties, totaling some $70, offered to every man who was accepted by the mustering officer.[82] This was the initial security needed by men who were leaving families behind them. And there was considerable appeal in an advertisement of Harrison's, indicating that his recruiting office was his own law office, and adding the exhortation:

Boys, think quick, and decide as patriots should in such an emergency. Fathers, cease to restrain the ardor of your sons, whose patriotic impulses prompt them to aid our country in its hour of trials. Ladies, give the stout and hearty young men who caught your smiles, to understand that "the brave alone deserve the fair."[83]

While his days were devoted to business pursuits as well as to the task of enlisting friends and neighbors, Harrison frequently spent the evening in speech-making. According to the press, these oratorical efforts were productive of volunteers, but after July

80 Samuel Merrill, *The Seventieth Indiana Volunteer Infantry* (Indianapolis, 1900), p. 1.

81 Indianapolis *Daily Journal,* July 16, 1862. "Lt. Benj. Harrison received many accessories to his list, and his office presented a lively appearance." The other counties besides Marion were Hendricks, Johnson, and Shelby. All were active in raising companies.

82 Indianapolis *Daily Journal,* July 18, 1862. Reporting on Harrison's Co. A, the paper said: "Three responsible gentlemen have agreed to obligate themselves to pay $50 to each of the men with family who enlist in this company. In addition the county pays $10 to each recruit, and the city will make a similar appropriation."

83 *Ibid.*

20, patriotic speeches were not needed. A new stimulus was found to foster Indiana's growing war fever: the daily headlines.[84] They sounded the alarm of the rapid Southern advance toward Indiana, and soon editorials appeared: "Indiana Invaded," "Newburgh Taken," "Evansville Threatened," "Rebels in Possession of Henderson, Kentucky," and "Up Hoosiers and Defend Your Homes." Such warnings carried more sting than did the challenge of a patriotic speaker, and they reached a wider audience.

Under these circumstances, it was less than two weeks before Second Lieutenant Harrison was ready to file his muster roll with the Adjutant General. The document listed eighty-five members, including officers, non-commissioned officers and privates. Upon its presentation, Governor Morton commissioned Harrison "to the office of Captain in and for the 70th Regiment . . . on the 22nd day of July."[85] This promotion was doubly appreciated in the Harrison household, for the new Captain could choose his brother-in-law, the experienced and reliable Henry Scott, as a First Lieutenant in the outfit.[86] That evening, Company A, joined by four other newly recruited companies, reported to Colonel Burgess on the commons northwest of the old state fair grounds. Here the Seventieth Indiana located their camp.

Having secured for his men the services of an experienced drillmaster from Chicago,[87] Captain Harrison did not immediately report to camp. Actually, there were many bits of unfinished business that occupied his attention, and he could care for these while "assisting in enlisting the other companies completing my regiment."[88] The most difficult task was obtaining a competent substitute to handle his Reporter's duties. His family income depended mainly upon the successful conduct of this office. Fortunately, the man whom Harrison desired most and the one whom he approached first, John Caven, accepted the trust. Im-

[84] "The War in Kentucky," "Morgan Captures Cynthiana," "The Guerrillas 25,500 Strong," "Bridges Burned," "An Entire Company Killed or Taken Prisoner." Indianapolis *Daily Journal*, July 19, 1862.

[85] This signed commission is preserved in Harrison MSS, Vol. 4, 681.

[86] Indianapolis *Daily Journal*, July 23, 24, 1862; also Harrison MSS, Vol. 4.

[87] Wallace, *op. cit.*, pp. 181–82. The drillmaster's pay came out of Harrison's own pocket. He wrote afterwards: "I enlisted a Company myself in 1862, and spent a good deal of money in doing it." B. Harrison to Capt. Joseph Beckman, April 1, 1888, Harrison MSS, Vol. 24, 4959 (Tibbott transcript).

[88] *Ibid.*

mediately, but without legal contract,[89] Harrison designated him Deputy Reporter.

There was one other pivotal figure in Harrison's plan to secure Carrie and the children from want while he was at the front. This was Fishback, his devoted law partner. The young officer was faced with a dilemma which Fishback himself characterized aptly when he wrote: "I must confess your example has inspired me with the duty of going myself as much as your advice has inclined me to remain."[90] Although there seemed to be no ready solution to this problem, unforeseen events determined Fishback to remain "and practice law as formerly in the style of Harrison and Fishback."[91] Harrison wrote to Carrie:

Tell Mr. Fishback . . . he and my other friends must manage the matter of my Reporter's office this fall as seems best. I hope he will succeed in making sufficient collections to keep you well supplied with money.[92]

By early August, everything was in readiness. The Seventieth Indiana Regiment was not only full, but had a surplus of 250 men;[93] and, as far as Harrison personally was concerned, adequate provision had been made for his family, his profession and his elective office. Consequently, on August 8, after being commissioned a full Colonel,[94] Benjamin Harrison assumed his command. Though he was a novice in military drill and discipline, his appointment received a favorable press. The *Journal* observed:

Col. Ben Harrison will make a good regimental commander, having the requisite amount of energy and ability to apply himself to the new work before him, and with a little experience will master those details of drill and discipline so essential to the good management of a thousand men.[95]

89 Harrison Scrapbook, Vol. 52, p. 94, the testimony of Caven in an unidentified newspaper clipping. The fact that there was no legal or registered agreement proved a serious oversight, once the matter of Harrison's successor reached the Indiana Supreme Court.

90 W. P. Fishback to Col. Benjamin Harrison, August 25, 1862, Harrison MSS, Vol. 4, 696.

91 *Ibid.*

92 Benjamin Harrison to his wife, August 21, 1862, Harrison MSS, Vol. 4, 689–91.

93 Indianapolis *Daily Journal,* August 8, 1862.

94 This commission is also preserved in Harrison MSS, Vol. 4.

95 Indianapolis *Daily Journal,* August 9, 1862.

Four days later, Harrison and his regiment were under marching orders to join the Union concentration of troops at Louisville, toward which a Confederate army under Bragg was then moving.[96] Confusion struck the city, as numerous friends and relatives of the members of the regiment began to arrive from all parts of central Indiana. Some came too late even to enjoy one of the four dress parades which Harrison and his men staged before breaking camp.[97]

The memorable evening was that of August 12 and, although sorrow vied with patriotism, in some respects it was a gala event:

The band of the 19th Infantry was on the ground and officiated at the dress parade, discoursing most appropriate music. After the parade William P. Fishback came forward with a beautifully wrought sword which he presented to Col. Harrison on behalf of some friends of this city, accompanying the act with an appropriate speech, to which Harrison responded feelingly and eloquently.[98]

Not to be outdone, the ladies of Indianapolis prepared a colorful regimental banner and delegated Judge David McDonald to present it to the men through their Colonel. On behalf of his regiment, Harrison, "in becoming terms," accepted the gift. The principal civilian address of the evening was by John L. Ketcham, another close friend of Colonel Harrison. Ketcham justified the cause in which the men were about to engage, and concluded by presenting a huge American flag, "another gift of the fair ladies." For the third time Colonel Harrison replied, calling upon his men, as a reporter related,

. . . to answer with three cheers, that they would never turn their backs upon that flag, but defend it to the last. This appeal was answered by three cheers and a tiger, most heartily given by all the men.

The color guard was then called up and the flags turned over to it with that injunction on the part of the Colonel, to protect them in the hour of danger at every hazard.

96 *House Document No. 154*, p. 111; also Indianapolis *Daily Journal,* August 11, 1862.

97 Actually, their real military assignment had occurred when Harrison's and Meredith's companies marched into the Union Depot and escorted a trainload of Confederate prisoners to Camp Morton (August 5, 1862). The *Journal* of August 7, 1862, remarked: "it was the first military duty done by these two new companies and it was well done."

98 Indianapolis *Daily Journal,* August 13, 1862.

Col. Harrison's concluding address was most eloquent and patriotic, and vociferous cheering followed its conclusion.[99]

When the ceremonies were over and the last visitor had left the camp, the hour was so late that the departure was rescheduled for nine o'clock the following morning.

Promptly at seven the next morning, Wednesday, August 13, the regiment broke camp. At its head rode Colonel Harrison, astride "a fine sorrel horse." Sidewalks and cross streets were crowded as the men took up their line of march from the camp to the Jeffersonville, Indiana, train. The regiment, new Enfield rifles in hand,[100] reached the train between eight and nine o'clock, but it was long after ten before the men were arranged in the cars and made ready for starting.

Company E claimed the honor of shedding the first blood, when, just as the engine was about to start, Private William Cooper, with an eager fist, taught a citizen not to utter unpatriotic sentiments while farewells were being spoken. Again, while the Louisville-bound train was wending its way southward, a huge bull planted himself on the track and disputed its passage. The next moment the regiment had bowled over its second opponent.[101] The men laughed boisterously over the incident, but they were not lulled into any false sense of security about what might await them.

At home, reports of the rapid rebel advance were headlined in the press: "The crisis is alarming. . . . Gov. Morton is moving with all energy to meet it . . . all the troops that can move will be sent at once to Kentucky . . . and they will go amply prepared in all but discipline. . . ."[102] With her hero husband in the midst of danger, Carrie spent many a restless night.

99 *Ibid.*

100 Merrill, *op. cit.*, p. 4.

101 *Ibid.;* also Indianapolis *Daily Journal,* August 14, 1862.

102 Indianapolis *Daily Journal,* August 16, 1862. Even as the regiment marched to the train on the 13th, bystanders commented favorably on its ability, but everyone added: "If it can have a week or two of instruction before engaging actively on the field, it will have acquired a proficiency in drill that will have prepared it for almost any emergency." *Ibid.*, August 14, 1862.

CHAPTER IX

The Soil of Kentucky

THERE USUALLY COMES a moment in the conscious development of every human soul when some serious choice, or important decision, or difficult renunciation must be made. Such a moment came to Benjamin Harrison and to his regiment of Hoosier Volunteers while they rode the Louisville-bound cars on that hot August day in 1862. They had ample time for reflection.

As the train rumbled and lurched southward from Indianapolis, crawling laboriously, few realized better than this freshly commissioned colonel that the group under his charge was a regiment in name only. He knew that he was confronted with a difficult task, and he was particularly conscious that it would require a thorough organization on the part of himself and his staff to make soldiers out of men accustomed to the comforts of home. Perhaps nothing less than a complete mental and physical revolution would be necessary before these mechanics, farmers and business men could be fashioned into a well-drilled and disciplined unit.

The scene at the Indianapolis depot was a particularly trying time for loved ones never before separated. Several claimed that they would rather go into the hottest battle than go through the departure ceremonies again.[1] Yet the ruling spirit of the regiment, according to one correspondent from the ranks, was "not a feeling of fear, but a holy reverence for the sacredness of home, which will nerve men to strike harder blows, take better aim, and make longer marches, than the merely instructed soldier."[2] As this is the moral fiber out of which good soldiers are made,

[1] Indianapolis *Daily Journal,* August 20, 1862. These sentiments appeared in a letter written to the editor on August 16, 1862.
[2] *Ibid.*

Harrison concluded that, though his task was difficult, it was far from impossible.

This journey of the regiment to Louisville was, as Ben wrote to Carrie, "safe and reasonably pleasant . . . we were greeted at every town and farmhouse with cheers and waving handkerchiefs."[3] Indeed, along the entire route and at every station, it was evident from the "anxiety manifested, the moistened eyes, and the sustained applause of almost every community that the 70th carried with it dear friends from every county in the District."[4]

When the troop train arrived at Jeffersonville, Indiana, an aide of Brigadier General J. T. Boyle presented Harrison with orders to proceed directly to Louisville. The regiment proceeded to the ferry, crossed the Ohio River, and marched through Louisville to a large farm some three miles outside the city. This was a fairly open area and close to the Nashville railroad depot. It marked the end of a tiring trip. "Our men were so fatigued," Harrison relates, "that they did not put up their tents but turned in on the ground. Some of them did not take their blankets out of their knap sacks but just used it for a pillow."[5]

Complete physical exhaustion guaranteed sleep. Colonel Harrison, however, was a bit perplexed, and before yielding to sleep he made a rapid mental survey of the situation in which he found himself. Here at his side were sleeping more than a thousand men, "the first into the field"[6] under Lincoln's call of July 1. They were encamped now in "country overrun by enemies of the Government," and Ben pondered the fact that during the entire three-mile march through Louisville "most of the citizens looked on in sullen silence,"[7] though from one residence "ladies

---

[3] Benjamin Harrison to his wife, August 16, 1862, Harrison MSS, Vol. 4.

[4] Indianapolis *Daily Journal*, August 20, 1862. The Indianapolis *Daily Sentinel*, the Democratic organ of the city and state, carried very little comment on the Seventieth until much later in the war.

[5] Benjamin Harrison to his wife, August 14, 1862, Harrison MSS, Vol. 4. A more detailed description appeared in the Indianapolis *Daily Journal*, August 20, 1862.

[6] Samuel Merrill, *The Seventieth Indiana Volunteer Infantry*, p. 4. The troops were in Louisville less than a month from the time the first man was enlisted. Also in Indianapolis *Daily Journal*, March 14, 1901, it was reaffirmed that this was "the first regiment from any Northern state to enter the region where disloyalty prevailed."

[7] Merrill, *op. cit.*, p. 5: "Little enthusiasm was manifested in Louisville. It seemed to be regarded as a small matter for Indianians to come armed for the protection of Kentuckians from robbers and murderers, though what Union feeling is manifested, appears to be genuine. But there is not enough of it!"

came out bearing waiters full of cakes and pies, which they offered to the boys." Only the "Negroes could not restrain their
joyous laughter and cheers."[8] This sobering first contact with the
"secesh" mentality failed to dampen Harrison's enthusiasm or
lessen the pride he felt. Late in the night he wrote Carrie his
secret thoughts:

> We are proud of her [Indiana] and hope to make her proud of us
> before we return from the war. I hope you all remember us at home
> and that many prayers go up to God daily for my Regiment and for
> me. Ask Him for me in prayer, my dear wife, first that He will enable
> me to bear myself as a good soldier of Jesus Christ; second, that He will
> give me valor and skill to conduct myself so as to honor my country
> and my friends; and lastly, if consistent with His holy will, I may be
> brought "home again" to the dear loved ones, if not, that the rich
> consolation of His grace may be made sufficient for me and for those
> who survive. . . . We will improve the time of our stay . . . and be better
> prepared to render effective service when called upon.[9]

In his concluding sentence Harrison was merely voicing the
almost universal belief that the regiment would be kept some
time at Louisville. Yet, twenty-four hours after arrival, a courier
from headquarters handed the Colonel marching orders that
were effective immediately. The regiment's destination was Bowling Green, Kentucky, a strategic military center located some
thirty miles above the Tennessee border. A soldier has left his
vivid impressions of the action-filled moments after the order to
strike tents was issued:

> In five minutes Col. Harrison had out his troops to prepare for
> marching, and in an hour our tents were struck, 40 rounds of ammuni-
> tion drawn, and the entire Regiment in line, a drenching rain falling
> at the time. It was an encouraging sight to see the boys with their
> heads erect, weathering the storms like veterans. We marched to the
> depot and took passage in a train, miserable, filthy box cars,[10] some
> of them without seats, and what seats they had, appeared to have been
> stolen from country school houses.[11]

8 Indianapolis *Daily Journal*, August 20, 1862.

9 B. Harrison to his wife, August 21, 1862, Harrison MSS, Vol. 4.

10 Merrill, *op. cit.*, p. 5, related: "these cars had been used to convey cattle, and
the author of Knickerbocker's History of New York would have described them as
fragrantly cushioned for military occupants."

11 Indianapolis *Daily Journal*, August 20, 1862.

Harrison recorded the fact that his regiment finally "got off at 6 P.M. . . . all on one train with one engine." In no sense, however, could he call their departure "an encouraging sight." To his wife he also confided his feelings of personal chagrin:

I was too much mortified and amused to see the ignorance and awkwardness of some of our men and officers when I gave the order for the battalion to load before getting on the cars at Louisville. Some of them got the wrong end of the ball down and some rammed the paper down into the ball and got it lodged. I got mad and went along the lines scolding, but finally concluded to take it good naturedly and make a joke out of it.[12]

This move to Bowling Green was fraught with more than ordinary peril. Danger was imminent because of the activity of Confederate Colonel John H. Morgan, head of a marauding cavalry band of 1,200.[13] Only two days before Harrison was ordered from Louisville, Colonel Morgan and his hard-riding rebel band had captured Gallatin, Tennessee, and by destroying railroad bridges and several sections of track had effectively severed communications between Nashville and Louisville.[14] Union intelligence reported that Morgan and his command were headed north from Gallatin, and it was conjectured that Bowling Green was his next military objective.

Harrison was fully apprised of Morgan's northern movement, but this knowledge in no way lessened the danger of attack and interference. While the tyros of the Seventieth Indiana were willing and eager for actual combat, the sobering fact still remained that their familiarity with firearms was restricted to hunting equipment. Weapons of war still mystified them. As Harrison and his men jolted along that night of August 14 through "an enemy's country with raw recruits lying on loaded guns,"[15] it

12 B. Harrison to his wife, August 16, 1862, Harrison MSS, Vol. 4.

13 R. U. Johnson and C. C. Buel (eds.), *Battles and Leaders of the Civil War* (New York, 1888), III, Part 1, pp. 26–28. Perhaps the best account of Morgan's Cavalry during the Bragg invasion of Kentucky is given by Brig. Gen. Basil W. Duke, C.S.A. He relates that Morgan's duty "was the destruction of the railroad track and bridges between Nashville and Bowling Green, for the purpose of retarding Buell's movements when the latter should begin his retreat to Louisville."

14 *Ibid.,* p. 39.

15 Merrill, *op. cit.,* p. 5.

might be difficult to decide whether the danger was greater from within or from without. Harrison himself confessed that "we rode in constant expectation of being pitched into some creek, or riddled by musketry. We all slept quietly, however, trusting, in my case at least, to a good providence to protect us."[16]

On the home front, however, and especially at Indianapolis, the friends of the regiment were filled with alarm. No sooner had the news of the assignment to Bowling Green reached the city than the rumor was strong that "Harrison's men were badly used up by Morgan and taken prisoners."[17] This report worried Carrie greatly, and her fears mounted frantically until allayed by her first note from her husband in the field: "We arrived here safely this morning about nine A.M. and am now, after a hard day's work, getting our camp arranged in order. I have only time to write this brief note to tell you of our safety."[18]

After the flood of false rumors had subsided, Indianapolis rested easily in the truth that the initial assignment in enemy territory had been executed without incident. Harrison's report from Bowling Green was to the effect that they were "pleasantly encamped on a beautiful slope near the town,"[19] and the men were soon writing home that they were "well supplied with all that a soldier can wish."[20] Translated into the reality of camp life, this latter report signified the men could acquire everything desirable in the eating line: "peach cobblers, chicken pies, milk and so forth ... for the boys are all flush and can't stand the pressure of sheet iron biscuit and fat bacon."[21]

During the first week of encampment the regiment was kept under arms for several hours each day. The frequency of alarms both day and night, the excitement and tenseness of the camp rising from Morgan's supposed proximity, gave a zest for drilling that nothing else could supply. After only a week, according to one observer, the Seventieth Indiana in the promptness of its

16 Benj. Harrison to his wife, August 16, 1862, Harrison MSS, Vol. 4.

17 Benj. Harrison to his wife, August 21, 1862, Harrison MSS, Vol. 4, 689–91.

18 Benj. Harrison to his wife, August 15, 1862, Harrison MSS, Vol. 4.

19 Ben also told Carrie that Morgan's forces, or at least his main force, was probably still at Gallatin, Tennessee, some forty miles to the south. He thought, however, a "few of his assassins were prowling about." Benj. Harrison to his wife, August 16, 1862, Harrison MSS, Vol. 4.

20 Indianapolis Daily Journal, August 21, 1862. P. T. J. M. to the Editor.

21 Indianapolis Daily Sentinel, September 4, 1862. Letter to the Editor.

movement and in soldierly appearance "would rival many older regiments."[22]

Upon arrival at Bowling Green, Harrison's regiment had been assigned to a provisional brigade under the command of Colonel S. D. Bruce, a pleasant gentleman from Kentucky.[23] Bruce instructed Harrison that, as his prime task was to fashion an effective fighting unit, neither discipline nor tactical instruction was to be minimized. His confidence in their numerical superiority was shared by Harrison, who lost no time in informing his wife that "we have abundant forces here I think to whip him [Morgan] handsomely . . . at least we would like to try our chance with him."[24]

Perhaps the most substantial reason why this young and inexperienced colonel could indulge his feeling of security was that this provisional stop-gap brigade was now occupying the almost impregnable fortifications constructed earlier by Confederate General Simon B. Buckner and 10,000 men.[25] Buckner's fortifications, moreover, were still in first-rate condition, and, if an attack had been made by Morgan's guerrillas or by his entire force, the place would have been a bulwark of defense. It is little wonder, then, that these troops, although still unchristened by battle, "were on the lookout for lively times."[26]

The succeeding weeks of camp life at Bowling Green served as an effective proving ground for character training as well as for military drill. Only on Sunday was the strict daily order for drilling somewhat relaxed. Otherwise, reveille was sounded at five, and each company had an hour's drill before the six-o'clock breakfast. A second drill period of two hours' duration was preceded by mounting guard, officers' drill and police duty. Nor was the afternoon routine any less strenuous: dinner at twelve noon; non-commissioned officers' drill from one to two; battalion drill from two to four; supper at five; dress parade from six to seven; roll call at eight and lights out at nine.[27]

22 Indianapolis *Daily Journal,* August 21, 1862.

23 *Ibid.,* November 7, 1862.

24 Benj. Harrison to his wife, August 16, 1862, Harrison MSS, Vol. 4.

25 Rossiter Johnson, *Campfire and Battlefield,* p. 76. As a result of the Battle of Mill Springs and the fall of Fort Henry, Buckner was compelled to abandon Bowling Green, and the area fell into Union hands.

26 Indianapolis *Daily Journal.* Bode to the Editor, August 20, 1862.

27 Merrill, *op. cit.,* pp. 6 ff.

The road to military perfection was steep and difficult, and what the young soldiers hated above all was the rigid discipline. Even the regimental historian, Samuel Merrill, felt compelled to characterize his colonel's attitude on discipline as distinctly severe:

> Discipline was severe, for the commander, Colonel Benjamin Harrison, knew that without discipline a thousand men are no better than a mob. He proposed to form a battalion that in the day of battle would move as if animated by one soul. He had the intellect and will, and he accomplished the work.[28]

During these months of intense preparation Harrison and his command were fortunate in having the services of Major S. C. Vance, a superior drillmaster.[29] Under his able supervision the troops moved with clock-like precision, and before long Colonel Harrison manifested his pleasure at their progress. With a certain amount of pride and a sense of personal achievement, he informed Carrie that his "field and staff officers are getting along very pleasantly . . . the utmost harmony and good feeling prevails. I have no apprehension of any trouble or disagreement. We are enforcing a very strict discipline in the camp and the Regiment is progressing very finely in the drill."[30]

Several compliments were paid to the regiment for "good order and soldierly bearing," he told her, but the young colonel quickly discovered that, although the good name of the regiment was being secured, it was at the price of his own popularity. A real crisis developed over the use of whiskey by the soldiers. Colonel Bruce had "drawn the strings tight on saloons"[31] in Bowling Green. Such establishments were "forbidden to sell or to give soldiers, (commissioned officers are not considered soldiers . . . they get their 'nips' at all times), nor can a commissioned officer treat or give to a private." The soldiers found extreme difficulty getting their "morning's warming."[32] Naturally, all kinds of dodges were

---

[28] *Ibid.*, p. 71.

[29] Major Vance, of Indianapolis, received his commission on August 9, 1862. He resigned on April 10, 1863, and re-entered the service as colonel of the 132nd Regiment.

[30] Benj. Harrison to his wife, August 21, 1862, Harrison MSS, Vol. 4.

[31] Indianapolis *Daily Journal*, November 7, 1862.

[32] These details are from a letter dated Bowling Green, Ky., October 25, 1862, published in the Indianapolis *Daily Sentinel*, November 7, 1862.

practiced, and, when successful, proved detrimental to the good order of the regiment. The problem grew more serious, and when the following incident took place, Colonel Harrison took a very firm stand. The Indianapolis people read the story this way:

A young commissioned officer who had fellow feeling for a fellow soldier, was standing with a non-commissioned officer . . . [on] a cold, damp, ugly day, debating that interesting question how they could get a smile. They decided on the following trick as worth a trial: . . . Straps walked in . . . pouring out about three fingers, drank half . . . stopped to flatter the bar creature on keeping such excellent Burb. In walked Mr. Non-Com. with a note for Mr. Com. who left this standing on the counter while he read it. Non-Commissioned hurried down what was left and walked out . . . they smiled several times and at several places that evening.[33]

Similar instances of misconduct angered Colonel Bruce to such an extent that Harrison confided to Carrie "I think he has taken a strong dislike to the Regiment and will have further trouble with it."[34] In reality, Bruce was not too displeased, but he did seize the opportunity of impressing Harrison with the necessity of strict observance. The younger man was susceptible to the advice of Bruce, and by mid-September Harrison had shown himself a stern disciplinarian and had overcome much of the feeling that his subordinates had harbored against him. He wrote to his law partner, William Fishback:

I believe that you will find that every officer has come to respect me and that traces of difficulty have been obliterated. I have had no trouble in discipline of any company but Capt. Meredith's. He has a good many hard city boys and is a *very poor* disciplinarian himself. . . . I have broken two of his corporals, put one of his lieutenants under arrest, and have a large squad always in the guardhouse. They are beginning to know me now.[35]

Harrison's rough handling of the men in Captain Meredith's company had a sobering effect not only on the men disciplined but also on the captain himself, whose change of heart left a lasting impression on the regiment. Meredith had been thoroughly

[33] Indianapolis *Daily Sentinel*, November 7, 1862.
[34] Benj. Harrison to his wife, September 5, 1862, Harrison MSS, Vol. 4.
[35] Benjamin Harrison to W. P. Fishback, September 7, 1862, Harrison MSS, Vol. 4.

humiliated by Harrison's reprimand and punishment. Accordingly, it required courage as well as character before the chastised captain could address himself to his colonel again. Having found himself, he wrote to Harrison:

It is not for myself alone I plead, but for my wife and children and my parents. I am as sincerely anxious to reform, Col., as you are to have me reform . . . for the sake of those who love me, let me "try again." I will take any obligation you may dictate to abstain entirely from the use of liquor in all shapes during my connection with the army, and will take it in the face of the whole regiment. I do not pretend to excuse myself, I only ask a chance to redeem myself, to make myself worthy of your esteem.[36]

From that day there was a perceptible improvement in the discipline of the Seventieth Indiana. Camp Ben Harrison at Bowling Green, Kentucky, quickly earned a reputation for sobriety and respectability, so that, upon the arrival of such distinguished lady visitors as Mrs. Harrison, Mrs. Vance and Mrs. Will Wallace, an edifying good order prevailed.[37]

September saw Ben knuckle down to the two principal objectives: that his men should be finished soldiers and that their leader should be a competent tactician. With unfailing regularity he marched and drilled his troops by day; by night, long after taps had sounded, he studied and perfected himself in theoretical tactics and in the art of war. Without military knowledge in July, this young lawyer had, by the end of September, grown perceptibly in his new profession.

Early in the month the commander and his men felt "quite gloomy about the news from the Potomac."[38] For them this definitely was their first dark hour in the war. Nor did Harrison's correspondents from Indianapolis send any encouraging news. Fishback was not only deeply despondent but also highly critical of the Administration in Washington:

[36] Meredith's plight was a sad one. On August 24, 1862, he wrote: "I have been in disgrace now nearly six days, hardly feeling justified in speaking to a fellow officer . . . treated very cooly by many of them, and have suffered the most bitter mortification." W. Meredith to B. Harrison, Harrison MSS, Vol. 4.
[37] Indianapolis Daily Sentinel, August 31, 1862. This was Carrie's first visit with Ben in the field. The ladies called for all the mending the boys had to do, fixed all the things up, and took thanks for pay, which the boys heartily gave.
[38] Benj. Harrison to his wife, September 5, 1862, Harrison MSS, Vol. 4.

We have divers rumors here from different seats of war. It is said the President is fearful, which means that the Cabinet have been un-amused at one of his dirty, flat . . . yarns. We are informed that the Rebels are "bagged" . . . "in a trap," etc. . . . but the report has shown in several similar cases that the game has been strong enough to carry away trap, bag and all. After our generals have done skirmishing with and outguessing each other, we may expect to hear of some strategy that will confound the foe.[39]

Another week of watchful waiting passed at Bowling Green before a faint ray of hope appeared. Finally, on the 19th, a rumor that "McClellan has whipped Jackson" lifted Harrison's spirits. His new-found hope he communicated to Carrie: "I do not fully credit it . . . [but] if it be true, and we can whip them speedily and terribly in Kentucky, the darkness will be turned into day and my hopes of speedy success be more cheering than ever before."[40] A week later, the rumor was confirmed; the news had been despatched to Washington that "Lee had been shockingly whipped . . . with his loss at 15,000."[41] He read in the Louisville and Indianapolis papers at least part of McClellan's jubilant wire to General Winfield Scott which stated: "R. E. Lee in command. The rebels routed, and retreating in disorder this morning. We are pursuing closely and taking many prisoners."[42] Scott's en-thusiastic acknowledgment was surpassed only by Lincoln's tele-graphic accolade to McClellan: "Your dispatch of today received. God bless you and all with you. Destroy the rebel army if pos-sible."[43]

As usual, Carrie was the first to share in her husband's joy and revived anticipation of a quick Union victory:

The loyal people of this vicinity and the soldiers were highly elated with the good news we received yesterday from the Potomac, and in-deed from all divisions of our army. If the armies of Kirby Smith . . . [and] Bragg care to be *thoroughly* defeated in Kentucky and "little Mac" will only follow up the rebels to Richmond, this Civil War can be speedily ended. I hope the people of our country will recognize God's hand in this deliverance and not boast themselves of the valor

39 William P. Fishback to Benj. Harrison, September 12, 1862, Harrison MSS, Vol. 4.
40 Benj. Harrison to his wife, September 19, 1862, Harrison MSS, Vol. 4.
41 Kenneth P. Williams, *Lincoln Finds a General*, I, 383.
42 *Official Records*, Series I, Vol. XIX, Part ii (Serial No. 28), 294–95.
43 *Official Records, op. cit.*, pp. 27, 53.

of our soldiers and the skill of our leaders and refuse to see the good providence of the God of battles which has now made that valor and skill efficient.[44]

Subsequent events diminished this confidence. There was even cause for despair when his "little Mac," who could "have thrown against Lee a force which would have utterly overwhelmed him," procrastinated and eventually lost a golden opportunity for a quick and possibly decisive Northern victory.[45]

Under the circumstances, however, Harrison could ill afford to carp at McClellan's undistinguished record at this period. The Seventieth Indiana, through no fault of its own, had also compiled a war record that was in no sense enviable. Even local Indianapolis newspapers began to picture the regiment as "skylarking all day" and at night "sleeping as sound as if they were in their old camp"[46] at the Hoosier capital. The troops themselves were bitterly disappointed with their uneventful existence, especially when other Indiana volunteers found themselves in the heat of battle despite General Buell's cautious and severely criticized opposition to the rebel advance under General Bragg.[47] One of the regiment's imaginatively inclined members wrote:

Columbus was not more rejoiced when the Islands of his long dream rose before him than we were to see the advance of Gen. Buell's army rolling into Bowling Green yesterday morning.

We have for the last week been feeling rather over conscious about the lungs, being the only regiment here. The other troops stationed here were sent to Louisville, leaving us to perform all the picket and provost duty, which is very interesting, such as guarding cornfields and peach orchards.[48]

Toward the close of September the Bowling Green Camp grew alive at the prospect of combat. This sudden change was due

[44] Benj. Harrison to his wife, September 26, 1862, Harrison MSS, Vol. 4.

[45] Williams, *op. cit.*, II, 497, 816–817. For a more friendly interpretation of McClellan see H. J. Eckenrode and Bryan Conrad, *George B. McClellan: The Man Who Saved the Union* (Chapel Hill, N. C., 1941).

[46] Indianapolis *Daily Sentinel*, September 4, 1862.

[47] The Indianapolis *Daily Journal*, October 1, 1862, carried a sharp indictment against Buell, when it was prematurely reported that he had been removed: "The salvation of the West depends upon the removal of so inefficient a General. The army despises him, and well they may. From the beginning he has been a laggard . . . he never meant to fight Bragg. He had plenty of opportunities to cut him all to pieces."

[48] Indianapolis *Daily Sentinel*, October 10, 1862.

largely to the pressure of the ubiquitous Colonel John Morgan.[49] His forces resumed their program of tearing up railroad tracks and burning bridges, with consequent great inconvenience to Federal forces stationed in Kentucky. Deprived of communication with Indianapolis for nearly a month, the Seventieth Indiana found itself the victim of a new disease, easily diagnosed as homesickness. No one was spared, though some attacks were milder than others. Colonel Harrison was among the more serious victims:

How precious home seems to us all now that we are strangers to all of its comforts! The tender affection you have ever felt for me, and which I so often crossed with wounds, is now the source of my strongest longing . . . and the dear children whose caresses sometimes seemed obtrusive when I enjoyed them everyday, now in their dumb images excite the strongest longing to feel the pressure of their little arms and lips—Dear Gifts of God, a wife and two dear babes.[50]

Only marching orders could shake off nostalgic musings. They came on September 30, 1862.

Harrison was in one of his characteristically reflective moods when he wrote his wife that "a soldier can never guess what the orders of tomorrow may be."[51] He had spoken advisedly, inasmuch as his own intelligence department consistently reported: "Bands of guerrillas within 20 or 30 miles of Bowling Green."

Colonel Bruce, Harrison's superior officer, had been informed that Captain Dortch, a Confederate leader of some local renown, was in the vicinity of Russellville, Kentucky. Evidently, the rebel commander was given to understand that there were no Federals nearer than Bowling Green, 30 miles away, and that these forces

49 To use the well-chosen language of Catherine Merrill: "Morgan was at home everywhere. He entered at night the house of a friend within Federal lines, slept in the best bed, and departed with only a sly recognition. He walked on the streets of a town which was full of Federal soldiers, chaffered with the tradespeople, gave them a wink, and received from them the result of their observations as to the numbers or movements of the enemy. He went into a Federal telegraphic office, sent a dispatch to a friend, or an enemy in the North, and walked off unsuspected, or with threats imposed silence until his safety was secured. He waylaid a train, destroyed the cars and took the passengers prisoners. But his most common performance was a sudden swoop on Federal pickets." Quoted in Merrill, *op. cit.,* p. 18.

50 B. Harrison to his wife, September 26, 1862, Harrison MSS, Vol. 4.

51 He repeats this same idea in the following letters to his wife: September 9, 19, 20, and 26, 1862, Harrison MSS, Vol. 4.

were assigned almost exclusively to guard duty. Consequently, Dortch resolved to venture into Russellville "for a frolic and a few days rest." The only precaution he deemed necessary to prevent surprise was the burning of a little railroad bridge at Auburn, 12 miles from Bowling Green.[52]

Early on the morning of the 30th, Bruce ordered Harrison to Russellville.[53] At nine o'clock, 500 men of the Seventieth Indiana and about one hundred from the Eighth Kentucky Cavalry and from Company K of the Sixtieth Indiana, all under the command of Colonel Harrison, tumbled into stock cars bound for Russellville. Extremely pressed for time Harrison, nevertheless, managed a short letter to Carrie:

God bless you all and strengthen me for the duties of the day . . . should I never see you and the dear children again, you must comfort yourself by the rich grace of God, which is *all* sufficient, and that the dear little ones be taught to meet me in heaven. Keep my memory green in their young hearts. Again God bless you. Yours as ever in the tenderest love.[54]

As the train approached the watering station at Auburn, Harrison's command encountered the partially destroyed bridge that spanned Black Lick ravine. The enemy had been at work, but not too effectively. In three hours the forty-foot structure was fully restored.[55] While the bridge was being repaired, Colonel Harrison detailed several searching parties to comb the vicinity for information and to cut off all possible communication with Russellville. These squads executed their task effectively. Not only had two companies surrounded the village and prevented

52 Wilbur F. Barclay, a lengthy, signed newspaper article in the Russellville *Herald and Enterprise*, April 9, 1890.

53 Merrill, *op. cit.*, p. 24. Colonel Bruce's information was that a new Confederate regiment was also raised at Russellville.

54 B. Harrison to his wife, October 2, 1862, Harrison MSS, Vol. 4.

55 In his official report to Colonel Bruce, Harrison highly commends "Captain Fisher of Co. I, being an old railroad builder, was designated by me to superintend the work, and right well did he justify the choice. In less than three hours he had felled the trees, put them in their place, and laid the rail upon the superstructure, so that the train passed safely over. I cannot commend too highly the skill and industry of Captain Fisher in so rapidly accomplishing this work without which the expedition must have been a failure. Captain Carson of Co. G also rendered valuable assistance in the work." A copy of this official report is in Merrill, *op. cit.*, pp. 27–31.

Photograph by George N. Barnard

BATTLEGROUND OF RESACA, GEORGIA

Lithograph by Kurry and Allison, 1889

BATTLE OF RESACA

information being sent to Russellville of the Federals' nearness, but they had also secured a strategically valuable diagram of the approaches to Russellville. Before departing from Auburn, Colonel Harrison drew up a plan of attack with Captains Givens and Morrow.

In his official report to Colonel Bruce, Harrison painstakingly described each incident connected with this prudent reconnaissance at Auburn. He had nothing but high commendation for the officer whom he had ordered to take a company and search thoroughly the house of Captain Wood of the Confederate Army. He gave explicit instructions to "collect axes, tools, etc." and to "capture any enemies lurking thereabouts."[56] What Harrison omitted in his report was the fact that Wood's dwelling was large and full of enemies—all females, the Captain being blessed with ten unmarried daughters. The regiment's historian was not so delicately inclined. He wrote that "the searchers were not to be envied, followed as they were from parlor to bedroom, from cellar to garret by beautiful anathematizing damsels."[57]

After detailing some fifty men to protect the bridge, the expedition headed for Russellville. Within two miles of the town, a "negro riding furiously along the side of the track" informed the Colonel that "rebels were then encamped in a grove on the righthand side of the track . . . about four hundred strong."[58] More important, they had had no notice of the oncoming expedition.

This was Harrison's first opportunity to exercise his book knowledge of military tactics. He threw off four companies under Major Vance on the left of the road. They were to come in on the rear of the town and block any attempted retreat. The youthful Colonel ordered the train to advance with the remainder of his command to within approximately one mile of the town. Here, as he related to his wife,

I threw off the residue of my troops, and turning off to the right of the railroad, through a cornfield, I deployed Co. A, Capt. Scott, as skirmishers, and advanced cautiously toward the rebel camp.[59]

56 Harrison to Bruce, October 1, 1862, cited in Merrill, *op. cit.*, p. 25.
57 *Ibid.*
58 B. Harrison to his wife, October 3, 1862, Harrison MSS, Vol. 4.
59 *Ibid.*

At what he deemed the proper moment, Harrison gave the order to advance and open fire. The attacking Hoosier battle line swept forward and fired briskly. The astonished foe could direct only a feeble return volley before they beat a hasty and confused retreat. Many attempted to flee through the town of Russellville and thus effect an escape by the back roads. Here they met Major Vance's command, which "opened upon them hotly in the streets."[60]

At the close of their first actual engagement, they were not ashamed of their record. They had "killed thirty five and wounded many more." The Seventieth suffered one casualty, but "took the rebel camp, forty-five good horses, about fifty guns, mostly short guns, a large number of saddles and other accoutrements too numerous to mention, besides a dozen prisoners."[61]

After Major Vance had successfully completed his assignment he joined Harrison, who now had possession of the public square and the main buildings of Russellville. Pickets were posted and squads detailed to search certain houses where escaped rebels were reported by Negroes to be in hiding. Harrison, accompanied by Captain Morrow, took personal charge of one of the searching parties, and thereby hangs an interesting tale nowhere to be found in the Colonel's official account to Bruce.

In his report to Colonel Bruce, Harrison devotes only one line to the results achieved by his searching party: "I succeeded in capturing ten prisoners, which number would have been largely increased, but night coming on, further search became impracticable."[62] Fast-approaching darkness, however, was only a partial explanation of why the search had to be abandoned. The remaining part of the story, and perhaps the most interesting section of it, was not revealed until almost a quarter of a century later.

Colonel Harrison had been informed that a Southern sympa-

60 *Ibid.* According to the official report, "Vance's troops caught sight of the fleeing rebels and were brought forward by the Major on the double quick, each company taking a different street, all debouching into that upon which the rebels were retreating. As the broken squads of rebel horsemen passed the posts of the respective companies they delivered their fire with great steadiness and precision, killing and wounding a large number." Merrill, *op. cit.,* p. 29.

61 B. Harrison to his wife, October 3, 1862, Harrison MSS, Vol. 4.

62 Harrison to Colonel Bruce, October 1, 1862, in Merrill, *op. cit.,* p. 30.

thizer named Dr. Barnes was responsible for burning the bridge at Auburn. Moreover, Addison Cash, a free Negro, gave Harrison to understand that Dr. Barnes had directly aided Captain Dortch and that this gentleman was now being harbored at Russellville by a rich and sympathetic Southern matron. Inasmuch as the doctor was a civilian, this charge was a serious one. If he were caught, "it subjected him to trial by court martial, and probable immediate execution under military law."[63] Thus was precipitated a struggle of wits. The young colonel wanted no mistakes made in this inquiry. He chose Captain Morrow, well known in Russellville and extremely familiar with the lay of the land, as his companion in the search. Harrison also took personal charge of the party which rapidly approached Aunt Lucy Blakely's house, the suspected refuge of Dr. Barnes.

Dr. Barnes, a man of high intelligence, clearly understood the seriousness of the charge against him. While in hiding on the outskirts of the town, he was alerted to the fact that Harrison was pursuing him. Doubting the security of his first sanctuary, Barnes hastily mounted a swift horse and made a dash for freedom. Almost immediately, he found himself trapped by Union troops coming from the opposite direction. He dismounted and finally reached the door of a mansion where he begged for asylum. Aunt Lucy, the owner of the house, was absent, but her Cousin Lou, acting mistress of the estate and a loyal supporter of Jefferson Davis, quickly extended welcome. She told Dr. Barnes to hide under the raspberry bushes. "When night comes, I will send for your horse and you can escape."

Within the hour, Colonel Harrison's band of searchers, informed by Negro servants of Barnes's hideout, rode up and the Colonel addressed one of the household maids: "Girl, have you seen Dr. Barnes come in here?"

"Sir," snapped the lady of the house before the servant girl could find her tongue, "I have not lived in the North where I suppose you were reared, and I do not know what is considered good

[63] Russellville *Herald and Enterprise*, April 9, 1890. The remainder of this story as told in the following pages is based exclusively on the newspaper account. Even if it were apocryphal (there is no evidence that it is), the tale is sufficiently characteristic to merit inclusion in this work. The traits of Harrison manifest in this incident occur again and again, and can be well substantiated by evidence in the Harrison MSS.

breeding there, but we of the South would consider it grossly improper to interrogate a servant in the presence of her mistress without at least asking leave."

"I beg your pardon, Madame," stammered Harrison, bowing and coloring deeply, "I intended no disrespect. I did not see you standing at the door when I called the girl, and in my haste to obtain the information I desire I cannot stand much upon ceremony."

Harrison's reference to ceremony was, in one sense, his undoing. Cousin Lou admitted later: "I saw from the manner and tone of the speaker that I had a gentleman to deal with, and I took courage. My plan of action was now quickly formed. I would engage him in conversation, and keep him there as long as possible, and if I could not baffle him entirely, I would trust to Providence to bring deliverance out of delay."

"Indeed, Sir," Cousin Lou began, "can a gentleman ever afford to waive that ceremony which affects the rights of ladies upon any plea of urgency?" Without waiting for an answer, Cousin Lou added, pretending not to have heard Harrison's original question to her maid: "I suppose you are seeking something to eat like the rest of your men. If you will come in, I will have something prepared for you. If any one is excusable for a breach of etiquette, it is a hungry man, and if mending your appetite will mend your manners, I shall be happy to perform that service for you. That is, I will feed you, if there is anything left. We cooked two days for Captain Dortch, and your men got that; and now two of them are in the kitchen helping themselves to what is left. But I think I can find something for you, if you will come in."

The colonel bit his lip in vexation. "Madame, we are not a foraging party. We are seeking Dr. Barnes and we desire to learn whether he is in your house. As I am not permitted to inquire of the girl, may I ask you, Madame, if he is here?"

Cousin Lou proceeded to accommodate Colonel Harrison, but in her own tantalizing way. "Oh, ask your questions where you think you will be more likely to get a truthful answer. I waive ceremony. Ask the girl by all means." Whereupon, Louise, the frightened maid, was directed to "answer the gentleman's questions." The girl was already in a state of panic and, when pressed by Harrison, her invariable response to each question was: " 'Fo' de Lawd, Miss Lou, I do' know nuthin' 'bout it." As Harrison hesitated in his questioning, Cousin Lou broke in: "Louise, did Dr. Barnes come in here?" With stereotyped accuracy the maid's answer was " 'Fo' de Lawd, Miss Lou, I do' know nuthin' 'bout it." And that was all that could be got out of her.

After she had won this round in her strategic battle with the military inquirers, Cousin Lou decided to rub a little salt into their wounds. "Well, gentlemen, is there anything more I can do for you? It is not my custom to entertain visitors at the front gate. Walk in, gentlemen, rest and refresh yourselves. I think there is wine cake on the sideboard."

"Thank you, Madame," the slightly exasperated Northern leader gravely responded. "Our business is too pressing to permit such an indulgence. I beg pardon, Madame, but you must allow me to renew the question I asked you awhile ago. Dr. Barnes has committed a flagrant breach of military law, and we must secure his person. I have good reason to believe he is secreted in your house. I demand to know if that is true."

With an air of cunning, the lady not only insisted that Harrison had been misinformed, but also that she did not intend to have her house searched. According to her story, the house was to enjoy immunity from search. She told Harrison: "Aunt Lucy Blakely has promised me, in return for favors rendered to her when the Confederates occupied Russellville, that Federals should never search my house; and she has given orders to that effect to Capt. Morrow. If he were here, he would tell you so." Cousin Lou feigned not to recognize Morrow who was standing at Harrison's side. She claimed she saw from Morrow's expression that he assented, and would be a witness, if necessary. Evidently, the good Captain Morrow was under some obligation to Aunt Lucy, who was the wife of the leading Union figure in southern Kentucky. Her influence was all-powerful.

She asked the unbelieving colonel: "Do you suppose that I would take the risk of having a fugitive caught in my house under such circumstances? Do I not know what the consequences would be to me and to my husband? Call me a rebel, sir, but do not call me an idiot."

"But, Madame," said the colonel, with a significant judicial emphasis, "you may not know the facts. Dr. Barnes was seen to enter your gate, and we must have him."

"Sir," replied Cousin Lou, primly, "I am a Christian woman.

From my childhood I have been taught to speak the truth, and to dread the fate of liars. I tell you once more, Dr. Barnes is not in my house and you must believe me."

With this chance mention of religion and Christianity, Harrison started down the road of the vanquished. "I, also," he said in a more cordial tone, "profess to be a Christian. I have long been a member of the church, but military duty—"

"What church?"

"I am a Presbyterian, Madame."

"Presbyterian!" sputtered Cousin Lou. "The Presbyterians are sound on perseverance, but they have no right to ignore the plain commands of the Bible."

"Indeed, Madame, and what is the great sin of omission of which we are guilty?" His look of annoyance gave way to one of amused surprise at the turn the conversation had taken.

"Why, Sir, your church does not practice baptism."

"Your mistake," replied the colonel, who had behind him six years of Sunday School experience, "no unbaptized person is admitted into the Presbyterian Church, and most of our members are baptized in infancy." There was a merry twinkle in the eyes of this elated elder when he mentioned infants. Such a show of interest and enjoyment convinced Cousin Lou that for once at least a baptismal controversy would serve a good purpose.

"Infant baptism! Why, Sir, I will go and get my Bible, and if you will show me a single passage where infant baptism is taught, I will take my bonnet and join you in this search for Dr. Barnes." Before the Colonel could make his protest against further delay, Cousin Lou hurried off to the house. Later she said she believed that Harrison would not violate the truce by entering the yard in her absence. Having remained in the house as long as she dared, the self-appointed Scripture expert returned, Bible in hand.

After a long and learned exchange of Biblical quotations, during which Cousin Lou stretched time by reading aloud entire chapters, Harrison became restless. "Your arguments are doubtless all right, Madame, but I did not come here to argue about baptism. My business is to find Dr. Barnes. He was seen to enter your yard. I must have him."

There was no budging Cousin Lou. "Well, gentlemen, if you will not come in, I must ask you to excuse me, as I have some household duties to perform." With a low and graceful bow the victor closed the gate, deliberately secured the latch. As she walked towards the house, she heard Colonel Harrison's squad go away.

Her job was all but completed. The doctor was still hiding in the garden when she took him some wine, and told him what time the horse would be ready for him. As the appointed hour approached, Cousin Lou drew her last herring across the Union trail. She instructed her personal maid Dinah to pick up a rooster and make him squawk as loud as she could. This would help drown any noise of clatter at the gate or the horse's hoofs on the pike. This last ruse was as successful as the others and the doctor made his escape.

After their first taste of victory at Russellville, a general sense of confidence and satisfaction pervaded the ranks. Harrison let it be known about Bowling Green that his men were justified in being "pleased with our success." The military and tactical mistakes which he had noted were caused by excessive generosity and enthusiasm. Hence, he confided to his wife:

The Regiment did splendidly, except that there was not as much order as I would have liked in marching to the line of battle . . . there being a little too much eagerness to get into the fight.[64]

To curb and channel the regiment's spirit of bravery was a much more pleasant task than attempting to create fortitude and generosity in hearts that might have been cowardly and selfish. Harrison also revealed a note of personal satisfaction because "he had made some credit with the regiment in the fight." While the results achieved at Russellville were good, two subsequent expeditions to that area were fruitless. "The rebels in the place fled before we got there," he regretfully told Carrie.

This surge of consolation had run its course within three short weeks of the Russellville triumph. The intervening period saw repeated and rather intense efforts to capture Morgan, or at least some part of his marauding cavalry. Each try failed. Always, the more swiftly moving enemy eluded carefully planned traps. It was at the end of these futile attempts that Harrison, "having

[64] B. Harrison to his wife, October 3, 1862, Harrison MSS, Vol. 4.

spent two whole nights riding on an engine," put his finger on
the heart of the difficulty—an inadequate cavalry force. "It is
shameful that we have not a cavalry force dashing enough to pursue and capture the scoundrel."[65]

Toward the latter part of October, however, the perennial
problem of the elusive Morgan and of the sporadic raids by his
command assumed a minor significance when compared with the
trouble and discontent brewing on the home front. Throughout
the nation, but especially in Indiana, a political battle was taking
place in which "a vindicated, indignant, and almost revengeful
Democracy was pitted against a humiliated and bitterly disappointed Republican-dominated Union Party."[66] This political
death struggle had ramifications and repercussions in all walks of
life. Benjamin Harrison, who was far removed at Bowling Green,
and whose physical appearance with "long hair, whiskers and a
moustache of very savage proportions"[67] would have made him
almost unrecognizable in Indianapolis, suddenly found himself
the subject of a violent political and legal dispute. He was seriously threatened with the loss of his office as Supreme Court
Reporter.

This move to oust Harrison and deprive him of its income,
despite the fact that he had appointed John Caven as his deputy,
was not unforeseen. As early as August 22, when he had been at
Bowling Green but one week, Colonel Harrison was informed
that the Indiana Democrats were instituting court action to have
his elective office declared vacant because he now held a lucrative
office,[68] a colonel's commission in the U. S. Army. In anticipation
of a court ruling to this effect, the Democrats decided to nominate
Michael Kerr, the opponent whom Harrison had soundly defeated in 1860, as Court Reporter.

This news was shocking enough to Ben, who relied heavily
upon this source of income for his family's support. The mere
possibility of losing out worried him, though he felt confident

65 B. Harrison to his wife, October 21, 1862, Harrison MSS, Vol. 4.

66 Kenneth M. Stampp, *Indiana Politics during the Civil War*, p. 158.

67 B. Harrison to his wife, October 21, 1862, Harrison MSS, Vol. 4.

68 In Kerr *v.* Jones (19 Indiana Reports 351) Judge Perkins actually decided the
case upon the fact that Benjamin Harrison was *not* a Colonel in the militia, but a
colonel in the army of the U. S. Therefore, he held two lucrative offices simultane-
ously and this contravened the State Constitution of Indiana. Either his colonelcy
or his reportership had to be abandoned.

that the Republicans of Indianapolis would stand by him and see him through this legal difficulty.[69] It is not difficult to imagine his chagrin when the Union Central Committee of the Republican Party not only failed to support his claims,[70] but even by-passed Caven, the deputy whom he had selected and employed.[71] The Committee agreed to a coalition candidate, a certain "Pop-Gun" Smith, to contest the office with the Democrat Kerr. Ben got his first intimations of this move from the pages of the Indianapolis *Daily Journal* on August 22, 1862. He wrote to Carrie:

I see by the Journal of yesterday that the Union Central Committee has nominated "Pop Gun" Smith for Reporter. I think this is *shameful treatment* . . . they are only too glad to sacrifice me to help the prospects of their own election by putting on the ticket another *Democrat.* . . . The cowardly rascals make some present advantage by this, but I am willing to trust God and the honest people, while I am found in the discharge of my duty.[72]

As for the office itself and its honors and emoluments, Harrison was willing to let these go, he added, provided only he could keep the consciousness that he was "rendering a humble service to my country in this hour of her sore trial." Ben looked at the problem philosophically,

If God spares my life to return home again to civil life, I shall not fear that He will enable me to gain as much competence. I hope, however, to make out of the office yet enough to pay for my house and lot, and can readily do so, if my friends at home will only aid me a little in getting two volumes out.

Three weeks had slipped by in which Colonel Harrison's time was "constantly occupied with matters of discipline, drill and

[69] B. Harrison to his wife, August 23, 1862, Harrison MSS, Vol. 4, and more explicitly in Harrison to W. P. Fishback, September 7, 1862, Harrison MSS, Vol 4.

[70] W. P. Fishback to Harrison, August 25, 1862, Harrison MSS, Vol. 4, "You have probably heard already that the Central Committee placed the name of Smith of Fort Wayne on the state ticket for Reporter. The members here, three in number, voted for Caven, in accordance with your suggestion, but the eight other members controlled the selection. I suspect that other members on the ticket suggested the matter . . . the argument smells somewhat of the trickery of [Jonathan] Harvey."

[71] "Say to John Caven that I do not ask and will not have his labor without a fair compensation, and he must get from the proceeds of the work what will fairly remunerate him." B. Harrison to W. P. Fishback, September 7, 1862, Harrison MSS, Vol. 4.

[72] B. Harrison to his wife, August 23, 1862, Harrison MSS, Vol. 4.

study of tactics."[73] Though his light was usually the last to be extinguished, he was unable to answer any letters. Consequently, the Reporter matter went from bad to worse. In a letter to his law partner, he admitted that he still "felt a great deal of disappointment at the realization of the loss of an office which had been so pleasant and profitable . . . just when I was beginning to realize its benefits. . . . I would not feel so much anxiety about it, but . . . it is *vital* to me and my dear little family."[74]

Despite Governor Morton's promise of assistance,[75] Harrison became exceedingly worried as the October state elections drew near.

This unhappy combination of financial worry and military responsibility rested heavily with Harrison. Yet, after three months of growth in his new profession of soldier, he was a wiser and most certainly a much more mature person because of the experience he had undergone during the discharge of duty in the field. His losses, he reflected, were

Only apparent and not real. And this reflection never fails to comfort me when I feel sad . . . and to remove all gloomy apprehensions of the course I have taken . . . and regrets are the source of most of our sorrows.[76]

Although "the fire in the rear"[77] was beginning to burn brightly as the winter of 1862 approached, and Indianapolis looked for a counter-revolution to be inaugurated at home by the newly

[73] B. Harrison to W. P. Fishback, September 7, 1862, Harrison MSS, Vol. 4. Ben had received two important letters from Fishback on the subject, but could not find time to answer either of them.

[74] *Ibid.*

[75] Harrison wrote to Fishback: "The Governor told me that he would do just as I wanted . . . and I have no doubt that he will." *Ibid.* Will Wallace, however, had no faith in Morton. Will Wallace to Harrison, Nov. 6, 1862, Harrison MSS, Vol. 4. As matters turned out, Wallace's judgment was more accurate than Harrison's.

[76] *Ibid.*

[77] This was a popular expression among Unionists during the fall and winter of 1862, the term "fire" referring, of course, principally to the Democracy of the Northwest, and secondarily to all opponents of the war. William Wallace to Benj. Harrison, October 30, 1862, Harrison MSS, Vol. 4: "I am clearly of the opinion that it would have been better for the country had a draft been resorted to. By this means there would not have been left a fire in our rear almost as much to be dreaded as the fire on the front." See also Wood Gray, *The Hidden Civil War*, p. 18, where he describes Senator Sumner's interview with Lincoln in the black winter of 1862: "The President tells me he now fears 'the fire in the rear'."

entrenched Democrats,[78] there was one fact Harrison could not forget either now or during the rest of his life. For, as Fishback had put it, "only the loyal and the patriotic are in the army . . . an element that can scourge from the face of the earth the traitors at home should it become necessary."[79]

[78] Fishback wrote to Harrison on October 16, 1862: "our danger now is at home . . . [disloyal] men feel their power in numbers, and you must not be surprised if the counter revolution is inaugurated at home." Harrison MSS, Vol. 4.

[79] *Ibid.*

CHAPTER X

On Secessionist Ground: The War in Tennessee

ALTHOUGH Colonel Harrison's regiment had marched into the heart of the Confederacy in response to frantic demands for fresh troops to defend Kentucky against Bragg, its only claim to fame, so far, was from several moderately successful forays at Franklin, Morgantown, Munfordsville and Russellville.[1] During the last months of 1862, the men faced a dangerous enemy, not on the battlefields of Kentucky, but on the homefront in Indianapolis. Harrison soon discovered that several Southern sympathizers in and about Indianapolis were conducting an effective epistolary campaign among some of the members of his regiment. Every artifice was employed to encourage both disobedience and desertion from the Union ranks. This homefront attempt to sabotage the ranks was a serious matter, which grew proportionately as the South became more stubborn in the defense of its rights, and as the casualty lists on both sides lengthened.[2]

Especially at the time of the state elections in October many doubts beset the people of Indiana. Old political loyalties were resurrected, and men publicly denounced the "unjust" war. A draft was announced, postponed, and announced again, while the Democrats electioneered with a newly discovered vigor.[3]

[1] General Harrison to General E. A. Carman, February 8, 1876, Harrison MSS, Vol. 7. In response to General Carman's request of January 10, 1876, Harrison wrote a summary of the Seventieth's war service. It is detailed and concise, and was prepared for inclusion or for use in Carman's history of the 20th Army Corps, under General Hooker.

[2] John B. Martin, *Indiana; an Interpretation*, p. 61.

[3] The columns of the Indianapolis *Daily Sentinel* were filled with reports and editorial comments on the unconstitutionality of drafting men to fight in an unjust war. The Democrats made much of the civil liberties argument. They complained that Governor Morton was trampling on civil liberties at every chance. Also see Martin, *op. cit.*, p. 62.

They claimed to stand for constitutional liberty, freedom of opinion, of speech and of press, which, they clamored, had been trodden under foot. In reality, they were opposed to the war, and on election day they carried the state by a majority of almost 10,000, electing seven out of eleven Congressmen as well as both houses of the Legislature. Undoubtedly, this repudiation of Republicanism can be set down as a positive reaction against the war. Democrats had repeatedly asserted that this was an "abolition war;"[4] and on September 22, when Lincoln finally yielded to radical pressure and issued his preliminary proclamation of emancipation, the reaction of Indiana was overwhelmingly hostile.[5] Even Governor Morton's pronouncement that the President's act was nothing more than a "stratagem of war"[6] failed to pour oil on the troubled political waters. A majority of the Indianans had not put aside old prejudices and dislike of the Negro and the Black Republicans who were now self-confessed abolitionists.

The election had a disastrous personal result for Harrison. Kerr, the Democrat, was victorious for the office of Reporter. Fishback wrote: "Caven thinks the Supreme Court will oust you . . . if we contest the point, Kerr will claim Volume 18 now in progress. If Pop Gun had been elected, I think the Court would have left you in without doubt."[7] Actually, within a month, Kerr claimed the proceeds from Volume 17 as well as Volume 18 of the Reports. Ben wrote to Carrie: "I would like to give M. Kerr a caning better than anything I know of."[8]

It was against this background of political change that Harrison first detected the spirit of unrest among his own troops. The propaganda campaign on the home-front had its effect in the camp at Bowling Green. Almost daily, some of the boys received letters calculated to make them desert the colors either on the score that the war was unjust or that they had never been properly

4 J. P. Dunn, *Greater Indianapolis*, I, 230–31.

5 Kenneth M. Stampp, *Indiana Politics during the Civil War*, pp. 147–48: "The immediate hostile reaction in Indiana promised to validate Secretary Smith's warning that the measure would certainly cause the Republicans to lose his state." Actually, "most of the Hoosiers were not inclined at that time to accept the measure upon any grounds."

6 Indianapolis *Daily Journal*, October 10, 1862.

7 W. P. Fishback to B. Harrison, October 17, 1862, Harrison MSS, Vol. 4.

8 B. Harrison to his wife, November 21, 1862, Harrison MSS, Vol. 4.

mustered into the service of the United States Army.[9] So effective was the campaign that a loyalty crisis was being precipitated.

Several enlisted men bitterly resented this sniping by Copperheads who were staying safely at home. Harrison was quick to capitalize on the indignation. His first move was to call a mass meeting of his entire regiment and to ask General Paine to preside. This was a wise choice. Men applauded generously, as speakers rivaled each other in proclaiming loyalty to the Union cause. As the junior officer on the platform, Colonel Harrison made the concluding address. That he was at the tail end of a long program of speech-making made little difference to him. Here was a real opportunity to show that he was a leader of men, not merely one in the ranks. With a pent-up fervor Harrison lashed out at the dishonesty of the letter-writers, and immediately "riveted the attention of that mass of men, held it undivided for about an hour, and was cheered vociferously when he closed."[10]

The regiment's sagging morale was bolstered and the colonel climbed immeasurably in the esteem of his own men. No sooner had he finished his remarks than General Paine walked over to Captain Samuel Merrill; and, slapping the younger man on the back, he exclaimed: "By George, Captain, that Colonel of yours will be President of the United States some day."[11]

A false report had also circulated in the Indianapolis press that sickness had removed more than half the regiment from active service. While Harrison felt that he could cope with the bad feeling created by communications from home, he worried because "dysentery, measles and some typhoid fever are disabling many of my men."[12] It was under these circumstances of doubt, discontent and physical suffering that the fires of disloyalty burned most brightly within certain companies. Officers were charged with having little sympathy for the men; and some of the men them-

9 In a letter dated Bowling Green, Ky., November 10, 1862, that appeared four days later in the *Daily Sentinel,* one paragraph read: "There has been a great deal of excitement at camp during the past few days. It seems that the Regiment has never been mustered into the United States service . . . the boys say they are going home to be mustered in. . . . I will not say what the reasons are for being dissatisfied, for that would bring some of the leading officers bad repute." Also see B. R. Sulgrove, *History of Indianapolis and Marion County* (Philadelphia, 1884), p. 317.

10 Samuel Merrill, *The Seventieth Indiana Volunteer Infantry,* p. 49.

11 Freeman Cleaves, *Old Tippecanoe,* p. 123.

12 B. Harrison to his wife, October 17, 1862, Harrison MSS, Vol. 4.

selves were easily convinced that they were free to leave the army, since, it was alleged, they had not been properly mustered into service. Others of a more skeptical nature wrote to "eminent lawyers in Indiana concerning the matter."[13]

At first, Harrison was patient in his efforts to bolster the spirits of a regiment partially torn with sickness, and understandably, as he thought, discontented with their inglorious role of inactivity. He labored diligently to have his unit assigned to an active brigade. His heart was set on moving south and on to the field of battle. Though the winter of 1862–63 was hard, he confided his secret ambition to his wife:

I am myself willing to put away the thought of winter quarters and be kept in active operations in the field, if we can be used effectively against the enemy. . . . I am for the most active and continuous fighting. Let us fight them today, tomorrow and the next day and every day until they are killed and captured, and the sham confidence for which they are fighting, is only remembered as a horrible dream in history.[14]

These efforts were actually misconstrued by some of the men in his outfit. One wrote to the *Sentinel* that "Harrison thinks, doubtless, that if he gets us in a division that he can make us soldiers whether we are mustered, paid or clothed; but he will find out before we go far, that we are unwilling to serve under him until we are mustered in."[15] Views such as these, and the ever-present knowledge that they were originated by people at home, caused him to unloose a volley of vituperation:

We feel real malicious towards the traitorous and cowardly scoundrels who not only refused to share with us the perils and glories of our dear country's service, but extend sympathy and encouragement to the red-handed traitors of the South who are seeking ours and our country's life. Most earnestly do I pray God to turn away the sword and faggot from our dear state and dear homes, but at the same time we are ready to meet the enemies of our country even in Indiana, "with bloody hands and hospitable graves." . . . I have some hope, though it is faint, that those who have now attained power, may, when they feel the public responsibility upon them, laboriously maintain the war. Should they fail to do so, they will soon perish before

13 Indianapolis *Daily Sentinel*, November 14, 1862.
14 B. Harrison to his wife, October 17, 1862, Harrison MSS, Vol. 4.
15 Picket (Co. A) to the Editor of the *Sentinel*, November 14, 1862.

the avenging breath of a million veteran soldiers of liberty, who have
sworn to defend the government against all her enemies and opposers.
. . . I turn away from thoughts so agonizing.[16]

Fortunately for the colonel's reputation, one of his own officers,
his brother-in-law Captain Scott, was in Indianapolis on leave
just when the spirit of rebellion in the Seventieth was being aired
in the press. Not only did Scott readily prove that all the charges
against Harrison and the officers of the regiment were *"in toto
untrue,"* but he also made a special point of defending his superior officer:

Among the unkindest charges was the one against Col. Harrison,
that he was trying to get our regiment to move with the army, thinking that he could make us soldiers in this way whether mustered,
paid or clothed. I venture the assertion that there has never been an
officer more zealous than Col. Harrison in having his regiment properly clothed and equipped, sending two daily messengers to the city
for oil-cloth blankets, one to Louisville for over-coats, and laboring
in season and out of season to have his command comfortable and
happy. He labored, it is true, to get his command to move, but it was
to leave a town now rendered a pest house with the sick of our great
army . . . 5,000 strong . . . in 20 hospitals.[17]

While the war on the home-front was being hotly waged, the
military were in a confused state. No clear-cut plan of campaign
was executed by either side.[18] Though the Confederate Braxton
Bragg seemed on the point of taking Louisville as late as mid-
September, he allowed himself to be diverted, and swung his
columns toward Lexington. On the other hand, General Buell,[19]
who had promptly occupied Louisville, performed no signal service until the campaign was climaxed by the battle of Perryville[20]
on October 8, 1862. Yet, even this battle could not be counted

16 B. Harrison to his wife, October 21, 1862, Harrison MSS, Vol. 4.

17 Capt. H. M. Scott to the Editor of the Indianapolis *Daily Journal*, November
18, 1862. As an officer of the regiment, Scott said he felt called upon to refute the
false charges.

18 James G. Randall, *The Civil War and Reconstruction*, p. 526.

19 After succeeding Sherman in November, 1861, as commander of the Army of
the Ohio, Buell arranged and developed it into a well-disciplined fighting machine.
Even Williams, whose standards for commanders are high, says, *op. cit.*, II, 478: "he
was an accomplished soldier in many ways."

20 Randall, *op. cit.*, p. 527.

as a clear victory for either side. Perhaps the only gratification was the report that the Confederates had decided to abandon Kentucky.

When the Confederates actually began their withdrawal to Tennessee, Harrison's hopes skyrocketed. Now, an early movement southward was probable, with chances for real fighting imminent. When Washington determined to guillotine all unsuccessful generals,[21] Harrison's wishes were near fulfillment. Buell's failure[22] to anticipate Bragg's invasion of Kentucky as well as his neglect in pursuing the confederate general after Perryville, brought his removal from the command of the Department of the Ohio.[23] He was succeeded by General William S. Rosecrans.

With this new appointment Harrison and his men were extremely pleased. The order which placed Rosecrans in command also created the Department of the Cumberland, embracing that portion of the state of Tennessee lying east of the Tennessee River, and such parts of Georgia and Alabama as should be occupied by Federal troops.[24] The Seventieth Indiana, as well as every other regiment in the field, needed no briefing on the strategy underlying this general reorganization of the western forces. Even the rawest recruit realized that a big push into the deep South was in the offing, and Harrison's Hoosiers hoped to play a significant part. This time they were not to be disappointed.

On October 30th, General Rosecrans came to Louisville and assumed his new command, and three days later, while Colonel and Mrs. Harrison were enjoying their second visit together at Bowling Green,[25] he rode into camp. The new commander announced a three-fold division of his army, under the command, respectively, of Major Generals McCook, Thomas, and Critten-

21 Kenneth P. Williams, *Lincoln Finds a General*, II, 477.

22 R. V. Johnson and C. C. Buel (eds.), *Battles and Leaders*, III, Part 1, p. 19; Henry M. Cist, *The Army of the Cumberland* (New York, 1882), pp. 76–77.

23 Rossiter Johnson, *Campfire and Battlefield*, p. 230. Stampp, *op. cit.*, p. 160, declares that, "besides falling victim to civilian meddling and western discontent, Buell was something of a scapegoat for disappointed Union party politicians." This viewpoint is verified by Harrison's letter to his wife, October 21, 1862, Harrison MSS, Vol. 4.

24 Cist, *op. cit.*, p. 77.

25 Will Wallace to Benj. Harrison, October 30, 1862, Harrison MSS, Vol. 4.

den. Three divisions were assigned to each wing, while the center was composed of five. Three days later, the Seventieth Indiana Volunteers found themselves a substantial part of the center. Harrison wrote: "On the 10th of November, 1862 the 70th was assigned to Ward's Brigade, Dumont's Division, 14th Army Corps, and moved with its command to Scottsville, Kentucky, and thence on the 24th of November to Gallatin, Tennessee."[26]

The three-day march from Bowling Green to Scottsville, Kentucky, was made through a

country destitute of any respectable improvement and seemingly incapable of any. . . . We saw very few houses and they were the makeshifts of the frontier. Every now and then we would pass a cow path coming out from the thick woods and thicker underbushes about which would be collected fifteen or twenty children who must have been startled from a bed of leaves by the rattle of our drums. They gazed with rustic wonder on the troops as they passed, and thought they had never seen such multitudes on multitudes of soldiers.[27]

Captain Merrill later related that

in the march he [Harrison] was always merciful, protesting against unnecessary haste. Frequently he would take the guns and accoutrements of some poor worn out soldier and carry it before him on the saddle. Often I have seen him dismount and walk while a sick soldier occupied his place on the horse.[28]

Many of the men were still on the sick list; some, scarcely able to walk. Harrison "walked fully one half the distance"[29] to Scotts-

26 Harrison to General E. A. Carman, February 8, 1876, Harrison MSS, Vol. 7. General Dumont, Harrison's new division commander, was a personal friend. He had served with distinction as Lieut. Colonel of the Fourth Indiana Volunteers in the Mexican War, was elected to Congress in October, 1862, and re-elected in 1864. Sulgrove, op. cit., pp. 308–12.
27 B. Harrison to his wife, November 11, 1862, Harrison MSS, Vol. 4.
28 Indianapolis Journal, June 29, 1888.
29 This was not an uncommon experience. In later years, several members of his regiment recalled such kindness. Dan Ransdell, ex-county clerk and a member of the Seventieth, not only recalled seeing Harrison dismount and march, but claimed: "I remember once he did me that kindness. I have always loved him and admired him, and I might say that I have always insisted that he would be one day President of these United States." An unidentified newspaper clipping in Harrison Scrapbook Series, Vol. 6, Harrison MSS. This story was also reprinted in a campaign pamphlet, Public and Private Life of Gen'l. Benj. Harrison, p. 15.

ville. This example was not lost upon most of the staff members, who perforce, followed suit,[30] thus boosting the morale of the regiment and winning the respect and admiration of their subordinates. Ben confided to Carrie:

I think, though no such motive prompted the act, that this cause has enlarged my popularity with the men. They begin to see that I will sacrifice at any time my own comfort for their good.[31]

Arrival at Scottsville, however, brought little consolation. The thought in most minds was that of moving further south as soon as possible. The area around the town struck Benjamin Harrison as "one of the most desolate and barren portions of the world" with the "produce of the country . . . completely exhausted."[32] Due to the very limited opportunities that this sector offered for drill, both officers and men soon grew tired of lying about camp.[33] This enforced inactivity allowed more than ample time for speculation as to future movements; and just before Rosecrans instructed General Thomas to advance Dumont's division to Gallatin, Tennessee,[34] Harrison had written home that "there is some talk about reorganizing our brigadiers and putting us in another brigade and giving the command of it to me."[35] Realizing that he was still untested by real fighting in the field, and still lacked that quality of self-confidence so essential to a successful commander, Harrison showed little interest in the suggested promotion. He mulled over the matter and entrusted his conclusion to his wife:

[30] One did not. This drew Harrison's critical fire: "the Major rode his horse all the way, and had besides two wheeled vehicles with his traps and his negroe driving it, . . . he is a *very selfish man* and the officers are finding him out and laugh a good deal at his disposition to grasp everything he can get his hands on." Harrison to his wife, November 14, 1862, Harrison MSS, Vol. 4.

[31] *Ibid.*

[32] Harrison to his wife, November 18, 1862, Harrison MSS, Vol. 4.

[33] The complaint was that there was no field of level ground within miles that was large enough to move even a regiment. *Ibid.*

[34] Cist, *op. cit.,* p. 77. General S. S. Fry was also to join Dumont with his division in order to "push rapidly forward the repairs of the railroad to Nashville."

[35] Harrison to his wife, November 18, 1862, Harrison MSS, Vol. 4. The basis for this talk seems to be that his unit "takes the shine of all the brigade in mounting, in dress parade and . . . in battalion drill."

I am not ambitious for a high command and am perhaps a little lacking in confidence in my real powers. . . . Gen. Ward, our brigade commander, is a very clever man, but has very little idea of military matters.[36]

Rosecrans' order of November 24th, directing Ward's brigade to Gallatin, ended all immediate speculation, but found the colonel of the Seventieth an uncomfortably sick man. The weather at Scottsville had been excessively cold and damp during the regiment's stay; further Harrison had eaten some fresh pork that induced ptomaine poisoning. On top of this misfortune came renewed shafts of criticism from Indianapolis.[37]

What particularly piqued Harrison was an attack in the press by Alexander Thuer, a member of his own company and a former newspaper editor.[38] Thuer said that he especially despised Harrison for the religious influence that he attempted to exert in the regiment. It is true that Harrison had exercised such influence. He had often acted as chaplain. One comrade said: "He was a true man of old Presbyterian stock . . . he was the only general officer I knew of at whose headquarters family prayers were regularly held."[39]

Thoroughly disheartened and still somewhat dyspeptic, Harrison lost his usual calm and self-control. After he had belatedly blasted his critic as a "blatant infidel," in a bitter letter to Carrie,[40] he felt better. He explained other "letters to the editor" in the columns of the *Sentinel* and the *Journal* as coming from soldiers whom he had been compelled to discipline. He was sensible enough to look upon these attacks "as a mode of venting their rage," yet his oversensitive nature rebelled at what he deemed rank injustice. He drew some satisfaction in tagging his press opponents as "miserable egotistic fools," and finally adopted a practical and simple philosophy: "The day of these dogs will soon be

36 *Ibid.* By mid-1863, Harrison had changed his opinion of General Ward most radically.

37 The violent attacks in the Indianapolis press annoyed Harrison greatly. B. Harrison to his wife, November 21, 1862, Harrison MSS, Vol. 4.

38 Thuer had been appointed by Col. Burgess as postmaster. Subsequently, he was removed by Harrison for drunkenness, and in his place was appointed a Mr. Elgin, a preacher. This appointment was the cause of Thuer's vitriolic attack on Harrison.

39 Indianapolis *Journal* account republished on p. 14 of the campaign pamphlet.

40 B. Harrison to his wife, November 21, 1862, Harrison MSS, Vol. 4.

over. I know that I have the confidence and respect of every officer and man whose esteem is worth having."

On the evening of November 24, 1862, in obedience to Rosecrans' order the regiment broke camp at Scottsville, Kentucky. Shortly before four A.M. on the 25th the troops were alerted, and while the Fortieth Brigade,[41] also part of Dumont's division, was getting under way, the rest of the battalion was formed in a close column. At this point General Dumont rode up to the Seventieth and made a speech which, according to one hearer, was "just such a one as you would expect from a Hoosier General to a Hoosier Regiment."[42] Upon the men this veteran of two wars urged discipline and subordination; with the officers he insisted upon promptness and firmness. Every man knew the general to be sincere when he expressed his desire to have the Seventieth remain with him until "peace should again smile upon the land." He pledged his word that, if the opportunity offered, he would lead them "to glory and to victory." At the conclusion of the speech, Harrison proposed three rousing cheers as a mutual pledge that they would not disappoint the expectations of their general. Enthusiasm ran high as the regiment began the thirty-three mile march to Gallatin, Tennessee.[43]

When approximately nine miles from Scottsville, the Seventieth reached the Kentucky-Tennessee line. The regiment paused momentarily; then, with colors flying and the band playing "Dixie," each company commander came forward and set foot on this new territory. To the accompaniment of waving hats and tremendous cheering, the entire regiment crossed, whistling "Dixie" as they marched.[44] Nine more miles were covered before the division halted for the night.

The intervening fifteen miles were covered leisurely on the 26th, and at 4:00 P.M. the last of Dumont's command reached Gallatin, the county seat of Sumner County, located three miles from the Cumberland River and directly on the line of the Louisville and Nashville Railroad. Much to their good fortune and to

[41] The Fortieth Brigade was under the command of Col. O. A. Miller and was comprised of his regiment, the 98th Illinois as well as the 72nd and 75th Indiana Regiments. Cist, op. cit., p. 264.

[42] Indianapolis Daily Journal, December 6, 1862.

[43] B. Harrison to his wife, November 28, 1862, Harrison MSS, Vol. 4.

[44] Indianapolis Daily Journal, December 6, 1862; also Merrill, op. cit., p. 46.

the jealousy of the other troops, the Seventieth was chosen by General Dumont as his bodyguard and consequently was assigned the best camping site near Headquarters.

On the following day, which was Thanksgiving, Harrison, having duly reflected on "a rich harvest of joy . . . a united family around our own hearthstone," rose manfully to the festive occasion and ate heartily. Shortly afterwards, with the plaintive air of an overstuffed schoolboy, Ben wrote to Carrie:

Yesterday being Thanksgiving Day, the Major set out a turkey etc., and invited us all to dine with him which we did. Though sick myself, the sight of these home delicacies was too much for me and I went into them pretty strong. Just as we had finished, there came an invitation from General Ward for us all to go to his headquarters at 4 P.M.[45]

This letter contained several allusions to the poor state of his health.

I have alluded to the condition of my health and ought perhaps to be more explicit, to avoid unnecessary uneasiness. I have a slight attack of yellow jaundice and feel at times very badly in body and quite despondent in spirit. I have dropped more than one tear since writing this letter and feel ashamed of their flow, but cannot dry them up. I am taking a blue pill every day and hope before we leave here to be quite well again.

No sooner had Dumont's division taken up quarters at Gallatin than the intelligence department reported a rebel concentration near Murfreesboro, only a two-day march southeast of Nashville. This bit of news encouraged Harrison: "I am for a fight and go home policy."[46] But a few days later, while still waiting for fighting orders, he had to content himself with a dreamer's letter to Carrie, wherein he contemplated "a neat cottage home in which to enjoy my *pension* when I come home with *one leg*." He kept his hopes high, convinced as he was that the order to march would come before long, and he added: "I don't care how soon." His confidence was based on his belief that "we have an

45 B. Harrison to his wife, November 28, 1862, Harrison MSS, Vol. 4.
46 Harrison to his wife, November 30, 1862, Harrison MSS, Vol. 4.

army in the field which if skillfully led would crush the rebellion in 90 days, but the leader seems to be wanting."[47]

Harrison, in his prognostication that a serious engagement was close at hand, was entirely correct. He was wrong, however, in his belief that Dumont's division and his own regiment would share in the fighting. Just two weeks before General Rosecrans moved out of Nashville with 41,000 effectives to strike Bragg's forces near Murfreesboro, the Union general detailed Harrison's troops from Gallatin to Drake's Creek, from which point they were to guard twenty-six miles of railroad from Gallatin to Nashville.[48]

This assignment was deemed of extreme importance by Rosecrans, who from the first day of his command of the Army of the Cumberland had bent every effort to keep the Louisville and Nashville track in good condition. No one understood better than Rosecrans that Buell's most serious problem was that of safeguarding his communications to his base of supplies.[49] Harrison, disappointed by the orders to keep this life-line open, and considering it a "big contract," nevertheless criticized the move as the "sheerest madness."[50] But there they stayed. "We are still encamped upon the grassy banks of this classic stream . . . doing little but picket and guard duty." His chief complaint was being "kept on a stretch of mind and body day and night." The cold was so penetrating that he uttered the fervent wish that his troops would not be *"condemned* to spend the winter in such service . . . most trying and dangerous, and at the same time the *least honorable* of any."[51]

Harrison even contemplated a ride to Nashville for a personal request to Rosecrans that he be given an opportunity to fight against Bragg's army. Upon reflection, however, he decided to wait at least until after Christmas Day. On its eve, his first away from home, he succeeded in putting aside all thoughts of battle, and wrote to Carrie one of his characteristically beautiful letters:

. . . And this is Christmas eve; and the dear little ones are about this time nestling their little heads upon the pillow, filled with the high

[47] Harrison to his wife, December 4, 1862, Harrison MSS, Vol. 4.
[48] Harrison to his wife, December 12, 1862, Harrison MSS, Vol. 4.
[49] Cist, *op. cit.,* p. 81.
[50] Harrison to his wife, December 12, 1862, Harrison MSS, Vol. 4.
[51] Harrison to his wife, December 15, 1862, Harrison MSS, Vol. 4.

expectations of what Santa Claus will bring them, and Papa is not there. How sad and trying it is for me to be away at such a time as this, and yet I cannot allow my complaining spirit to possess me. There are tens of thousands of fathers separated like me from the dear ones at home, battling with us for the preservation of our noble government which, under God, has given us all that peace and prosperity which makes our homes abodes of comfort and security. I am enduring very heavy trials in the army, but I believe that I was led to enter it by a high sense of Christian patriotism and God has thus far strengthened me to bear all cheerfully. I can never be too thankful for the heroic spirit with which you bear our separation and its incident trials and hardships. I know you must be very lonesome and oppressed with many anxieties, but God will give you strength to bear them all and will, nay I believe already has, drawn you closer to Himself as the source of all comfort and consolation. It is a blessed promise that *"all things shall work together for good to those who love God."* Let us have faith to receive the promise in all its *royal* fulness.[52]

Six days later, the engagement at Stone River (the Battle of Murfreesboro) began, and at Drake's Creek, forty miles away, concern for the outcome threw a pall over Harrison's New Year's Day thoughts:

I have felt very little of that festive spirit which usually belongs to this day. We have heard all day, the heavy bombing of artillery in the direction of Nashville and the great results of which hang upon the battle being fought and the dreadful carnage which the day witnessed, only a few miles away, have sobered and even saddened my mind. And then we have each a brother in the fight and God knows, not we, what may have been the issue to them.[53]

This note to Carrie was almost a premonition; a week later he learned that her brother, John Scott, had been severely wounded, one of the exceptionally high number of casualties.[54] Ben wrote that he was sending "whiskey, tea and a jar of peaches" to him, "being all the *delicacies* my chest could furnish." After words of consolation, he admitted to Carrie:

I almost envy John his honorable wound, and hope we may soon exchange the ease and quiet of our present camp for the hardship

[52] Harrison to his wife, December 24, 1862, Harrison MSS, Vol. 4.
[53] Harrison to his wife, January 1, 1863, Harrison MSS, Vol. 4.
[45] Of Rosencrans's forces, 1,677 were killed and 7,543 wounded; Bragg lost 1,294 killed and 7,945 wounded. Thomas L. Livermore, *Numbers and Losses in the Civil War in America, 1861–1865* (Boston, 1901), p. 47.

and dangers of the field . . . not that I am ambitious of military fame, but because I want to feel that I am accomplishing something for the cause, which I sacrificed to espouse.[55]

Since Bragg was compelled to evacuate Murfreesboro and ultimately to retire from middle Tennessee, this engagement is usually regarded as a Union triumph. As one Civil War authority points out, however, "the Union army which achieved the 'victory' did not strike again for six months."[56] To Harrison the prospects for 1863 appeared encouraging, for he told Carrie:

God seems to be smiling upon the efforts of our army in the West, and it does seem that the rebellion in that quarter is in a fair way of being *speedily* and *thoroughly* crushed out. If we could only hear more of some of the great success in the *East,* our cause would seem to be brilliant . . . we must not be too much elated over our successes, nor think, as we have many times before, that the fighting is over and cause successful. There will I have no doubt be thousands of lives lost yet on the battlefield before all life is crushed out of this monstrous hydra of treason. I have no doubt that we will all see fighting enough before we are permitted to lay down the weapons of our warfare, and resume the pursuits of peace.[57]

During the first six months of 1863, the military operations of the Army of the Cumberland were necessarily of a minor character, inasmuch as the exhaustion consequent upon the severe fighting at Stone River prevented any immediate serious offensive. The divisions were kept in camp until their respective losses in arms, material and men could be recouped.[58] Harrison and his command continued their assignment of guarding the railroad between Gallatin and Nashville. In mid-February they were ordered to Gallatin, after which came four months in camp. What one correspondent from the Seventieth had said earlier still applied:

Our Regiment has again quit traveling; again we have stopped and tied up at a post. Our services seem to be appreciated as guards . . . probably we have a talent that way, if we stay in the service long, we certainly will be entitled to rank as the "Old Guard."[59]

[55] Harrison to his wife, January 8, 1863, Harrison MSS, Vol. 4.
[56] Randall, *op. cit.,* p. 528.
[57] Harrison to his wife, January 8, 1863, Harrison MSS, Vol. 4.
[58] Cist, *op. cit.,* p. 136.
[59] Bode to the Editor, Indianapolis *Daily Journal,* December 26, 1862.

Lew Wallace has described these four months, for Harrison, as "a period . . . evenly divided between hunting guerrillas and drilling his men."[60]

In spite of the monotony, Ben could assure Carrie that he got "along with less grumbling than you would imagine."[61] An examination of Harrison's heavy correspondence for this period reveals two principal reasons why he did not especially notice the ennui of the camp. He seems to have discovered pleasure in novel reading, even though he devoted a great deal of time to books on tactics, strategy, and the art of war in general.

Harrison was compelled to admit that some of the observations by Dr. Bishop of Miami days about fiction were not entirely true. Not only did the colonel now deny that novel reading was "inferior and productive of evil," but he unblushingly reversed his collegiate conclusion that "it unfits the mind for close application to many subjects." Fun-loving Carrie must have chuckled as she read Ben's latest confidence that "in Gallatin I borrowed a large bound volume of Bulwer's novels and have found them very entertaining when tired of tactics and regulations."[62] Later, he wrote from Nashville:

I am fairly driven to write to you tonight by sheer loneliness. I bought today "Little Dorritt" [sic], and have been pouring [sic] over Dickens' description of the squalor and wretchedness of the Debtor's Prison, and of rainy, dripping, soggy days . . . in London, which consorting with my own loneliness, the pelting rain, and sodden ground of my own camp has made me quite miserable.[63]

These excursions into the imaginative realm of the novel were rare in comparison with the almost daily drudgery of long hours devoted to the study of the military art. This was of his own choosing, and he refused General Ward's offer of a provost marshalship in order to pursue his tactical studies more closely.[64] On a brief trip to Louisville, he related, "I bought several military books[65] . . . and am engaged now in studying them. They enable

60 Lew Wallace, Life of Gen. Ben Harrison, p. 184.

61 Harrison to his wife, January 18, 1863, Harrison MSS, Vol. 4. He was able to write an average of three letters a week through this year.

62 Harrison to his wife, January 18, 1863, Harrison MSS, Vol. 4.

63 Harrison to his wife, October 15, 1863, Harrison MSS, Vol. 5.

64 Harrison to his wife, February 14, 1863, Harrison MSS, Vol. 4.

65 Six of these are now in the library of the Harrison Memorial Home in Indianapolis. They bear the inscription by Harrison: "Gallatin, Tenn., Feb. 3, 1863."

me to spend my leisure both pleasantly and profitably."[66] This resolve to master the theory and art of war, while demanding many hours of serious study, was not surprising to the men who knew Harrison best. General Wallace wrote:

It must be remembered that he was as fresh in arms as the greenest man in the ranks. He was systematic and painstaking, however, and buckled to the mysteries of the tactical "schools," as he had in college days to geometry.[67]

As far as Benjamin Harrison was concerned, the master tactician in 1863 was Hardee,[68] and there can be no doubt that the latter's authoritative work, *Rifle and Light Infantry Tactics*, became a second Bible in camp. Harrison's adjutant, Jim Mitchell, as well as the regiment's Lieutenant Colonel, Jim Burgess, each possessed copies. With unfailing regularity, these men, accompanied by other staff officers, were summoned to Harrison's tent in the evening where he questioned them on each chapter. When it came to field tactics, Harrison "required them to illustrate the manoeuvers upon a board, chalk in hand. 'Hardee,' was of course, the umpire for the settlement of questions."[69] Naturally, Harrison supplemented Hardee with the works of later military authorities, such as Casey's three volumes on *Infantry Tactics*.[70]

Study and instruction were not restricted to the manuals usually prescribed. Harrison read omnivorously the accounts of the celebrated campaigns and battles in European as well as in American history. At regimental headquarters, *Modern War: Its Theory and Practice* by Imre Szabad (U.S.A.)[71] stood side by side with the English translation of General de Jomini's *The Political and*

[66] Harrison to his wife, February 14, 1863, Harrison MSS, Vol. 4.

[67] Wallace, *op. cit.*, p. 184.

[68] This work, prepared under the direction of the War Department by Brevet Lieut. W. J. Hardee, was published in Philadelphia in 1855.

[69] Wallace, *op. cit.*, p. 184. Copies belonging and inscribed to Mitchell and Burgess are now in the library of Harrison's Indianapolis Home.

[70] Published in 1862 by D. Van Nostrand, New York, "for the instruction, exercise and manoeuvers of the soldier, the company, a line of skirmishers, battalion, brigade or corps d'armee."

[71] Published in 1863 by Harpers, New York. A copy with the inscription, "Benj. Harrison, Col. 70th Ind. Vols., Gallatin, Tenn., Feb. 3, 1863," is in Harrison's library.

Military History of the Campaign of Waterloo.[72] While Schalk's *Summary of the Art of War* was widely consulted at camp, it ranked no higher with Harrison than de Jomini's other military classic, *The Art of War.*[73]

Several studies on field fortifications were also scrutinized. Perhaps D. H. Mahan's treatise,[74] with detailed instructions on "the method of laying out, constructing, defending and attacking entrenchments," proved most valuable, in the light of Harrison's successes during the Atlanta Campaign of 1864.

Because the sometimes "lazy, spiritless life of a garrison soldier"[75] did not agree with Harrison's habits of mind and body, highly geared as he was to intellectual activity as a civilian, he studied all the harder. By late August, his own and his command's progress in military learning had not gone unnoticed. While the Seventieth was at Nashville, Major Brigney made a routine inspection of the entire division and let fall several remarks showing that he deemed Harrison "a first rate officer" who "would be a Brig this fall."[76] A month later Harrison was in brigade school.[77] Although he confided to Carrie that "I study and read until I tire of both and am left a prey to loneliness and discontent,"[78] he drew some consolation from the fact that he was able to stump his instructors:

I have had the pleasure of attending several of his [Ward's] schools and am puzzling the old fellow to death with questions. Instead of learning us anything, he is confusing and unsettling all that we have learned. . . . Harryman is always on hand and comes to the General's rescue whenever he can, but I have several times stumped him too.[79]

Anyone who knew Harrison's propensity for study and his self-confessed lack of skill in the social amenities might justly suspect that this assiduous application to military theory would

[72] Capt. S. V. Benet, Ordnance Dept., U. S. Army, was the translator. Baron de Jomini was aide-de-camp to the Emperor of Russia.
[73] Translated from the French by Capt. C. H. Mendell (U. S. A.). This copy is also in the library of the Harrison Home.
[74] *An Elementary Course of Civil Engineering* (New York, 1835). Mahan was Professor of Military and Civil Engineering at the United States Military Academy.
[75] Harrison to his wife, October 15, 1863, Harrison MSS, Vol. 5.
[76] Harrison to his wife, August 26, 1863, Harrison MSS, Vol. 5.
[77] Harrison to his wife, October 4, 1863, Harrison MSS, Vol. 5.
[78] Harrison to his wife, October 15, 1863, Harrison MSS, Vol. 5.
[79] Harrison to his wife, October 13, 1863, Harrison MSS, Vol. 5.

have warped the man. This could well have been the case. Even back in April he had reported to Carrie the results of a party given by General Paine.[80] He admitted:

It was quite a gay assemblage. Dancing and card playing went round merrily and we had some very fine music. The music and a very nice supper were the only pleasures in which I participated. Though frequently urged to dance, and especially by a very buxom and pretty wife of one of our Indiana surgeons (Mrs. McGinnis from Evansville) I persistently declined. I really felt out of place in such a social gathering and must have seemed very dull to others as I was in fact. I believe I have lost all of my manners and all faculty of making myself agreeable in general society.[81]

He candidly admitted loneliness on several occasions. While stationed in Nashville he wrote: "If I were a frequenter of the theatres, or of the more questionable places of amusement with which this city abounds, I might enjoy our location as well as some of the officers I know."[82]

Fortunately for himself, Harrison did not long remain on a road to social ostracism and personal unhappiness. His resolution to improve himself in this regard was gently prompted by the ever-vigilant Carrie at Indianapolis.[83] She probably took great pride in his subsequent letters, for Ben was soon given ample opportunity to prove the sincerity and strength of his determination to lead a more balanced existence. General Paine continued to give parties at his cottage home, and as a rule the staff of the Seventieth were invited. Frequently, the entertainment provided was "rare and racy"; at other times, a round of singing was merely followed by a round of drinking. Harrison claimed that he learned how to enjoy himself as a witness, if not as an actual participant.[84]

80 When General Dumont was removed from command due to illness on December 10, 1862, General Paine was placed in charge of the division.

81 Harrison to his wife, April 5, 1863, Harrison MSS, Vol. 4. "My close application to hard work before coming into the army and my separation from all society since have made a very dull, matter of fact sort of personage out of me."

82 Harrison to his wife, October 15, 1863, Harrison MSS, Vol. 5.

83 Carrie used to tell Ben of his faults along these lines. He insisted that she need never apologize for such kindness. Harrison to his wife, December 10, 1862, Harrison MSS, Vol. 4.

84 Colonel Dustin insisted that Harrison be present, and sometimes had to hoodwink him into attending social functions. Harrison to his wife, April 10, 1863, Harrison MSS, Vol. 4.

His ability to make an impromptu speech had been discovered at a party when Colonel Dustin of an Illinois regiment presented General Paine "with a splendid Henry Clay Banner of the campaign of 1844 ... captured from some rebel house."[85] After Paine's gracious acceptance, a call was made upon Harrison. After some persuasion, he made a speech alluding "to Grandpa Harrison and to me a descendant. . . . Then I was fairly in for it." Carrie was encouraged by the sequel, as she read:

I made a short response and you will be pleased to know that I was very highly complimented and very rapturously applauded. . . . My reputation as a speaker is on the rise, however it may be in a military point of view. Some of the officers got quite *mellow* and I laughed more than I did for a year before at the antics of some of them, particularly Col. Dustin.

Referring to the bourbon that flowed freely, Harrison was at pains to assure Carrie that "I touched it very lightly myself," as did Surgeon Amos Reagan and Adjutant Jim Mitchell. "We came to camp duly sober, Col. Jim was a little funny, but not noticeably so."[86] When Carrie visited the camp during May and September, 1863, she found Ben leading a more normal existence. While he always found a "drunken revel disgusting," by November he could honestly confess that he enjoyed a "pleasant, cheerful dinner of the kind where only wine enough is taken to give vivacity to the mind."[87] Harrison had successfully climbed several rungs in the social ladder. With a twinkle in his eye he admitted that his "speech making and toast drinking . . . surprise" those who do not know me and who "from my quiet reserve at table have probably voted me a bore."[88]

The Seventieth Indiana, once more reunited with Ward's brigade, was assigned to Nashville, Tennessee, on August 19, 1863.[89] Here, as part of General Granger's reserve corps, it was engaged almost exclusively in guarding trains bound for Chattanooga,

85 *Ibid.*

86 *Ibid.*

87 Harrison to his wife, November 27, 1863, Harrison MSS, Vol. 5. His idea of a "good" dinner was the Thanksgiving Day repast served in a Nashville restaurant: "Venison, Turkey, Quail, Oysters in several styles, sparkling Catawba etc."

88 *Ibid.*

89 Harrison to Gen. E. A. Carman, February 8, 1876, Harrison MSS, Vol. 7.

while Rosecrans' command again went to the front.[90] The remaining four months of 1863 were spent there, with only fatigue and picket duty to lend variety to an otherwise completely enervating assignment.[91] Although Col. Harrison was thoroughly disgusted by this "scavenger" duty, as he termed it, he could say "that every day in camp should be used in preparation for that *other* day, always to be kept in mind—the day of battle."[92]

At last, after various delays and minor assignments, General Ward's command was called to the front. On January 2, 1864, it lost its unspectacular status as a member of the reserve corps by temporarily becoming the 1st Brigade of the 1st Division of the 11th Army Corps. In this reorganization Harrison commanded the brigade, while Ward led the division. Before the 11th Army Corps reached the front, it was fused with the 12th and this new consolidation was named the 20th Army Corps. In this organization Ward resumed command of the 1st Brigade, now part of the 3rd Division. With this outfit the Seventieth Indiana Infantry, under Harrison, was destined to serve until the close of the war.[93] After a year and a half of monotonous, although invaluable, experience, they were ready for combat.

Fortunately for the camp-weary Hoosiers, Ward's brigade and Harrison's regiment fitted admirably into the ambitious and ultimately successful plans of the new military dispensation in Washington, headed by General Ulysses S. Grant. Grant's appointment on March 9, 1864, to the supreme command of all the Union armies also elevated William Tecumseh Sherman to the head of the Division of the Mississippi.[94] Although there had been bitter campaigns and important battles before the spring of 1864, with Grant and Sherman directing the main armies in the east and west, chances now brightened for an early ending of the war.

90 Wallace, *op. cit.*, p. 185.

91 Harrison to his wife, August 21, 23, 25, 26, 29, October 1, 4, 1863, Harrison MSS, Vol. 5.

92 Wallace, *op. cit.*, p. 185.

93 Harrison to Gen. E. A. Carman, February 6, 1876, Harrison MSS, Vol. 7.

94 William T. Sherman, *Memoirs* (New York, 1875), II, 5: "On the 18th day of March . . . I relieved Lieutenant-General Grant in command of the Military Division of the Ohio." Randall, *op. cit.*, p. 551: "The comradeship of Sherman and Grant bespoke a high morale in Union ranks. They were 'as brothers,' says Sherman, both trained as professional soldiers but 'made' on the anvil of war, both associated with western victories, each giving credit to the other and ready to cooperate in the closing strokes of a well-planned, comprehensive campaign."

The prevailing concept of the war was changed as General Grant devised campaigns in combination, a strategy calculated to occupy the Confederates on their right, left and center and to keep them so busy that there could be no passing of help from one section to another. Consequently, with the conviction that Northern numerical superiority should prevail, simultaneous blows at the Confederate Army of Northern Virginia and the Army of the Tennessee were projected. Grant came east to command the Army of the Potomac and Sherman traveled to Nashville to take charge of his forces.[95]

Sherman had come to his new command fully determined that the Army of the Cumberland should be reorganized. He ordered the consolidation of the 11th and 12th Army Corps and placed "Fighting Joe" Hooker[96] in command of what was now christened the 20th Army Corps.[97] Hooker, who was bent upon a change of personnel within the corps, was adamant in his demand that Major General Daniel Butterfield should lead one of the three divisions that comprised the new corps.[98] Fortunately for Harrison, Joe Hooker got what he wanted. As the time of the reorganization approached, Hooker despatched Butterfield, his Chief of Staff, to find out why Ward's brigade was still posted at Nashville. Butterfield arrived in the city on February 11, 1864, and Harrison wrote to his wife:

There was a revival of the marching story this week, but I cannot tell you what it may result in. Gen. Butterfield (Hooker's Chief of

95 Jacob D. Cox, *Atlanta* (New York, 1882), gives the essential military and administrative background, but it should be supplemented by Henry Cist, *The Army of the Cumberland*. Walter Hebert, *Fighting Joe Hooker* (Indianapolis, 1944), especially Ch. 20, and Lloyd Lewis, *Sherman: The Fighting Prophet* (New York, 1932), are colorful and accurate accounts. For the background of Sherman's Georgia campaign see Otto Eisenschiml and Ralph Newman, *The American Iliad* (Indianapolis, 1947).

96 Hooker's sobriquet was well earned; he maintained that the highest form of human enjoyment was "campaigning in an enemy's country." See Hebert, *op. cit.*, p. 272, wherein he cites D. E. Sickles, *An Address Delivered in Boston before the Hooker Association of Massachusetts* (Norwood, 1910), p. 25.

97 According to Hebert, *op. cit.*, p. 272, and *Official Records*, Series 2, XXXII, pp. 363–66, the 20th Army Corps was organized as follows:

1st Division: Alpheus S. Williams; Brigade Commanders: Joseph F. Knipe, Thomas H. Ruger, Hector Tyndal;

2nd Division: John W. Geary; Brigade Commanders: Charles Candy, Adolphus Bushbeck, David Ireland;

3rd Division: Daniel Butterfield; Brigade Commanders: William T. Ward, Samuel Ross, James Wood, Jr.

98 Hebert, *op. cit.*, p. 271.

Photograph by George N. Barnard

Courtesy Library of Congress

PASS IN THE RACCOON RIDGE, WHITESIDE

Photograph by Matthew B. Brady   *Courtesy Harrison Memorial Home*

HERO-TRIO AT PEACH TREE CREEK
Brig. Gen. Benjamin Harrison, Maj. Gen. William Ward, and
Brig. Gen. John Coburn

Staff) was up here a day or two since and making inquiries into the matter and has now gone back to report. He says Gen. Grant expressed surprise that we had not been sent forward. We shall probably know within a few days what to expect.[99]

And on February 12th, Butterfield wrote to Hooker:

My opinion in the premises is that the interests of the service would be best promoted by moving General Ward's Brigade, if not his division to the front. Their present condition near Nashville, with its temptation to soldiers, will not be improved. The command is represented to be in a very high state of discipline and perfection in drill.[100]

Within a fortnight, Hooker ordered Ward's brigade to set out from Nashville and join its corps. In Ward's absence, Harrison took command, and within a few days he was on his way to Lookout Valley to join Hooker's command.

[99] Harrison to his wife, February 12, 1864, Harrison MSS, Vol. 5.
[100] Official Records, Series 2, XXXII, pp. 376–77.

CHAPTER XI

In the Face of the Enemy

W ITH THE SPRING of 1864 the three-year old Civil War entered a new phase. A new-born spirit of aggressiveness in the North seemed to support Grant as he assumed command. The foray of might which he planned would rain sledge-hammer blows on Southern troops throughout Virginia and would place Lee on the defensive at Richmond. Sherman's task was to force open the gate leading to the lower South. He had no particular city to capture, not Atlanta, nor Augusta, nor Savannah. His objective was the army of Confederate General Joseph E. Johnston, "go where it might."[1]

Sherman, in whose campaign Harrison was to play so conspicuous a role, spent the early weeks of spring in assembling under his direct command three good-sized armies.[2] Major General John M. Schofield's Army of the Ohio was the smallest unit, comprising 14,000 men and 28 guns. Next in numerical rank was Major General James B. McPherson's Army of the Tennessee, with 24,000 men and 96 guns. The most formidable element was the Army of the Cumberland, numbering 61,000 men and 130 guns, under the command of Major General George H. Thomas, already the "renowned Rock of Chickamauga."[3]

Opposed to these forces was General Johnston, the peer of Lee in defensive generalship[4] and the "storm center" of the Confed-

---

1 William T. Sherman, *Memoirs*, II, 26.

2 *Ibid.*, pp. 23–24; Jacob D. Cox, *Atlanta*, p. 25.

3 Two recent biographies of General Thomas have appeared: Richard O'Connor, *Thomas: Rock of Chickamauga* (New York, 1948), and Freeman Cleaves, *Rock of Chickamauga: The Life of General George H. Thomas* (Norman, Okla., 1948). More manuscript research went into Cleaves' work, which seems both better organized and more critical.

4 James G. Randall, *The Civil War and Reconstruction*, p. 511, modified this and claimed Johnston was "almost" a peer, while Cox, *op. cit.*, p. 26, says Johnston was second to Lee, if "second."

erate Army.[5] Although outnumbered, for Sherman's forces numbered close to 100,000, Johnston determined early to employ his 70,000 troops[6] in constructing entrenchments, one behind the other, to be resorted to in the event of compulsory retreat. His strategy was to maintain his usual "lynx-eyed watchfulness" over his foe, so as to tempt the latter constantly to assault the entrenchments that were so well fortified that one man in the line was equal to three or four on the attack.[7] Each commander knew the skill and reputation of his opponent, and in April both hoped that this spring would be a season of hope and success.

While Johnston and his Confederate subordinates, Hood, Polk, Hardee, and Cleburne, were digging in and disposing their forces in the vicinity of Dalton, Georgia, the Army of the Cumberland shook itself out of winter quarters.[8] Harrison started Ward's brigade from Nashville on February 24, 1864.[9] The march to Georgia promised to be wearying, for the terrain was mountainous. Harrison, however, had his own ideas regarding the conduct of the march. After only one week on the road at an average marching pace of ten to thirteen miles per day, it was evident that good time had been made by troops who were still sufficiently rested "to be delighted with the daily routine."[10] Even Harrison, now weighing 140 pounds and looking the picture of health, maintained that the march would "greatly improve my health, though it didn't seem to need any."[11] The only real casualties on the route after the first hundred miles were the underfed and none too hardy mules. After being exposed to a chilling rain and a hard pull through mud ankle-deep, many simply lay down on the grass and died.[12]

[5] Alfred P. James, "General Joseph Eggleston Johnston, Storm Center of the Confederate Army," *Mississippi Valley Historical Review*, 14 (1927–28), 342–59. See also Cox, *op. cit.*, pp. 25 ff.

[6] This eternal controversy about the number of Confederate troops in Johnston's army is admirably handled in a lengthy footnote by Randall, *op. cit.*, p. 551.

[7] Cox, *op. cit.*, p. 27.

[8] O'Connor, *op. cit.*, pp. 259 ff.

[9] At Murfreesboro, Harrison relinquished command of the brigade to Gen. Ward, who, accompanied by the 102nd Illinois, had caught up with his troops after a few days' absence. Harrison to his wife, February 27, 1864, Harrison MSS, Vol. 5.

[10] Harrison to his wife, February 27, 1864, Harrison MSS, Vol. 5.

[11] *Ibid.*

[12] By contrast, Harrison stated: "We have slept in wet blankets which were frozen in the morning and I am still perfectly well, and not even a cold." B. Harrison to his wife, March 2, 1864, Harrison MSS, Vol. 5.

When the Seventieth passed through Shelbyville, Tennessee, large numbers turned out to see these "veterans" yet unscarred by battle. In the audience were a number of Hooker's eastern soldiers, who viewed the Indiana troops with critical eye. Evidently, the outfit passed muster quite successfully, for the easterners were not slow to say within Harrison's hearing that "The Indiana Regiments made the best march through they ever saw and were the best looking Brigade."[13] Of course, the men were pleased and went into camp that night in fine spirits. Yet this was only a lull before the storm of hardship and disappointment. Heavy rains came to make the wagon trails nothing better than a sea of mud.

I thought I had seen things *a little rough,* but . . . yesterday's march and yesterday in camp at Tullohoma surpassed anything I had ever *dreamed* of. It rained . . . and the holes in the road were up to the axles of the wagons. Some of the wagons did not get in until noon the next day and the rear guard were forced to stand all night in a swamp and without fire to do any good. I went out four miles the next day to help them and took a ration of whiskey to them. Last night when we and all our bed clothes were wet it turned cold and froze quite hard and this morning we got up stiff all over.[14]

During the remainder of the march through southern Tennessee, Ward took over his brigade once again, and Harrison's responsibility was at an end. Yet the Brigadier General from Kentucky might well have wished things were otherwise, for he had committed at least three serious errors on the march that drew the fire of Harrison's criticism. Even before the brigade reached mountainous country, Harrison complained that "Gen. Ward has been a perfect nuisance as usual."[15] What particularly annoyed him, he wrote, was Ward's custom of starting ahead with a mounted company in the morning, and each time failing completely to communicate any orders to his regimental commanders. Even when the brigade's destination would be made known, Ward was not sure "by what road" to proceed.

The troops' strong feeling against Ward reached its peak on March 4. His brigade, rapidly reaching out for Alabama and

---

13 *Ibid.*

14 *Ibid.*

15 *Ibid.* Harrison frequently aired his misgivings about Ward to the confidential ear of his wife.

Georgia, was directed to pass through some desolate mountain country with the understanding that they should then pitch camp in the valley of Big Crow Creek, 18 miles north of the Alabama line, and on the railroad leading to Stevenson. Ward preceded the marching columns on horseback in order to determine the road. Before long, he had lost his way in the mountain passes. The wagon train, well advanced along a desolate trail, had to be turned around and brought back several miles. "The roads are terribly bad and it seems a wonder that a single wagon came over safely," Ben wrote. His added remarks to Carrie are interesting:

> I worked like a Turk correcting his errors and finally got the troops and the train on the right road. The Gen. got a good deal of *cussing*, I hear, for the blunder, and right well did he deserve it. As to myself I am told that I was greatly praised for the energy I displayed in bringing things right. I marched the troops right across the mountain from one road to another where I venture no horseman ever rode before . . . but as we saved several miles march, it was thought to be a good thing. Gen. W. was greatly surprised when I sent a staff officer to report that the Brigade was on the new road and ready to march forward.[16]

Yet, when it came time to explain Ward's blunder, Harrison's humor did not fail him. Admitting that the desolate countryside yielded no army rations, he naïvely explained the Brigadier's mistake by adding:

> Gen. Ward rides on ahead and buys up all of the chickens. I think he and his staff must have been tracking a chicken when they lost the road yesterday. If we had not stumbled on a house in the hills, we would have been going yet on the Battle Creek Road.[17]

On the next day, however, when Ward succeeded in losing the road again, Harrison put aside any semblance of charity, attributing this second error in two days to Ward's heavy drinking.[18] Under the circumstances this charge may or may not have been true. The brigade had been instructed to march along Crow Creek, "the crooked stream whose windings we were compelled

16 Harrison to his wife, March 5, 1864, Harrison MSS, Vol. 5.
17 *Ibid.*
18 Harrison to his wife, March 7, 1864, Harrison MSS, Vol. 5.

to follow from the summit of the mountain to Stevenson." After Ward's mistake had been detected and his orders countermanded, the march was completed without further mishap. In the reflective mood sometimes induced by a glowing campfire, Ben wrote to Carrie:

> We marched to within one mile of Stevenson, following all the way the valley of . . . Big Crow Creek . . . often having to go a mile around to get a quarter on our way. The banks of the stream are in many places swampy and the road follows along the base of the hills, and makes the circuit of every little cove in the mountains. Gen. Ward said he hadn't been drinking anything (?) but that the road was so crooked that it made him drunk. Perhaps in consequence of this he lost his road again and ordered me to cross the creek at Anderson. . . . After working for an hour and getting 20 men wet all over in trying to construct a bridge, we found out there was a good road (the one that we had been following) that didn't cross the creek at all and I turned the troops back and took that road.[19]

Captain Merrill called the road from Bridgeport, Alabama, to Wauhatchie, Tennessee, the "region of dead mules."[20] Harrison's recollection of the day is vivid:

> We had a terrible day's march from Bridgeport here. The road was lined with dead mules and horses and the stench was sickening. Dr. Reagan got to vomiting and I had hard work to keep my stomach quiet. We got our water for coffee out of a creek in the morning; and when we started to march up it, found dead mules in and along the creek at the rate of a hundred to a mile. We joked it off, however, as only soldiers can, and suffered no detriment from our cups of mule tea.[21]

Having covered twelve miles in this tiresome trudge, Harrison's command reached the Wauhatchie encampment on a picturesque hillside beneath the frowning heights of Lookout Mountain. Here in a narrow valley, "with Lookout Range on one side and Raccoon on the other," the Seventieth received its warmest welcome. On hand to greet the untried Hoosiers were Major General Oliver O. Howard, Commander of the 11th Army Corps, and his entire staff. There was even a brass band. Although

19 *Ibid.*
20 Merrill, *The Seventieth Indiana*, p. 75.
21 Harrison to his wife, March 11, 1864, Harrison MSS, Vol. 5.

the troops were exhausted by the march under a scorching sun
and through a polluted atmosphere, Ward's entire brigade passed
in review. Harrison confided to his wife that Howard "seemed
very much pleased with the Brigade and treated us with greatest
cordiality."[22] This was the beginning of a friendship that ma-
tured with the passing years.[23] Howard was a man of parts whom
Sherman praised as "one who mingles so gracefully and perfectly
the polished Christian gentleman and the prompt, zealous and
gallant soldier."[24] A delighted Harrison wrote:

We (self, staff and field officers) took dinner with him yesterday
and witnessed a review of one of his Brigades. He rode all about his
camp with us . . . in a word made us feel perfectly at home. He asked
a blessing at table and bore himself like a Christian gentleman.[25]

Camped on the ground of "Hooker's fight where he scaled
Lookout" during the celebrated battle above the clouds, Harrison was soon feeding the fires of ambition and glory within his
own heart. One afternoon, he accepted the invitation of General
Howard to ride over and examine the battlefield. The lesson of
heroic sacrifice was not lost upon Ben; for that same evening from
the quiet of his tent he despatched a significant message to his
wife: "I feel as if I had a character to make . . . and shall work
night and day to do it and hope to have my labors appreciated."[26]
Within a week, he was appointed Commandant of the post at
Wauhatchie.[27] During the next month and a half, while holding
this office as well as directing the activities of Ward's Brigade,
the colonel worked "like a beaver" both in adjusting the camp
and in adapting himself to the methods of Howard's 11th Army

22 Harrison to his wife, March 11, 1864, Harrison MSS, Vol. 5. Their new location was about six miles from Chattanooga.

23 Immediately after his election to the presidency, Harrison received a letter
from Howard who said in part: "I remember you, when in your young manhood,
you were maneuvering your regiment near Bridgeport, Ala. It was the first time I
looked into your cheerful face. I felt stronger that you with a noble regiment were
there." November 7, 1888, Harrison MSS, Vol. 45.

24 Lloyd Lewis, *Sherman: The Fighting Prophet*, p. 349.

25 Harrison to his wife, March 11, 1864, Harrison MSS, Vol. 5. See Hebert, Walter,
Fighting Joe Hooker, pp. 262–66. Otto Eisenschiml and Ralph Newman, *The
American Iliad*, has a splendid account of the battle of Chickamauga and Missionary Ridge where the fighting in the West took place. For Howard's part, see pp.
532–37.

26 Harrison to his wife, March 11, 1864, Harrison MSS, Vol. 5.

27 Harrison to his wife, March 15, 1864, Harrison MSS, Vol. 5.

Corps. He earned a slight reputation as "Administrative Ben,"
but no one took the liberty of saying so to his face.

Sunday in camp afforded Harrison his only respite from the
drudgery of administration. Usually, a preaching service was held
at headquarters at five; and, after the chaplain had given his message, General Howard, "a very decided Christian and a total abstinence man,"[28] would make a short address. Hooker, never too
guarded in his remarks, said, "Howard would command a prayer
meeting with a good deal more ability than he would an army."[29]
Harrison found this procedure to his personal liking; the general
was apt to "urge some strong consideration against profanity and
other vices,"[30] and second, his manner and mode of speech were
"easy, gentle and persuasive."[31] There is considerable evidence
that acting Brigadier Harrison drew abundant consolation from
these and kindred services. Each succeeding letter to Indianapolis contained some reflection on the progress of his spiritual life.
On the final Sunday as a member of the 11th Army Corps under
Howard, he wrote to his wife:

This is a beautiful Sabbath and my heart *yearns* to sit with you in
the house of God at home, and to go with my dear little ones to the
Sabbath School I love so much, but, if it cannot be . . . I must endeavor
to find such grace as God will afford me in my private meditations in
my lonely cabin, or at a brief service in the open air. Oh, how I do
pine for home . . . God only grant that there be no "vacant chair."[32]

While at Wauhatchie, Harrison's star was in the ascendant.
The high command under Howard liked his ability to get things
done, while subordinates in camp were pleased with an administration that provided good food and comfortable quarters.[33] This
honeymoon of contentment, however, was threatened with an
abrupt termination by the consolidation of the 11th and 12th
Army Corps into the 20th Army Corps. General Oliver Howard,
Harrison's intimate friend and potential Warwick, was transferred, to make room for Major General Joseph Hooker.[34] This

28 Harrison to his wife, March 22, 1864, Harrison MSS, Vol. 5.
29 Hebert, *op. cit.*, p. 294.
30 Harrison to his wife, March 29, 1864, Harrison MSS, Vol. 5.
31 Harrison to his wife, March 22, 1864, Harrison MSS, Vol. 5.
32 Harrison to his wife, April 3, 1864, Harrison MSS, Vol. 5.
33 Harrison to his wife, March 24, 29, April 3, 7, 10, 1864, Harrison MSS, Vol 5.
Also Merrill, *op. cit.*, pp. 76–79.
34 Hebert, *op. cit.*, p. 271.

change came as a distinct blow to Harrison; and he was none too happy in the loss of Howard's leadership:

> It was a source of real regret and sadness to me to lose Gen. Howard. . . . I really learned to *love* him, and he is the only military leader I felt so towards. He was so much a *gentleman,* refined, kind and rigidly conscientious in the discharge of his duty. All of his actions seem to spring from principle. As a military leader . . . his great characteristic was a cool disregard of danger in the path of duty.[35]

When he referred to Hooker, Howard's successor and the new Commander of the 20th Army Corps, Harrison had few good words. Undoubtedly, his first opinion of "Fighting Joe" was somewhat colored, when he learned that Hooker liked General Ward. With the removal of Howard's restraining influence, Harrison feared that "whiskey . . . would be the *ascendant* now, if the stories about Hooker are well founded."[36] During the first few weeks under this new military regime he stayed far from Hooker's headquarters. "Indeed, I have only been [there] . . . once and that once shortly after we came here. I do not like to call there now, as he might think I was *toadying* to keep my place."[37]

Harrison's fear that Hooker would reward General Ward was fully realized once the total reorganization was effected. In mid-April, Ward resumed command of the 1st Brigade of Butterfield's 3rd Division, while Harrison returned to the command of his own regiment.[38] The colonel was not nearly as displeased by his own demotion as he was "heartily disgusted" that "the incubus we have carried so long"[39] should be his superior officer once more. He had a solution for his problem; and having swallowed his disappointment, he told Carrie:

> . . . there is no use of grumbling. . . . I have a duty to do, and I *shall do it,* however unpleasant it may be. . . . I have received a very flattering expression from the officers of the different Regiments in regard to

[35] Harrison concluded his encomium of Howard by saying that "he seemed to have put his life in God's keeping with perfect trust." Harrison to his wife, April 10, 1864, Harrison MSS, Vol. 5.
[36] Harrison to his wife, April 7, 1864, Harrison MSS, Vol. 5. It is evident that Harrison entertained a growing dislike for Ward as a "lazy sot" and one who was always "beastly drunk."
[37] Harrison to his wife, April 10, 1864, Harrison MSS, Vol. 5.
[38] *Ibid.* The orders were officially issued to Harrison on April 15, 1864. "Direct to me hereafter 70 Ind. Vols., 1st Brig. 3rd Div., 20 A. C. Army of the Cumberland."
[39] Harrison to his wife, April 7, 1864, Harrison MSS, Vol. 5.

my command of the Brigade, which must atone in large measure for the loss of my command.[40]

In time, Harrison came to like Hooker, and became a frequent guest at "Fighting Joe's" dinner table. He felt somewhat vindicated when Hooker called him aside for a long conversation, in the course of which the general advanced the confidential information that the regimental commanders had bestowed liberal praise upon the acting Brigadier from Indiana, and told Carrie:

He said they [the regimental officers] gave me the *whole credit* of making the Brigade what it is, and that it was not divided with anyone. I was glad to hear that the truth was *partly* known, though I told him that I thought the Regimental Commanders were entitled to more credit than anyone else.[41]

Although he still maintained that Ward was a poor brigade commander, he was moved to confess that:

Perhaps my ambition was soaring too high, for a soldier who had never seen any service, and this clipping of my wings may do me good.
With God's blessing I hope, when I head the 70th into battle to strike some good blows for my country, and it will then be time to claim a larger command.[42]

During the spring, both the Union forces under Sherman and the Confederate forces under Johnston made elaborate preparations for the battle that all knew was close at hand. April teemed with rumors in Harrison's camp, all telling of a rebel offensive under Gen. Joe Johnston, to be launched near Ringold, Georgia, on the Chickamauga River. Definite news, however, was most difficult to obtain; and while a pitched battle at Ringold never materialized, the anxiety suffered by both sides was intense.[43] In late April, a rebel chaplain deserted Johnston's forces and, upon entering the Union camp, reported the Confederate Army at no less than 60,000 effective troops. This piece of information caused Harrison to warn his wife that General Johnston "will

40 *Ibid.*
41 Harrison to his wife, April 7, 1864, Harrison MSS, Vol. 5.
42 *Ibid.*
43 Merrill, *op. cit.*, p. 81.

give us warm work; but we will be more than a match for him, if we can only keep our long line of communications."[44]

Actually, Johnston had concentrated his troops at Dalton, Georgia. Sherman's intelligence reported that this strategic center was strongly fortified, whereupon the Union leader put aside any intention of "attacking the position seriously in front."[45] This strategy, as Harrison explained it, was founded "on the plain proposition that if we can flank the fortified position of the enemy at Dalton, we will do so rather than to assault it in the front."[46]

Even before the signal to march, almost every man at Wauhatchie sensed the nearness of the Confederate forces now concentrated for the first general engagement of the Atlanta campaign. In the heavy mail pouch ticketed for Indianapolis was a long letter to Carrie, one paragraph of which told the whole story:

We have been having very warm weather for several days and the trees are bursting into the full foliage as if by magic, after being kept back for so long by the cold rains and winds. These steep and craggy sides of Lookout will soon be hidden by a leafy curtain. Is it not a strange contrast that while nature is budding into a sweet and joyous life, man should be preparing a carnival of death? . . . I fancy these stalwart soldiers of the hillsides are unfurling their leafy banners to welcome us, and that the songsters in their branches are singing to cheer us, as we march on, the conquering soldiers of freedom. . . . In nature there is no life except the seed be cast into the earth and die, and so in our national life, this sad time of death shall yet yield its fruit in a purer, higher and surer national life. . . . May God help us who stand for our country in the coming conflict to quit ourselves like men.[47]

Carrie's anxiety had been increased by stories which had appeared in the Indiana press. Her husband reassured her by adding:

You must not feel uneasy or be alarmed at any rumors you may hear of fighting. I will telegraph you after any fight we may be engaged in, and let you know how I fared, and will inform you of the truth as soon as any body could possibly hear it at home. . . . I shall

44 Harrison to his wife, April 24, 1864, Harrison MSS, Vol. 5.
45 Sherman, op. cit., II, 32.
46 Harrison to his wife, April 26, 1864, Harrison MSS, Vol. 5.
47 Harrison to his wife, April 26, 1864, Harrison MSS, Vol. 5.

take all proper care of myself both on the march and in battle and have a strong faith that God will keep me safely.[48]

Grant and Sherman saw to it that everything was in complete readiness for their simultaneous thrusts at Lee and Johnston. Grant's original "D-Day" was April 30th. Consequently, on the 28th Sherman moved his headquarters to Chattanooga and prepared to take the field in person.[49] Grant canceled his original plans and set May 5th as the day to move on both fronts. This extra delay enabled Sherman to maneuver his three armies to more advantageous positions. While Thomas directed his Army of the Cumberland toward Ringold in anticipation of rebel resistance, Harrison and the Seventieth left Wauhatchie, crossed over the Chickamauga battleground, and reached Lee and Gordon's Mills on May 1, 1864.

On May 4th, he moved to within five miles of the rebel position at Buzzard's Roost. From this outpost Harrison could hear the firing at Tunnell Hill. After a single day in camp, the Seventieth was ordered to the front, but progress was slow because the enemy had blockaded the way with timber. The next day Harrison's advance guard encountered hostile scouts, and "routing them and capturing some prisoners, arms and horses," they marched to within six miles of Dalton, where the bulk of the Confederacy's finest soldiers awaited them.[50]

His self-description, meant only for Carrie's eyes, is eminently clear.

To give you an idea of how we look on the move, let me describe myself. Behind my saddle I have a comfort rolled up in my rubber coat . . . strapped as small as possible. In front of my saddle I have my blue coat rolled up and strapped on. The small cavalry saddle bags are filled to their utmost capacity . . . my little tin bucket for making tea, swings clattering by my side. About my person I have my sword and belt, cantine and haversack. The bundle behind my saddle is so large that it is a straining effort to get my leg over it in getting on or off and when in the saddle I feel like one who has been wrapped up for embalming . . . it is *very* disagreeable.[51]

48 *Ibid.*

49 Sherman, *op. cit.*, II, 30–31.

50 Harrison to his wife, May 5, 1864, Harrison MSS, Vol. 5. Merrill, *op. cit.*, Ch. 7, details the entire action day by day. See also Cleaves, *op. cit.*, pp. 205–14.

51 Harrison to his wife, May 5, 1864, Harrison MSS, Vol. 5.

May 8th was a Sunday. One private with his feet on the ground and his head in heaven wrote that "there was a large turnout to preaching this morning in God's first temple, for the poor fellows of our Regiment feel pretty solemn at the prospect of a coming battle."[52] On the 9th and 10th, Hooker's Corps went into action as the battle raged at Tunnell Hill and Rocky Face Ridge; but the Seventieth was held in reserve. Heavy firing ceased on the 10th, and news reached Harrison that the enemy was falling back to Resaca to make a real stand. The next day, the entire 1st Brigade slipped through Snake Creek Gap to confront the foe at Resaca.

Generals Sherman, Schofield, Hooker, Thomas, McPherson and Kilpatrick had outlined their strategy in council. Shortly after dawn on May 13, 1864, Harrison's command moved closer to Resaca; their orders to move into the second line of battle.[53] As he advanced his companies, Harrison was later to report:

Gen. Kilpatrick passed us with his cavalry command, and in less than an hour came back wounded, in an ambulance. We moved out and formed on Gen. McPherson's left . . . and very soon engaged the enemy. We did not participate in the fight and were not under fire that day except from enemy's batteries which dropped a few shells among us.[54]

Tomorrow would be his turn. Now it was Friday the 13th; and late that night Benjamin Harrison, in a mood of rare emotion, penned a beautiful letter to his wife:

I must write you tonight as we look for battle tomorrow, and God only knows who shall come safely through it. . . . May God in His great mercy give us a great victory and may the nation give Him the praise. . . .
You will perhaps like to know how I feel on the eve of my first great battle. Well, I do not feel in the least excited, nor in any sense of shrinking. I am in my usual good spirits, though not at all insensible to grave responsibilities and risks which I must bear tomorrow. I am thinking much of you and the dear children and my whole heart comes out towards you in tenderness and love and many earnest prayers will I send up to God this night, should you lose a husband

52 Merrill, *op. cit.*, p. 83.
53 From the diary of William Wilhite, cited by Merrill, *op. cit.*, pp. 84–85.
54 Harrison to his wife, May 20, 1864, Harrison MSS, Vol. 5.

and they a father in the fight, that in His grace you may find abundant consolation and in His providence abundant temporal comfort and support. I know you will not forget me, "should I be numbered among the slain," but let your grief be tempered by the consolation that I died for my country and in Christ. If God gives me strength I mean to bear myself *bravely*—come what will, so that you may have no cause to blush for me, though you should be forced to mourn.

But I have said these things only against the possibility of death, and not in any spirit of despondency, nor to awaken needless anxiety in your heart. Probably this letter will not be sent forward until the issue of the battle is known and I will precede it by a telegram if I can get one through, though this is doubtful. You must not burthen your heart with too much anxiety, as doubtless you will be in suspense for some days before you hear from me. Let us calmly put our trust in God and wait the issue. If it be prosperous for our country and for me, let us lift a glad song of praise, and if adverse to either, let us humbly bow to the decrees of Him who doeth all things well.

... I must make this letter short, as we need a good rest tonight and shall probably be awakened early in the morning. I might say much more, but this is enough. I love you, my dear wife, with all the devotion of a full heart, and my children as the apple of my eyes. But the obligations of a soldier are upon me, and these dear domestic ties are only the stronger incentive to quit myself well in the fight.

May the large storehouses of God's grace and providence always be open to you and them. My blessing rests upon you. Remember me affectionately to Irwin, Jennie and their families, also to Mr. Nixon, Mr. Sharpe, Mr. Ray and all of my family in the old P[resbyterian]. Ch[urch]. who may inquire for me, and particularly to the members of my old Bible class and the dear Sabbath School. Should I come alive through the fight to get home . . . I hope to see you all in good time. Farewell and God bless you.[55]

55 Harrison to his wife, May 13 (?), 1864, Harrison MSS, Vol. 5.

CHAPTER XII

The Atlanta Campaign

IN THE CONFEDERATE VIEW, Resaca was the "first battle of magnitude in the celebrated Georgia campaign."[1] Around this little Georgia town General Joe Johnston had formed a horseshoe-shaped defense line, somewhat like the formation called for by the Union strategists at Gettysburg. All around were hills, swamps, ravines, and "dense thickness"[2] so that the Confederate general calculated wisely that any direct frontal attack by Union forces was tantamount to suicide. Consequently, since he held so tremendous a tactical advantage, he determined to cling closely to his heavily fortified position and possibly tempt Sherman to launch a costly assault.

On May 14, 1864, Sherman was tempted and he did not resist. He at once began to press his foe around Resaca with a view to outflanking him. This Union decision to take the offensive made the rebels rejoice; and one man in gray wrote:

> To their music we slept, by their thunderings we were awakened and to the accompanying call of the bugle we responded on the morning of May 14 to engage in the death grapple with Sherman's well-clothed, well-fed and thoroughly rested veterans who moved against us in perfect step, with banners flying and bands playing, as though expecting to charm us.[3]

Sherman's strategy,[4] calling for a frontal attack in order to draw

[1] Otto Eisenschiml and Ralph Newman, *The American Iliad,* p. 609, record this as the opinion of Confederate Lieutenant L. D. Young.
[2] The New York *Press,* March 14, 1901, gives an excellent historical setting and background for the fight at Resaca.
[3] Eisenschiml and Newman, *op. cit.,* p. 609.
[4] Sherman was entertaining the main part of enemy forces in front, while he planned their undoing by sending Dodge's Corps down the river to the rear to cut Confederate communications and to intercept their retreat. William Sherman, *Memoirs,* II, 37.

Joe Johnston's fire, resulted in several collisions costly to the Union cause. Securely entrenched along a line of hill crests, the Confederate infantry and artillery calmly waited until the advancing Union columns were within seventy-five yards before opening a murderous fire. Despite the terrible carnage and the horribly shattered lines, the Union forces rallied again and again.[5]

To Hooker's army, and in particular Ward's brigade, fell the thankless task of attempting to silence one especially obnoxious rebel battery commanding the approach to Resaca. Orders were issued to Colonel Harrison that the Seventieth Indiana, at a signal from General Ward, was to storm the hill and knock it out. The hill was not particularly steep; the difficulty was in crossing a ravine "all choked with stunted pine trees and undergrowth, without break or path."[6] Harrison discovered that, before his regiment could even reach the enemy position, "they had to run down hill, and make their way through a dense pine thicket, traverse a few hundred yards of open field and thence on up the hill to the Confederate redoubt."[7] While reconnoitering and awaiting the moment of command, Harrison found the aim of enemy sharpshooters "most provokingly accurate [as] bullets kept whistling over our heads all day long . . . often striking a tree and falling at our feet."[8]

He now faced his first major military assignment under fire; and although there are numerous accounts of his conduct,[9] none is more accurate than his own description sent to an anxious wife five days after the battle.[10] The order to advance came from General Ward, while "we were lying behind the crest of the hill." Down the exposed slope the Seventieth moved, not without heavy casualties, "halting at the bottom under the cover of a fence to

5 Eisenschiml and Newman, *op. cit.*, p. 611: "Three times during the morning and early afternoon were these attacks made upon our [Confederate] lines. It was a veritable picnic . . . protected as we were by earthworks with clear and open ground in front."

6 Lew Wallace, *Life of Gen. Ben Harrison*, p. 190.

7 *House Document No. 154*, p. 112.

8 Harrison to his wife, May 20, 1864, Harrison MSS, Vol. 5.

9 In addition to a number of newspaper accounts, now a part of the Harrison Scrapbook Series, the best accounts are by Wallace, *op. cit.*, pp. 189–99; *House Document No. 154*; Samuel Merrill, *The Seventieth Indiana*, pp. 99–114.

10 Harrison to his wife, May 20, 1864, Harrison MSS, Vol. 5. Except for identified source references, all quotations in the next few pages, until his letter of June 14, are from this missive.

reform my line." Here the stark reality of the situation struck the colonel:

I saw that the Regiment on my left had not come down. . . . [I] passed word up to General Ward to know what was the matter. He sent me word that he did not intend to pass over the hill,[11] but only to advance to the crest.

Harrison found his position extremely precarious. Bitterly cursing Ward and his command as "stupid and maudlin," he took stock of the danger. As for being reunited with Ward's brigade, Harrison explained that he was

. . . where I could not get back without being exposed to a *terrible* fire . . . even where we were, there was no safety except in lying perfectly flat on the ground. As I lay here, the bullets would strike into the bank just above me and roll the sand down upon my head.

The perplexed colonel was far from pleased when he heard one of the brigade staff calling to him from the summit of the hill that General Ward desired the return of the regiment. The risk involved in getting up the hill was again described by Harrison as "terrible":

It was very steep and I could only get up the hill by pulling by roots and bushes. . . . You had better believe I scrambled up *pretty fast* . . . the sharpshooters did not fail to pay their compliments to me all the way up.

By retiring the men singly or in small squads under the cover of night he was able without further casualties to resume his former line behind the crest of the hill.[12] The rest of the night was spent in the construction of rifle pits along the front line.

At dawn on the 15th, Harrison's men were relieved. Ward's

11 "Instructions had been received from your headquarters . . . to assault the works in our front at some time during the day . . . supposing that the order to advance involved such an assault," Harrison advanced over the crest of the hill, down the slope. Harrison to Ward, May 20, 1864, Merrill, *op. cit.*, pp. 106–12.

12 In his official report to General Ward, Harrison totaled his losses for the day: "On the skirmish line, killed, enlisted men, 1; wounded, enlisted men, 3; in advancing over crest of hill to our supposed assault, killed, enlisted men, 2; wounded, enlisted men, 10; wounded, Lt. Martin, Company I, slightly in the leg." The complete report is given in Merrill, *op. cit.*, pp. 106–12.

brigade was deployed in support of Howard's left. Almost immediately, the weary men were ordered to storm a battery of enemy rifle pits. For Harrison there was no mistaking of orders this time. The brigade was formed under the cover of a woods, and Carrie Harrison read the sequel:

... one regiment behind another ... my Regiment in advance and Coburn's and Wood's Brigades of our Division supporting our left ... we started to descend the hill and the enemies' batteries soon opened upon us ... getting into the valley which was a cleared field we caught a heavy fire of musketry, but the men pressed on bravely and without flinching.

The enemy's breastworks were almost completely hidden on the side of a thickly wooded hill. Reconnoitering, however, was hardly necessary, inasmuch as fire from the rebel battery clearly revealed their position. Harrison, taking off his cap and waving it high above his head, "cheered his men on."[13] Moving forward on the double and subjected to a murderous enfilading fire, the men maintained perfect order. With no sign of faltering, they charged the hill into the very face of the enemy battery. The undaunted Hoosiers, who had waited almost two years for this opportunity, now drove forward until the Confederate gunners were struck down at their guns. The ensuing struggle was indelibly printed in Harrison's memory:

Having gained the outer face of the embrasures, in which the enemy had four 12-pound Napoleon guns, my line halted for a moment to take breath. Seeing that the infantry supports had deserted the artillery, I cheered the men forward, and, with a wild yell, they entered the embrasures, striking down and bayoneting the gunners, many of whom defiantly stuck by their guns until struck down.[14]

There was still another strong line of breastworks, hidden from view by a thick pine undergrowth, save for one point which had

13 Dan M. Ransdell remarked that Col. Harrison always cried "come on boys" and never "go on boys," Indianapolis *Journal*, June 29, 1888.

14 With the passing years Harrison's respect for the courage and bravery of the Confederate soldiers at Resaca increased. In 1876 he wrote to General Carman that "the rebel gunners who manned this battery stood their guns nobly . . . several of them refusing to surrender and striking at our men with their rammers, were bayoneted at their guns." Harrison MSS, Vol. 7.

been used as a gateway. To storm this line would be their acid test. Opposing the Seventieth Indiana was a division of veteran Confederate troops under the command of General J. B. Hood, a man whose bravery was not tempered by caution.[15]

Dan Ransdell remembered seeing "Harrison standing up there right in front of the rebels, waving his sword in one hand and brandishing a revolver in the other."[16] The colonel ordered and led the assault. Later, he reported:

> When we first entered the embrasures of the outer works, the enemy fled in considerable confusion from the inner one, and had there been a supporting line brought up in good order at this junction, the second line might easily have been carried and held. My line having borne the brunt of the assault, it was not to be expected that it could be reformed for the second assault in time. The enemy in a moment rallied in rear of their second line, and poured in a most destructive fire upon us, which compelled us to return outside the first line to obtain the cover of the works.[17]

At this point, confusion creeps into an otherwise clear narrative. A command, probably from a Confederate officer to his own men, was heard and repeated: "Retreat, they are flanking us." Several battalions of Ward's brigade were coming up to support Harrison's regiment, but, on hearing the cry, many scrambled down hill. Apologetically, Harrison reported:

> I strove in vain to rally my men under the enemy's fire on the hillside, and finally followed them to a partially sheltered place behind a ridge on our left . . . preparing to lead them again to the support of those who still held the guns we had captured.

At the foot of the hill, Harrison was informed that General Ward had been wounded,[18] leaving him to command the 1st Brigade. He reformed the brigade "and then urgently asked General Butterfield for permission to take it again to the works we

[15] James G. Randall, *The Civil War and Reconstruction*, p. 553.

[16] Indianapolis *Journal*, June 29, 1888.

[17] Harrison to Ward, May 20, 1864, an official report cited by Merrill, *op. cit.*, pp. 109–10.

[18] On December 15, 1884, Harrison wrote to John Ward, the General's son: "I saw your father, General Ward, on the battlefield at Resaca a few moments after he was wounded in the arm. He did not go to the hospital at all . . . whatever surgical treatment the wound had was at his own quarters" (Tibbott transcripts).

had carried and still held, and bring off the guns we had captured." Butterfield, however, had other plans.

He refused permission, but ordered me to support Coburn's Brigade
which was on a hill nearby. Just as we were forming, the enemy made
a charge. . . . I ordered the men not to fire if the enemy reached the
hill but to push him back with the bayonet.

Though the issue was joined on this second front, at nightfall
no decision had been reached. In the meanwhile, 300 or so from
the Seventieth remained just outside the rebel lunette and held
fast to the guns captured earlier in the day. At a late hour on
the 15th, this rugged band under Captain Henry Scott, Carrie's
brother, was withdrawn, but not before handing off the enemy
guns to a fresh party of reinforcements.[19] That night, General
Joe Johnston effected a strategic retreat across the Oostenaula
River. Resaca fell to the Federals and the first important phase
of the Atlanta campaign came to a successful close.

Monday morning, May 16th, was to carry sad and bitter memories for the regiment. The battle-scarred group, itself afflicted
with heavy losses, was ordered to the battlefield "to bury our own
and such Rebel dead as we could find." Perfect respect and attention attended the brigade's first mass burial, but to Harrison the
scene was "most appalling" because a "fire had broken out in the
woods at night and many of our dead were horribly burned which
gave additional gastliness [sic] to their stiffened corpses." After
the interment of the last body, Harrison wrote: "we dragged our
captured cannon to Resaca and turned them over . . . with about
1200 small arms, to the Ordnance Department."

In analyzing the part his regiment played in the fight for Resaca, Colonel Harrison rejoiced that "we have no cravens in our
band"; but he harbored a deep dread that the brigade would be
censured for retiring amid the confusion on the afternoon of
May 15. These fears, however, were groundless. General Hooker
rode up and told Harrison that he regarded the charge as "very
brilliant and successful,"[20] while General Sherman referred to

---

[19] Harrison to General Carman, February 8, 1876, Harrison MSS, Vol. 7.

[20] Also Hooker to Hon. E. M. Stanton, Secretary of War, October 31, 1864, Harrison MSS, A.C. 4950 Add.

capturing a 4-gun intrenched battery as "handsome fighting on the left."[21] Even more valued by Harrison than this praise from superiors was the warm personal tribute from the men in the ranks. At Resaca, where he "was exposed to death as much as any man could be," his own soldiers christened him "Little Ben," a sobriquet which in their understanding connoted courage and daring, and which clung to him all through the Atlanta campaign.

Congratulations from the home front were not long in catching up with Benjamin Harrison and his men. The Cincinnati as well as the Indianapolis newspapers carried highly laudatory accounts of Harrison's Resaca baptism under enemy fire. With the possible exception of his wife's warm and appreciative note of praise and thanksgiving, no letter pleased Benjamin more than his father's. Tremendously encouraged by this paternal approbation and benediction, Benjamin undertook to reveal his thoughts to Carrie. Speaking of the "one from Pa," Harrison wrote:

He seems to be very proud that I have won some distinction in my new profession. I am glad that I have been able to show them all that I could hold a creditable place in the army as well as in civil life, and that if not the most petted one in the family, its famous name is as safe in my keeping as in that of any who now bear the name. We must not however think too much of the praises of the newspapers, nor forget that to God who sustains me belongs all the honor.[22]

General Sherman, however, expressed bitter disappointment over the issue at Resaca. His pride was hurt by the realization that Johnston had outmaneuvered him. So complete and so well-organized was the Confederate withdrawal from Resaca that Sherman found several of his officers, as well as a goodly number of his men, on the brink of discouragement.[23] Action, therefore, was imperative and Sherman called a meeting of his staff. He warned them that Johnston would not be easily overcome and that immediate pursuit of the Confederate force was essential.[24] This decision to hound Johnston until he was trapped was an

21 R. U. Johnson and C. C. Buel (eds.), *Battles and Leaders*, IV, Part 1, p. 266.

22 Harrison to his wife, June 14, 1864, Harrison MSS, Vol. 5.

23 Henry Stone, "The Atlanta Campaign," *Papers of the Military Historical Society of Massachusetts*, 8 (1910), 389.

24 Walter Hebert, *Fighting Joe Hooker*, p. 276.

invitation to three months of hard fighting wherein each engagement was "seemingly hotter than the one preceding."[25]

In less than a month Benjamin Harrison was destined to engage in more battles than either William Henry Harrison, his
grandfather, or Andrew Jackson, had fought in a lifetime.[26]

In the final analysis, it was Sherman's dissatisfaction with a
rather empty victory at Resaca that allowed Harrison to become
a fighting soldier rather than a mere textbook colonel. Johnston's
initial escape at Resaca rankled. Even a decade later, Sherman
admitted:

Of course, I was disappointed not to have crippled his army at that
particular stage of the game; but as it resulted . . . rapid successes
gave us the initiative and the usual impulse of a conquering army.[27]

New Hope Church, Georgia, was the scene of Harrison's first
serious engagement after Resaca. Here, on May 26–28, the
Union forces, especially Hooker's Corps, made several fierce attacks upon the enemy, only to find that the deadly canister-shot of
sixteen Confederate field pieces and the musketry fire of 5,000 infantry at short range, made the location a veritable "hell hole."[28]
The Federals sustained heavy losses, as each day Hooker sent part
of Butterfield's division into action. The Seventieth shouldered
its share of the burden. On one occasion, as the regiment formed
its line for an attack, it was compelled to advance across undulat-
ing fields into rather thin woods. Under a heavy fire from a safely
secured and almost hidden enemy, the men crawled to a spot
where the bushes had been cut down so that the top of the enemy's works was visible. Harrison gave the command to fix bayonets, saying: "Men, the enemy's works are just ahead of us, but
we will go right over them. Forward! Double-quick! March!"
Every man sprang forward, several to sudden death. By day the
battle raged, and by night, when the firing ceased, torches and
candles threw a dim light over the incoming stretchers, while
surgeon's tables and instruments formed ghastly silhouettes.[29]

25 Wallace, *op. cit.*, p. 202.
26 *Ibid.*
27 Sherman, *op. cit.*, II, 36.
28 Joseph E. Johnston, "Opposing Sherman's Advance to Atlanta," in Johnson
and Buel, *op. cit.*, Part 1, p. 269. *Battles and Leaders*, Vol. 4, Part 1, 269.
29 These details are from Merrill, *op. cit.*, pp. 124–25.

On June 15, 1864, at Golgotha Church in the vicinity of Kene-saw Mountain, Harrison's regiment executed a charge more dar-ing even than those at New Hope Church. Carrie undoubtedly shuddered as she read her husband's account written three days after the battle:

My Regiment was advanced without any support to within three hundred yards of a strong rebel breastwork where they had eight pieces in position and nicely covered and we being entirely exposed. We stood there fighting an unseen foe for an hour and a half without flinching, while the enemy's shells and grapes fell like hail in our ranks, tearing down large trees and filling the air with splinters. Two or three of my men had their heads torn off close down to the shoul-ders and others had fearful wounds.[30]

Under orders to hold their position until nightfall, the Seventieth did not fail. At the appointed hour, Harrison's men fell back in perfect order, taking their dead and wounded with them. The skill with which they executed this maneuver would have done justice to a veteran regiment, yet the move was almost disastrous, for the brigade's surgeons had become separated from the main body of troops. The wounded, sheltered in a little frame house to the rear of the front lines, waited patiently for relief. When the absence of the surgeons was reported to Harrison, Lew Wal-lace says the Colonel "turned surgeon himself."[31] This squares with the detailed account that Harrison rendered to his wife:

Our Surgeons got separated from us, and putting our wounded in a deserted house, I stripped my arms to dress their wounds myself. Poor Fellows! I was but an awkward surgeon, of course, but I hope I gave them some relief. There were some ghastly wounds. . . . I pulled out of one poor fellow's arm a splinter five or six inches long and as thick as my three fingers.[32]

Wallace has painted a vivid description of Harrison in his sur-geon's role:

Taking off his coat and rolling his sleeves to his elbow, he set to staunching the wounds. He says, speaking of the circumstances: "I

[30] Harrison to his wife, June 18, 1864, Harrison MSS, Vol. 5. Harrison charac-terized this as a "hard fight" and numbered the losses in killed and wounded at 50 men.
[31] Wallace, *op. cit.*, p. 204.
[32] Harrison to his wife, June 18, 1864, Harrison MSS, Vol. 5.

don't know whether I did any service; I tried to." He caused some tents to be torn up for bandages, and worked industriously several hours before the surgeons appeared. When they came into the improvised hospital, they found him covered with the blood which he had striven to stop.[33]

Once more the Southern troops were withdrawn in accordance with Johnston's plan of strategic retreat. Yet, each Federal victory brought Atlanta within closer striking distance. Still more important, however, was the excellent fighting spirit created within the ranks. Their colonel expressed it well: "I wouldn't like to leave my Regiment to the command of another in a fight. I have got to love them for their bravery and for dangers we have shared together. I have heard many similar expressions from the men towards me."[34] Harrison's anxiety, his solicitude, and his sympathy for every man under his command had not gone unnoticed. Consequently, on May 29, 1864, when he became chief of the 1st Brigade, his promotion was greeted with genuine joy and appreciation.[35]

Harrison assumed his new responsibility as brigadier just at a time when his command was to see its heaviest fighting in a campaign that was proving "very exhausting to the troops."[36] His own health was good, and he added that he could stand the pace at least for another month "if a rebel bullet don't come my way." It was during the Atlanta Campaign, near Marietta, Georgia, that Harrison had become poisoned, "making it necessary for me to wear a glove all the time." It is interesting to note that this susceptibility to poison in the hand remained with him until his death, and it undoubtedly accounts for his wearing kid gloves as a source of protection against infection and cold. This practice worked to his disadvantage in 1876, while campaigning for the governorship of Indiana. He was dubbed the aristocratic "kid-gloves" Harrison, and this sobriquet lost him many votes among the laboring classes.

By July 7th he had moved with his men to within ten miles of Atlanta, Sherman's objective. From the heights "we can see

[33] Wallace, *op. cit.*, p. 204.
[34] Harrison to his wife, June 18, 1864, Harrison MSS, Vol. 5.
[35] *House Document No. 154*, p. 114.
[36] Harrison to his wife, July 5, 1864, Harrison MSS, Vol. 5.

the steeples of the churches in Atlanta;"[37] but he hazarded the opinion that at least twenty days of hard campaigning remained for his weary brigade. The progress was slow and extremely dangerous. He wrote to Carrie:

We had a sharp artillery fight on the Marietta road on Sunday last. My Brigade was in the advance and lost several men killed. I had several very narrow escapes. One shell struck so near me that it threw the ground all over me.[38]

In his despatches from the field, Harrison frequently noted the wonderful skill that Joe Johnston had demonstrated in erecting defensive works that were almost impregnable. Johnston, he wrote, "has successive lines prepared in advance, or rather in the rear, and when we flank him out of one line, he has only to fall back to another a few miles to the rear . . . then we are forced to make such movements as will force him to retreat again, and so the campaign has dragged along."[39] And he could only marvel at the way in which Johnston made a safe retreat, thus saving his army from demoralization, "though there had not been a single brilliant or successful 'offensive return' since the campaign opened."

He was equally quick in defending Sherman against critics who blamed the Union leader "for what they call *inactivity.*" Harrison challenged Sherman's critics "to serve under him for a few days and make a survey of, or an *assault on,* one of Johnston's lines of defensive works and they would take another view of it." Undoubtedly, they would have changed their opinion if they had been able to read but one paragraph that Harrison penned to his wife concerning the peril faced by any column assigned to assault a fortified Confederate line:

. . . As you have never seen one of these field works, I must try to give you an idea of what an assaulting column has to overcome. In the first place in advancing you will come at 1000 yards from the enemy's works into a "tangle," that is, all the small trees and some

[37] Harrison to his wife, July 7, 1864. Harrison MSS, Vol. 5.

[38] *Ibid.* The best military history for this section of the Atlanta campaign is perhaps Jacob D. Cox, *Atlanta,* pp. 89–115.

[39] Harrison to his wife, July 10, 1864, Harrison MSS, Vol. 5. Other contemporary accounts can be found in Merrill, *op. cit.,* pp. 113–38; Lloyd Lewis, *Sherman: the Fighting Prophet,* pp. 355–66.

large ones are felled cross-wise so that you have to make your way through a *continual succession of tree-tops.* As you get nearer, say 300 yards, you come to an abatis which consists of tree-tops . . . bushy ends towards you, all the leaves trimmed off and every branch and twig sharpened so that it will catch in the clothes. If you succeed in getting through this, you will find about 20 yards from the rifle pits two lines of stakes about 12 feet long, set about four feet in the ground and inclining towards you, the upper end being sharpened and the stakes set so close that a man can't pass between them. If you can stand the deadly stream of musketry fire until you can dig up or cut down these stakes, you will have no other obstacle save the climbing of the breastworks and a line of bayonets jetting up inside . . . they [also] have what the boys call "horse rakes" . . . made by boring large auger holes through logs 20 feet long or so, at right angles, and putting through them long oaken stakes or pines sharpened at both ends, so that however many times you may turn the thing over, there is always an ugly line of sharpened stakes sticking out towards you.[40]

Harrison concluded this summary with a barb at the civilians who were criticizing Sherman's slow push to Atlanta. "I should like to see a few thousand of the 'On To Atlanta' civilians of the North charging such a line of works. Most of the tender-skinned [*sic*] individuals of this class would require help to get into the works if they were *empty.*"

Sherman's relentless push through Georgia during the intense heat of June and July, 1864, brought Harrison to a small ridge just beyond Peach Tree Creek, two miles north of Atlanta. In this rugged terrain, picturesque in name and in beauty, "Old Cump" Sherman dug in and made plans to strike another blow at his foe.[41] As in the past weeks, Harrison and Sherman walked the skirmish line together. During the past seven weeks of offensive warfare, the colonel had found his superior officer "very companionable and pleasant;"[42] and so, at this last stronghold outside of Atlanta, they observed and plotted one more flanking movement by which they hoped to entrap the wily Johnston.[43]

40 *Ibid.*

41 By the end of May, Sherman counted his losses at 9,000; while Johnston had lost 8,500. Lewis, *op. cit.,* p. 364.

42 Harrison to his wife, May 28, 1864, Harrison MSS, Vol. 5. Their friendship carried over into civil life, and was renewed on many occasions when Senator John Sherman and Harrison served in the Senate together.

43 Sherman's skill in flanking awed the Southerners. See Lewis, *op. cit.,* p. 360.

Although their patience was at an end, this time they determined not to assault until they were morally certain of "bagging the fox." They had drawn little consolation from the campaign up to this time. An average daily gain of slightly over a mile is not the progress that engenders pride in military men.[44] Still more annoying was the political significance underlying Johnston's delaying tactics. If he could keep Sherman from winning a victory before early November, the Northern peace party would be immeasurably strengthened in their effort to carry the presidential election. This alone, Johnston believed, "would have brought the war to an immediate close."[45]

Military and civilian observers in the South were far from agreeing, however, on the wisdom of Johnston's defensive policy. Several thought that he had tipped his hand too fully and too early. Moreover, the more skeptical civil leaders gave scant credence to Johnston's conviction that by slow and skilful retreating "he might some day catch Sherman in an awkward position and ruin him."[46] Now, as the Southern army fell back upon Atlanta, the city Jefferson Davis had pronounced vital to the life of the Confederacy,[47] demands were made that Johnston should fight or resign. In mid-July, under the pressure of severe criticism and at the urging of President Davis, Johnston resigned in favor of General John B. Hood, who immediately proclaimed a "fight Sherman now-or-never policy."[48] The first opportunity for Hood to implement his plan for an offensive thrust was at Peach Tree Creek on July 20th. He thought he spied a weak spot in the newly formed Union line, and he ordered a surprise attack. The only obstacle to a serious break through Union lines was Ward's 1st Division, and holding the front lines was the brigade commanded by Colonel Benjamin Harrison.

Early on the 20th, the Union army had successfully bridged Peach Tree Creek, so that by noon the entire army had crossed the "unfordable" stream and had extended its line of battle along

44 Harrison to his wife, May 31, 1864, Harrison MSS, Vol. 5. His brigade was then near Altoona, and "only about fifty miles from Atlanta." This was the danger zone, and Ben admonished Carrie "to look to my insurance . . . an additional premium may be required."

45 Lewis, *op. cit.*, p. 366.

46 *Ibid.*

47 Eisenschiml and Newman, *op. cit.*, p. 619.

48 Lewis, *op. cit.*, pp. 381–83: "Johnston surrendered his offices to Hood, explaining with cold courtesy that he had planned to fight Sherman at Peach Tree Creek."

a ridge about 400 yards from the creek on the south.[49] At first, Ward's division was ordered to remain in the creek bottom, fixing its line approximately 300 yards to the rear of the remainder of the army. This left a gap of a quarter of a mile between Geary's division on the right and Newton's on the left.[50] In the eyes of Hood's scouts, this slight gap in an otherwise straight and tightly drawn line of battle might well have appeared to be a weakness. The area directly in front of the ridge was an open field extending clear to the rebel lines. In accord with their orders, Ward's division had formed behind the ridge at the creek bottom. At ease, some men were cooking, some sleeping, and others just relaxing. It was at this moment that the rash and reckless Hood[51] made his bold bid to knife through Sherman's lines and cut the Federal army in two.

When the first report of the sudden enemy sortie reached General Ward, who was not only in the rear but also on the far side of Peach Tree Creek, he refused to believe that the South was taking the offensive. An eye-witness, L. T. Miller, relates the interesting sequel:

About this time Generals Coburn and Harrison, each commanding a brigade, reported to General Ward their belief that the enemy was advancing and would occupy the ridge. General Ward, notwithstanding this information, and although requested by Harrison and Coburn, declined to give them orders to move their brigades forward.

At this juncture I heard this conversation between Generals Harrison and Coburn. I was commanding the 33rd Indiana—Coburn's old Regiment—and was on the right of the Regiment. They rode up to where I was. General Harrison said to Coburn: "John, I am going to place my men on that ridge, if you will support me?" "I'll see you through," replied General Coburn, and turning about, ordered me to move the 33rd immediately forward, which I did. Just then Harri-

[49] Cox, *op. cit.*, pp. 144–47, gives an excellent description of the geography northeast of Atlanta and explains the military importance of the various streams and ridges in the vicinity.

[50] The full report is printed in Merrill, *op. cit.*, pp. 153–59. Harrison gives an even more detailed account in his letter to General Carman, February 8, 1876, Harrison MSS, Vol. 7.

[51] Lewis, *op. cit.*, p. 383: "Sherman had at his elbow three men who had known Hood intimately at West Point. McPherson, Schofield and Howard agreed that Hood, for all his lack of limbs, would attack; in school he had been rash, erratic, headstrong, precipitate and not intellectual."

son put spurs to his horse and dashed forward up the hill, in front of his brigade, and both brigades cheering ran rapidly . . . up the hill.[52]

It was at this moment that hours of intense study and discipline brought their reward. Leading his brigade on the double-quick, he issued only one command. He told his veteran troops to engage the enemy in hand-to-hand fighting, and to re-establish, if at all possible, the integrity of the Union line.[53] He waved his men forward, shouting:

Come on boys, we've never been licked yet, and we won't begin now. We haven't much ammunition, but if necessary we can give them the cold steel, and before we get licked we will club them down; so, come on.[54]

Up the slope he led them. Prompt support by Coburn's and Wood's brigades enabled Harrison's command to gain the brow of the ridge, where the Federals closed with the hard-charging enemy, many falling to the ground in hand-to-hand combat. Bayonets, muskets and pistols served as clubs. "Many fell—now a flag would go down, only to be raised by another—the Rebel officers were urging their men forward, but the long charge, and our hot fire had broken the order of the line."[55] Harrison continued to inspire his men and, finally, by his own personal courage and leadership, precipitated the final lunge that caused the rebel lines to waver. No sooner had they begun to yield ground than they were hurled down the far side of the hill. The Union lines held firm. Captain H. A. Ford attests: "But for him I think our army on that field would have been cut in two, and at least one wing of it rolled up and badly shattered."[56]

The day was saved, and, though he probably did not realize it, Benjamin Harrison was a hero. On the day after Peach Tree

[52] Indianapolis *Daily Journal*, July 1, 1888, an interview given by L. T. Miller, then residing at Wichita, Kansas. In recalling the facts of this bloody struggle, he bestowed upon Harrison the title, "Hero of the Battle of Peach Tree Creek."

[53] Capt. H. A. Ford maintained that a breakthrough by the foe, charging down a slope on unprepared Union lines, would have created hopeless disorder in the Union camp, and the battle would, in all probability, have been lost. Indianapolis *Journal*, July 1, 1888.

[54] *House Document No. 154*, p. 115.

[55] Harrison to General Carman, February 8, 1876, Harrison MSS, Vol. 7.

[56] Indianapolis *Journal*, July 1, 1888.

Creek, General Hooker rode the lines manned by the 3rd Brigade of his 1st Division. Meeting Colonel Harrison and shaking hands with him, "Fighting Joe" blurted out a promise he was quick to fulfill: "Harrison, by God, I'll make you a Brigadier for this fight."[57] His subsequent warm letter of commendation, directed to Secretary of War Stanton on October 31, 1864, was responsible for Harrison's promotion to the rank of Brigadier General, Volunteers:

I desire to call the attention of the Department to the claims of Col. Benjamin Harrison, of the 70th Indiana Vols., for promotion to the rank of Brigadier General, Volunteers.

Col. Harrison first joined me in command of a brigade of Ward's division in Lookout Valley preparative to entering what is called the Campaign of Atlanta. My attention was first attracted to this young officer by the superior excellence of his brigade in discipline and instruction, the result of his labor, skill and devotion. With more foresight than I have witnessed in any officer of his experience, he seemed to act upon the principle that success depends upon the thorough preparation in discipline and esprit of his command for conflict, more than on any influence that could be exerted on the field itself, and when collision came his command vindicated his wisdom as much as his valor. In all of the achievements of the 20th Corps in that campaign Col. Harrison bore a conspicuous part. At Resaca and Peach Tree Creek the conduct of himself and command were especially distinguished. Col. Harrison is an officer of superior abilities, and of great professional and personal worth. It gives me great pleasure to commend him favorably to the Honorable Secretary, with the assurance that his preferment will be a just recognition of his services and martial accomplishments.[58]

Promotion, however, was not the most important thing in Harrison's mind after the Confederate reverses. His frequent letters to Carrie manifested an intense longing "to get moored again in the sweet and quiet harbor of home."[59] Furloughs, of course, were out of the question until Atlanta should capitulate; and early in August the prospects for a speedy Union occupation were far from bright. Even with Union batteries opening fire on the city, the Confederates continued to hold on tenaciously.

[57] Harrison to General Carman, February 8, 1876, Harrison MSS, Vol. 7.

[58] A copy is in the Harrison Collection (Library of Congress), A.C. 4950, the gift of A. T. Volwiler. This letter is also cited in full by Wallace, *op. cit.*, p. 222, and in *House Document No. 154*, p. 116.

[59] Harrison to his wife, August 8, 1864, Harrison MSS, Vol. 5.

By mid-August, Harrison's morale had sunk to a new low. The siege of Atlanta, especially while Sherman moved south around the city, was both boring and annoying to a man who still wanted "to fight and go home." He complained to Carrie:

My life drags along very wearily now, and my heart needs the frequent refreshing of a good letter from home, and you ought not to withhold it from me. The ceaseless care and watching, together with the privations and hardships of this campaign of over 100 days has exhausted a good deal of my mental and nervous energy; and when not worked up by some unusual danger or responsibility, I feel a little depressed and homesick. I want rest, both in heart, mind and body, and this I can only get in the temple of my heart at home and in some slight degree from your letters.[60]

Carrie's serious illness at this time caused Harrison great anxiety and left him in particularly low spirits. Though Sherman was allowing no able-bodied officers to leave his post, Harrison thought that "by hard begging" he might be able to get "a short leave of absence,"[61] if his wife's condition became more critical. Such action, fortunately, proved unnecessary; for on August 20, Harrison's thirty-first birthday, word came from Indianapolis that Carrie was well along the road to recovery. Harrison's spirits went up "in a bound."[62] The news of Carrie's improvement and the receipt of two letters from her, coupled with the fact that "it is my *birthday*," suggested many memories and drew from Benjamin a letter which in his more conservative and less joyous moments he would have hesitated to write. It reveals the inner thoughts of a man who prided himself on never wearing his heart upon his sleeve:

I feel as if I ought to write today not only to acknowledge the receipt of these letters . . . but because it is my *birthday* and suggests many memories of the past, among the happiest of which your sweet form is closely interwoven. Perhaps you will not remember the day, as it is not the anniversary of any event so important to you as to *me*, but still perhaps you will think of me a little oftener and more tenderly than usual. I am *thirty-one* years old today, and nearly eleven years of this, we have been man and wife. For how many more years God has decreed my life to be lengthened out, He only knows, and whether

60 Harrison to his wife, August 12, 1864, Harrison MSS, Vol. 5.
61 Harrison to his wife, August 14, 1864, Harrison MSS, Vol. 5.
62 Harrison to his wife, August 20, 1864, Harrison MSS, Vol. 5.

they shall be as full of blessings as those that are gone. But whether they may be many or few, I hope they will bear witness of a faithful discharge of duty both to those I love on earth and my Father in heaven. Who is there that could not mend his life, if he could live his years over again, and how many think more of the errors of the past than of the promise, and of the opportunities of the future. I hope to be a better husband and father, a better citizen and a better Christian in the future than I have been in the past.

You may think it strange that I promise nothing to my present profession as a soldier. The reason is that I hope my mission as a soldier will end before another birthday. Certainly my present term of enlistment will expire before next August 20th, and unless Gen. Hooker should accomplish his threat of making me a Brigadier General, I will be a citizen again. For after three years of the best service I could render, if they don't promote me, I shall think the public does not need my help in that department and shall try to help myself in some other pursuit.

The very complimentary notice which Gen. Hooker made of me in conversation with Halstead was, of course, very gratifying to me; but in all candor I do think "Uncle Joe" was somewhat extravagant and hope he will not push me *too* rapidly, as that has been the ruin of more than one good officer in the war. On your account and my children, I should like to wear the "lone star," when I can feel that I have *won* it, but my own ambition does not soar very high; and as such favors have been generally obtained through political influence and hard begging, I fear we need not look with much confidence to my obtaining it. The high compliment which Gen. Hooker has bestowed upon me, and the confidence which I have won among the brave officers and men of my command is worth more to me than a Brigadier's star, though the public will of course look to the latter as the evidence of the former. . . . I have talked enough about myself and my humble military career. Lest your affection might lend you to exaggerate my merits as a soldier, let me assure you that I am not a Julius Ceasar [*sic*], nor a Napoleon, but a plain Hoosier Col., with no more relish for a fight than for a good breakfast and hardly so much. . . .

Write to me often and tell me everything. I am in excellent health; and since I have heard of your recovery, in fine and hopeful spirits. May God abundantly bless you and the dear children and bring me to your arms again when my duty is done. Love to all friends.[63]

Within a fortnight, Atlanta fell.[64] On September 2, 1864, Harrison scribbled the glad tidings to his wife: "Atlanta is ours . . .

63 Harrison to his wife, August 20, 1864, Harrison MSS, Vol. 5.
64 For contemporary accounts of the Union occupation after their hard campaign of three months, see Eisenschiml and Newman, *op. cit.*, pp. 626–33.

Photograph by George N. Barnard

CONFEDERATE WORKS IN FRONT OF ATLANTA, GEORGIA

RUINS IN COLUMBIA, SOUTH CAROLINA, AS SEEN FROM THE CAPITOL

ABRAHAM LINCOLN

A portrait that hung over Lincoln's body as it lay in state (State House, Indianapolis). It was a special favorite for Harrison and hangs in his Memorial Home.

STATE HOUSE, INDIANAPOLIS, APRIL 30, 1865

Where Lincoln's body lay in state

and I send you a piece of cedar plucked from a door yard in Atlanta yesterday."[65] Two days later, he wrote: "We have just received a congratulatory order from Gen. Sherman over the occupancy of Atlanta and an instruction that the campaign is ended."[66] In the conviction that his troops had earned a rest, Sherman gave it to them. Colonel Harrison's long awaited furlough came in orders to report to Governor Morton for special duty.[67]

On the next morning Harrison left Atlanta and reported to Morton on September 20th. As a military hero he was returning to his own people, but to his wife and two growing youngsters this meant little or nothing. They could only think that now, after two years of continuous service in the field, he was to be with them again. In the Harrison home, where joy and thanksgiving reigned, only one disturbing thought danced behind three pairs of moist eyes: would he go back again?

[65] Harrison to his wife, September 2, 1864, Harrison MSS, Vol. 5.

[66] Harrison to his wife, September 4, 1864, Harrison MSS, Vol. 5.

[67] Special Field Orders, No. 71; copy in the Harrison MSS, Vol. No. 1065; also, Wallace, *op. cit.*, pp. 223–24.

CHAPTER XIII

Twin Triumphs: Indianapolis and Nashville

HARRISON'S RETURN to Indianapolis could not have been timed more auspiciously. Widespread dissatisfaction with an apparently indecisive and useless war was completely swept away by the September flood of Union victories. Scarcely had the fall of Atlanta on September 2nd been appreciated, when the news of General Phil Sheridan's brilliant victory in the valley of the Shenandoah reached the Indiana capital. Newspapers recorded the joy in the "hearts of all true patriots"[1] because, in decisively defeating General Jubal Early, Sheridan had dissipated the serious threat of another Confederate raid on Washington. "These triumphs, together with Farragut's capture of Mobile, convinced the volatile public that the stalemate was broken."[2] No longer were the majority of Hoosiers asking "how long the futile bloodshed would continue," and no longer was an ear given to the "Democratic cry that the Lincoln Administration was a failure."[3] The Republicans were jubilant, and in the light of the twin successes they proclaimed that "for us there is no step backward."[4]

In the Democratic camp spirits were low. While Harrison was journeying homeward, the Republican Indianapolis *Journal* made political capital of this sudden sweep of Union victories. In triumph and defiance, the state Republicans claimed that "the

[1] Indianapolis *Daily Journal*, September 23, 1864.

[2] Wood Gray, *The Hidden Civil War*, pp. 189–90; also D. S. Freeman, *Lee's Lieutenants* (New York, 1942–44), III, 580–83.

[3] Kenneth Stampp, *Indiana Politics during the Civil War*, p. 229.

[4] Indianapolis *Daily Journal*, September 23, 1864.

echo of every gun fell on Copperhead ears like the death knell of their hopes."[5] Such blows at Copperheadism within his own state undoubtedly warmed Harrison's heart. He had never fully recovered from the shock of his removal as Supreme Court Reporter by a Democratic court in November, 1862. Though he had succeeded in pushing this disappointment into the background during his two years of active service, Harrison had not forgiven the Copperheads, for he was convinced that their intrigue accounted for his ouster. Evidently, a good many Republicans shared the colonel's belief because, without consulting him, the Union State Convention on February 23, 1864, had renominated him for this same office.

Official notice of this did not reach him until nearly six weeks after the convention had adjourned. Stationed in Tennessee's Lookout Valley, Harrison mulled over the acceptance for three weeks.[6] Finally, on April 27, 1864, he reached an affirmative decision and made it known in a letter to Jacob T. Wright, Chairman of the Union State Central Committee. Harrison's acceptance, however, was only conditional. After perfunctory thanks to the party leaders for the honor conferred upon him, he felt constrained to express his real feelings on the subject of his candidacy. Consequently, he wrote the following "open letter" and gave his consent to its publication:

. . . You ask me to signify my acceptance of the nomination. It was known to you, and was doubtless known to all the members of the Convention, that I vacated the office for which I am now placed in nomination, in the summer of 1862, to accept the position I now hold in the military service of the country. I did not abandon the office then without many regrets; it was in the exact line of my profession, agreeable to my tastes and habits, and was reasonably lucrative, much more so than my present position.[7]

In several more closely reasoned paragraphs Harrison gave ample evidence that the rigors of military life had in no sense dulled his legal acumen or his sense of practical patriotism. While he confessed that "it would meet my highest ambition, if I might be permitted to resume the office when this war for our nation's life

5 *Ibid.*, September 8, 21, 22, 1864.
6 Harrison to his wife, April 26, 1864, Harrison MSS, Vol. 5.
7 Harrison to Jacob T. Wright, April 27, 1864, Harrison MSS, Vol. 5.

has been closed in the *complete* triumph of our arms," he attached one important reservation to an otherwise wholehearted acceptance. It was to the Colonel's credit that he added:

While allurements of home and peaceful pursuits are not to be turned aside without an effort, yet I could not reconcile it with my own sense of duty to quit the army for *any* civil office or pursuit, unless incapacitated by disease or wounds from efficient service in the field. Should the war be ended, or virtually so, during the campaign now opening, as many hopeful ones believe, or should my usefulness in the army be, from any cause brought to an end, then I should be much gratified to resume the duties of Reporter.[8]

The Republican leaders acquiesced in Harrison's conditional acceptance, disregarding his own suggestion that it might be more advisable "that another name be substituted for mine on the ticket . . . at once."[9]

Once Atlanta was in Union hands, Harrison could start his homeward journey. His future political welfare, as well as that of Republicans in the state and in the nation, hung in the balance. The scales, however, were tipped heavily in his favor.

Harrison's trip home was not without incident. Accompanied by many of the less serious casualties of the Atlanta campaign,[10] he left Georgia on September 12, 1864. The pace was as rapid as war conditions permitted, but the fear of surprise raids by roving bands of detached Confederate cavalry considerably delayed the push to the north. Part of the journey was made by steamer along the Ohio River. Special warnings had been issued that all river transports should be fully armed and should protect passengers and property by every means possible. One river cap-

---

[8] *Ibid.* Previous to this paragraph Harrison had charged Wright with the responsibility of seeing that all important party members be informed on the exact state of his mind in accepting the nomination.

[9] *Ibid.* Harrison added that "if you should conclude to retain my name on the ticket I shall, if elected, be glad to serve the people in the office of Reporter, *provided* it should then appear that I cannot serve them better in the army."

[10] Governor Morton had pledged to obtain furloughs for Indiana voters on active service. Lincoln and the War Department refused his blanket request. Consequently, Morton, "as a last resource, suggested that all the troops who were unfit for service, should be sent home and not be kept in hospitals out of the state. To this Lincoln assented." Consequently, many with only superficial wounds made the journey to Indianapolis with Harrison. W. D. Foulke, *O. P. Morton,* I, 366.

tain reported that even in this late hour of the war "it was very common . . . for guerrillas to lie in wait in convenient ambuscades along the river for the purpose of killing what people they could on the boats, and at various times . . . to capture and destroy . . . vessels."[11]

As the journey up the Ohio progressed, Harrison experienced some of the peace and quiet that he had yearned for so ardently during the summer months. He had the companionship of several other officers, though many of these were convalescents. One afternoon, while they were all seated at dinner, the usual tranquility of the passage was rudely shattered. As the vessel rounded one of the many bends in the Ohio, it ran into an ambuscade. "Shots from the shore came whistling through the thin sides of the dining room, and in a moment all was confusion."[12] Passengers scurried for safety. Apparently, the only one who did not realize the danger was an attractive young lady. She had been seated at the captain's table and, when she heard shots, she left the cabin to satisfy her curiosity. Colonel Ritchie, sensing the peril of the fair lady, followed her. To his surprise, he found that Colonel Harrison was already on the hurricane deck with "a revolver in each hand . . . blazing away with great enthusiasm and vigor at the people on the shore." Ritchie claimed that Harrison "stood there in a storm of bullets and banged away until the boat was out of range."

This reckless abandon impressed Ritchie the more because, as he later reported, the Indiana colonel appeared perfectly unconscious that he had done anything extraordinary. Whether one views Harrison's action as plain foolhardiness or as high gallantry, it matters little; aboard ship, he had become a hero. When the story was noised about Indianapolis, the home folks magnified the deed out of all proportion. It certainly did not harm Harrison's political chances.

On September 20th, Harrison arrived in Indianapolis. "After witnessing," as he said, "the scenes of desolation and decay in the

---

[11] This is the testimony of Colonel W. T. Ritchie, who was engaged in the transportation of army supplies in the West. From an unidentified newspaper clipping in the Benjamin Harrison Scrapbook, Vol. 9, p. 99, Harrison MSS.

[12] *Ibid.* The following details are from Ritchie's account.

track of a great army, the sight of the busy streets and peaceful residences of Indianapolis was like a gleam of paradise."[13] Yet, once he had greeted his wife and two children, he was compelled to admit that "he found himself almost a stranger in his native town, lost in a labyrinth of new and eloquent buildings, and the busy world of commerce. The growth of the city seemed to be the effect of some magician's wand." His fellow citizens gave him a warm welcome, and the Indianapolis *Journal* editorialized the return of "Col. Ben Harrison, of the gallant 70th ... who enjoyed an enviable reputation in civil life, which has received a fresh luster by his conduct as a soldier."[14] The story of his loss of the Reporter's position made fine political capital and was stressed with telling effect.

Within a week of his arrival, the *Journal* listed a speaking schedule that commenced in Lawrenceburg on September 29th and carried candidate Harrison to Rockport, Vincennes, and Terre Haute.[15] While the Hoosier hero was stumping the southern and western portions of the state, another military man, one also destined for the White House, General James A. Garfield, canvassed the northern sector.[16] Although Indiana was far from realizing the fact in 1864, presidential timber abounded in that state campaign, as Andrew Johnson was also one of the more prominent orators for the Republican cause.[17]

After his first speech in the familiar environment of Lawrenceburg, Harrison knew that he was in for a stiff fight. He found that the Democrats, bitterly incensed by the "sensational and effective exposé of the Sons of Liberty or the Knights of the Golden Circle,"[18] were now aroused to vindictive fervor in prosecuting the

13 Indianapolis *Daily Journal*, October 20, 1864. This was the occasion of Harrison's famous speech at the Tabernacle for the re-election of Abraham Lincoln.
14 The editorial note was published in the Indianapolis *Daily Journal*, Thursday, September 29, 1864, under the caption: "Our Soldier Candidate." It added: "Col. Harrison abandoned the lucrative and pleasant office of Reporter of the Supreme Court for the toils and dangers of the battlefield. The late Union State Convention nominated him for re-election, and during his brief furlough, he will visit as many points as practicable and address the people. The Colonel is an excellent speaker and will do good service on the stump, as he has on the battlefield."
15 Harrison's speaking appointments appeared on the front page of the Indianapolis *Daily Journal*, from September 27th until October 4th.
16 Indianapolis *Daily Journal*, September 27, 1864. Garfield was listed as speaking at Peru, Rochester, Plymouth, Westville, and South Bend.
17 Stampp, *op. cit.*, p. 237.
18 J. P. Dunn, *Greater Indianapolis*, I, 236. Stampp, *op. cit.*, pp. 149–50, points out that the Knights of the Golden Circle supposedly sprang from the parent stem

state campaign. While some Republican orators delighted in tagging each and every Democrat as charter members in these organizations suspected of treason, the Democrats themselves raised the cry of Republican dictatorship and military despotism. The fight in the press was just as fierce as it was in the hustings. The *Daily State Sentinel,* in championing the Democrats, featured several vitriolic editorials. The *Sentinel* warned its patrons that "every vote cast for Morton and the Republican candidates is an endorsement of the corruptions, the frauds, the reckless extravagance, and the suicidal policy of Lincoln and his adherents."[19] Though the issue was stated as a choice between free government under the Democrats or military despotism under the Republicans, the campaign was hotly waged over the personalities involved. Three days before election, Democrats were strongly urged to vote out "their worthless public servants, *Morton* and *Lincoln.* They have both been tried and found wanting."[20]

Public opinion, however, leaned heavily to the Republicans. The successful overthrow of a group suspected of treason and almost wholly identified with the Democratic party practically guaranteed Republican success at the polls, both in the important October state elections and in the November national contest.[21] Before the victory at Atlanta, Union speakers elaborated the theme that the "ballot of loyal men would have to sustain the armies in the field; a vote for the Administration was a vote squarely against secession and secession sympathy, and against the rebellion."[22] After the military successes in September, Harrison and many local army officers stumped the state and "gave additional testimony to the unity of the soldiers behind Governor

---

in the Confederacy itself, and was the most publicized of the local "treasonable" societies.

[19] Indianapolis *Daily State Sentinel,* October 11, 1864. The editorial columns savagely attacked Morton as "the most desperate and unscrupulous politician that ever disgraced the political station in Indiana. From the date of his first apostasy from the Democratic party, and his advocacy of the Know-Nothing faction and its proscriptive dogmas, he has been head and front of the wiliest conspiracies against liberty. He has stopped at nothing to accomplish his purposes."

[20] *Ibid.,* October 8, 1864.

[21] See Kenneth M. Stampp, "The Milligan Case and the Election of 1864 in Indiana," *Mississippi Valley Historical Review,* 31 (1944–45), 41–58. Also Felix G. Stidger, *Treason History of the Order of the Sons of Liberty* (Chicago, 1903).

[22] Stampp, *Indiana Politics during the Civil War,* p. 237.

Morton and the Union Party."[23] The political situation was most closely approximated by the *Daily Journal:*

As the election approaches, the people are preparing to vindicate the policy of an Administration that has struggled through the most appalling difficulties, and has with defiant front encountered rebels in arms and traitors at home, overcoming the one and confounding the machinations of the other. An Administration dear to all true and loyal men, successful, glorious, just in the act of binding the Republic in an eternal union, will never be deserted.[24]

For Harrison, political haranguing was a mixed pleasure. Even before his return from the field and before his actual presence on a political rostrum, he had confided to his wife:

I think the Union papers and speakers are making too much noise and parade about the treasonable designs of the Copperheads. It would be better to say less and *do* more. . . . In my opinion the place for our loud talking Union men to fight the Copperheads is here before Atlanta and before Richmond. If they would fill the call and give Sherman one hundred thousand and Grant three hundred thousand, we could take in Hood and his whole army . . . , and Grant would soon have Richmond and then the Copperheads would be dead and no one would know who killed them.[25]

Here was a man after Governor Morton's own heart. Harrison was not only interested in winning the election, but he desired to fill the Union ranks without resorting to a draft. Consequently, when the colonel of the Seventieth Indiana reported to Morton for special orders on September 20, 1864, he was given a twofold assignment to commence immediately after his brief furlough. First of all, he was ordered to support his candidacy and his party by electioneering; secondly, he was to canvass the state for recruits. Harrison found this twofold task entirely to his liking, especially his commission to recruit.[26] It is interesting to note that in one of his last letters before his furlough Col. Harrison had written to Indianapolis: "I would like to make a speech to one of your large *enthusiastic* Union meetings in the Circle. The

23 *Ibid.*
24 Indianapolis *Daily Journal,* September 23, 1864.
25 Harrison to his wife, August 24, 1864, Harrison MSS, Vol. 5.
26 *House Document No. 154,* p. 116.

first thing that I would say would be 'Gentlemen, *everyone of you* over 18 and under 45 years ought to be in the army, instead of sitting here among these patriotic ladies.'"[27] He was correct in surmising that such language would not win him much popularity, especially among the able-bodied Republicans who had not seen active service. Nevertheless, he was convinced that such a blunt statement would mirror perfectly the "feelings of those who are separated from their families, not singing 'rally round the flag,' but *rallying* around it, and dying in its defense."[28] He added: "I really begin to feel *contempt* for those who talk so eloquently for the Union and won't come and *fight for it*. I begin to believe that the only genuine patriotism in the country is found among the old men, the ladies and the soldiers." However strong Harrison's feelings may have been on this subject, no evidence appears either in the press or in his own letters that he ever voiced his challenge.

As the campaign drew to a close, Morton, Harrison and the Republican-Union ticket worked feverishly. For Morton, victory would vindicate his wartime measures, and for Harrison it would be a clear sign of popular repudiation of his ouster by the Supreme Court. On election day, Tuesday, October 11, 1864, the Democrats played their last trump against candidate Harrison. On its second page, the *Sentinel* carried an editorial headed: "Hon. J. Scott Harrison of Ohio."

This distinguished citizen and patriot, the father of a gentleman who is running in this state on the Abolition ticket for Supreme Court Reporter, assures the Democratic Executive Committee, of Hamilton County, Ohio, that he is with "the Democracy in this contest, and will support the October and November Democratic tickets." The honorable gentleman, if he lived in Indiana, would not therefore, vote for his own son.[29]

The parting shot by the Republicans was an election day reminder that Napoleon B. Taylor, Harrison's opponent, was a "third degree member of the treasonable order of the Sons of

27 Harrison to his wife, August 24, 1864, Harrison MSS, Vol. 5.
28 *Ibid.*
29 Indianapolis *Daily State Sentinel*, October 11, 1864.

Liberty."[30] There is no way of calculating the effect of these last-minute attacks. We do know, however, that the Hoosier electorate supported Morton and Harrison by giving them a 20,000 margin of victory.[31]

Indiana was now almost solidly Republican, and to show his appreciation Morton staged a tremendous victory rally at Indianapolis on October 14th. The re-elected governor made the principal address, keynoting his remarks with the claim that the State Republican triumph "had dealt the rebels a staggering blow."[32] No one left the rally that evening without sharing Morton's conviction that Lincoln would defeat McClellan in the coming presidential election, and that the President's re-election would virtually end the war.[33] Lest over-confidence pervade the Republican ranks, the party organ warned every voter in the state:

Let no one suppose that because one battle has been gained there is no more work to be done. The fight has just begun in good earnest, and from this time until after Abe and Andy have been elected by an overwhelming majority, the walls of the Tabernacle will echo three nights in a week with the voices of Union speakers and the cheers of a Union audience.[34]

Ben Harrison's was the first voice heard in the hall known as the Tabernacle. With neither his knowledge nor his consent, on October 19, 1864, an announcement appeared: "Meeting at the Tabernacle. . . . Ben Harrison Speaks Tonight."[35] Surprised and chagrined by so brief a warning, Harrison had no choice but to accept. When he arrived, the strains of Lozier's new victory song, "Have You Heard from the People," were still echoing.

Harrison opened his remarks by launching a savage attack against the Copperheads, "the men who are making such an outcry about the burdens of war," yet "bear none of them." He was cheered when he said that "those who bear the burdens—the

[30] Indianapolis *Daily Journal,* October 11, 1864.
[31] Stampp, *Indiana Politics,* p. 253. The Republicans won control of the General Assembly and elected 8 of the 11 Congressmen.
[32] Foulke, *op. cit.,* 370.
[33] Indianapolis *Daily Journal,* October 15, 1864.
[34] *Ibid.,* October 19, 1864.
[35] *Ibid.,* October 19, 1864.

brave soldiers in the field—make no complaint." "Copperheads,"
he continued,

have a great deal to say about the cruelties of war. It is a cruel war—
preeminently cruel—cruel in its inception, as being against a government which only touched subjects to bless them; cruel in its savage
ferocity with which it is waged on the part of the rebels; cruel in that
it has brought desolation and grief to the hearthstone of almost every
household in the land. But all these horrors should not affright us,
or make us hesitate one moment in our duty.[36]

In reviewing the origin and the cause of the war, Harrison
maintained that the North had not wanted war, and had held
back so long "before it took up the gauntlet so defiantly flung
in its face, that it looked like timidity." Now that the issue was
squarely joined, he said, there could be no turning back. Harrison was not speaking for himself. He protested that he represented the "voice of the men who have borne the burden" and
who have just voted to "crush the rebellion." With respect to the
doctrine of state sovereignty as one of the principal articles in the
creed of the Democratic Party, Harrison characterized it as a most
"dangerous heresy, and a deadly poison to national life." He
called upon the people of Indiana to repudiate this doctrine in
the national elections. To his statement that state supremacy
could be practically blocked by suppressing the rebellion and
theoretically blocked by defeating the Democratic Party, his audience gave whole-hearted approval.

By far the most popular part of Harrison's speech was his strong
defense of President Lincoln. Charging that objections to the
presidential policy were being made in the interest of treason,
the colonel high-lighted his remarks by declaring that "the progress of Mr. Lincoln has been but the progress of the people."
He even went so far as to say that the President's Emancipation
Proclamation "did but reflect the will of the people which clearly
demanded a change of policy." Throughout the remainder of
his address Harrison gave testimony to the benefits that followed
upon that proclamation. Witness, he said, Sherman's long line
of communication, "where black men, in a hundred ways, did the
work which would have otherwise fallen upon our brave sol-

[36] *Ibid.*, October 20, 1864.

diers." This section of his speech was a well-phrased eulogy on the Negro's part in the war. "Not a negro has escaped and made his way into our camps but has brought more aid to our cause than the entire brood of whining, carping Copperheads who object, in the interest of treason, to the employment of the black men."

The *Journal* report called Harrison's effort "eloquent and profound." His audience, however, most probably remembered this speech as one of Harrison's most partisan harangues. The bloody shirt was in evidence, as the little colonel swung into a fiery peroration. He declared that, if McClellan were elected, "the Copperheads would strip the uniforms from the backs of these dusky soldiers and send them back to slavery." Although he was against involuntary servitude, except as a punishment for crime, in his eyes the sin of Southern traitors was so deep and damning "that centuries of servitude could not atone for it." He went further, stating that, if, after the war, anyone must be enslaved, "he was in favor of making the traitor white a slave to the loyal black." Partisan statements like these Harrison was to regret, especially during his presidency. His invective in 1864, however, drew loud cheers from the audience. As they heard the hardened soldier dealing death-blows to the persons of his political opponents, the crowd no longer remembered him as the calm and conservative barrister of two years back.

As the presidential canvass wore into its final phase, Harrison doubled his effort in behalf of Lincoln. Whether he spoke in small towns or in large cities mattered not at all.[37] His long experience on the stump made him a valuable asset to Lincoln's cause. Finally, on November 7th, Indiana joined her sister states in the North in giving Lincoln a popular majority of 400,000 votes over McClellan;[38] the Hoosier majority was 20,000. Morton and Harrison were delighted with the results, for Republicanism was now firmly entrenched in both state and nation.[39] To the

[37] The Indianapolis *Daily Journal,* October 26, 1864, listed Harrison as speaking at Columbia City, Whitney County, November 1; Warsaw, Kosciusko Co., November 21; Lafayette, November 3; and Newport, Vermillion Co., November 4.

[38] James G. Randall, *The Civil War and Reconstruction,* pp. 621–22. Though the election was hailed as a landslide, there were large minorities for McClellan in New York, Pennsylvania, Ohio, Indiana, and Illinois.

[39] Stampp, *Indiana Politics,* p. 253.

war hawks of 1864, Lincoln's re-election brought complete assurance of a fight to the finish.[40]

The question of Harrison's return to active service now confronted the colonel's superiors, his friends, and above all, his family. Morton was uncertain in what office Harrison could render the best service; Indianapolis friends who had cast their ballots for him wanted Harrison to remain in order to take up his duties as supreme court reporter; his family did not interfere, but the colonel knew their secret thoughts. Deeply gratified by his re-election, he weighed the possibility of resigning his commission. His first love was the courtroom, though he had grown very fond of the men in the Seventieth Indiana. The promise of profound peace at home strongly urged him to an immediate acceptance of the Reporter's position.

Harrison's die was cast, though he did not know it, on the day of his loudest acclaim in Indianapolis. While Republicans were congratulating themselves on Harrison's firebrand address in the Tabernacle, two events in the South conspired to effect his speedy return to the fighting front. One was a Confederate council of war held at Gadsden, Alabama, on October 20, 1864; the other, a special letter from General Ward, Harrison's former commanding officer, to Governor Morton.[41]

Ward was now in Nashville, Tennessee, serving with the army of General George H. Thomas.[42] With undisguised concern, the Kentuckian told Morton that veteran substitutes were needed from the Indianapolis area. Moreover, with a frankness bred from familiarity with Harrison, Ward asked Morton to assign the colonel to the task of filling up the "33rd, the 70th and the 85th Indiana Regiments." Morton agreed, and Harrison, already engaged in recruiting, now doubled his efforts to sign up veterans

40 Randall, *op. cit.*, p. 624, points out: "On the main issues of the day Lincoln and McClellan were not opposites. They agreed essentially as to reconstruction. There was no peace-at-any-price ballot in the election."

41 S. K. Harryman to Col. Benj. Harrison, October 20, 1864, Harrison MSS, Vol. 5. On the council at Gadsden, see John P. Dyer, *The Gallant Hood* (Indianapolis, 1950), pp. 281–82.

42 On September 29, 1864, Sherman had sent Thomas to Chattanooga and Nashville to reorganize the middle Tennessee defenses against the forays of Nathan B. Forrest. Hooker's old 20th Army Corps and, therefore, Harrison's old command, were left at Atlanta. Dyer, *op. cit.*, p. 280.

for at least a short term of service, if not for the duration. As for Harrison's return to active duty, Ward instructed his adjutant to write the colonel a personal letter,[43] in which he argued that, even if Harrison had committed himself to the people of Indiana by agreeing to accept the office of supreme court reporter, the proposed promotion to brigadier general would relieve him from such obligations. Ward craftily added that "with the recommendations already forwarded, a word from the Governor to the President would probably be sufficient to obtain the promotion." With Hooker, Ward, and Morton active in his behalf, Harrison knew his promotion was certain, despite the fact that the waters passing through official channels frequently move slowly. While this praise from superior officers was most satisfying, the compliment offered by the men in the ranks was undoubtedly a source of even greater consolation. They wanted his return to command either in his "present or in superior rank."[44]

Ward's message all but compelled Harrison to return immediately. The event, however, that protracted Harrison's destiny as a soldier was the all-night strategy conference between Generals Beauregard and Hood. There, a new Southern strategy was born. Hood was going into Tennessee with "a hope to establish our line eventually in Kentucky."[45] This bit of daredeviltry on the part of the Texan, John Bell Hood, was to be executed by the same courageous Confederate army that had been compelled to evacuate Atlanta. The last hope of the Confederate cause in the West rested squarely on the shoulders of the towering blond-haired veteran of Gettysburg and Chickamauga, whose left arm dangled almost useless at his side, and whose right leg was little more than a stump. The task of stopping Hood fell to General George H. Thomas. Sherman had grown tired of chasing the Texan who could "turn and twist like a fox, and wear out my army in pursuit";[46] instead, he faced his army about and began his destructive march to the sea.

[43] S. K. Harryman (Ward's adjutant and secretary) to Harrison, October 20, 1864. Harrison MSS, Vol. 5.

[44] Ibid. Morton may have fulfilled his part in Harrison's promotion by a verbal recommendation to President Lincoln. No written document has been uncovered.

[45] Dyer, op. cit., p. 281.

[46] Henry Stone, "Repelling Hood's Invasion of Tennessee," R. U. Johnson and C. C. Buel (eds.), Battles and Leaders, IV, 441.

Once he had determined to return to the battlefield, Harrison lost no time in leaving Indianapolis. On the day after Lincoln's re-election, November 8, 1864, he entrained for the South, according to orders,[47] to join his regiment at Atlanta and march with Sherman to the sea. Harrison, however, never made contact with the 20th Army Corps at Atlanta, and consequently, never shared with his comrades of the Seventieth Indiana the feeling that "they had a part in driving the dagger into the heart of the Rebellion."[48]

Wallace records that "the failure of a hack to make connection with a southgoing train at Indianapolis" prevented Harrison from joining his command. Taking the next train, he got as far as Dalton, Georgia, only to find the railroad torn up and further progress impossible. While at Dalton, Harrison was ordered to report to General Charles Cruft at Chattanooga where he was immediately given command of the 1st Brigade.[49] Upon his arrival there, he found several other contingents cut off from their regular commands, and assembled there by special order.[50] In command of what was soon to be called a provisional detachment was Major General James B. Steedman, a veteran of Chickamauga fame.[51] Though this odd assortment of troops had been hastily thrown together to answer Thomas' call for more strength, it was welded rapidly into a sharp fighting unit, ready to march at a moment's notice.

The moment was not long in coming. All during Sherman's march through Georgia the impetuous Hood was unfolding his plans for a counter-offensive in Tennessee. During the last week of November, Hood tried desperately to prevent Schofield from effecting a union with Thomas at Nashville. The Texan was convinced that, if he could block this important junction of two large Union armies, "complete victory would be in Confederate

[47] "Executive Dept., Indianapolis, Indiana, November 9, 1864: Col. Ben Harrison, 70th Ind. Vols., having discharged the special duty under the within orders is hereby relieved from duty and will report to his regiment. O. P. Morton, Gov. of Indiana," Harrison MSS, Vol. 5.

[48] Samuel Merrill, *The Seventieth Indiana*, p. 213.

[49] Lew Wallace, *Life of Gen. Ben Harrison*, pp. 224–25.

[50] *Ibid.*, p. 225.

[51] Among the troops listed in this provisional detachment were the 1st and 2nd Colored Brigades under the respective commands of Col. Thomas J. Morgan and Col. Charles R. Thompson. Johnson and Buel, *op. cit., Battles and Leaders*, IV, 473.

hands and Hood's dazzling dream of marching to the Ohio and then joining with Lee would come true. Such a victory would completely neutralize Sherman in Georgia and compel him to abandon the state. Get in between Schofield and Thomas; whip the former; then turn on the latter and take Nashville. That was Hood's plan."[52] This bit of Southern strategy, brilliantly conceived, met with dismal failure in execution. During the night of November 29, 1864, Schofield's large and well-equipped army successfully slipped from under the very nose of General Hood and bivouacked along the Columbia Pike near Spring Hill.[53] When dawn broke on the 30th, a chagrined and mortified Hood swore that he would avenge his humiliation. Then and there he determined to catch his elusive foe immediately and deal him a crippling blow.[54]

From early morning to late afternoon on the 30th, Hood and Cheatham drove their men in pursuit of Schofield. Just eighteen miles south of Nashville, Schofield was compelled to rest his weary troops. He called a halt at Franklin, selecting an excellent defensive position and fortifying it well.[55] At about 3:00 P.M., Hood made contact with Schofield's skirmish line. Never one to delay, Hood, against the advice of his staff officers, immediately issued the tragic command: "Drive the enemy from his position into the river at all hazards."[56] There followed a series of desperate attacks that served only to immortalize Southern valor. The attack was a costly failure: Hood lost well over 6,000 men; Schofield, only 2,000.[57]

On the night that Schofield eluded Hood, Harrison's brigade was ordered from Chattanooga to Nashville to re-enforce Thomas against Hood. Save for a few necessary garrison guards, Chattanooga was evacuated of able-bodied troops in response to Thomas' call for more men. No one had to inform Harrison

[52] Dyer, *The Gallant Hood*, p. 285. Thomas' army was scattered all over Tennessee, the largest unit being his own force of some 18,000, in and around Nashville, and the forces of Schofield and Stanley, at Pulaski, numbering some 25,000.

[53] *Ibid.*, p. 286.

[54] A. J. Lewis, "Into Tennessee," New Orleans *Times-Democrat*, March 5, 1893, as quoted in Dyer, *op. cit.*, p. 289.

[55] Henry Stone, "Repelling Hood's Invasion of Tennessee," Johnson and Buel, *op. cit.*, IV, 450.

[56] John Bell Hood, *Advance and Retreat: Personal Experiences in the United States and Confederate Armies* (New Orleans, 1880), p. 293.

[57] Randall, *op. cit.*, p. 675.

just how serious was Hood's threat on Nashville. Moving troops and empty towns were evidence enough. The march was hard; food and fuel were scarce, "for hardly any part of the western country had been foraged upon as much as middle Tennessee."[58]

Harrison and his brigade arrived at Nashville at a propitious moment. General Thomas' headquarters reflected the joy that reigned in the city from the moment of Hood's serious reverse at Franklin. Though the gallant Confederate leader was laying siege to the city, there was an air of expectancy and triumph about the Union camp. Both Thomas and the recently arrived Schofield extended a warm welcome to General Steedman and his provisional detachment of over 5,000 men. Harrison said that Thomas knew Steedman as a fighting man and was determined that he should play an important role in the battle for Nashville, now looming larger and larger.[59] Both Thomas and Hood were poised to strike at the end of the first week in December, but the weather turned fiercely cold and sleet turned into snow and ice.[60] Harrison wrote to his wife: "If Hood falls back, we will, of course, follow him, and if this weather continues, it will be a terrible campaign."[61]

The freezing weather continued, and there was little activity in either camp. Acute suffering afflicted both armies, some soldiers dying on the picket line, and a good many others were so badly frost-bitten that they never recovered.[62] Harrison felt a personal responsibility for the men under his command, searching by day "to supply my command with wood to keep them from freezing."[63] At night, he walked the picket lines, dispensing from a large can the hot coffee that he himself had prepared. This special act of kindness was never forgotten in the circle of Harrison's friends in the post-war years.[64] Despite the hatreds of war, Harrison also felt keenly for the ill-clad foe under Hood. To Carrie he mused: "If the rebels are not well clothed, they must

[58] Freeman Cleaves, *Rock of Chickamauga*, p. 253.

[59] Harrison to his wife, December 9, 1864, Harrison MSS, Vol. 5.

[60] Dyer, *op. cit.*, p. 298.

[61] Harrison was quite disconsolate over the fact that most of Carrie's letters to him were not coming through, but "were hidden away in the accumulating Chattanooga mail." Harrison to his wife, December 9, 1864, Harrison MSS, Vol. 5.

[62] Wallace, *op. cit.*, p. 227.

[63] Harrison to his wife, December 12, 1864, Harrison MSS, Vol. 5.

[64] Wallace, *op. cit.*, p. 227, cites the typical gratitude of one of these pickets, Richard Smock.

be suffering immensely from cold and exposure . . . both sides seem to be ice-bound."[65]

While both sides waited patiently for the weather to break, Harrison found time as well as topics for speculation. As usual, his wife was the confidante of those battles that are fought within the heart and never find their way into official reports or records. "I am getting along pretty well with my new command, but I am still very anxious to get to my proper one." He also wondered about his promotion to brigadier general, reluctant at the same time to go to General Thomas' headquarters and to make inquiries about himself. He concluded, finally, to "wait till I hear of what is done at Washington and keep my expectations in check in the meanwhile."[66]

All during this enforced delay, the impatient and exacting Grant kept wiring from Virginia that he wished Thomas to launch an immediate attack upon Hood.[67]

On December 13th, when a moderation of weather brought increased activity in Hood's camp, an attack was imminent. General Steedman, in charge of the left-wing defenses of the city, ordered Harrison's brigade to erect and fortify a breastwork covering the entire front of his line. All of the 13th and part of the 14th, they slaved to accomplish their assignment. Harrison later reported that the patriotism and warm co-operation of the citizenry made their task successful, and made them fight "like tigers for that . . . land."[68] He also tells how it was necessary to cut across and even appropriate civilian property in this work. He seems to have won a lifelong friend in the person of Judge Trimble, who gave Harrison an American flag to use for his garrison colors, adding, "Colonel, if it is necessary for the defense of Nashville, take the bottom brick in my house."

The battle of Nashville began at dawn on December 15, 1864. Late the night before, Thomas carefully outlined his plans for battle. Harrison, as a part of Steedman's force, was to move at daylight against Cheatham, commanding the Confederate right. A. J. Smith's corps was scheduled to make a simultaneous attack

---

[65] Harrison to his wife, December 12, 1864, Harrison MSS, Vol. 5.
[66] *Ibid.*

[67] Cleaves, *op. cit.*, p. 259. Also Randall, *op. cit.*, p. 675. "Grant sent urgent but unheeded orders to Thomas demanding a battle, and finally sent Logan to supersede him." Thomas attacked, however, before Logan arrived on the scene.

[68] Wallace, *op. cit.*, p. 226.

on the Confederate left under Stewart. Thomas assigned General T. J. Wood to center as the pivot for the flanking movement. General Schofield was to be held in reserve for use wherever needed.[69] In the face of an early morning fog,[70] Steedman moved out cautiously against Cheatham, with Harrison's brigade in the lead. Behind the Hoosier colonel moved the two Negro brigades.

Skirmishers from Harrison's brigade thrust aside enemy pickets and attempted to charge a Confederate battery planted in a rocky ravine, but Cheatham's men did not yield on the 15th. Despite this, the Union army achieved a decided advantage at the end of the first day's fighting. No little credit was given to Steedman's provisional detachment; it "had more than accomplished its first day's task."[71]

That night a badly battered Hood dug in for the last time. Falling back two miles to hills strongly fortified, the courageous Southern leader completely realigned his forces in both wings, and contracted his battle line from six miles to three. Cheatham was now sent to bolster the badly shattered left wing. At dawn the battle was renewed, but by noon the die was cast. As soon as the North attacked Hood's left from front and rear, the Confederate cause was lost. The fatal breakthrough was quick in coming. Then the disastrous rout began. "Nobody knows who followed whom to the rear. All were mingled in inextricable confusion—the Army of the Tennessee had degenerated into a mob clawing its way down the Franklin Pike toward safety."[72]

General Thomas despatched all available infantry and cavalry in pursuit of Hood. Harrison's brigade, which had been transferred to reserve, was affected by these general orders and was directed to march to Murfreesboro, "there take the trains and push forward with the utmost speed."[73] His mission was clearcut. He was to try to reach the Tennessee River before Hood, and by destroying pontoons was to intercept the rebel retreat.

[69] *Official Records,* Series I, Vol. XLV, Part 1, p. 38. Thomas's complete strategy is contained in his report of January 20, 1865.

[70] Cleaves, *op. cit.,* p. 262.

[71] *Ibid.,* p. 264.

[72] Dyer, *op. cit.,* p. 301. Cleaves, *op. cit.,* p. 267, indicates that the two-day battle cost the Confederate army 13,189 men, including 4,462 prisoners, as well as 53 guns; the Union loss was set at 3,057.

[73] Wallace, *op. cit.,* p. 228.

Although Harrison's command undertook the chase southward with great enthusiasm, they found it extremely difficult. Partially covered by Forrest's cavalry, the fleeing foe had hastily organized a rear guard which gave some semblance of order to their retreat. With remarkable skill, Hood's retiring columns threw every possible obstacle in the path of the Federal pursuers. Harrison's chase was effectively stalled by rail, as alert Confederates burned wood piles and destroyed water tanks. Only at the cost of precious hours could he detail ax-men to chop up rails to feed the engine. Further delay ensued while "creek buckets were used to fill the tanks with water."[74] Only late on the morning of December 17th could the Union pursuers make effective contact with the enemy, and, even then, brave bands of Louisianians stubbornly stood their ground, successfully breaking the impact of the Federal assault. In later years Harrison appreciated the Southern courage that staved off certain disaster to a barefoot infantry sliding as fugitives along icy roads.

The pattern of pursuit did not vary, because rear guard Confederate forces fought and fell back again and again for the next seven days, with Federal pursuers only a few hours behind Hood all the way. Try as they would, Harrison's slower infantry could not catch up with the enemy. The roads were either glazed with ice or "bottomless with mud," while many of the streams could only be "crossed by wading."[75] Prospects of intercepting the enemy grew dimmer by the day, and there seemed little chance of bagging Hood's remnants.

The capricious weather continued, and in the rain, ice, and mud the gap between the pursuers and the pursued widened. Finally, on Christmas Eve, the cavalcade of Confederates safely crossed the Tennessee River. Notwithstanding this failure to achieve their principal mission, Steedman's division and Harrison's brigade pushed forward in the ardent hope of striking a final blow at the once-magnificent fighting machine of General Hood. Arriving at the banks of the Tennessee, the Federals had to bridge the river in the face of a hostile battery. This they successfully accomplished, continuing their almost hopeless pursuit to Decatur, and as far as Courtland, Alabama.[76] Here the Union

74 *Ibid.*
75 *Ibid.*
76 *Ibid.*, p. 229.

cavalry did their best work of the whole pursuit. After they had destroyed an important pontoon bridge, they were able to flank a large remnant of Hood's army. The Southerners who stood to fight it out received a sound drubbing. Despite this modicum of success, Harrison and the slower infantry never again caught sight of Hood.

On New Year's Eve the campaign ended officially, and Harrison's contingent was recalled.[77] While Thomas ordered most of his army into winter quarters, Harrison was directed first to report to General Cruft at Chattanooga, where, on January 16, 1865, he received from Major General Thomas the command that warmed his heart: "Col. Ben Harrison, 70th Indiana Infantry, will proceed without delay to Savannah, Ga. and rejoin his proper command for duty."[78] For more than two weeks he had waited impatiently for these orders to rejoin General Sherman at Savannah, the city that had been given to President Lincoln as a Christmas present.[79] If Sherman was already dreaming of the hour when he could march North and unite his army "with that of General Grant before Richmond," Harrison was looking beyond Richmond and the surrender of the South. His eye and his heart were set upon Indianapolis.

When he was packed and ready to begin his trip to Georgia, Harrison received belatedly but willingly a handsome Christmas gift from Major General Thomas. His orders were reissued to allow him a brief furlough at Indianapolis, whence he was to entrain for New York, and then proceed by steamer to Savannah. This unexpected leave to visit Carrie and the children was a real boon. As he left for home, Harrison's superior officer, Brigadier General Charles Cruft, bade him a warm farewell. Then the general went to headquarters and wrote the following to the War Department:

. . . in parting with Col. Benjamin Harrison, 70th Indiana Vols., it affords me pleasure to say that he has served the country, during the

[77] Cleaves, *op. cit.*, p. 276.

[78] Special Orders No. 16, Department of the Cumberland; copy in Harrison MSS, Vol. 6, 1091.

[79] Otto Eisenschiml and Ralph Newman, *The American Iliad,* p. 655: "Sherman presented Savannah to President Lincoln as a Christmas gift and then prepared for further exploits. He could either join Grant by water or else march by land through the Carolinas. He himself preferred the latter."

recent short but arduous and brilliant campaign (as commander of a Brigade in the Division under my command) most faithfully and creditably. He has proven himself on all occasions to be an excellent officer. His long and meritorious service entitles him to remembrance at the hands of the Government and to speedy promotion. I recommend that he be made a Brigadier General and guarantee that he possesses all the qualities requisite to successful administration of the office. I have known Col. Harrison for several years and speak from personal knowledge.[80]

[80] Copy in the Harrison MSS, Vol. 6, No. 1092.

CHAPTER XIV

Brigadier General Harrison and Desolated Roads

HARRISON'S RETURN to Indianapolis immediately after the successful Nashville campaign bore a striking resemblance to his homecoming after the fall of Atlanta. Some Hoosiers maintained that his courage and skill in handling a brigade on the Nashville front had assured him of a brigadier's "star," whether official Washington chose to recognize it or not.[1] Still others listed Benjamin Harrison with Colonel John Coburn as Indiana's "most deserving and best colonels."[2] Such sentiments of appreciation and praise moved Harrison to dismiss all feelings of regret that he had been prevented from joining Sherman and his original command at Atlanta. No longer did he consider his absence from the Seventieth Indiana, as it marched from Atlanta to Savannah, a stroke of misfortune. Although he sorely missed his own regiment and his old brigade, whose military fame was now assured, Harrison found ample compensation in the warm reception he was given in the Indiana capital. He found it stimulating when a body of his fellow citizens heralded him as "having gone through a harder and not less glorious campaign with Thomas"[3] than he would have experienced with Sherman on the march to the sea.

---

[1] George W. Grubbs to Col. Harrison, February 21, 1865, Harrison MSS, Vol. 6: ". . . believing the 'star' won on more fields than one, permit me to congratulate you."

[2] John Defrees to Harrison, February 18, 1865, Harrison MSS, Vol. 6, claims that this was the opinion in the U. S. Senate as well as in Indiana. Defrees was Superintendent of Public Printing in Washington and wrote Harrison that "we have battled over your cause and that of John Coburn several times."

[3] George W. Grubbs to Col. Harrison, February 21, 1865, Harrison MSS, Vol. 6.

While no official action had been taken on the several recommendations that Harrison be promoted to the rank of brigadier general, he himself was not overconcerned, since public opinion and influential men were on his side, and the notification of his deserved promotion was just a matter of time. As Major Grubbs had written, with the South Carolina campaign about to start, and with a new opportunity for Harrison to head his old and tried brigade once again, "the full honor" could not be far distant. As Harrison rode into Indianapolis, he fully realized that Sherman was now entering upon the last stage of the great march which was to unite the Army of the West with that of the East before Richmond. He shared Grant's and Sherman's belief that, if this march were successful, the Confederacy was doomed. Sherman did not hope or expect to accomplish it without a struggle, and Harrison wanted to be there for the first attack.

Harrison did not delay long at Indianapolis. Anxious to rejoin his command, yet reluctant to leave his family, he finally decided to have Carrie and the two children accompany him as far as New York. Aside from the presence of two healthy children, this second honeymoon, made at the expense of the Government, differed vastly from the one of some twelve years previous. The intervening years had seen Ben and Carrie make rapid strides. The unknown lawyer of '54 was not only known, but actually cheered, as he waved farewell once again to Indianapolis and a host of friends. He seemed to sense that his own honor and future were secure.

Before they reached Honesdale, Pennsylvania, where Carrie's sister, Elizabeth Lord, and her family awaited their arrival, Benjamin confided to Carrie that nothing would please him more than to march northward from Savannah with the general who had taken Atlanta. He had learned that Sherman was to make for Hilton Head, a coastal city, really an island, southwest of Charleston. Harrison was set upon rejoining his command at that point.[4] Carrie, fearful but understanding, encouraged him. Certainly, her hero-husband could join Sherman's army of 60,000 by early February. While she scarcely could have envisioned his marching 420 miles farther, across swamps, over narrow mud roads and through unbroken forests, Carrie was content to feed the fire of

4 S. M. Bowman and R. B. Irwin, *Sherman and His Campaigns: A Military Biography* (New York, 1865), p. 335.

her husband's military ambition. Nor was it hard for her to picture her own pride and joy as supporting Grant against Lee in Virginia, especially if he were instrumental in cutting off Georgia and the Carolinas, the chief sources of Confederate supplies and re-enforcements. The reverie ended abruptly at Honesdale.

During the last week of January, 1865, for the first time since mid-July, 1862, Harrison found himself unfit for active service. Within a few hours of his arrival, scarlet fever struck the colonel and his family. The attack was serious and immediate quarantine dispelled all hope of a quick reunion with Sherman. The doctor certified that he would be unable to rejoin his command in less than thirty days.[5] Harrison's illness was bad, but his disappointment was worse.

Under the excellent care and attention of Mr. and Mrs. Lord's family,[6] the Harrisons recuperated more rapidly than the physician predicted. After two weeks of confinement, he began to show signs that his ordinarily robust constitution was on the mend. Perhaps good care and constant medical attention were not solely responsible for the swift recovery, for Harrison's will to recover was significantly stimulated by his official appointment as brigadier general by brevet. John Defrees helped Harrison more than he realized by a timely letter informing the general that his nomination had been unanimously confirmed by the Senate, and by a consoling postscript: "I have not heard a single word to your prejudice, but on the contrary, you stand well."[7]

Fully recovered by the beginning of the last week in February, Harrison now found his confinement increasingly irksome. Moreover, a score of congratulatory messages constantly sharpened his desire to ride once more at the head of his brigade. Friends in Indianapolis, so wrote his law partner "Pink" Fishback, were "much pleased with your deserved promotion, and you have the prayers of many that you may be spared to return again to more

5 Harrison MSS, Vol. 6.

6 Harrison mentions this in several later letters to his wife, Harrison MSS, Vol. 6, February 25, March 1, and March 4, 1865.

7 John Defrees to Brig. Gen. B. Harrison, February 18, 1865, Harrison MSS, Vol. 6. As founder of the newspaper, the Indianapolis *Atlas*, Defrees was in complete touch with local as well as national affairs. Harrison and other Indiana men used him as a contact man with President Lincoln whose nomination he helped to achieve at Chicago in 1860. See Kenneth Stampp, *Indiana Politics*, p. 6.

peaceful pursuits."[8] Ben's promotion also elicited from John Scott Harrison a letter fairly bursting with paternal pride. Yet, fatherly prudence dictated a strong admonition: "Be extremely careful of yourself and [do] not suffer anxiety to rejoin your command."[9] He was further urged to await a full convalescence and not to attempt to travel before complete recovery. It was typical of his father to add: "you can do your country no good laying [sic] in a hospital."

Despite his father's advice and without his physician's permission, Brigadier General Harrison left Honesdale for New York early in the last week of February. Greatly fatigued by the long train ride to Lackawaxen, Harrison was too proud to admit the fact. Rather, his first letter to Carrie and the children quickly passed over his own condition and dwelt at length on the kindness of a conductor who happened to hail from Indianapolis.[10] Harrison put up at the Merchants Hotel in New York City, relaxing there until orders should be issued from Washington. On February 25th the New York *Herald* bore the glad tidings that all officers belonging to Sherman's Army were to report immediately at Hilton Head.

The next morning Harrison sailed from New York on the steamer *Fulton*. On boarding the vessel he was surprised to find that army orders put him in command. The trip was uneventful, and the ship docked at Hilton Head on March 2, 1865. At this important land and naval base, now in Union hands, General Harrison had only a two-hour stay before taking passage on a small steamer that slowly nosed its way inland up the Broad River. The vessel's destination was Camp Sherman, situated near Blair's Landing, thirty miles from the coast. Dusk and a thick fog compelled the captain to drop anchor in mid-stream, though only half of the distance had been navigated.

Fog still shrouded the steamer the next morning, and, to chase away disappointment, the general proposed an oyster fishing ex-

8 W. P. Fishback to Gen. Benj. Harrison, February 18, 1865, Harrison MSS, Vol. 6. Also Grubbs to Harrison, February 21, 1865, *ibid.*

9 J. S. Harrison to Benj., February 22, 1865, Harrison MSS, Vol. 6. Harrison's father was quite surprised that his son was a victim of scarlet fever. "I had always thought that you had passed through the ordeal of Scarlet Fever—and indeed—all other diseases which are peculiar to infancy and early youth. Jennie and Carter had scarlet fever, when about ten or twelve years old, and quite severely too. You must have been away from home at the time."

10 Benj. Harrison to his wife, February 25, 1865, Harrison MSS, Vol. 6.

pedition. Harrison, who had never seen an oyster bed before, wrote to Carrie:

... we were soon pulling through the fog with the undersigned at the helm. We found plenty of oysters and loaded our boats down with them. The tide was out and we could reach the beds along the margin of the water without dipping for them. I had never seen an oyster bed before and they were quite a curiosity to me. The shells grow together in great bunches, the larger oysters being inside, and great clusters of smaller ones grown fast around them. The shells are very sharp; hands and boots suffered a good deal in the expedition.[11]

For Harrison the fun had just begun. With their heavy loot slowing them down, the oyster crew made for the steamer. Here they procured several empty buckets and "picked out some dozen bucketfuls of the best and got the engineer to *steam* them for us, so as to partially cook them and assist in opening the shells."

I soon got to be expert in opening them and took two or three dozen with *great* relish; which was perhaps not to be wondered at, as we had no supper or breakfast. The oysters are not large, but have a very good flavor. They are called along the coast Coon oysters—from the fact that the Coons eat them at night along the shore. Some times the oyster catches the Coon, by closing his shell on his paw, which is perhaps a fair retaliatory measure on his part.[12]

Before long, the morning fog had lifted, enabling the small steamer to dock at Blair's Landing. Harrison marched his contingent two miles to Camp Sherman, where General Prince was commandant over several thousand men prepared to reinforce Sherman. Upon reporting to Prince, Harrison boldly requested that he be permitted to join his old command without further delay. When Prince replied that he was ignorant of Sherman's exact position, Harrison was undaunted. He pleaded for leave to make his way alone, if necessary. Prince promptly vetoed this plan by explaining that no one was to leave the Blair's Landing base until the Confederates "now lurking in the woods and swamps"[13] could be starved or driven into the open. This attitude seemed to Harrison nothing more than overcaution. He cen-

[11] Harrison to his wife, March 4, 1865, Harrison MSS, Vol. 6.
[12] *Ibid.*
[13] Lloyd Lewis, *Sherman: The Fighting Prophet*, p. 499.

sured his senior officer for what he termed a lack of interest.[14]

Prince had his way, and Harrison was kept at Camp Sherman. In a couple of days he found himself in command of all arriving contingents, doing the same routine training job that he had done at Chattanooga the month before the Nashville campaign. If anything, his set-up at Blair's Landing was worse than that at Chattanooga. It was not so much the character of the troops as the location of the camp. As far as he could see, South Carolina was an endless succession of swamps and salt marshes. Moreover, the mosquitoes were so bad and sharp-biting gnats so numerous that, at the end of two weeks, he could truly write "I fit and blid for my country every day."[15]

Problems other than climate and terrain pressed Harrison. A number of "bounty jumpers," having obtained their loot, attempted to desert, but hemmed in, as they were, by swamps and rivers, it was almost impossible for them to get away. One night, eight of them deserted and made a raft on which to cross the river. Only four could ride the raft and the other four sent their clothes over on it and attempted to swim. One was drowned in crossing and the nearly naked three waded back to camp through swamps. One had only a shirt and another an overcoat. The culprits were brought to General Harrison for judgment. He seized this opportunity to warn his command against further attempts at desertion, and his solution, as he revealed it to Carrie, was quite simple: "I paraded them under guard before their command just as they were for two hours to show their comrades what desertion came to."[16]

Three days became three weeks, and still no news from Sherman. The camp near Blair's Landing increased in numbers daily. By the middle of March more than 5,000 well-drilled reinforcements anxiously awaited the signal to break camp and, further inland, 3,000 additional troops were ready to move with them. Battalion drill and dress parade were dull routine for veterans of Atlanta and Nashville. As the days dragged on, Sherman's fail-

[14] Harrison to his wife, March 4, 1865, Harrison MSS, Vol. 6: "Gen. Prince was assigned to General Sherman after the army reached Savannah and has no command with the moving column, and I don't think he feels the same interest in getting there as some of us do."

[15] Harrison to his wife, March 17, 1865, Harrison MSS, Vol. 6.

[16] *Ibid.*

ure to communicate with either Prince or Harrison irked the Hoosier.

The chief source of Harrison's melancholy was the dearth of letters from home. Carrie was still the faithful correspondent, but the news and sentiment contained in her roving letters never reached Blair's Landing; they were held at the 20th Army Corps Headquarters some 200 miles away. Toward the end of March, Carrie learned his plight:

If I were receiving letters from you by every steamer, the labor would be much more easy and pleasant. As it is, my life is one of unvarying monotony, and the companions by whom I am surrounded are strangers to you, and their doings and sayings of no interest to you. With you it is not so; the friends who surround you and make part of your daily life are my children or my very dear friends, and everything that concerns these is of interest to me. Your daily domestic life I feel to be a part of my life, and I love to know every little event of it to feed my love of home upon, and direct my imagination when I go in fancy to my absent home. My life here is an indolent one, offering very little scope for ambition or energy. The office business is very light, and my out-of-door duties consist of an occasional visit to my picket line and the camp.[17]

Much as Harrison yearned for Carrie, the children and his Indianapolis friends, he feared, so he admitted, "to anticipate the joy of returning home to remain, or 'for good' as the children say, lest some casualty of disease or battle" should shatter "these fond anticipations."[18] Despite every indication to the contrary, this period of enforced confinement and inactivity was, in reality, a blessing in disguise. Granted that Harrison was sad, despondent and deeply introspective, this was a mental climate which he needed in order to mature and plot his future course. Not even the brigadier general's commission could shake his determination to retire "at the expiration of my present term.... I am growing older and perhaps injuring my constitution more than I am now aware of, while I am not growing wiser in anything likely to be of use to me in future life."[19]

Yet, he was on the threshold of change, and the change was

17 Harrison to his wife, March 28, 1865, Harrison MSS, Vol. 6.
18 Harrison to his wife, March 17, 1865, Harrison MSS, Vol. 6.
19 Ibid.

one Carrie had yearned to see. The years 1857–61 had been financially bearable, but no wife enjoys seeing her husband an utter slave to his work. There was silent suffering and resignation on Carrie's part. Her husband would not always be forced to devote two-thirds of his day to actual practice, office routine, and home study. When the change would come she did not know. The letter from South Carolina, however, fanned the flame of hope. Harrison himself wrote of a strong resolution to amend his ways in the postwar world:

> Sometimes I fear that I might find the monotonous and the plodding life of a lawyer too much lacking in excitement to satisfy me after three years in the army, as many before me have done, but I mean to be a more domestic and sociable man than I have ever been before, and I am sure that I shall find in the delights of home and family all that my heart longs for. On one point my mind is fully made up, and that is that I will never again make myself a *slave* to my business as I did for several years before going into the army. I am sure we shall be a happier family with a smaller income and more time spent in domestic and social intercourse.[20]

He had calculated that the publishing of the Supreme Court Reports would be full employment; consequently, he determined not to engage in an active law practice immediately upon his return. If he found it better to do so after a while, he promised to "limit my practice so as not to be overburdened." Harrison did not dwell too long on a future whose character was still uncertain. He advised Carrie that "there are yet dark battle scenes between me and the fruition of these hopes which I so much cherish. We will trust God and do our present duty."

While Harrison was drilling reinforcements at Blair's Landing, Sherman was on the march—from Columbia to Fayetteville, then east, away from Raleigh, toward Goldsboro, North Carolina. Near this city, on March 19, the hero of Atlanta fought a sharp engagement with Johnston in the vicinity of Bentonville, driving the enemy back and taking the railroad connecting Wilmington and Beaufort. Sherman's famous march was ended. His courageous army was strategically placed and heavy reinforce-

20 *Ibid.*

ments were near at hand. Further action, however, waited on an important conference with Grant and developments in the strategic Petersburg-Richmond sector.[21]

Under the circumstances Harrison was compelled to abandon his oft-repeated dream of marching to Sherman in the latter's hour of need. Sherman had no need. His army was well and still could march, even if great swaths had not been cut in the Carolinas. Harrison had all but given up hope, when a steamer put in at Hilton Head with orders to transport all available troops to join Sherman in North Carolina.

Highly elated, he confided to General Prince that he did not remember witnessing the dawn of a happier day. The Old West Pointer eyed the young general, and remarked that their present camp was a perfect *paradise* compared with any place on the coast of North Carolina. Concerning North Carolina Harrison had no information, but even the intimation that South Carolina was in any sense a paradise greatly disturbed him. Carrie shared her husband's indignation when he wrote that if this is Prince's idea "of paradise, the generally received idea of it ought to be corrected, and should no longer stand for a synonym of either *beauty, innocence,* or *happiness,* unless they are found in swamps, miasma, the company and control of bad men, laziness and a *bilious* habit."[22]

Harrison's eager departure was delayed only by his obligation to remain until the last transport was despatched. The time, however, was filled up with comment on the significance of peace negotiations already sanctioned by President Lincoln.[23] He put little trust in the rumors. Even when the New York *Tribune* urged Lincoln to offer peace terms again and again until they should be accepted, Harrison was convinced that the presidential efforts would ultimately fail. He had his own solution. "Let Sher-

[21] John G. Randall, *The Civil War and Reconstruction,* p. 676. Wilmington had been evacuated on February 22 and Fort Fisher had already been reduced. At this time Grant was threatening Lee at Petersburg.

[22] Harrison to his wife, March 28, 1865, Harrison MSS, Vol. 6. The "bad men" reference was to the activities of the sutler whom General Prince had employed, and to whom he had given the monopoly of selling to 7,000 troops. This purveyor charged exorbitant prices which Harrison had in vain attempted to have regulated by a Counsel of Administration. The outrageous swindling continued, and Harrison let it be known in camp that he had no control over the matter.

[23] See Randall, *op. cit.,* pp. 676–78.

man, Grant and Sheridan," he wrote, "push on their conquering columns and peace will come spontaneously. . . . My belief is that the war will never be ended by negotiation with the rebel leaders."[24]

Underlying Harrison's opposition to formal peace negotiations at this time was a deep fear that such proceedings would precipitate a complicated and belligerent fight over the fundamental question of reconstruction policies. Better, he thought, that the fear of the Lord should compel total surrender by Southern leaders:

When their "fear cometh," and they flee, leaving the people and the army to their own guidance, they will lay down their arms and seek their homes, if permitted, and we shall have a peace more permanent, that it has not been bought by concessions which may hamper the future management of the difficult question that will come before Congress.[25]

Before the last troop transport sailed from Hilton Head, Harrison mounted his charger for a farewell canter through the countryside. He had a favorite rendezvous—a large and once beautiful plantation about three miles from Blair's Landing. Dismounting, he sauntered leisurely through the "desolate ruins of a once splendid mansion." Flowers of all variety were in bloom, but "some splendid avenues of oaks" were the "sole remaining tokens of the rich and haughty slave holder's once courtly house and grounds." The weed-choked garden, however, yielded Harrison a parting souvenir. He plucked two rosebuds. That same evening he sent them to Carrie, charging her "to retain one of the buds yourself and imagine my whispering in your ear with the simple gift all that could be delicate and affectionate in a lover, in his first declarations."[26]

On April 5 the last group of regulars had set sail for Wilmington. While Harrison was packing his few belongings, the steamer *Champion* put in. The one letter out of its mail addressed to him was a rare treat on two scores: it was from Indianapolis, which, as far as Harrison had been concerned, had been wrapped in silence for over three months; and its author was Irwin Har-

24 Harrison to his wife, March 28, 1865, Harrison MSS, Vol. 6.
25 *Ibid.*
26 *Ibid.*

Photograph by Matthew B. Brady or Assistant

GRAND REVIEW COMMENCES AS COLUMNS MARCH DOWN PENNSYLVANIA AVENUE

Courtesy Library of Congress

Photograph by Matthew B. Brady or Assistant

VIEW AT REVIEWING STAND IN FRONT OF EXECUTIVE MANSION

Photograph by Matthew B. Brady or Assistant

LOOKING DOWN PENNSYLVANIA AVENUE FROM CORNER OF FIFTEENTH STREET

MRS. BENJAMIN HARRISON, 1865

rison, the retired soldier in the family. The general's brother wrote that all was well on the domestic front:

The little world in and around Indianapolis wags on the same old way, and I see your old profession brotherhood passing to and from their homes. I often look for you, and then remember and see you in your soldier's cloth, doing and daring to do, for your country's honor.[27]

With Irwin's letter in his pocket and nursing the phantasm of Indianapolis, Harrison boarded the *Champion* at Hilton Head. On the 10th they set sail, and after a pleasant two-day run, the steamer docked at Wilmington.

There, pandemonium had broken loose. Not merely had the news of Richmond's fall been confirmed, but the report of Lee's surrender to Grant at Appomattox as well. Wilmington was late in receiving the tidings, but her celebration was equal to that of any city sheltering Northern sympathizers.[28] General Joseph R. Hawley, commander of the Wilmington district, was on hand to greet the new arrivals. The ship's landing was an excuse for another wild celebration. Harrison and his staff were guests "and rode in grand style about the city." The parade lasted several hours, and the private celebrations somewhat longer. Officers vied with their men in expressions of jubilation. Throughout the night the atmosphere remained charged with victory, and even Carrie must have raised an eyebrow when her usually sober-minded and conservative husband described his part in the mounted and foot races of the officers. The finish line, Harrison was quick to point out, was General Hawley's house "where we went in to enjoy a collation." Carrie was also informed:

There was plenty of wine and so forth and we soon had a merry party. I was called out to respond to a toast to Sherman's army and after a short speech toasted the *Ladies*, two of whom, Mrs. General Hawley and Abbott were present. Before the party broke up I had to make another speech.[29]

Evidently, Harrison won the esteem of his fellow officers in Wilmington. General Dodge, whose famous career as a great rail-

27 Irwin Harrison to Benjamin Harrison, March 30, 1865, Harrison MSS, Vol. 6.
28 Harrison to his wife, April 15, 1865, Harrison MSS, Vol. 6.
29 *Ibid.*

road builder and financier still lay in the future, was happy to number the Hoosier among his friends. So was General Hawley, destined to be Harrison's colleague in the United States Senate.[30]

As much as Harrison liked Wilmington and his genial companions, he begged and obtained special orders on April 14 which gave him permission to "go to Goldsboro, N. C., and if opportunity offers, there to join his command with General Sherman's army."[31]

Finally, on April 19, after six months of vain effort, he reached the command he had left at the end of the Atlanta campaign. As he strode towards brigade headquarters, he was preoccupied with thoughts of the warm homecoming that his own old command would give him. He scarcely noticed that the Raleigh streets were singularly clear of civilian and soldier alike. Uneasy over this strange quiet, he sought the reason. He was stunned when he discovered it. General Sherman had just issued a purposely delayed bulletin: President Abraham Lincoln had been assassinated.[32]

Slowly, he entered his own headquarters. No one seemed to take any notice of his arrival. Harrison saw what Sherman and every other officer witnessed. "For hours . . . men wept, or were stunned, or stood gritting their teeth and demanding that the armistice be ended so there might be one last savage battle."[33] Sherman's bulletin, however, exonerated the Confederate army from complicity in the assassination plot, and the first impact of the shocking news gradually lost its force. Dismay yielded to sympathy and curses became prayers. Memorial services for the President were conducted at headquarters. It was at the camp of

[30] Hawley represented Connecticut in the United States Senate from 1881 to 1905, entering that body with Benjamin Harrison, serving through the latter's administration as President, and then serving thirteen more years in the Senate after Harrison left Washington. Hawley was able but inconspicuous, served his country well as a consistent protectionist and advocate of sound money. In 1892, Hawley telegraphed the Minneapolis Convention that renominated Harrison: "Personally I was and am for Harrison first and last." J. R. Hawley to S. Fessenden, June 8, 1892. J. R. Hawley MSS, Vol. 21, No. 4962, Library of Congress.

[31] Special Orders Number 63, dated Headquarters, Wilmington, N. C., April 14, 1865; copy in Harrison MSS, Vol. 6, No. 1122.

[32] William Sherman, Memoirs, II, 350–51.

[33] Lewis, op. cit., p. 537. Sherman who watched the effect closely, and wrote that he "was gratified that there was no single act of retaliation; though I saw and felt that one single word by me would have laid the city in ashes and turned its whole population houseless upon the country, if not worse."

the 1st Brigade that Harrison delivered a eulogy on Lincoln.[34] Summoned by the members of the Seventieth Indiana, he made a very brief speech. Unfortunately, not a single word has been preserved, and eye-witnesses relate only that it was "brief, . . . remarkably well put, and often to the point of eloquence."[35] Almost forty years later, after his own presidential term, Harrison delivered a similar address—in a Chicago banquet hall.[36] Eulogizing the deeds of the martyred chief executive, Harrison knew no restraint:

The Civil War called for a president who had faith in time, for his country as well as for himself; who could endure the impatience of others and bide his time. A man who could by strong but restrained diplomatic correspondence hold foreign intermeddlers and at the same time lay the sure basis for the Geneva award, a man who could in all his public utterances, while maintaining the authority of the law and the just rights of national government, breathe an undertone of yearning for the misguided and the rebellious; a man who could hold the war and the policy of the government to its original purpose—the restoration of the states without the destruction of slavery—until public sentiment was ready to support a proclamation of emancipation; a man who could win and hold the love of the soldier and the masses of the people; a man who could be just without pleasure in the severities of justice, who loved to forgive and pardon. . . .

Qualities of heart and mind combined to make him a man who has won the love of mankind. He is beloved. He stands like a great lighthouse to show the way of duty to all his countrymen and to send afar a beam of courage to those who beat against the winds. We do him reverence. We bless tonight the memory of Lincoln.[37]

[34] No copy of this address can be found. Contemporaries remembered it and alluded to it frequently, and Harrison himself only narrates the circumstances under which he was called to make the address in a letter to his wife, April 20, 1865, Harrison MSS, Vol. 6.

[35] The testimony of Captain H. A. Ford, which appeared in the Indianapolis *Journal,* June 29, 1888, a reprint from the Detroit *Tribune.* The clipping is in the B. Harrison Scrapbook Series, Vol. 6, Harrison MSS.

[36] Lincoln Day Banquet of the Marquette Club, Chicago, February 12, 1898.

[37] Benjamin Harrison, *Views of An Ex-President,* pp. 472–78.

CHAPTER XV

The Grand Review

NEXT TO THE love feast Harrison had with the stack of Carrie's letters waiting for him at headquarters, the event that pleased him most was the cordial reception given him by General Ward. "I find he has been a very true friend to me in my absence. I shall never permit myself to say a word against him again."[1] Quite a courageous resolution this—when one recalls Harrison's bitter complaints of '63 and '64.

In excellent health and boasting his heaviest army weight, 145 pounds, Harrison did not retire without first acquainting Carrie with the details of his army homecoming:

... I found a most cordial welcome here both from my superiors and inferiors and was compelled to make them a little speech last night. They all expressed the most cordial feeling and the most enthusiastic gladness at my return. It was very gratifying to know that they missed me, and also to be assured that they all gave me credit for a desire to get back. Sherman has completed the terms with Johnston which, if ratified at Washington, will, he says, bring peace from the Potomac to the Rio Grande. And in the meantime we have a suspension of hostilities. We are fixing upon a camp for a stay of ten days or two weeks, and then we expect to march toward home. Yes!, thank God, towards *home,* our work done, our country saved. There is some talk that a portion of the army will march to the Potomac . . . and part back through Georgia. Which way we may go I cannot tell, but I hope towards the East, as I have no fancy for a Georgia trip. My impression is that the Regiments that came out when we did, will be mustered out by the first of June, and that the Colored Troops, the Regulars and the Veterans will be kept as Garrisons for such places as they may think necessary to garrison. It is a most joyous anticipation and I pray nothing may happen to dash our cup of joy.[2]

For a week after he had resumed command, Harrison's brigade remained in camp at Raleigh. On April 25, when peace negotia-

1 Harrison to his wife, April 20, 1865, Harrison MSS, Vol. 6.
2 *Ibid.*

tions fell through, Sherman's army was set in motion again,[3] since caution dictated the speedy erection of roadblocks at strategic points in the vicinity of Raleigh. Consequently, Harrison's brigade was ordered to Jones' Cross Roads, fifteen miles southwest of the city, to guard against a Southern withdrawal in the event that new negotiations should also fail. This movement, however, was wasted energy. Johnston and Sherman, on the 26th, agreed to a set of terms "as generous, simple, and almost as brief as those Grant had given Lee."[4] Grant quickly acquiesced in the agreement, and Sherman, intending to treat the South with increasing liberality, wrote to Johnston:

Now that the war is over, I am as willing to risk my person and reputation as heretofore to heal the wounds made by the past war, and I think my feeling is shared by the whole army.[5]

Johnston accepted what he termed an "enlightened and humane policy."

Two days later, April 30, the Union army in and near Raleigh began the march to Richmond and Washington. Orders were issued that the march was to be "conducted with a view to the comfort of the troops and suggested fifteen miles per day as the limit, unless circumstances should require a longer march."[6] Upon starting out, Harrison had written Carrie not to expect any letters "from me again before we reach Richmond which we expect to make in two weeks."[7] Nine days later, and five days ahead of schedule, Harrison was writing from Richmond that "the march was not made as easy or as comfortable to the troops as the orders suggested."[8]

In his official report Harrison registered only a mild complaint against the needlessly long marches, noting merely that "the troops were very much wearied and exhausted."[9] Carrie, how-

---

[3] Samuel Merrill, *The Seventieth Indiana*, pp. 278–81.

[4] Lloyd Lewis, *Sherman: The Fighting Prophet*, p. 556. Northern terms gave ten days' rations to all surrendered soldiers and loaned them enough farm animals to insure a crop. Sherman issued special field orders to "encourage the inhabitants to renew their peaceful pursuits and to restore the relations of friendship among our fellow-citizens and countrymen."

[5] *Ibid.*

[6] Harrison's official report, Merrill, *op. cit.*, p. 278.

[7] Harrison to his wife, April 28, 1865, Harrison MSS, Vol. 6.

[8] Merrill, *op. cit.*, p. 278.

[9] *Ibid.*

ever, bore the burden of her husband's real complaint. He had written from Clover Hill, Virginia, twenty-two miles south of Richmond:

One week ago today we left Raleigh and have ever since been "marching on" towards Richmond. . . . We have been making long marches, though the march was ordered to be made with deference to the comfort of the troops. Our average distance per day has been about 20 miles. Reveille at 2½ A.M., and on the road at 4½. I don't like such early rising, and see no necessity for such hard marching. The 14th Corps has been trying to get up a race, and I suppose our Corps Commander has urged us forward to keep up with them.[10]

Despite his understandable growling, Harrison found the march on the whole "very pleasant . . . road good and the weather fine and cool save one day." Moreover, he had high praise for the discipline of his troops. At Raleigh, orders had been issued against all foraging from the country and no soldier was to enter private houses on any pretext. Reporting upon his own brigade, Harrison testified that "the orders were faithfully observed." While one or two cases of thieving came to his knowledge, he could honestly say that "it was really surprising to see an army so long accustomed to living off the country and to irregularities necessarily resulting, at once resume their habits of order and good discipline, and it is highly creditable to the Army."[11]

One of the unforgettable scenes of the rapid rush toward Richmond was the meeting and commingling of Southern and Northern troops. As a member of Harrison's regiment described it:

The men from General Lee's army, whom we met in large numbers, were ragged and had nothing to eat and no blankets, but the weather was warm, and little bedding was needed by old soldiers. When we met them, as we were going into camp, we invited them to sleep with us, and at such times talked over the events of war till far into the night. We always found these ex-rebels friendly and glad that the war was over, and the parting in the morning would be like leave-taking of old friends.[12]

10 Harrison to his wife, May 7, 1865, Harrison MSS, Vol. 6.
11 Merrill, *op. cit.*, p. 279.
12 U. H. Farr's diary, quoted by Merrill, *op. cit.*, p. 271.

Once the swift-moving corps had crossed the Roanoke River, only sixty miles separated them from Richmond. On May 8, Ward's division went into camp just eight miles south of the conquered capital. That evening the weary troops received word that General Halleck would review all the Washington-bound troops. No complaint was voiced more pointedly than Harrison's indignant protest:

> We have had no chance to re-fit our men and shall make a rather shabby appearance when compared to the spruce soldiers of the Potomac Army who are to be turned out to receive us. However, our shabbiness will be respectable, when the origin of it is known to be our wonderful marches and bold departures from our base.[13]

This prediction was completely verified, and after the Richmond review no one dared any longer to look upon Sherman's army as "a rough rabble of disorganized cut-throats."[14] Rather, the opposite opinion prevailed and a dignified reception was given the army whose tightly knit columns moved with perfect order through the city streets. Richmond never forgot Sherman's troops and Harrison never forgot Richmond. Here he officially received his commission as Brevet Brigadier General.[15]

Pushing ahead from Richmond was a trying ordeal. The battle-scarred route to Washington served only to revive the horrible memories of slaughter and carnage now stored in the minds of men who had once fought under McDowell, McClellan and Grant against Lee's command. Especially revolting were the skeleton-strewn battlefields around Spotsylvania and Chancellorsville. Splintered trees and riddled stumps could not hide from Harrison and his brigade several patches of ground "thickly strewn with dead Union soldiers."[16] Deeply shocked by these "horrible sights," Harrison refused to describe them in detail.

---

13 Harrison to his wife, May 9, 1865, Harrison MSS, Vol. 6.

14 Merrill, op. cit., p. 272.

15 "I received my commission as Bvt. Brig. Genl. at Richmond and was greatly relieved to have it at hand." Harrison to his wife, May 20, 1865, Harrison MSS, Vol. 6. The delay was caused by Lincoln's assassination. On April 29, 1865, John Defrees had written to Harrison: "I called at the War Dept. today to see about your commission. It had not been returned to the War Dept. from the Executive Mansion until a few days ago. A great many comm. were on Mr. Lincoln's table unsigned at the time of his death." Harrison MSS, Vol. 6.

16 Merrill, op. cit., p. 273.

It is to Sherman's credit that his army gave these honored dead
a belated but decent burial.

Through the Wilderness, across the Rappahannock, and northward into Alexandria, marched Sherman's stalwarts, begrimed
and thirsty. Harrison wrote: "We were all so much fatigued and
worn out that we had not fixed up any desks or tables and I can
only write you a brief pencil note on my knee. The last three days
of our march were very exhausting owing to intense heat and
scarcity of water."[17] No sooner had camps begun to mushroom
along the Virginia side of the Potomac than a three-day downpour drenched the squalid, sweaty corps. After the storms, the
ordinary Washington weather prevailed. Yet, even the hot, sultry
days that exasperated the natives failed to dampen the enthusiasm in camp. One topic alone was discussed—the Grand Review
of Sherman's army scheduled for Wednesday, May 24.

Even General Harrison, who did not hide his distaste "for such
crowds and parades," predicted that the Grand Review "will
probably be the grandest military parade this country will ever
see." Personally, he wrote Carrie, "I would not prolong my separation from you and the children one hour to see it." For the men
who had fought and won the war, "all these shows and red-tape
delays in getting us home," were not pleasing.[18]

No forecast of the grandeur of the review even approached the
actual brilliance of the military spectacle that thrilled the nation's capital for two days. On Tuesday the 23rd, the East had
its day, as the Army of the Potomac marched by the immense
throngs on Pennsylvania Avenue. President Johnson and his
cabinet occupied the center of the wooden stands before the
White House. Close by were governors, senators, and celebrities
from every part of the Union. Blaring bands heralded the appearance of General Meade, the hero of Gettysburg. Then came
General George Custer at the head of his honored brigade of
regular cavalry. The crowds cheered wildly as each unit of Eastern troops hove in sight. In the wooden stands sat General Sherman, carefully planning for the morrow. That would be his day
and the day of the West.

17 Harrison to his wife, May 20, 1865, Harrison MSS, Vol. 6.
18 Harrison to his wife, May 21, 1865, Harrison MSS, Vol. 6.

Before more than one half of the Army of the Potomac had passed, Sherman made one important mental note. Too many of the Eastern troops turned their "eyes around like country gawks to look at the big people of the stand." They did not march well, because of the faulty music from two civilian orchestras—"pampered and well-fed bands that are taught to play the very latest operas." Come what might, his army must outmarch the Easterners. Tomorrow, "his officers and men would keep eyes fifteen feet to the front and march by in the old customary way." At this moment, General Meade came to the reviewing stand, and Sherman humbly remarked: "I'm afraid my poor tatterdemalion corps will make a poor appearance tomorrow when contrasted with yours." Meade agreed that this might be the case, but he sought to ease Sherman's sorrow by assuring him that the people would make allowances.[19]

Indeed, the people were prepared to go far beyond Meade. Wednesday May 24th was bright and mild, and the capital was still bedecked with flags. Larger and more interested crowds waited impatiently for the review of Sherman's army. For many of the spectators both Sherman and his army were enshrouded in mystery. Thousands had been intrigued by the exploits attributed to the Army of the Tennessee, now for the first time setting foot in Washington. The reporter for the Washington *Chronicle* explained the mystery and the interest that gripped the crowd when the Army of the Tennessee was mentioned. For months they had heard about this valiant host,

down amid the miasmatic marshes of the Mississippi; in the slime of the Yazoo and the Tennessee; fighting battles above rolling clouds; disappearing beyond the ken of the telegraph; now supposed to be victorious, and again a cause of apprehension and doubt; marching unrecorded hundreds and hundreds of miles . . . so that the distance lends enchantment to the view . . . seldom authentically heard from save in connection with the news that some rebel stronghold had surrendered to its General's strategy and to its own indomitable energy. . . . The marches it has made; the victories it has won, the difficulties it has surmounted, have perhaps never been equalled by any army since the days of Xenophon's Anabasis.[20]

[19] These details are from Lewis, *op. cit.*, pp. 572–73.
[20] As reprinted in the Indianapolis *Daily Journal*, May 29, 1865.

People wanted to see this section of Sherman's army in the flesh, and General Harrison told his command the reason: "The highest honors are due to the men who bore the cartridge and the gun. What were your officers without you? Much pride as we may take in Sherman, it was Sherman's Army, and not Sherman, that accomplished the great work."[21] Fired to enthusiasm, Harrison's brigade broke camp early on the 24th.

At exactly 9:00 A.M. a cannon boomed. "Sherman shook a spur; his horse stepped forward, drumsticks made the air flutter like flying canister or wild-geese wings. Bands blared into 'The Star-Spangled Banner.' Around the corner of the Capitol the Westerners came."[22] Deafening cheers met each succeeding wave of marchers. It was a day for heroes. Proud Sherman admitted that the show his army staged thrilled him to his fingertips. Even he had at last disobeyed his own orders by stealing a backward glance at his own troops to see those "legions coming in line, every man locked in steady formation—formal for perhaps the first and last time in their lives."[23] If he boasted that this was the happiest and most satisfactory moment in his life, then he mirrored perfectly Harrison's thoughts: "We took the shine off the Army of the Potomac and in marching *altogether* excelled them . . . the Review was a grand thing for Sherman's Army."[24]

From the conclusion of the review until the end of his life, thirty-six years later, General Harrison never once tired of telling of the glories of Sherman's army and of the joys of May 24, 1865. With his own courageous Seventieth Indiana Regiment in mind, Harrison would discourse for hours on the achievements of the army under Sherman. They were rooted, he maintained, in that undeniable versatility of Yankee character which adapts itself to the circumstances in which it finds itself: the tremendous marches and protracted fighting of the Georgia Campaign, or, as he saw on May 24, the transition from relaxed discipline and "bumming" to order and discipline.[25] Even Harrison's final brigade report breathed an undeniable pride:

21 Indianapolis *Daily Journal*, June 17, 1865.

22 Lewis, *op. cit.*, p. 573.

23 *Ibid.*, pp. 574–75.

24 Harrison to his wife, May 25, 1865, Harrison MSS, Vol. 6.

25 Indianapolis *Daily Journal*, June 17, 1865. A reporter took down a portion of Harrison's impromptu homecoming address.

The review was creditable to the troops and gave to those who had never seen Sherman's army a new and unexpected view. They had looked for an army of "Bummers," wild, undisciplined and unskilled in the precision of military movements. They saw, instead, an army that could be "Bummers" par excellence when necessity required, and when that necessity was removed, could at once exhibit a subordination and precision in drill and movement excelled by no other army.[26]

Many things in the military array excited the crowd's warm admiration. One newspaperman wrote:

All were delighted, all were pleased at the spectacle which this army afforded. We all knew it to be warlike, but all were surprised to find it so military . . . ocular proof that armies of men, warlike in spirit, may be taken from the plow and the desk to the march and the field of battle, and be returned to their country perfect soldiers, even in the military details of a soldier's duty. Sherman may say of his army what, in 1815, Wellington said of his: "With that army I could go anywhere and do anything."[27]

The very way in which Sherman managed his dark bay mount with his left hand, while waving appreciatively with his right, set the tone. Behind Sherman's staff and escort rode General Logan, Commander of the Army of the Tennessee, whose celebrated 15th and 17th Corps drew the most sustained applause. Next came the Army of Georgia, headed by General Slocum. Hooker's old 20th Army Corps, now led by General Mower, and General Jeff Davis' 14th Corps brought up the rear.

Perhaps the greatest interest, however, was manifested in the so-called "Bummer Brigade," foragers—actual "bummers"—an essential part of the 20th Corps during the Georgia and Carolina campaigns. It marched slowly behind General Geary's infantry, led "by a sable warrior on a diminutive donkey." In their ranks were mules on whose backs were perched goats, occasional roosters, and even a poodle. One observer reported "this brigade observed no military rules as we perceived, but it kept a wonderfully sharp lookout. In culinary matters it seemed supreme. Pots, pans, kettles, saucepans, spoons in abundance."[28]

[26] Merrill, *op. cit.*, pp. 279–80.
[27] Indianapolis *Daily Journal*, May 29, 1865.
[28] *Ibid.*

General Harrison, who rode directly behind General Ward and his staff, and kept one eye on the "Bummers" and the other on the crowd, later remarked:

The Eastern people who assembled at Washington to witness the review of Sherman's Army, expected to see a disorganized rabble marching through the streets, without being able to distinguish one company from another. . . . But they beheld a vast column marching along with a precision step and uniform soldierly bearing of which the Army of the Potomac could never boast.[29]

The note of personal triumph and satisfaction was not missing in Harrison's letters home. He wrote to Carrie:

There were a great many western people in Washington, and they cheered the Western army most enthusiastically. I was called by name and church about twenty times on the march by friends of whom I could only recognize a few. Some young officer, whom I did not know, ran out to speak to me and said he had seen my family only a few days ago. Who was it? It was a grand review, but I am glad that it is over and that we can now give our attention to the work of mustering out.[30]

The most trying period in Harrison's army career occurred during the last week of May and the first two weeks of June, 1865. The thrill and satisfaction of the Grand Review quickly wore off, and within four days Carrie knew she had reasons for anxiety. He wrote: "I feel so nervous and expectant when I have a prospect of getting home after a long absence, that I cannot sit down to any ordinary work of routine with patience or interest. There is only one thing that interests me now, and that is the progress being made in our muster out papers."[31] Try as he might, Harrison was unable to hasten the process. Captains and clerks worked day and night to finish their rolls, but the form and routine seemed endless. The red tape distressed Harrison and left him in ill humor. His real difficulty stemmed from a fundamental lack of adaptability to any set of circumstances that spelled inactivity. Carrie had no difficulty in imagining her husband's restlessness:

29 Indianapolis *Daily Journal,* June 17, 1865, a section from the first speech General Harrison delivered before his neighbors and friends in Indianapolis.
30 Harrison to his wife, May 25, 1865, Harrison MSS, Vol. 6.
31 Harrison to his wife, May 29, 1865, Harrison MSS, Vol. 6.

I have been reading a little by snatches, and becoming discontented with that method of keeping down my consciousness of discomfort and heat, have taken to pencil and paper under the shade of our withered arbor in the hope that a little conversation with you and indulgence in home thoughts, may put me in a pleasanter humor with myself and my surroundings.[32]

His quiet sense of humor, however, did not entirely abandon him. With Presbyterian insight he managed to quip that "though the 'neither hot nor cold' state may not be commendable in matters of faith, yet in the natural world it seems to be highly desirable."

Many of Harrison's fellow officers found abundant diversion in the social life at Washington City, but not the general. Enough dinner invitations came his way, but with the exception of two evenings with his old friend, John Defrees, Harrison declined all the others. "Washington," he confided to Carrie, who knew the tune by heart, "is like every other city I have ever visited, a very dull and uninteresting place to me, except so long as I have business to engage my time. You know I am a very poor pleasure and curiosity seeker. I was near Charleston for a month, and though I could have gone any day, I never visited it." Mrs. Harrison was not surprised, for she alone could understand how her husband, with plenty of time on his hands, could "ride past the Capitol a dozen times" and never enter the structure. Also she probably excused him when he added: "I shall probably go home without seeing more than its exterior."[33]

While Harrison was camped outside of Washington, the trial of the Lincoln conspirators was being held within the city. Even this event, with all its legal and patriotic implications, could not shake the general from his lack of interest in all things that did not directly bear upon his speedy return to Indianapolis. General Lew Wallace actually extended him a special invitation to attend the trial, but to no avail. Concerning his unsociability, Harrison made only one observation to Carrie:

If you were here I should try to overcome this habit, as I feel I have not been generous to you in allowing my selfish habits to keep you so much away from places of amusement and curiosity, but as I am

[32] Harrison to his wife, June 4, 1865, Harrison MSS, Vol. 6.
[33] *Ibid.*

alone I may allow my habits sway for a little time, before I begin the *great reform* which I am to inaugurate when I get home. You will see by my frequent allusions to this matter that I have been giving a good deal of thought to the construction of a spiritual model of a proper husband and family man.[34]

Not too consistently, however, Harrison yielded to the pressure of social amenities on three occasions. Of the two dinner parties held by John Defrees in his honor, one was a quasi-state dinner, to which all Indiana men in Washington were invited. Only the circumstance that he was the honored guest rendered Harrison's presence a certainty, and even then he did not "much fancy" the idea. Defrees learned his lesson, and the second time he succeeded in wooing the general from camp, he restricted the dinner to the family circle. Harrison's laconic remark to Carrie was, "a very pleasant dinner, but not particularly noticeable."[35]

Chaplain Allen of the Seventieth Indiana was only moderately successful in his efforts with Brigadier General Harrison. He failed to prevail upon the general to address a memorial meeting of chaplains. Even the thought of speaking on the same platform with General Howard was not a powerful enough incentive. "I don't feel like speechmaking; indeed, I never do, and though the meeting will be one in which I should be glad to appear, I shall not go."[36] On another occasion, Allen employed his good offices with singular success. He had met a Mr. Wright of Bladensburg, a Washington suburb, and when the elderly man revealed that he was "an old and warm friend" of President William Henry Harrison, Allen urged Ben to pay Wright a courtesy call. After he had raised the usual number of objections, Harrison yielded to the importunings of the gentleman of the cloth and agreed to visit his grandfather's friend. It turned out to be Harrison's most successful social venture, and certainly Carrie must have clapped as she scanned her husband's account of the meeting:

Well, I went out to take a little ride last evening, and in returning through the town I stopped to see him [Mr. Wright]. He was very

34 *Ibid.*

35 *Ibid.*

36 When one considers Harrison's personal friendship for both Chaplain Allen and General Howard, it argues to an increasing dislike for public speaking. Harrison to his wife, May 29, 1865, Harrison MSS, Vol. 6.

cordial and took me to his house where he introduced me to his daughters and insisted on me taking supper, though he had already had one. He lives in a frame house built in 1732, that was formerly used for a tavern. It was very plain and old fashioned but quite tidy and neat and his daughters appeared to be very intelligent and agreeable girls. The most *enthusiastic* Union people I have ever met. The old gentleman gave me a log cabin cane of very quaint and original construction, and though not of any great intrinsic value, quite an interesting and valuable relic. I shall not try to describe it for you, but will let you see when I get home. I have promised to call again and will take my band down to serenade them. He had four sons in the Union Army and seems to take the highest pleasure in sharing everything with a soldier.[37]

Discharge day finally dawned for Harrison and the Seventieth Indiana on June 8. W. A. Benotti, Washington military agent for Indiana, had succeeded at last in clearing all papers and affidavits. General Harrison was anxious to possess but one important document: "To all whom it may concern: Know ye, that Benjamin Harrison, a Colonel and Brev. Brig. Genl., 70th Regiment of Indiana Infantry Volunteers, who was enrolled on the 7th day of August, one thousand eight hundred and sixty-two, to serve three years or during the war, is hereby discharged from the service of the United States this eighth day of June, 1865, at Washington, D. C."[38] When he pocketed this paper, his military career was ended. Benjamin Harrison, "[thirty-two] years of age, five feet seven and one half inches high, fair complexion, blue eyes and light hair,"[39] was, in virtue of this piece of paper, once again a civilian. As he walked back to headquarters to pick up his haversack and a few personal belongings, including presents for the children, he recalled the words of Sherman's farewell address: "As in war you have been good soldiers, so in peace you will make good citizens."[40] And just two days earlier, the expectant citizens of Indianapolis read the message: "Prepare to grasp the hard hands of the Hoosiers who heard the call for the '600,000 more,' in 1862."[41]

37 *Ibid.*

38 A copy of this document is in the Harrison MSS, Vol. 6, No. 1140.

39 *Ibid.*

40 A reprint of Sherman's address appeared in the Indianapolis *Daily Journal,* June 1, 1865.

41 *Ibid.,* June 6, 1865.

Early on the morning of June 9, Baltimore and Ohio freight
cars welcomed General Harrison and his homeward-bound regiment. The train lurched and rattled through the hills of Maryland and West Virginia, but, for the first time since 1862, the
cars seemed only to purr. At dusk on the evening of June 10 they
gladly boarded a steamboat headed for Lawrenceburg, Indiana,
a spot Harrison remembered well from his younger days.

A throng of citizens from Lawrenceburg and nearby towns
were waiting to greet their native sons. Evidently, John Scott
Harrison was too ill to join the welcoming committee. His disappointment at not seeing Benjamin immediately was deep, but
he readily admitted that Carrie and the two children enjoyed
special priorities on his affection. John Scott Harrison understood perfectly why his son boarded the first train for Indianapolis, but he was grieved that his own well-made plans for a
celebration did not materialize. He had hoped to honor his son,
but instead had to communicate his surprise by letter:

Your Grandma[42] when she gave me the medal voted your grandfather by Congress for his military services, said that after my death,
it was to go to you—bearing the old family name of Benjamin. I do
not feel disposed to clutch this relic until death releases my grasp,
and had intended to call together a limited number of your Ohio
and Indiana friends . . . and present the family relic to your charge,
for I really thought that you had by your efficient service in the late
war fairly won the *immediate* possession of the medal.[43]

When the members of the Seventieth Indiana rolled into the
Indianapolis depot, they soon knew that their friends and relatives had not been inactive. Every detail for a huge demonstration had been arranged far in advance of their arrival. Every
citizen in the Indiana capital was determined that "the men who
fought the great battle of the Republic to a successful and glorious issue,"[44] would be honored in a fitting way. As the members
of Company A alighted, a lusty cheer shook the station.

42 Mrs. William Henry Harrison had died while Benjamin was with the army in
Tennessee.
43 John Scott Harrison to his son, July 5, 1865, Harrison MSS, Vol. 6.
44 As early as June 9, Quartermaster-general Stone had alerted the people of Indianapolis and made known detailed plans to welcome the returning heroes.
Indianapolis *Daily Journal*, June 9, 1865.

Harrison found the reward for which he so ardently yearned—the embrace of his family. This first exchange of affections had to be curtailed, for an honorary escort was forming to conduct the veterans to the arsenal, "where we turned over our guns to the United States officials, and then went to the Soldiers' Home for dinner."[45]

In the week of receptions that followed, General and Mrs. Harrison had their hour of triumph. Not only was the general mentioned by name at the various victory rallies, but the *Daily Journal* editorialized his return, giving a résumé of his military accomplishments and noting that "he was so well appreciated by his superior officers that he was appointed Brevet Brigadier General. His success as a military man was confidently expected by those who knew his talents and industry in civil life, and their expectations were completely realized."[46]

Climaxing the festivities was a joint demonstration held in honor of four returning Indiana regiments, the 22nd, 70th, 74th, and 82nd, on Friday, June 16. Governor Morton, the principal speaker, was in rare form. The flowery exaggerations of his speech made his audience smile and somewhat embarrassed the returning heroes. He declared that the "crossing of the Alps by Napoleon . . . dwindles into insignificance when compared with Sherman's march to the sea, or Grant's Vicksburg campaign." Even Harrison, student of history as he was, must have put his tongue in his cheek when the Governor rounded out one oratorical period with the claim that "the passage of the bridge of Lodi is another of the wonders of history. It was a mere skirmish compared with the storming of Fort Fisher, or the fortifications around Petersburg. This war will furnish the grandest chapter in the history of military achievements which the world has ever seen. The destiny of millions unborn has been shaped by it."[47]

[45] Merrill, *op. cit.*, p. 277.

[46] Indianapolis *Daily Journal*, June 14, 1865. Harrison shared the editorial spotlight with General Fred Knefler, who was also a leading Indianapolis attorney. After he had narrated their joint military accomplishments in some detail, the editor concluded by saying that "Indianapolis has a right to be proud of the officers and men she has sent to the field, and none are more worthy of the honor than Generals Knefler and Harrison."

[47] Indianapolis *Daily Journal*, June 17, 1865. The reporter who covered the meeting aptly remarked that "Gov. Morton manifests a remarkable fertility of resources in matter of speechmaking, not having as yet, occasion to repeat any of his speeches, nor any parts of them, in fact."

Sun-browned veterans who "had put a girdle round about the earth" loudly cheered the Governor. Not since the celebrated charge at Resaca had so much lung power been expended. When Morton sat down, Harrison, whom he had singled out for special praise, was called on to speak. Carrie was in the audience and she thrilled to see her husband arise and command such attention. General Harrison aptly remarked that "the soldiers had been too long engaged in speaking with the muzzles of their rifles to listen to speeches. Yet he couldn't refuse to say a word or two to them."

He began by playing down Morton's allusion to enlisting when he did. After all, he said, "thousands here deserved more praise" than he did. He explained that he "did not turn out at the first outbreak of the rebellion, when, in over-confidence, we thought 75,000 men adequate to the suppression of the rebellion." His decision came, he explained, when "the gigantic proportions and the malignant purpose [of the Confederacy] became fully developed. It was not ambition, nor gain, but patriotism," that led him and his comrades forth.

He preferred, he went on, to dwell on the scene familiar to all his hearers—that of three years before, when, in less than thirty days, 1,020 men from Marion County were in Kentucky in quick response to Lincoln's call:

I well remember three years ago, under the shade of these trees, when I made my first appeal to the men of Marion County. Now we are here again, sheltered by these same trees, but oh! how much brighter the skies. . . . God has been bountiful to us in prolonging our lives to see this day. Many who went out with us are not here. We buried them in Southern soil, but thank God the secession flag does not wave over them. They sleep in the soil of the great Republic.

Profound silence greeted General Harrison's next remarks:

Do you remember the enclosure, my Comrades, at the foot of the hill at Resaca, up which we made that fearful charge? How we gathered their torn blankets around them, and tenderly composed their limbs for the last sleep, casting branches of evergreen in their graves! They lie there still, and along by the wayside lie others. They were not permitted to return with us, but they left behind them honorable records. I almost feel that I would rather lie within that little mound at the foot of the hill, than to have had no participation in this struggle. These brave men lived to accomplish more for the good of their country than most men who go down silvered to the grave.

After his stirring tribute to the dead, the general spoke boldly of the apprehensions (entertained in the city) of violence on the part of returned soldiers. First he turned to his own men and said: "People here have been quaking with terror, in apprehension of your return, in anticipation of riot and bloodshed." Then he faced his audience and with a challenge in his voice, proclaimed:

But I tell you these men are just as good as you are, my timid friends. They own property here, and have just as much interest in preserving the peace as you. They will go into business here, and if you outstrip the men who followed Sherman to the sea, you will have to brighten your wits and quicken your pace, and they mean to be felt in politics as well as business. Not that they mean to monopolize the offices. But if anyone who is a candidate for office shall be shown to have been lukewarm in the good cause, the boys will brand him with the word written on the shoulders of played-out horses—"condemned."[48]

Resounding cheers answered his words. When cannons began to thunder their salute, the crowd quieted down and rapidly dispersed.

Before General Harrison could join Carrie and the children for a leisurely stroll to their home, Mayor Caven rushed up to congratulate him and to inform him that the Citizens' Committee in charge of the Fourth of July celebration, had selected him as the special orator for the occasion.

At last, the general and his family were alone. They were Ben and Carrie again, and one did not have to be a mind reader to sense the deep enjoyment and peace they experienced in one another's presence. They had waited three years for this hour; yet, unlike many others, they did not plan for the future. This had already been settled almost a month ago, and the general himself had set the pattern. Carrie had the blueprint in her pocketbook. It was a letter Ben had written from Washington, and for days now she had it memorized:

[48] *Ibid.*

... you do not seem willing of late to give me credit for the affection I do really feel for you and our home,[49] but if you could read my heart you would be satisfied that I do not speak half that I feel, and that no object of ambition or gain could ever lead me away from the side of my dear wife and children. I have no doubt from intimations I have received that I could go to Congress for our District at the next election, but positively I would not accept the office, for the reason that it would take me away from home so much. If my ambition is to soar any more after I come home, you will have to give it wings, for I certainly long only for a life of quiet usefulness at home. You do not know how much I have thought since I left you last as to how I might make my home brighter and happier for you and the children. It has been in my mind on the march, on my cot, and even in my dreams. I know I have the best intentions and the strongest resolutions to devote myself more to your happiness than I have ever done since our marriage, and if I should fail, if you will meet my failure with a kind reminder of what I have promised, I have a good hope that every asperity may be banished from our family intercourse and that we may always express in our lives the devoted affection which I know we have for each other and must have till death parts us. I know you love me Carrie, with more devotion than most women are capable of, and I, so far as my heart or person are worth your acceptance, have given them all to you. Why then should we allow a word or thought or act to express any other feeling. I wish you could give me some little article of apparel or ornament that might always be before my eyes to remind me of the resolutions and vows I have made but I think I have a better idea still, I will bring you a little keepsake when I come home from the war which you shall *always* wear, never putting it off til death shall separate us. And when I deliver it to you we will weave a spell about it that I shall make it to me a constant reminder of the resolutions and vows I have made in the army. Will you wear it and promise me always to hold it up before me when you see a cloud on my brow or hear hasty words from my lips? I have a good hope that by mutual help and by God's help, we may live the residue of our lives without having our hearts' sunshine clouded by a single shade of mistrust or anger. I know it is possible and I would rather succeed in such an effort than to have the highest honors of earth. . . .[50]

There was no need for an exchange of promises, as they walked home hand in hand. The light in Carrie's eyes was a proof of her

[49] To this lengthy letter Harrison appended an important P.S. "Dear Carrie: I have just received and read your letter of the 14th inst., and though this letter was sealed and stamped, I tore it open to thank you for the affectionate tone of your letter. I cannot tell you how *real good* it did my heart. God bless you for it. With a heart brimful of love, Yours, Ben."

[50] Harrison to his wife, May 21, 1865, Harrison MSS, Vol. 6.

renewed love and willingness to help her husband. She was determined that not only should he succeed in his efforts at home, but also, with her help, that he should have the highest honors of earth. Twenty-three years later, President and Mrs. Harrison were sure they had not failed.

Bibliography

BIBLIOGRAPHY

Manuscript Sources

The primary sources for the early life and Civil War career of President Benjamin Harrison include:

1. The extensive Benjamin Harrison collection housed in the Division of Manuscripts, Library of Congress. Closed to the public and research historians alike until 1948, this is the richest font of information. Described by the Division of Manuscripts card as: "Papers of Benjamin Harrison (1833–1901), lawyer, soldier, U. S. Senator, 23rd. President of the U. S. Family letters and other papers covering the civil war period, a large body of papers representing the period of his service as a U. S. Senator, legal and official papers covering his post-presidential career in law, letter-books, scrap-books, etc., dated 1858–1931."

A serviceable breakdown of these materials is as follows:

> 183 volumes (bound) of approximately 40,000 pieces which, in the judgment of the curator of the Manuscripts Division deal primarily with Harrison's public life and activities.

> 55 manuscript boxes (red) judged by library authorities as not pertaining to the public and/or political aspects of Harrison's life. They contain, however, much material essential to the biographer.

> 58 volumes (bound) of newspaper clippings, now known as the Benjamin Harrison Scrapbook Series. Invaluable material on every phase of Harrison's private as well as his public life.

> 18 manuscript boxes of Tibbott transcripts. Everard F. Tibbott, an Associated Press reporter, joined Harrison's staff in 1888. After Harrison left the White House, Tibbott became his efficient and faithful private secretary.

> 8 manuscript boxes: "The Tibbott short hand books." Long after Harrison's death, Tibbott transcribed these thousands of letters from his own stenographic notebooks. These are the contents of the above-mentioned eighteen manuscript boxes of Tibbott transcripts.

> 7 manuscript boxes of "Legal material from 1851–1900."

> 3 manuscript boxes of Harrison and Wallace Law Firm correspondence.

> 80 manuscript boxes of miscellaneous materials: personal bills, checks, notes, lectures, photographs, galley proofs, invitations, guest lists, pamphlets, telegrams, memorials, etc.

2. The next largest collection of Benjamin Harrison Papers is housed in the Indiana Division of the Indiana State Library (Indianapolis).

Sundry items are scattered in the approximately fifty collections catalogued and indexed, covering the years 1855 to 1901.

3. A small number of private and family papers, rich in biographical details, are on file at the President Benjamin Harrison Memorial Home, 1230 North Delaware Street, Indianapolis, Indiana.

4. The papers of William Henry Harrison Miller, Attorney General during Harrison's administration (1889–93) and Harrison's law partner for a quarter of a century, are now in the possession of the author. Invaluable for recollections.

5. Other manuscript sources in the Library of Congress especially pertinent to ancestral background, early life, and military career are:

    a. John Scott Harrison Papers.
    b. William Henry Harrison Papers.
    c. Joseph R. Hawley Papers.
    d. Louis T. Michener Papers.
    e. John Sherman Papers.
    f. The Short Family Papers.

Civil War manuscript material is abundant in the Indiana Division, Indiana State Library. Particularly useful are:

    a. John Coburn MSS.
    b. Schuyler Colfax MSS.
    c. Calvin Fletcher Papers and Diary, 1861–1862—Indiana Historical Society Library.
    d. Vallette Miller MSS.
    e. Oliver P. Morton MSS.
    f. Daniel D. Pratt MSS.
    g. Benjamin Spooner MSS. (photostats)
    h. Richard W. Thompson MSS.

By far the most serviceable letters for this study were the papers of Samuel K. Harryman, 1862–65; and war letters, camp life, campaigns, and experiences of the Seventieth Regiment, Indiana Volunteers, account of Sherman's March to the Sea.

6. Certain manuscript collections, though not cited in the footnotes to this volume, contain material pertinent to Harrison's character and place in history. They have been examined by the author with a view to forming an over-all mature value judgment of Benjamin Harrison. In the Division of Manuscripts, Library of Congress, the most helpful were the papers of:

Wharton Barker, Thomas F. Bayard, Jeremiah S. Black, James G. Blaine, the Blair Family, the Breckenridge Family, Benjamin H. Bristow, W. P. Bynum, Simon Cameron, Andrew Carnegie, William E. Chandler, James S. Clarkson, Grover Cleveland, Chauncey M. Depew, Don M. Dickinson, William Evarts, John W. Foster, William D. Foulke, James A. Garfield, Walter Q. Gresham, Eugene Hale, Eugene Gano Hay, John Hay, Horatio King, Daniel S. Lamont, William McKinley, Daniel Manning, Manton Marble, John T. Morgan, Justin S. Morrill, Richard Olney, Mathew S. Quay, Theodore Roosevelt, Carl Schurz, William T. Sherman, John C. Spooner, Benjamin F. Tracy, Henry Watterson, William C. Whitney, John Russell Young.

7. Other archival collections which yielded material were:

The papers of William Boyd Allison, Grenville M. Dodge, James S. Clarkson, and John A. Kasson—all in the Historical Memorial and Art Department of Iowa, Des Moines, Iowa.

The papers and the diary of John Bigelow and the papers of Levi P. Morton in the Manuscripts Division of the New York Public Library.

The papers of Nils P. Haugen, Henry Demarest Lloyd, Jeremiah Rusk, Ellis Usher, William F. Vilas in the State Historical Society of Wisconsin, Madison, Wisconsin.

The papers of Terence B. Powderly in the Mullen Library of the Catholic University of America.

The papers of Whitelaw Reid (privately owned).

The papers of James Cardinal Gibbons (in the archives of the Archdiocese of Baltimore, Baltimore, Maryland).

Pertinent newspaper material is found in the following: *American Eagle* (Paoli, Indiana), Boston *Daily Advertiser,* Chicago *Weekly Inter-Ocean,* Cincinnati *Commercial,* Cincinnati *Enquirer,* Cincinnati *Gazette,* Columbia (S. C.) *Record,* Detroit *Tribune,* Fort Wayne *Sentinel,* Indianapolis *Atlas,* Indianapolis *Daily Journal,* Indianapolis *Locomotive,* Indianapolis *News,* Indianapolis *Old Line Guard,* Indianapolis *Sentinel,* New Orleans *Times-Democrat,* New York *Daily Tribune,* New York *Evening Post,* New York *Mail and Express,* New York *Times,* Omaha *Bee,* Richmond (Va.) *State,* St. Louis *Post-Dispatch,* Washington *Chronicle,* Washington *Post,* the *Herald and Enterprise* (Russellville, Ky.), *Parke County* (Indiana) *Republican.*

In addition to a plenitude of identified newspaper clippings which form the bulk of the fifty-eight-volume Scrapbook Series in the Harrison Papers (Library of Congress), attention is called to a valuable three-volume Scrapbook Series in the Indiana State Library, the gift of Russell B. Harrison, the President's son. Its chief merit lies in the universal newspaper coverage given to the death and funeral of Benjamin Harrison in 1901. Russell Harrison had subscribed to several clipping services and carefully preserved the unfavorable as well as the favorable news and editorial comment.

Published Sources

Adams, Charles Francis. *Charles Francis Adams, 1835–1915: An Autobiography*. Boston and New York, Houghton, 1916.

Adams, Henry. *The Education of Henry Adams*. New York, Modern Library, 1931.

Alexander, De Alva S. *Four Famous New Yorkers*. New York, Holt, 1923.

Alumni and Former Student Catalogue of Miami University, 1809–1892, Oxford, Ohio, 1892.

Auchampaugh, Philip G. "The Buchanan-Douglas Feud," *Journal of the Illinois State Historical Society*, 25 (1932), 5–48.

Bailey, Louis J. "Caleb Blood Smith," *Indiana Magazine of History*, 29 (1933), 213–39.

Beale, Howard K. (ed.). *The Diary of Edward Bates 1859–1866*. (American Historical Association Annual Report, 1930, Vol. IV.) Washington, D. C., Government Printing Office, 1933.

———. "What Historians Have Said about the Causes of the Civil War," in Bulletin 54, *Theory and Practice in Historical Study: A Report of the Committee on Historiography*. New York, Soc. Sci. Res. Council, 1946, 53–102.

Benjamin Harrison Memorial Commission, Report of. (77th Congress, 1st Session, House Document No. 154.) Washington, D. C., Government Printing Office, 1941.

Beveridge, A. J. *Abraham Lincoln*. Boston and New York, Houghton, 1928. 2 vols.

Bond, Beverley W., Jr. *The Foundations of Ohio*. The History of the State of Ohio in Six Volumes. Edited by Carl Wittke. Vol. I, Columbus, Ohio State Archaeological and Historical Society, 1941.

Bowman, S. M., and R. B. Irwin. *Sherman and His Campaigns: A Military Biography*. New York, C. B. Richardson, 1865.

Boyd, James P. *Life and Public Services of Benjamin Harrison, Twenty-third President of the United States*. Philadelphia, Publishers Union, 1901.

Brown, Ignatius. *History of Indianapolis from 1818 to the Present.* (Published as part of *Indianapolis Directory, 1868*.)

Carter, Alfred G. W. *The Old Court House.* Cincinnati, P. G. Thompson, 1880.

Casey, Silas. *Infantry Tactics.* New York, D. Van Nostrand, 1862.

Chase, Salmon P. *Diary and Correspondence of Salmon P. Chase.* (American Historical Association Annual Report, 1902, Vol. II.) Washington, D. C., Government Printing Office, 1903.

Cist, Charles. *Sketches and Statistics of Cincinnati in 1851.* Cincinnati, W. H. Moore, 1851.

Cist, Henry Martyn. *The Army of the Cumberland.* New York, Scribner, 1882.

Cleaves, Freeman. *Old Tippecanoe.* New York, Scribner, 1939.

————. *Rock of Chickamauga: The Life of General George H. Thomas.* Norman, Okla., Univ. of Oklahoma Press, 1948.

Cortissoz, Royal. *The Life of Whitelaw Reid.* New York, Scribner, 1921. 2 vols.

Cottman, George S. "Lincoln in Indianapolis," *Indiana Magazine of History,* 24 (1928), 1–14.

Cox, Jacob D. *Atlanta.* New York, Scribner, 1882.

Crandall, Andrew W. *The Early History of the Republican Party, 1854–1856.* Boston, R. G. Badger, 1930.

Crook, W. H. *Memories of the White House.* Boston, Little, 1911.

Davis, Virgil E. "The Literary Societies in 'Old Miami' from 1825 to 1873." Unpublished Master's thesis, Miami Univ., Oxford, Ohio, 1950.

Donald, David. *Lincoln's Herndon.* New York, Knopf, 1948.

Dumond, Dwight L. *The Secessionist Movement.* New York, Macmillan, 1931.

———— (ed.). *Southern Editorials on Secession.* New York, Century, 1931.

Dunn, Jacob Piatt. *Greater Indianapolis.* Chicago, Lewis, 1910. 2 vols.

————. *Indiana and Indianans.* Chicago and New York, American Historical Society, 1919. 5 vols.

Dyer, John P. *The Gallant Hood.* Indianapolis, Bobbs, 1950.

Eckenrode, H. J., and Bryan Conrad. *George B. McClellan: The Man Who Saved the Union.* Chapel Hill, N. C., Univ. of N. C. Press, 1941.

Eisenschiml, Otto, and Ralph Newman. *The American Iliad.* Indianapolis, Bobbs, 1947.

Esarey, Logan. *A History of Indiana.* Indianapolis, B. F. Bowen, 1918. 2 vols.

Fite, Emerson D. *The Presidential Campaign of 1860.* New York, Macmillan, 1911.

Flint, Timothy. *Recollections of the Past Ten Years.* Boston, Cummings, Hilliard & Co., 1826.

Foster, Harriet McIntire. *Mrs. Benjamin Harrison.* Indianapolis (published privately), 1908.

Foulke, William D. *Life of Oliver P. Morton.* Indianapolis, Bowen-Merrill, 1899. 2 vols.

Freeman, Douglas Southall. *Lee's Lieutenants.* New York, Scribner, 1942–44. 3 vols.

Goebel, Dorothy Burne. *William Henry Harrison.* Indianapolis, Historical Bureau of Indiana Library and Historical Department, 1926. (Historical Collections, Vol. XIV, Biographical Series, Vol. II.)

Gray, Wood. *The Hidden Civil War.* New York, Viking, 1942.

Green, James A. *William Henry Harrison: His Times.* Cincinnati, Garrett, 1941.

Griffiths, John L. *An Address by.* (October 27, 1908, Indianapolis, Ind., on the occasion of the unveiling of the statue of Benjamin Harrison), pp. 21–31 in *The Addresses* by Charles W. Fairbanks, John W. Noble, John L. Griffiths; and in *The Poems* by James Whitcomb Riley. Indianapolis, Hollenbeck Press, 1909.

Hardee, W. J. *Rifle and Light Infantry Tactics.* Philadelphia, Lippincott, Gambo, 1855. 2 vols.

Harney, Gilbert L. *The Lives of Benjamin Harrison and Levi P. Morton.* Providence, R. I., J. A. and R. A. Reid, 1888.

Harrison, Benjamin. *Views of an Ex-President.* Compiled by Mary Lord Harrison. Indianapolis, Bowen-Merrill, 1901.

Harrison, John Scott. *Pioneer Life at North Bend.* Cincinnati, Robert Clarke, 1867.

Harrison, Short Review of Public and Private Life of Gen'l. Benj. (A campaign pamphlet.) Indianapolis (copyrighted by C. A. Nicoli), 1888.

Hebert, Walter H. *Fighting Joe Hooker.* Indianapolis, Bobbs, 1944.

Hedges, Charles (comp.). *Speeches of Benjamin Harrison.* New York, Lovell, Coryell & Co., 1892.

Henry, R. B. *Genealogies of the Families of the Presidents.* Rutland, Vt., Tuttle, 1935.

Hiatt, Joel W. (ed.). "Diary of William Owen." Indianapolis, 1906. (Indiana Historical Society Publications, Vol. IV, No. 1, 7–134.)

Hoar, George F. *Autobiography of Seventy Years.* New York, Scribner, 1903. 2 vols.

Holcombe, John W., and Hubert M. Skinner. *Life and Public Services of Thomas A. Hendricks.* Indianapolis, Carlon & Hollenbeck, 1886.

Holliday, J. H. *Indianapolis and the Civil War.* Indianapolis, Edward J. Hecker (printer and publisher), 1911. (Indiana Historical Society Publications, Vol. IV, No. 9, 525–95.)

Holloway, W. R. *Indianapolis*. Indianapolis, Journal Print, 1870.

Hood, John Bell. *Advance and Retreat: Personal Experiences in the United States and Confederate Armies*. New Orleans (privately printed by Hood Orphan Memorial Fund), 1880.

Huston, A. B. *Historical Sketch of Farmers' College*. Cincinnati, Cincinnati Students Association of Farmers' College, 1902.

Indianapolis Directory, 1855. (Groom's and Smith's *Indianapolis Directory, City Guide and Business Mirror; or, Indianapolis As It Is in 1855*.) Indianapolis, A. C. Grooms & W. T. Smith, 1855.

Indianapolis Directory, 1857. Indianapolis, A. C. Howard, 1857.

Indianapolis Directory, 1868. Indianapolis, Logan & Co., 1868.

Indianapolis, First Presbyterian Church, Centennial Memorial, 1823–1923. Greenfield, Ind., Wm. Mitchell Printing Co., 1925.

James, Alfred P. "General Joseph Eggleston Johnston, Storm Center of the Confederate Army," *Mississippi Valley Historical Review*, 14 (1927–28), 342–59.

Johnson, R. U., and C. C. Buel (eds.). *Battles and Leaders of the Civil War*. New York, Century Press, 1888. 4 vols.

Johnson, Rossiter. *Campfire and Battlefield*. New York, Bryan, Taylor & Co., 1894.

Jomini, Baron de. *The Political and Military History of the Campaign of Waterloo*. Translated by S. V. Benet, New York, Redfield, 1860.

———. *The Art of War*. Translated by C. H. Mendell. Philadelphia, Lippincott, 1862.

Julian, George W. *Political Recollections, 1840–1872*. Chicago, Jansen, McClurg, 1884.

Keith, Charles P. *The Ancestry of Benjamin Harrison*. Philadelphia, Lippincott, 1893.

Kenworthy, L. A. *The Tall Sycamore of the Wabash: Daniel Wolsey Voorhees*. Boston, Humphries, 1936.

Lewis, Lloyd. *Sherman: The Fighting Prophet*. New York, Harcourt, 1932.

Livermore, Thomas L. *Numbers and Losses in the Civil War in America, 1861–1865*. Boston, Houghton, 1901.

Lockridge, Ross F., Jr. "The Harrisons," published as Exhibit 2, pp. 19–210 in *Benjamin Harrison Memorial Commission, Report of (supra)*.

Luthin, Reinhard, H. "Indiana and Lincoln's Rise to the Presidency." *Indiana Magazine of History*, 38 (1942), 385–405.

———. *The First Lincoln Campaign*. Cambridge, Harvard Univ. Press, 1944.

McKee, Irving. *"Ben-Hur" Wallace*. Berkeley and Los Angeles, Univ. of Calif. Press, 1947.

Mahan, D. H. *An Elementary Course of Civil Engineering*. New York, John Wiley, 1853.

Marshall, Carrington T. *History of the Courts and Lawyers of Ohio*. New York, American Historical Society, Inc., 1934. 4 vols.

Marshall, Thomas R. *Recollections of Thomas R. Marshall: A Hoosier Salad*. Indianapolis, Bobbs, 1925.

Martin, D. V. "History of the Library Movement in Ohio." Unpublished Master's thesis, Ohio State Univ., 1935.

Martin, John Bartlow. *Indiana: An Interpretation*. New York, Knopf, 1947.

Merrill, Samuel. *The Seventieth Indiana Volunteer Infantry*. Indianapolis, Bowen-Merrill, 1900.

Milton, George Fort. *The Eve of Conflict*. Boston, Houghton, 1934.

Morison, J. E., and W. B. Lane. *Life of Our President Benjamin Harrison*. Cincinnati, published for Morison and Lane, 1889.

Nevins, Allan. *The Ordeal of the Union*. New York, Scribner, 1947. 2 vols.

"News from the Maryland Gazette," *Maryland Historical Magazine*, 17 (1922), 364–79.

Nichols, Roy F. *The Disruption of American Democracy*. New York, Macmillan, 1948.

Noble, John W. *An Address by*, pp. 7–18 in *The Addresses* by Charles W. Fairbanks, John W. Noble, John L. Griffiths *(supra,* see Griffiths). Indianapolis, Hollenbeck Press, 1909.

Nolan, Jeannette C. *Hoosier City: The Story of Indianapolis*. New York, Messner, 1943.

Northrop, H. D. *The Life and Public Services of Gen. Benj. Harrison*. Philadelphia, Globe Bible Publishing Co., 1888.

O'Connor, Richard. *Thomas: Rock of Chickamauga*. New York, Prentice-Hall, 1948.

Palmer, Walter B. *The History of Phi Delta Theta*. Menasha, Wisc., George Banta Publishing Co., 1906.

Pollard, James E. *The Presidents and the Press*. New York, Macmillan, 1947.

Porter, George H. *Ohio Politics during the Civil War*. New York, Columbia Univ., Longmans, Agents, 1911.

Povenmire, Kenneth W. "Temperance Movement in Ohio, 1840–1850." Unpublished Master's thesis, Ohio State Univ., 1932.

venson, David, and Theodore Scribner. *Indiana's Roll of Honor.* Indianapolis, 1864, 1866. 2 vols. (Vol. I published by Stevenson; Vol. II published for Scribner by A. D. Streight.)

lger, Felix F. *Treason History of the Order of the Sons of Liberty.* Chicago (published by author), 1903.

ddard, Henry L. *As I Knew Them: Presidents and Politics from Grant to Coolidge.* New York, Harper, 1927.

ne, Henry. "The Atlanta Campaign," *Papers of the Military Historical Society of Massachusetts,* 8 (1910), 341–492.

grove, B. R. *History of Indianapolis and Marion County.* Philadelphia, L. H. Everts & Co., 1884.

bad, Imre. *Modern War: Its Theory and Practice.* New York, Harper, 1863.

ylor, Charles W. *The Bench and Bar of Indiana.* Indianapolis, Bench and Bar Publishing Co., 1895.

wksbury, Donald G. *The Founding of American Colleges and Universities before the Civil War.* New York, Columbia Univ. Press, 1932.

rpie, David. *Sketches of My Own Times.* Indianapolis, Bobbs, 1903.

ham, Alfred H. "The Centennial of Miami University," *Ohio State Archaeological and Historical Quarterly,* 18 (1909), 322–44.

———. *Old Miami: The Yale of the Early West.* Hamilton, Ohio, The Republican Co., 1909.

a Horne, Thomas B. *Life of Major General George H. Thomas.* New York, Scribner, 1882.

lker, Charles M. *Sketch of the Life, Character, and Public Services of Oliver P. Morton.* Indianapolis, Indianapolis Journal Press, 1878.

llace, Lew. *Life of Gen. Ben Harrison.* Philadelphia, Hubbard, 1888.

r of Rebellion, Official Records of the Union and Confederate rmies.* Washington, D. C., Government Printing Office, 1880–901. Four Series, 70 vols., 128 books.

isenburger, Francis P. *Passing of the Frontier.* The History of the tate of Ohio in Six Volumes. Edited by Carl F. Wittke. Vol. III, Columbus, Ohio State Archaeological and Historical Society, 1941–44.

ite, William Allen. *Masks in a Pageant.* New York, Macmillan, 1928.

liams, Charles R. *The Life of Rutherford Birchard Hayes.* Columbus, Ohio State Archaeological and Historical Society, 1928. 2 vols.

Randall, James G. *Constitutional Problems ur*
    D. Appleton, 1926.
———. *The Civil War and Reconstruction*
———. *Lincoln the President*. New York, Dc
Rodabaugh, James H. *Robert Hamilton Bi*
    State Archaeological and Historical Society,
———. "Miami University, Calvinism, and
    ment," *Ohio State Archaeological and H*
    (January 1939), 66–73.
Roll, Charles. "Indiana's Part in the Nominati
    for President in 1860," *Indiana Magazine of*
Roseboom, Eugene H. *The Civil War Era, 185*
    the State of Ohio in Six Volumes. Edited by
    Columbus, Ohio State Archaeological a
    1941–44.
Sager, B. F. *The Harrison Mansion*. Vincennes
    Vigo Chapter, D.A.R., of Vincennes), 1928.
Schalk, Emil. *Summary of the Art of War*. Ph
    1863.
Scott, John W. *A History and Biographical*
    County, Ohio. Cincinnati, Western Biogra
    1882.
Sears, Louis M. "Slidell and Buchanan," *Amer*
    27 (1922), 709–30.
———. *John Slidell*. Durham, N. C., Duke Un
Sharp, Walter R. "Henry S. Lane and the Four
    can Party in Indiana," *Mississippi Valley*
    (1920–21), 93–112.
Sherman, William T. *Memoirs of General Wil*
    York, D. Appleton, 1875. 2 vols.
Smith, Ophia D. *Old Oxford House*. Oxford, C
    Press, 1941.
———. *Fair Oxford*. Oxford, Ohio, Oxford H
Smith, Theodore Clark. *Liberty and Free Soi*
    west. New York, Longmans, 1897.
Stampp, Kenneth M. "The Milligan Case and
    Indiana," *Mississippi Valley Historical Revi*
———. *Indiana Politics during the Civil War,*
    Historical Bureau, 1949. (Indiana Histor
    XXXI.)

St

St

St

St

Su

Sz

T

T

T

U

—

Va

W

W

W

W

W

W

Williams, Kenneth P. *Lincoln Finds a General.* New York, Macmillan, 1949. 2 vols.

Wilson, Woodrow. *George Washington.* New York, Harper, 1896.

Woodburn, James A. "Henry Smith Lane," *Indiana Magazine of History,* 27 (1931), 279–87.

World Almanac and Encyclopedia, 1894. New York, New York *World,* 1894.

World Almanac of 1949. New York, New York *World-Telegram,* 1949.

Zimmerman, Charles. "The Origin and Rise of the Republican Party in Indiana from 1854–1860," *Indiana Magazine of History,* 13 (1917), 211–69; 349–412.

Index

INDEX

Abolitionism, fever in Indiana, 35–36

Acton, Indiana, Harrison's first stump speech at, 122

Adams, Charles Francis, on Lincoln, 158

Adams, Henry, views on Harrison, 9 n.

Adams, President John Quincy, 4, 17

Aiken, William (Governor of South Carolina), 120

Allen, Chaplain, 310

American Eagle, on Harrison's opposition to Bell, 147

American Party, 116, 123, 131, 136, 146; election of 1856 and, 124–5; *see also* Know-Nothing Party

American Revolution, 36

Ancestry of Harrison, 11–13; Harrison's views on, 11, 11 n., 12

Anderson, John Alexander, 50, 53, 60–61, 69–70, 71–73, 74, 75–83; letters to Harrison of, 75–76, 103–4, 124

Anderson, Dr. William C., 46, 48, 78

Arnold, Benedict, 14

Art of War, The, by de Jomini, 228

Atlanta campaign, 243, 247–65; Harrison on the fall of, 264–65

Atlas (Indiana), 143, 289 n.

Banks, Nathaniel P., Speaker of the House of Representatives, 123

Barnes, Dr., 203–7

Bates, Edward, Republican presidential aspirant in 1860, 145

Bates House, 94, 131, 160

Beauregard, Confederate General P. G. T., 278

Beaver, General James A., 6

Beecher, Henry Ward, 28, 135

Bell, John, 146, 147, 154

Benotti, W. A., 311

Benton, William T., 73, 108

Bishop, Robert Hamilton, 45, 47, 48, 105, 226; career of, 31–34; influence on Harrison of, 35–40, 52 n., 61, 105 n.; "father of American sociology," 37 n.

Blaine, James G., 7

Blakeley, Lou (cousin), 203–7

"Bloody shirt" and Harrison, 276

Boggess, C. H., 109, 122

"Bounty jumpers," 292

Bowdoin College, 49

Boyle, Brigadier General J. T., 189

Bragg, Confederate General Braxton, 177, 186, 198, 216–17; Murfreesboro battle and, 223–25

Breckinridge, John, 146

Bridgeport, Alabama, Harrison at, 239 n.

Brigney, Major, on Harrison, 228

Brooks, Preston, caning of Senator Sumner by, 124

Brown, Hilton U., xix–xxi, 58 n.

Browning, Robert, Harrison's recollection of, 95, 102

Bruce, Colonel S. D., 193, 194–95, 199–202

Bryan, T. B., 85, 101 n.

Buchanan, President James, 125, 132, 145

Buckner, Confederate General Simon B., 193

Buell, General Don Carlos, 198, 216–17, 223; removed from command, 217

Buffalo Bill, 7

Bull Run, Battle of, 174, 176

"Bummer Brigade," 307–8

Burgess, Jim, 220 n., 227

Butterfield, General Daniel, Hooker's Chief of Staff, 232–33, 252

Butterworth, Benjamin, on Harrison's boyhood, 23

Campbell, Lewis D., 120

Career, Harrison on choosing a, 61–63

Carter, Robert (King) (great-great-great-grandfather), 13

Cary, Freeman G, 30–31, 33

Cary, Samuel Fenton, 30

Cary's Academy. See Farmers' College

Cash, Addison, aids Colonel Harrison, 203

Cass, Lewis, 39

Caven, John, 173 n., 184, 185 n., 208, 209, 213; Mayor of Indianapolis, 315

Centennial inauguration, 3–7

Chase, Philander, 17

Chase, Salmon P., 148

Cheatham, Confederate Major General B. F., 282–83

Chesnut, Mrs. Mary, 155

Chicago, 84–85

Chronicle (Washington), 305

Cincinnati College, 17, 67

Cincinnati, 15–16, 20; Horace Greeley on, 68–69, Harrison's dislike of city life in, 70–71; admitted to legal practice in, 84

Cincinnati Gazette, on Harrison's Lawrenceburg speech, 147

City Attorney (Indianapolis), Harrison's election as, 127–28

Civil War, Harrison on origin and cause of, 275

Clay, Cassius Marcellus, anti-slavery sentiments of, 139–40, 145

Clay, Henry, 138, 139; cited on slavery, 140

Claybaugh, Joseph, 59

Claypool Hotel, 160 n.; see also Bates House

Cleburne, Confederate Major General P. R., 235

Cleveland, President Grover, 5, 8, 8 n.

Cleves Presbyterian Church, 28

Coburn, General John, 260–61, 287

Cockrell, Francis Marion, 4

College Hill. See Farmers' College

Colley, Sims, 96

Colonies, the, 36

Columbia University, 49

Constitution, Harrison on the guarantees of, 8 n.

Cooper, T. N., cited on Harrison, 9

Cooper, Private William, sheds first blood for Seventieth, 187

Copperheads, 267; Harrison's views on, 272, 274–75, 276

Court Crier, Harrison appointed in Indianapolis, 94

Court of Claims, Harrison's ambition to be Commissioner of, 108

Crane and Mason cited, 108–9

Crittenden, Thomas L., 217–18

Cruft, General Charles, 279; commendation of Harrison by, 285–86

Cumback, Hon. Will, letters of Harrison to, 132 nn.

Cunningham, Rev. Mr., 129

Custer, General George, 304

Daily Citizen (Indianapolis), 136

Daily Journal (Indianapolis), 145, 175, 177, 181, 182, 185, 209, 220, 266, 270, 272, 276, 313

Daily State Sentinel (Indianapolis), 158, 175, 215, 220, 271, 273

Dartmouth College, 49

"Daughter of the Old Northwest," 48; *see also* Miami University

Davis, General Jeff (14th Corps commander, the Union Army), 307

Davis, Jefferson (President of the Confederacy), 203, 259

Davis, John, 151

De Motte, Mark L., 138

Declaration of Independence, 14

Defrees, John, 142 n., 287 n., 289, 309, 310

Delaware Indians, 91

Democratic Party, 115, 136; Douglas Democrats in 1860 campaign, 137; antiwar stand of, 175, 208, 212-13; in the elections: of 1856, 125-27; of 1860, 144-46, 151-52; of 1864, 266-67, 270-71, 273

Denny, Father Harmar, 59 n.

Detroit speech of Harrison, 7

Devil's Hole, 79; *see also* Niagara

Dibble, Work and Moore, 105

Dickens, Charles, 226

Divorce laws of Indiana, 106-7

Dodge, General Grenville M., 247 n., 297-98

Dortch, Confederate Captain, 199-203

Douglas, Stephen A., support of Kansas-Nebraska Bill, 118, 119; discussed by John Scott Harrison, 130-31; feud with Buchanan, 145; nominated for President, 146

Dred Scott decision, 142

Dumont, General Ebenezer, 181, 182, 221, 222, 229 n.

Dustin, Daniel, 229 n., 230

Early, Confederate General Jubal, defeated by Sheridan, 266

Eaton, Betsey Short Harrison (half-sister), 24, 25, 44, 50-51, 69, 75

Eaton, Doctor George, 69, 75, 78

Eaton, Harry, 164

Edmundson, Henry Alonzo, 120

Education, background of Harrison's early training, 10-11, 25-28; Robert H. Bishop's views on, 32-34; Harrison's views on, 34-35

Election of 1848, Harrison's views on, 39

Eleventh Indiana Volunteers, 168

Elliott, Charles, 49

Emancipation Proclamation, 213; Harrison's views on, 275

Essays, written by Harrison for Bishop, 35, 36-37, 39-40, 40-41

Everett, Edward, 146, 154 n.

Farmers' College, 29-41, 47, 49, 52 n.

Farragut, Admiral David G., capture of Mobile by, 266

Fillmore, President Millard, 124-25

Financial panic of 1854, 103

"Fire in the rear, the," 210-11

First Continental Congress, 13

Fishback, William Pinkney, 186, 195; on Harrison, 171, 174; critical of war administration, 196-97, 211, 213, 289; partnership with Harrison, 171-72, 174, 185

Foraker, General Joseph B., 7

Ford, Captain H. A., 261

Fort Sumter, 161, 162

Fort Washington (Cincinnati), 15

Forts Henry and Donelson, captured by Grant, 176, 193 n.

Free Soilers, 38–39

Frémont, John Charles, 11; Harrison's campaigns for, 115, 116, 124–25, 139

Fry, General S. S., 219 n.

Fuller, Chief Justice Melville W., 5

Gadsen, Alabama, Confederate Council of War at, 277

Gallatin, Albert, 8

Garfield, President James A., 7; campaigns in Indiana in 1864, 270

Gazette (Cincinnati), 147

Geary, General John W., 232 n., 307

Georgetown University, 49

Giddings, Joshua, 148

Golgotha Church, battle of, 255–56

Gordon, Major Jonathan W., 95–96

Grand Review, 304–8

Granger, General Gordon, commands reserve corps, 230–31

Grant, General Ulysses, 176, 231–32, 234, 244, 282, 297, 301

Greeley, Horace, 68, 136, 146

Grubbs, Major George W., 287 n.; cited on Harrison's "Star," 288

Gwynne, Abram, 67, 69

Halleck, General Henry W., at Grand Review, 303

Halstead, Murat, 30

Hamilton, Alexander, 4, 8

Hamlin, Hannibal, 146

Hammond, Governor Abram A., 156

Hardee, Confederate General William J., 235

Harrison, Anna Symmes (Mrs. William Henry Harrison) (grandmother), married to William Henry, 15; Presbyter-

Harrison, Anna Symmes—*cont.* ian faith of, 17, 28–29; influence of on John Scott Harrison, 17 n.; death of, 312 n.

Harrison, Anna Symmes (sister), 24, 42, 70, 128, 153

Harrison, Benjamin, the English emigrant, 12–13

Harrison, Benjamin, Signer of the Declaration of Independence, 13–14

Harrison, Caroline Scott (wife), 47–48; courtship of, 55, 60–61, 65, 66, 72–75, 77–82; religion of, 112–14; tribute on, 180–81; wife to Benjamin, 82–89, 91–93, 98–100, 133–34, 165–70, 196, 217, 230, 263, 288–89, 293–94, 313–17

Harrison, Carter Bassett (brother), 24, 128, 164

Harrison, Elizabeth Bassett (great-grandmother), 14

Harrison, Elizabeth Irwin (mother), 43–44; marriage of, 18; death of, 22, 45

Harrison, Irwin (brother), 24, 25, 29, 41–45, 80; army life of, 128, 168–69; letters to Benjamin by, 129, 133, 296–97

Harrison, James Findlay (infant brother), 24, 42

Harrison, James Irwin (infant brother), 24

Harrison, John Irwin (infant brother), 24

Harrison, John Scott (father), 88; career of, 17, 66–67, 83–84, 116–22, 123–28, 146–48; early and married life of, 16–22, 24–26, 29–30, 42, 46; financial worries of, 21–22, 29, 42, 46–47; boomed for presidency in 1856, 121; letters to Benjamin of, 43, 51–52, 53–54, 98, 118, 119, 120, 121, 126, 130–31, 147–48, 154, 166, 172, 175–76, 273, 290, 312

Harrison, John Scott, Jr. (brother), 24, 25, 116, 128, 164

Harrison, Mary (daughter), 6, 164; birth of, 134

Harrison, Mary Jane Irwin (sister), 24, 25, 42, 44, 51, 60, 128, 133–34, 164

Harrison, Russell (son), 16, 98, 100, 102, 121, 133, 164; birth of, 98

Harrison, Sarah Lucretia (half-sister), 24, 42, 44, 56, 128, 145

Harrison, William Henry (grandfather), 11, 20, 28, 142, 148, 254; life of, 14–17; inaugurated President of the United States, 4, 4 nn., 6; relationship with Benjamin, 26–27

Harrison, W. R., delegate to Republican National Convention of 1860, 145

Hartranft, Major General John F., 7

Harvard University, 49

Hawley, General Joseph R., 297–98

Hendricks, Thomas A., Democratic nominee for Governor in 1860, 137, 144, 150; debate with Harrison, 151–52; Harrison's view of, 151 n.

Henry, Patrick, 58–59

Herald (New York), 290

Hill & Co., James L., 173

Historians, Harrison on qualifications of, 38

Hoar, George F., 5

Holloway, W. R., Indianapolis city historian, 134

Honesdale, Pennsylvania, 73, 74, 98 n., 288, 290

Hood, Confederate General John B., 251, 259–60, 278, 279–85

Hooker, General Joseph, 242, 245, 252, 254; in command of the 20th Army Corps; Harrison's fear of, 232–33, 240–41;

Hooker, General Joseph—*cont.* commendation of Harrison by, 252, 262, 278

House of Burgesses (Virginia), 13, 14

Howard, General Oliver O., Harrison's recollection of, 238–39, 240–41

Impending Crisis by Helper, 135

Indiana, resources, 89; law in, 93–94; politics in, 114–15, 125–27, 131–33, 137–61, 208–16, 266–68, 270–77

Indiana Reports, 173, 213, 294

Indianapolis, 269–70; advantages for young lawyer, 85–86; Ben and Carrie's first impressions of, 89–92; antiwar sentiment in, 212–16; Harrison's welcome in 1864, 270; religion in, 110–14; slavery question in, 135–36; politics in; *see also* Indiana

Infantry Tactics by Casey, 227

Irwin, Archibald (grandfather), 18, 19 n.

Irwin, Mary Ramsey (grandmother), 18, 19 n.

Jackson, Andrew, 8

Jackson, Confederate General "Stonewall," 197

Jefferson, Thomas, 4, 8

Johnson, President Andrew, 270, 304

Johnston, Confederate General Joseph E., 234–35, 242–43, 244, 256, 301; defense tactics of, 257–58; Resaca Battle and, 247–48, 252, 253–54; resignation of, 259

Kansas-Nebraska Bill, 95, 117, 118; passage in Congress, 118–20

Kansas Territory, an indictment of Republicanism in, 129

Kenyon College, 17

Kerr, Michael C., 137, 138, 208, 213
Ketcham, John L., 186
Kilpatrick, General Hugh J., 245
Kitchen, Dr. John M., 92, 97
Kitchen, Mary, 92
Knights of the Golden Circle, 270; *see also* Sons of Liberty
Know-Nothing Party, 146; *see also* American Party

Lane, Henry S., 138, 141, 144; Governor and Senator, 156
Lane, Joseph, 146
Lawrenceburg speech of Harrison, 147
Lee, General Robert E., 177, 197, 198, 234, 244, 297
Lincoln, Abraham, 8, 137, 145; assassination of, 298–99; Harrison cited on, 275, 299; President, 145, 153, 154, 157–61, 163, 175, 177–78, 213, 274; Harrison's defense of, 275–76, 295; slavery stand of, 143–44
"Little Ben," sobriquet given Harrison at Resaca, 253
Logan, General John A., Commander of the Army of the Tennessee, 307
Longworth, Nicholas, 17
Lookout Valley, 233, 238, 267
Lord, Elizabeth (Scott), 47, 101 n., 288–89
Lord, Russell Farnum, first child named after, 98, 101 n.
Lynn, Thomas, 26

McClellan, General George B., 175, 176, 177, 197, 198; election of 1864, 274, 276–77
McClurg, Rev. John A., 87, 112 n.
McCook, General Alexander Mc., 217
McDonald, Judge David, 186
McDonald, Senator Joseph E., 7

McDowell, General Irvin, 303
McNutt, Joseph G., 30
McOuat, George, 94
McPherson, General James, 234, 245
Madison, James, 4
Mahan, D. H., 228
Mann, Horace, 96
Mansion House (Oxford, Ohio), 53, 82
Marshall College, 26
Masonic Hall, Harrison's speech at, 182–83
Masons and Odd Fellows, 110
Mathews, James, on Dr. Bishop, 31
May, Edward, 135
Meade, General George G., 304, 305
Meredith, Captain W., 186 n., 195–96
Merrill, Captain Samuel, 189 nn., 194, 214, 238; cited on Harrison, 218
Miami Indians, 91
Miami University, 31, 34, 44, 46, 47, 48–50, 52–65; commencement at, 63–65; history of, 48; life at, 49–50; Presbyterian influence at, 58–61, 63
Michener, Louis T., 11–12, 133
Michigan Club, Harrison's toast to "Washington, the Republican" at, 7–8
Miller, John F., 138, 139 n.
Miller, L. T., on Harrison at Peach Tree Creek, 260–61
Missouri Compromise, 118, 120
Mitchell, Jim, 227, 230
Modern War: Its Theory and Practice by Imre Szabad, 227
Moffat, Dr. J. C., 49
Morgan, Confederate Colonel John H., 191–93, 199, 208
Morrow, Captain, 202–7
Morton, Vice-President Levi P., 6

Morton, Oliver Perry, 6–7, 126, 132, 138, 141; Governor of Indiana, 156–60, 165, 177–82, 187, 210, 213, 272–74, 277, 313

Mount Pleasant Academy (Kingston, Ohio), 53

Mower, General Joseph A., 307

Murfreesboro, Tennessee, results of battle of, 225

Mustering out, 308, 311

Nashville, Battle of, 279–81, 282–85

National Constitutional Union Party, 146–47, 154 n.; *see also* "Old Gentlemen's Party"

Neal, Miss Mary P., 72–73, 73 n.

Negro in the war, Harrison's views on the, 276

New Hope Church, battle of, 254–55

New Orleans, taken by Farragut, 176

Newcomer, Doctor, 99, 100

Niagara, New York, 74, 79

Nixon, Oliver W., 30

Novel, Harrison's views on, 39–40, 226

Ohio River, life on the, 19

"Old Gentlemen's Party," 146

Old Temperance Tavern, 54

Owens, Mary, 166

Oxford Female Institute, 47, 54–55

Pacific Railroad bill, 119

Paine, General Eleazer A., 214, 229, 230

Panic (financial) of 1854, effect in Indianapolis, 103

Patriotism, Harrison on, 40–41

Peace negotiations, Harrison's opposition to, 296; failure of, 301

Peach Tree Creek, battle of, 259–62

Perryville, battle of, 216–17

Phi Delta Theta, 71; Harrison as Society's Second Founder, 58

Pierce, President Franklin, 128

Pioneer Life at North Bend by J. Scott Harrison, 10 n., 19 n.

"Point, The," 16, 17, 20–26, 41, 62, 65, 66, 83, 98–99, 102, 128, 153

Point Lookout burglary, 95

Political and Military History of the Campaign of Waterloo, The, by de Jomini, 227–28

Polk, Confederate General Leonidas, 235

"Poor Laws," 65

"Poor of England, The," commencement address by Harrison, 63–65

Porter, Albert Gallatin, 165, 173–74

Porter, Admiral David D., 6

Porter, Joseph, 25–26

Presbyterianism, 27–28, 41; at Miami University, 58–59; Harrison and, 59–60, 61–62, 166 n.; in Indianapolis, 112–14

Prince, General Henry, commandant at Camp Sherman, South Carolina, 291–92, 295

Princeton University, 49

Prohibition, 136

Pulszky, Madame Theresa, description of Indianapolis in 1852, 90

Raccoon Range, 238

Ramsey, James (great-great-grandfather), 18

Ramsey, John (great-grandfather), 18

Ransdell, Dan, 218 n., 250 n., 251

Rea, John H., 94, 103

Reagan, Surgeon Amos, of 70th Indiana Volunteers, 230

Record (South Carolina), on Harrison's place in history, 8, 132

Reid, Whitelaw, 49 n.

Republican Party, 11, 122, 130, 136; beginnings of, 115, 120; in elections: of 1856, 123, 124–26; of 1860, 138–45, 149–53, 157–58; of 1864, 266–68, 270–77

Resaca, Battle of, 245, 247–52

Richmond, fall of, 297

Rifle and Light Infantry Tactics by W. J. Hardee, 227

Riley, James Whitcomb, tribute to Mrs. Harrison, 181

Ritchie, Colonel W. T., 269

Rockville, Indiana, Harrison debates Hendricks at, 151–52

Robinson, John L., 94

Romney, Virginia, Union raid on, 168

Root, Harriet, governess and teacher, 25

Rosencrans, General William S., 217–18, 219, 220, 223

Ross, Lewis, on Harrison, 65

Russellville, Harrison commands expedition to, 199–207

Saylor, Milton, 52, 65

Schofield, Major General John M., 234, 245, 279–81

Scott, Henry (brother-in-law), 169, 170–71; Civil War service of, 168–69, 184, 252; defense of Harrison, 216

Scott, John, Jr. (brother-in-law), 47; wounded in battle of Murfreesboro, 224

Scott, Rev. John W. (father-in-law), 47, 54, 55, 73, 98; officiates at marriage of Carrie and Ben, 81, 82

Scott, Mrs. John W. (mother-in-law), 73, 98

Scott, General Winfield, 197

Secession, 155, 157–58, 271

Seventieth Indiana Regiment, 40, 183, 188–247, 279, 287, 306, Seventieth Indiana Regiment—cont.

312; Georgia campaign and, 248–53, 254–57, 260–62; Kentucky posting of, 186–216; Tennessee duty of, 218–23, 225–226, 230–33, 235–45

Seward, William H., 153, 155

Sheets, William (cousin), 86–87, 88, 92, 101 n., 112

Sheridan, General Phil, 266, 296

Sherman, Senator John, and Harrison, 258 n.

Sherman, General William T., 231–32, 242–43, 244, 298, 301; "Grand Review" and, 304–8; "march" of, 278, 288, 294–95; Resaca Battle and, 247–48, 252–54

Short, John Cleves (uncle), 21, 22, 29

Slavery, 117, 120, 136, 139–41; Harrison's stand on, 122–23, 140–41, 143, 276

Slocum, General Henry W., 307

Smith, General Andrew Jackson, at Nashville, 282

Smith, Caleb Blood, 142, 145

Smith, Cyrus B., 107

Smith, General Kirby, 177, 197

Smith, "Pop Gun," 209, 213

Smith, William Henry, 142 n.; on Harrison's speech at Lebanon, 143

Sons of Liberty, 270, 273–74; *see also* Knights of the Golden Circle

South Carolina, College of, 49, 155

South Carolina and secession, 155

State Republican Central Committee (Indiana), 131–33; Harrison, Secretary of, 136

State sovereignty, Harrison's views on, 275

Steedman, General James B., 279, 281, 282, 283–84
Stephens, Alexander H., 119–20
Stoddard, O. N., 49
Storer, Bellamy, attorney and congressman, Harrison's law mentor, 67–68, 69, 78, 83, 165; influence on young Harrison, 69 n.
Studebaker, Clem, compares Benjamin with grandfather, 5
Summary of the Art of War by Schalk, 228
Sumner, Charles, 124, 135–36, 139
Supreme Court Reporter (Indiana), Harrison and office of, 136–37, 153, 161, 167, 267–68; Kerr dispute over, 208–10, 213
Swing, David, 52, 148–49

Taylor, Bayard, 39
Taylor, Napoleon B., 273
Teal, Rebecca, 54
Temperance, Harrison's views on, 56–57
Thanksgiving Day, 1862, in camp at Gallatin, Tennessee, 222
Thatcher, Shaw & Co., 106
Thomas, General George H., 217, 219, 234, 245, 277, 278, 279–83, 285
Thuer, Alexander, 220
Transylvania University, 31, 33
Treaty of Greenville, 15
Tribune (New York), 136, 295
Turpie, David, 138, 144

Uncle Tom's Cabin, 135
Union Central Committee, faction of the Republican Party in Indiana, 208–9, 210
Union Literary Society, 57–58; Harrison elected to the presidency of, 57

Union Party. *See* Republican Party
Van Buren, President Martin, 38–39
Vance, Major S. C., 194, 201–2
Virginia, University of, 49
Voorhees, Daniel, 151–52

Wallace, David, 17, 96, 97, 104
Wallace, Lew, 17, 104, 255–56; commander Eleventh Indiana Volunteers, 168, 169, 227, 309; on Harrison, 226
Wallace, William, 121, 156, 169, 178–80, 182; partnership with Harrison of, 104–5, 105–7, 170–71
Wallace and Harrison law firm, 104–5, 106, 117, 165, 171
War of 1812, 36
Ward, General William T., 226, 231–33, 241, 248–49, 260, 270–78; Harrison's opinion of, 220, 236–38, 248, 300; wounded at Resaca, 251
Warner, General Bill, 7
Washington College, 47
Washington, D. C., 3–7; Harrison's views on, 309
Washington, George, 4, 8, 13, 14, 15 n.
Wauhatchie, Harrison at, 240
Wayne, "Mad Anthony," and William Henry Harrison, 15
Webster, Daniel, views on slavery, 140
Whig Party, 39, 115–16; Nebraska bill effect on, 118–19, 131; collapse of, 121
Willard, Governor Asbel P., 134
Wood, General T. J., 283
Woodworth, Mrs. Ruth, curator of Harrison Memorial Home, 100 n.
Wright, Mr., 310–11
Wright, Jacob T., 267

Wright, John Montgomery, Marshal of the Supreme Court
   1888–1915), 5
Wright, Governor Joseph A., 97

Yale University, 49

Y. M. C. A., 113, 136 n.
Yorktown Peninsula, Harrison's
   comment on campaign of, 177
Young Men's Mercantile Library
   Association (Cincinnati), Har-
   rison's membership in, 71